RRAC

SEP 28 2004

FISHES OF OKLAHOMA

D1608276

Fishes of Oklahoma

Rudolph J. Miller • Henry W. Robison

University of Oklahoma Press : Norman

Also by Henry W. Robison

(with Robert T. Allen) *Only in Arkansas: A Study of the Endemic Plants and Animals of the State* (Fayetteville, Ark., 1995)
(with Thomas M. Buchanan) *Fishes of Arkansas* (Fayetteville, Ark., 1988)

Library of Congress Cataloging-in-Publication Data

Miller, Rudolph J. (Rudolph John), 1934–
Fishes of Oklahoma / Rudolph J. Miller, Henry W. Robison.
p. cm.
Includes bibliographical references (p.).
ISBN 0–8061–3611–1 (alk. paper) — ISBN 0–8061–3610–3 (pbk. : alk. paper)
1. Fishes—Oklahoma. I. Robison, Henry W. II. Title.

QL628.O4M56 2004
597'.09766—dc22

2003064582

The paper in this book meets the guidelines for permanence and durability of the Committee on Production Guidelines for Book Longevity of the Council on Library Resources. ∞

Copyright © 2004 by the University of Oklahoma Press, Norman, Publishing Division of the University. All rights reserved. Manufactured in the U.S.A.

1 2 3 4 5 6 7 8 9 10

597.09766 M617f 2004
Miller, Rudolph J. (Rudolph
John), 1934-
Fishes of Oklahoma

CONTENTS

PREFACE

The primary purpose of this book is to provide a ready means of identifying the fishes of Oklahoma. The first edition, published in 1973, went through two printings and has been out of print for over 15 years. We have been told that the book has served the state well despite the gradual loss of currency in nomenclature and distribution accuracy but that its recent unavailability has been a real problem for Oklahomans wanting to identify local fishes. Hence we opted to update the book in all its substantive aspects rather than trying to produce a more comprehensive, all-inclusive tome on Oklahoma's fishes. We trust that some of the many outstanding ichthyologists in the state will soon undertake that project. For now, we are content to bring nomenclature up to date and to include revised distribution maps and new comments on the distribution, biology, and behavior of species little known in 1973. In addition, the senior author has produced a number of paintings of Oklahoma fishes, which are presented as color plates. We hope this second edition will enable most people not only to identify any fish from Oklahoma waters but also to learn something about the wonderful diversity of Oklahoma's fish fauna and the sheer beauty of many of our fishes.

In the foreword to the first edition we expressed a hope: "We believe that the imminent future holds the key to whether our society will be able to cope with the enormous ecological problems that are becoming increasingly important in determining the nature and quality of life in this country. As a relatively unindustrialized state with low population density, Oklahoma has not yet experienced the magnitude and overpowering complexity of such problems already experienced elsewhere in America. With the rapid institution of appropriate controls over the treatment and disposal of personal, municipal, and industrial wastes, it may be possible for Oklahoma to avoid the horror of seeing its natural resources irreparably abused."

Though we noted that fish kills were becoming more common even in the early seventies, we hoped that institutions carrying the responsibility for keeping our air, waters, and lands reasonably clean would carry out that responsibility. Unfortunately, it seems that environmental safeguards have a far lower priority in Oklahoma than residential development, corporate farming, industrial development, and job creation, even the most menial. The eastern part of the state seems at times like a giant chicken coop, the west bristles with enormous corporate hog farms, and our western rivers especially are dying from lack of water and a surfeit of animal wastes and agricultural pesticides. A few state agencies struggle to contain local tragedies, but they lack the power to stop the burgeoning pollution. Sadly, this has caused numerous fish species in the state to dwindle in numbers, some sinking into threatened status, one going extinct (*Macrhybopsis tetranemus*), and another losing four-fifths of its native range (*Notropis girardi*). The state's commitment to protection of a handful of scenic eastern rivers has led to efforts to reduce waste disposal in both Oklahoma and western Arkansas, but the project is limited in scope and may not be successful even in the rivers concerned, at least in the near future.

We noted 30 years ago that we wrote with some sense of urgency because fishes, especially native species, could provide a sensitive indicator of ecological change: "The number of species and the number of individuals of each kind permit the calculation of diversity indices, which many ecologists consider to be the best indication of the health of aquatic communities." Unfortunately, such studies have only recently been systematically conducted in our state, and the results have rarely been incorporated into political decisions on environmental policy even to the present. Though our hopes for restored environments are often dashed, we must remain optimistic for the future, for without optimism we may leave the field of contention to polluters and developers.

This book provides a means for identification of fishes via alternate procedures. The first, and probably most efficient, is through the use of keys to the families and species of Oklahoma fishes. With a little practice, the simple dichotomous keys may be used by anglers and other interested parties as well as by biologists. Alternatively, one can use the photographs, as in any field guide. Upon locating a photo that appears appropriate, the written description and range map can be used to determine whether the fish in hand matches the one illustrated in those critical characteristics distinguishing it from similar species.

Range maps may also give clues to the identity of a specimen, but some provisos are in order. A species probably will not be found in all waters within the range indicated on the map; and it may be found outside the indicated range. The maps have been updated largely on the basis of specimens in the Oklahoma State University and University of Oklahoma museums but may require modification as additional localities are sampled in the future. Fish are mobile and some species are expanding their range; places historically devoid of a particular species may yield specimens in the future.

ACKNOWLEDGMENTS

Besides all the people who helped with the first edition and are acknowledged there, we now owe thanks to a new generation. Special appreciation goes to William J. Matthews of the University of Oklahoma for reviewing the manuscript and keys and for important suggestions and comments on both. We are grateful to Anthony Echelle of Oklahoma State University for reviewing and testing the keys and for comments on some species accounts. Their willing and enthusiastic participation in and support of this project strengthened it throughout.

For providing information on various Oklahoma fish species, thanks go to Kim Erickson of the Oklahoma Department of Wildlife Conservation, Robert C. Cashner at the University of New Orleans, David Eisenhour of Morehead State University, Robert E. Jenkins of Roanoke College, and once more to William Matthews and Anthony Echelle. Robert Cashner and David Eisenhour also contributed photographs, and for additional photos we are indebted to Michael M. Stevenson of the University of New Orleans; Stephen T. Ross at the University of Southern Mississippi; William Roston of Forsyth, Missouri; Garold Sneegas of Lawrence, Kansas; and Julian Humphries of Cornell University. Pat O'Neil of the Geological Survey of Alabama was especially generous with several excellent photos.

For prepublication access to information on the current status of common and scientific names of Oklahoma fishes in the forthcoming American Fisheries Society publication on common and scientific names, we thank Joseph S. Nelson at the University of Alberta and Carter R. Gilbert at the University of Florida.

For providing interlibrary loan service and making special efforts to secure vital scientific papers and reports relating to Oklahoma fishes, we extend special thanks to Donna McCloy of Southern Arkansas University. A huge amount of appreciation goes to Jan Rader and Christa Brummett, also at Southern Arkansas University, for typing and various tasks relating to compilation of the manuscript. We thank April Gillilan for rendering the new maps.

We wish to express our most heartfelt gratitude to our wives, Helen Carter Miller and Catharine Robison. Without their patience and support (and occasional help on a seine) this book would not have been possible.

FISHES OF OKLAHOMA

INTRODUCTION

Distribution of Oklahoma Fishes

Oklahoma waters drain into two major river systems: the Arkansas River system in roughly the northern two-thirds of the state and the Red River system in about the southern third. The majority of the principal tributary streams have a basically west-to-east orientation, though this trend is often absent in uplifted portions of the state. Aquatic habitats thus seem to intersect many of the physiographic, geologic, and biotic zones that have been recognized by various scientists. A good summary of the faunal regions of Oklahoma may be found in Robert Webb's *Reptiles of Oklahoma* (1970), especially as these relate to reptile distribution. Another key reference is "The Biotic Districts of Oklahoma," by W. F. Blair and T. H. Hubbell (1938). These authors define biotic districts in terms of unique ecological associations and discuss these with respect to the distribution of mammals and orthopterans. As yet no comprehensive zoogeographic analysis of Oklahoma fishes has been made, although A. P. Blair's paper on the distribution of darters in northeastern Oklahoma (1959) is a worthy beginning. Unfortunately, the data compiled in the preparation of this book do not permit definitive analysis of fish distribution in the state. Yet certain distributional patterns have emerged, and we would be remiss in not pointing out a few of the more conspicuous of these patterns.

One factor that poses difficulty in interpreting distributional data is the profound influence of the many recently created artificial impoundments on fish distribution and abundance. Figure 1 shows the major stream and river systems of the state and indicates (in black) the larger impoundments completed and (in outline) those authorized for construction. Since many stream- and river-inhabiting species cannot survive the altered conditions of impounded waters while others seem to do better in large lakes, the present distributional patterns of Oklahoma fishes are certainly different from those of 40 or 50 years ago. Many of our distributional records are based on specimens collected by the Oklahoma Biological Survey or by individuals from various institutions prior to the period of accelerated dam construction.

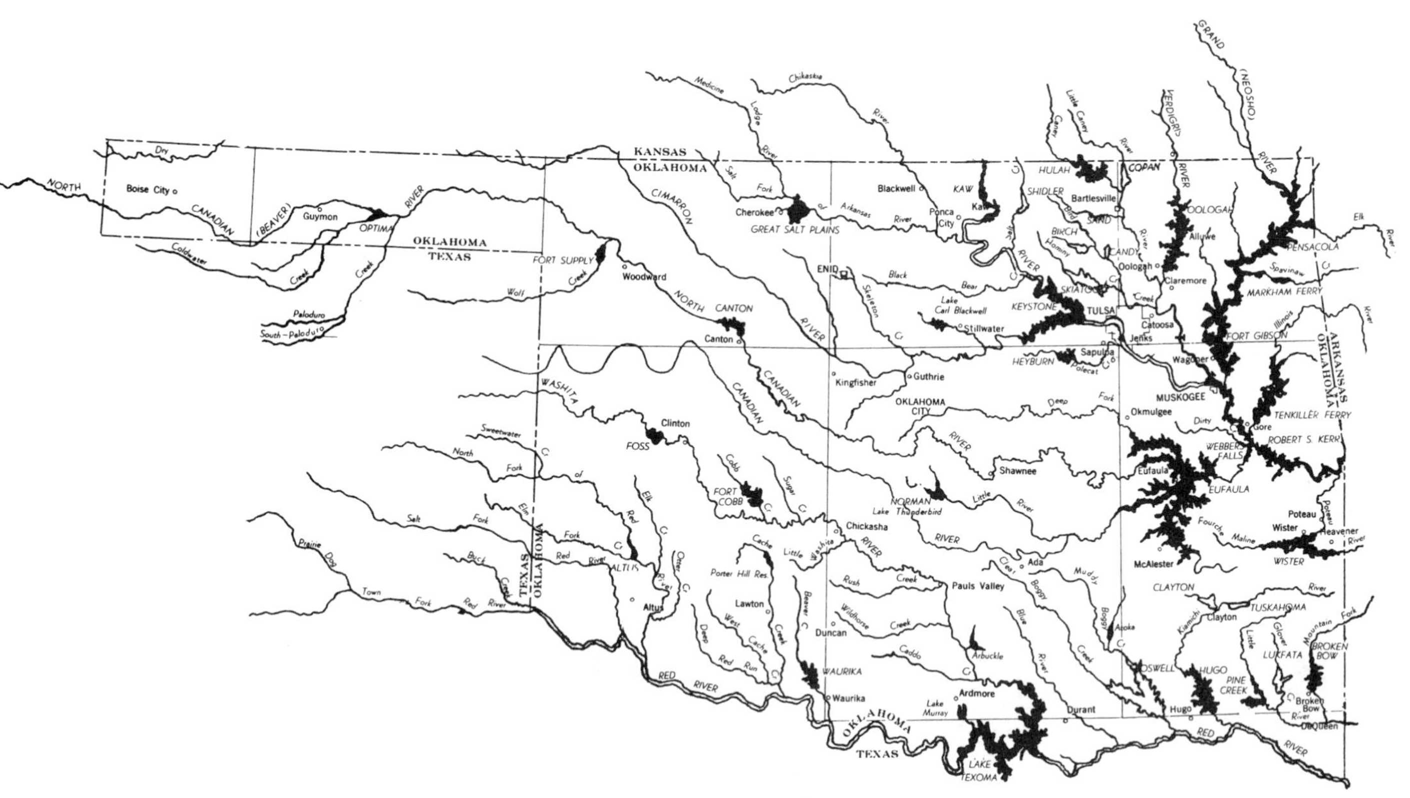

FIGURE 1. Major streams, rivers, and reservoirs in Oklahoma. Reservoirs in black are those completed or under construction, while those in outline are authorized. (Modified from a 1969 U. S. Army Corps of Engineers map of authorized projects for the Tulsa district)

Inasmuch as several of these impoundments have been completed relatively recently, evaluations of their impact on associated flowing water systems have been slow in coming. In a few cases their effects have been disastrous (see *Notropis girardi*). Any eventual study of the overall impact of such widespread impoundment in a Great Plains state will be of great value in providing models to assist in the future management of aquatic resources.

Relatively few species are found statewide. Most of the eighteen species that we would place in this category are extremely adaptable river and stream fishes like the gizzard shad, black and yellow bullheads, and channel catfish or are widely stocked, as are many sunfishes (*Lepomis*) and the largemouth bass. Reference to the range maps identifies other members of this group. Needless to say, one would be less likely to encounter bluegills, for example, in the Salt Fork of the Red River than in an adjacent farm pond. The converse would be true for the red shiner or plains minnow. This species cluster appears to have wide tolerances with respect to climate, physicochemical, and soil-type requirements, and members of the cluster are to be found wherever habitat needs (quiet or flowing waters, adequate food supply, appropriate gradient and bottom type, etc.) are met or wherever the species are stocked in permanent water.

A related group of fishes, including the two crappie species, may be found in all of the major impoundments of the state but are not common enough in the flowing waters or ponds in the west to be considered important major inhabitants of that portion of the state. We have arbitrarily included such species in a cluster of about 27 species that we consider to be inhabitants primarily of the eastern half of the state. This cluster includes species like the gars (except the alligator gar), goldeye, central stoneroller, golden shiner, smallmouth and bigmouth buffalo, flathead catfish, blackstripe topminnow, white bass, spotted bass, orangethroat darter, logperch, and others that can be identified from the range maps. Although some of these species can survive or even thrive in many of the western impoundments, or like the stoneroller inhabit a few western creeks with appropriate substrates and relatively low silt levels, most are unable to maintain viable populations in the western plains of the state. It seems likely that some combination of the heavy silt loads carried by the mud-bottomed streams of the central redbed plains region and the more extreme variations of temperature, salinity, and flow in western streams largely account for the limited distribution of this group, though careful study of individual species would be required to ascertain the precise nature of limiting factors in each case. The fact that a distinctive group of "eastern" species inhabits the streams in and adjacent to the Wichita Mountains in southwestern Oklahoma, including the bigeye shiner, southern redbelly dace, central stoneroller, black redhorse, golden redhorse,

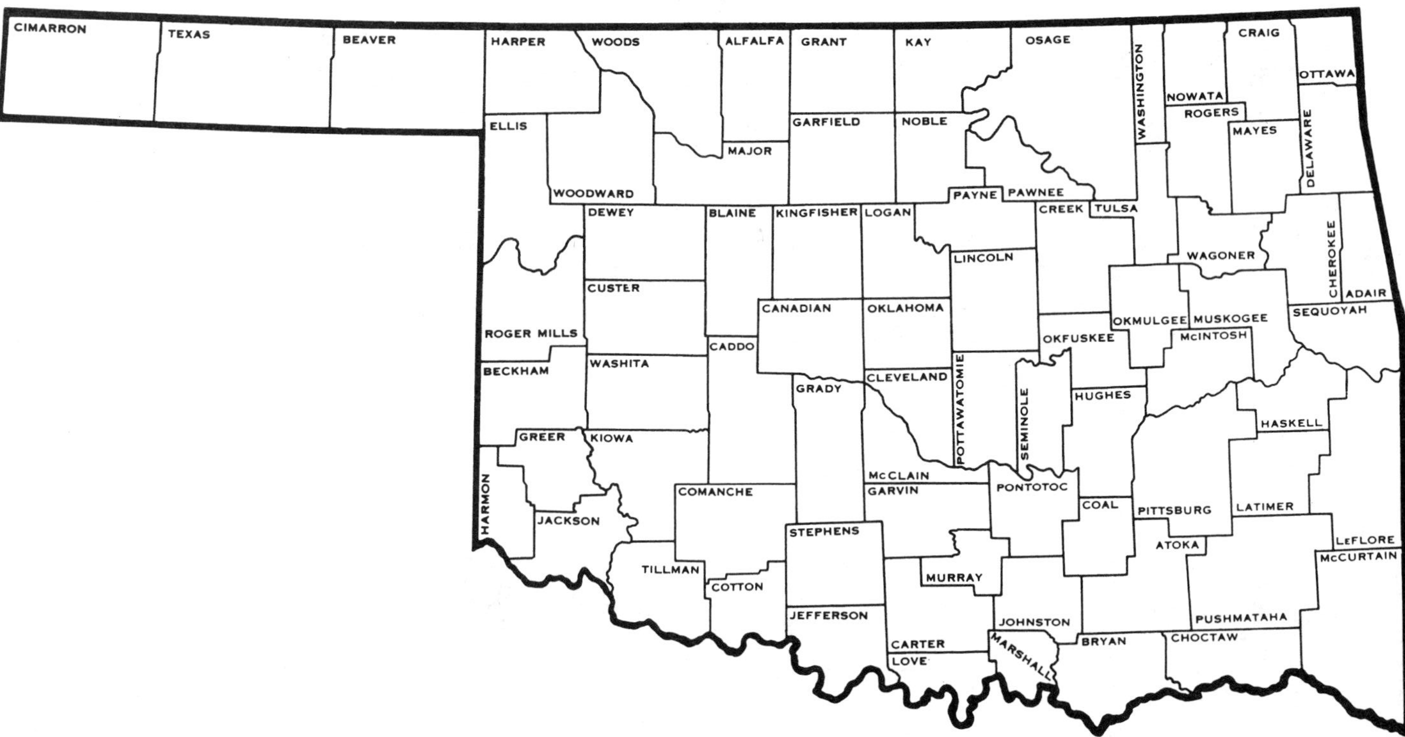

FIGURE 2. Oklahoma Counties.

spotted bass, logperch, and orangethroat darter, attests to the probability that relatively clear water with uniform flow and higher gradients could support a different fish fauna in uplifted regions even in the heart of the western plains. Physiographic and climatic features apparently have a more profound influence on the east-west distribution of Oklahoma fishes than do geographic factors.

A smaller group seems to occur in about the eastern third of the state, including the steelcolor shiner, freckled madtom, blackspotted topminnow, bluntnose darter, channel darter, and possibly the spotted sucker. Although the preferred habitat types may be distinctive among these species, most of them seem to be associated with either limestone or uplifted areas or both. The fact that they occur in both the Red River and Arkansas River basins suggests that they have been inhabitants of this region for a fairly long time, since the two systems have been separated long enough to allow the differentiation of a number of species (such as the rocky shiner in the Ouachita uplands, the leopard darter in the Little River, and the longnose darter in tributaries of the Arkansas) and subspecies (in the redfin shiner and orangethroat darter, for example).

One of the most distinctive fish assemblages can be found in the lowland waters of the Little River, Kiamichi River, and Red River systems of the Southeastern Coastal Plain region, called the Mississippi Biotic District by Blair and Hubbell (1938). This group includes the mooneye, blackspot shiner, ironcolor shiner, taillight shiner, peppered shiner, brown bullhead, pirate perch, western starhead topminnow, yellow bass, banded pigmy sunfish, flier, redbreast sunfish, dollar sunfish, redspotted sunfish, bantam sunfish, crystal darter, mud darter, swamp darter, and goldstripe darter. These species occur in the lowland streams, ponds, or oxbows of the Mississippi basin and/or southern coastal plains. Few are found west of Choctaw County, and most are known only from McCurtain County (fig. 2, map of Oklahoma counties).

Another distinctive assemblage occurs in the Ozark region of northeastern Oklahoma. The 21 species in this category include a mixture of endemic Ozark fishes found mainly in Oklahoma, Arkansas, Kansas, and Missouri (such as the wedgespot shiner, cardinal shiner, Neosho madtom, Ozark cavefish, Arkansas darter, and stippled darter) and species that are more widespread in clear, cooler waters of the northeast and in the highlands of the southeastern United States (such as the Ozark minnow, bigeye chub, gravel chub, spotfin shiner, creek chub, white sucker, northern hog sucker, stonecat, northern studfish, plains topminnow, rock bass, fantail darter, speckled darter, and banded sculpin). The redspot chub and shorthead redhorse are primarily Ozark forms but can be found in one or two other parts of the state. The Ozark species are undoubtedly limited to this area by a combination of the physical attributes of the region (clear, gravel-bottomed streams with frequent limestone outcroppings and an abundance of cold, clear springs) and the access route by which they entered the region. A number of facts indicate that at least some members of this fauna have had a much wider distribution in Oklahoma earlier in geologic time. Besides the occurrence of species like the redspot chub, shorthead redhorse, cardinal shiner, and southern redbelly dace in limited but widely separate regions elsewhere in the state, Pleistocene fishes (including the creek chub and white sucker) known from the Baerends fauna of Beaver County in the Oklahoma panhandle suggest that the climate in the high plains region was much cooler and that gravelly streams must have been present in this region during the Pleistocene (Smith 1954; 1963). Unfortunately, little is actually known about the drainage patterns of Oklahoma waters prior to recent times, though Metcalf (1966) has suggested that a major preglacial north-south river system may have existed in east-central Oklahoma.

It is possible that the total pattern of fish distribution reflects two or more invasions of the region, with the forms constituting distinctive Arkansas and Red River faunas being the most recent invaders. We hope a more detailed definitive study of the aquatic fauna of Oklahoma may clarify some of these relationships, but the data are at present too scanty to permit more than the aforegoing speculation.

Some interesting comparisons can be made among the species inhabiting different stream systems along the eastern edge of the state. Differences between the Ozark and Southeastern Coastal Plain faunas can be attributed to habitat differences and to the fact that most coastal plain fishes have been unable to penetrate the Arkansas system far enough to enter Oklahoma streams. Yet there are a number of species, some lowland inhabitants but many limited to clear, swift tributary streams, that occur in more than one of the major drainage systems of eastern Oklahoma, yet are not as widespread as the previously described group of inhabitants of the eastern third of the state.

A small group can be found in streams from the Ozarks to the Red River tributaries in the Ouachitas. Members of this group are the chestnut and southern brook lampreys, pallid shiner, ribbon shiner, creek chubsucker, river redhorse, black redhorse, smallmouth bass, cypress darter, and blackside darter, though the black redhorse has not been reported from the Poteau drainage. Most of these species seem to be inhabitants of clear, gravel-bottomed streams and rivers.

When fishes of the Poteau River are compared with those of the Ozarks and those of the streams draining the Ouachitas (Red River system), some interesting relationships emerge. Although there are ten species found in both the Red River tributaries and the Poteau and only seven shared by the Ozarks and Poteau, most of the latter are headwater or mainstream forms (slender and brindled madtoms; greenside, least, redfin, banded, and longnose darters), whereas most of the former are base-level or large-river inhabitants (bowfin, redfin pickerel, silvery minnow, pugnose minnow, Kiamichi shiner, tadpole madtom, scaly sand darter, harlequin darter, johnny darter, and dusky darter). At any rate, the apparent paradox of having a greater similarity in the fishes of river systems in different drainages can probably be best explained by assuming that most of the fishes found mainly in the Poteau and Ouachita-draining streams are essentially lowland fishes that moved up the Red and Arkansas rivers only to the eastern edge of the state and were unable to find suitable habitats in the major tributaries of the Ozark region.

The only species known from upland streams of the Ouachitas alone are the mountain madtom, Ouachita Mountain shiner, rocky shiner, and leopard darter.

Species known only from the Red River and its immediate base-level tributaries are the chain pickerel, chub shiner, blacktail shiner, western sand darter, crystal darter, and striped mullet. Only the Arkansas River shiner seems to be limited to the Arkansas River. The species that seem to be strictly western forms are the plains killifish, prairie chub, and Red River pupfish.

A final group of species seems to be associated with the larger rivers of the state, and several of them have also done well in the impoundments of these rivers. This group includes the shovelnose sturgeon, paddlefish, alligator gar (in the east), American eel, prairie chub, shoal chub, flathead chub, silver chub, river shiner, silverband shiner (in the east), highfin carpsucker, blue sucker, black buffalo, blue catfish, river darter, sauger, and walleye.

In summary, the patterns of distribution exhibited by Oklahoma fishes suggest the existence of several more or less distinctive faunal assemblages. Because fishes are limited by their dependence on water, often with specific physical or chemical constitution, and have often developed rather specialized ecological relationships, they cannot be impressed into the faunal regions or biotic districts that have been proposed on the basis of studies of reptiles or mammals. Neither do they correlate perfectly with physiographic features of the state. Nonetheless, when we consider that fishes are limited to streams, rivers, and lakes, it is noteworthy that there is considerable overlap in the patterning of faunal groups among the vertebrates that have been studied. We believe this similarity is due primarily to physiographic and climatic factors, whereas divergences are likely to be associated with the strictly geographic inhibitions imposed on any completely aquatic group of organisms. Thorough explanation of the distribution patterns of Oklahoma fishes, however, must await further zoogeographic, taxonomic, historical, and geological investigations.

What the Species Accounts Include

The bulk of this book consists of individual accounts of those species of Oklahoma fishes that are or have recently become established residents of the state. The majority of these species are native, but a number of them have been introduced either formally as game species by the Oklahoma Department of Wildlife Conservation (ODWC) or informally by anglers—often as bait fish. It is possible that a few of the 176 species discussed are no longer present as viable breeding populations, and several other rare species may well be on their way out as constituents of our fish fauna, but they are included because of the firm documentation of their presence in the state in the immediate past. A number of species not included have been recorded from the state and have been listed in the ODWC checklist of state fishes. The central mudminnow (*Umbra limi*), northern redbelly dace (*Phoxinus eos*), brook stickleback (*Culaea inconstans*), and rudd (*Scardinius erythrophthalmus*) have all been introduced into our waters as bait fish from Minnesota and elsewhere, but there seems to be no evidence that any except possibly the rudd (Pigg and Pham 1990) have become established in the state. The stargazing darter (*Percina uranidea*) has not to our knowledge been found in the state in recent decades despite intense collecting in the areas where Meek (1896) recorded it as common. Although a few specimens of the sheepshead (*Archosargus probatocephalus*) have been recorded from a number of lakes and rivers in various parts of the state, there is little evidence that the species is anything more than a sporadic visitor to the lower Red River system in Oklahoma. Finally, although the muskellunge (*Esox masquinongy*) has been stocked by the ODWC in several Oklahoma lakes, including Tenkiller and Pine Creek Reservoir, the success of these stockings is still in question at the time of writing.

Several exotic species have been introduced to the state accidentally or purposefully and may occasionally be caught by anglers or fish collectors. The white perch (*Morone americana*) has recently been introduced into the Arkansas River basin, from Kansas. If it breeds successfully in our waters it will become the first successful exotic (Kim Erickson, Pers. comm.). In a few cases, as in blue tilapia (*Oreochromis aureus*) and rudd (*Scardinius erythrophthalmus*), fair numbers may occur in a limited area at some point in time. Until these aggregations demonstrate their ability to reproduce and stand the test of time as established long-term breeding populations, we prefer not to recognize them as valid residents of the state. Other species that have been collected occasionally in the state are grass carp (*Ctenopharyngodon idella*), bighead carp (*Hypophthalmichthyes nobilis*), and a diverse array of South American and African fishes released into our waters by aquarists. The first two species are encountered often enough for us to have included them in the key to Cyprinidae. Should evidence accumulate that they have established themselves as breeding populations with a discrete range in the state, they may come to be included as valid members of our fish fauna. When such fishes are encountered, they should be taken to a university ichthyologist or to the Oklahoma Department of Wildlife Conservation for identification and record-keeping purposes.

Each species account contains a photograph or drawing of the species, a brief description that emphasizes diagnostic characteristics, a summary of the North American and Oklahoma distribution of the species, and a short statement about known aspects of its biology and habitat preferences. A range map is provided for most species. Areas where the species has been previously found and where it is likely to be encountered are indicated by shading. The ranges indicated on the maps are based on a variety of sources but primarily reflect collections by the Oklahoma Biological Survey and the staff and students of Oklahoma State University, the University of Oklahoma, and Tulsa University. Shaded areas on the maps are projections of the overall area within which a species is most likely to be found. Obviously, it will be found only in appropriate habitats within the projected range and may be found in some areas outside this range where the species has not previously been taken. A few records, from widely disjunct populations or with limited geographic breadth, are mentioned in the text but not the range maps.

Most of the photographs are based on freshly preserved specimens collected in Oklahoma. Unfortunately, for a number of the larger or less common species, we were forced to use older preserved material, and the quality of some of these pictures is not up to the standard we would prefer. Also, a few species are represented by halftones of paintings. A few of the photographs were of specimens collected outside Oklahoma, but none of these differed in pigment pattern or body shape from Oklahoma specimens in our care. They were used primarily because local specimens were in poor condition or were unavailable.

Paintings by the senior author are included in a separate section of color plates. These paintings portray the fishes as they appear immediately upon being taken from the water, and most are based on a composite of reference photos both published and unpublished, with the final painting (rendered in acrylic) reflecting the professional experience and knowledge of the artist. Some details, such as outlines of the scales, were purposely not emphasized when such features are not evident in live specimens. The paintings thus represent a depiction of the shape and color of an individual representative of the species. Needless to say, they do not represent individuals of different ontogenetic stages or sexes.

Statements about biology and habitat are based on a variety of sources, with references deemed especially significant cited in the text. In many cases, however, information derives from personal observations by the authors or from several sources providing similar information, and no attempt was made to cite all such sources. Good general references include Trautman's *The Fishes of Ohio* (1981), Cross's *Handbook of Fishes of Kansas* (1967), and Carlander's *Handbook of Freshwater Fishery Biology* (1977) as well as a host of earlier works like Forbes and Richardson's *The Fishes of Illinois* (1920). Recent books like Robison and Buchanan's *Fishes of Arkansas* (1988), Jenkins and Burkhead's *Freshwater Fishes of Virginia* (1994), Etnier and Starnes's *The Fishes of Tennessee* (1993), Mettee, O'Neil, and Pierson's *Fishes of Alabama and the Mobile Basin* (1996), and most recently Ross's *Inland Fishes of Mississippi* (2001) provide wonderful current information on fishes.

The common and scientific names of the fishes treated here are those presented in "Common and Scientific Names of Fishes from the United States, Canada, and Mexico" (Nelson et al., in press), except in a few cases where we disagree with the authors of that list about the scientific names of species, genera, or families or where current accepted nomenclature has dictated a departure from that list. Inasmuch as a revision of that work is in progress, we are trying to use names that reflect consensus in the current literature. In cases where we diverge from that consensus, we present our reasons.

Genera and species are arranged alphabetically within each family, and the families are arranged essentially in accordance with the scheme proposed by Greenwood, Rosen, Weitzman, and Myers (1966), with some modification for current ideas.

Preservation and Care of Specimens

A wide variety of techniques, including seining, angling, gill netting, and trapnetting, may be used to capture fishes. Since methods for collecting and preserving fishes are described in a number of readily available works (e.g., Cross 1967; Hubbs and Lagler 1958), we do not address the subject extensively. It is necessary, however, to know something about the standard methods for preserving and maintaining specimens that are to be retained in local collections or sent to established institutional museums.

The most useful containers for field collections are wide-mouthed plastic or glass jars of from one quart to one gallon capacity. Most plastic jars have screw-on-lids, which somewhat slows the opening and closing process, but have the advantage of being unbreakable. A 10 percent solution of formalin (90 percent water, 10 percent concentrated formalin—usually available at chemical supply outlets) is used in the container to kill and fix the specimens immediately after capture. Larger specimens (generally 7 to 8 inches or more in length) should be taken from the container after killing and slit open on the right side of the abdomen to ensure preservation of deeper tissues. In very large specimens, a series of small slits in the dorsal muscle masses on the right side are often required for good preservation.

A label of good quality, high rag-content paper should always be placed in the container immediately after the collection is completed. The use of a Kohinoor Rapiograph pen and Higgins Eternal Ink or Higgins Engrossing Ink or any pen with permanent black ink is generally recommended for preparation of permanent labels. The label should include the locality (state, county, section, township, and range, where known, or latitude and longitude from a GPS unit, if available); the name of the stream, lake, or pond where the collection was made; and information about the means of access to the collecting site (state or county road numbers, etc.) when possible. The collection date and names of the collectors (and their field numbers, if these are recorded on separate field note sheets) should also be put on the label. Field notes are usually compiled by most professionals and contain more detailed information on temperature, weather conditions, and the habitats encountered. The references cited give a detailed description of how to go about preparing and utilizing a comprehensive set of field notes.

Specimens should be kept in the original formalin solution for three to six days (longer for larger specimens), then soaked in fresh water for two to three days, until the formalin odor is largely gone. It is generally best to change the water several times during the washing process. The specimens should then be placed in 50 percent isopropyl alcohol or 70 percent ethyl alcohol. If the specimens are to be permanently stored, the original alcohol solution should be replaced by a fresh solution. Specimens to be maintained in a permanent collection should be kept in mason jars with polyethylene lids and polypropylene liners. The jars should be checked periodically for evaporation, and any fluid loss should be replaced.

Threatened Fishes

Conservation efforts in most parts of the world have largely focused on terrestrial habitats (Ryman et al. 1994), while aquatic habitats have received less attention from biologists (Folkerts 1997). Interestingly, aquatic fauna are proportionately more threatened than terrestrial species (Stein and Chipley 1996; Master 1990) and are more vulnerable to extinction. The fact that fresh water comprises less than 0.5 percent of the water on Earth gives us much concern as there is compelling evidence that North America freshwater biodiversity is diminishing as rapidly as that of some of the most stressed terrestrial ecosystems on the planet (Myers 1988; Ricciardi and Rasmussen 1999). Fishes are appropriate indicators of trends in aquatic biodiversity because their enormous variety reflects a wide range of environmental conditions (Moyle and Leidy 1992).

Conservative estimates suggest that 20 percent of the world's freshwater fishes are extinct or in serious decline (Moyle and Leidy 1992). Only 4 percent of all federally protected aquatic species with recovery plans have exhibited significant recovery (Williams and Neves 1992). Williams and colleagues (1989) reported that within North America the number of freshwater fishes considered by the American Fisheries Society to be endangered, threatened, or of special concern increased by 31 percent in the 1980s. The most important threats to aquatic organisms are generally given as, first, habitat destruction and fragmentation; second, pollution; and third, exotic species. Miller and co-workers (1989) dealt with North American fish extinctions and concluded that physical habitat alteration was the most common cause (implicated in 73 percent of extinctions) followed by introduced species (68 percent), chemical alteration of habitat (38 percent), hybridization (38 percent), and overharvesting (15 percent). Eastern species are most commonly affected by altered sediment loads from agricultural activities, whereas exotic species, habitat removal or damage, and altered hydrologic regimes predominate in the West (Richter et al. 1997).

The federal government protects organisms through the Endangered Species Act of 1973 (Public Law 93-205), which provides a program for the protection of species considered to be endangered or threatened with extinction. The act requires the listing of species according to specified criteria, prohibits the "taking" of any cited species, and encourages the preservation of habitats.

In Oklahoma, Robison and colleagues (1974) provided the first preliminary effort to clarify the status of the fishes in the state. A total of 34 forms were considered to be "threatened," five of which were deemed "rare and endangered." Later, this information was used by the Rare and Endangered Species of Oklahoma Committee (1975) to publish *Rare and Endangered Vertebrates and Plants of Oklahoma*. Today, both the Oklahoma Department of Wildlife Conservation (2001) and the Oklahoma Natural Heritage Inventory (2001) provide the public with lists of state threatened or endangered species based on federal and state laws. The definitions used by both organizations are based on Title 29, the Conservation Department's enabling legislation, section 800:25-19-6, Species Listing. Definitions for state species are as follows:

State Endangered Species:

A native species for which the prospect of survival or recruitment within the state is in imminent jeopardy. This determination is based primarily upon the status of the species within Oklahoma.

State Threatened Species:

A native species that, although not presently in danger of extirpation, is likely to become endangered in the foreseeable future in the absence of special protection and management efforts.

State Special Concern:

Definitions for these two categories are not from ODWC but from the Oklahoma Natural Heritage Inventory or ONHI (Ian Butler, pers. comm.).

CATEGORY I: A native species with a presently stable or increasing population that current evidence indicates is especially vulnerable to extirpation because of limited range, low population, or other factors.

CATEGORY II: A native species identified by technical experts as possibly threatened or vulnerable to extirpation but for which little, if any, evidence exists to document the population level, range, or other factors pertinent to its status.

Four fish species in Oklahoma are provided federal protection under the Endangered Species Act of 1973 (table 1) as federally "threatened" species: the Arkansas River shiner (*Notropis girardi*), Neosho madtom (*Noturus placidus*), Ozark cavefish (*Amblyopsis rosae*), and leopard darter (*Percina pantherina*). The Arkansas darter (*Etheostoma cragini*), is currently a candidate proposed for federal listing; however, it is considered a State Special Concern Category 2 species by the ODWC and the ONHI, which does not seem to make sense; we would urge a status of State Threatened Species in Oklahoma for this darter. In addition, the blackside darter (*Percina maculata*) is accorded State Threatened status, while the longnose darter (*Percina nasuta*) is considered endangered within Oklahoma.

One species not currently on the state lists but reported by Luttrell and colleagues (1999) to be extirpated from the state is the peppered chub (*Macrhybopsis tetranema*), which still occurs in nearby states. Because it has been extirpated, we have chosen not to include a species account for it but rather to mention it in the accounts for its congeners.

No state fishes are presently deemed State Special Concern Category 1. All 30 fishes of concern are currently placed in Category 2 (table 1).

TABLE 1.
Threatened Fishes of Oklahoma with Federal and/or State Conservation Status

COMMON NAME	SCIENTIFIC NAME	STATUS FEDERAL	STATUS STATE
Threatened or Endangered Species			
Arkansas River shiner	*Notropis girardi*	T	T
Neosho madtom	*Noturus placidus*	T	T
Ozark cavefish	*Amblyopsis rosae*	T	T
Blackside darter	*Percina maculata*		T
Longnose darter	*Percina nasuta*		E
Leopard darter	*Percina pantherina*	T	T
Federal Candidates and Species Proposed for Listing			
Arkansas darter	*Etheostoma cragini*	C	T
Extirpated from Oklahoma Listed Species			
Peppered chub	*Macrhybopsis tetranema*	Extirpated	
State Special Concern Category 2 Species			
Southern brook lamprey	*Ichthyomyzon gagei*		SS2
Shovelnose sturgeon	*Scaphirhynchus platorynchus*		SS2
Alligator gar	*Atractosteus spatula*		SS2
Mooneye	*Hiodon tergisus*		SS2
Alabama shad	*Alosa alabamae*		SS2
Bluntface shiner	*Cyprinella camura*		SS2
Spotfin shiner	*Cyprinella spiloptera*		SS2
Cypress minnow	*Hybognathus hayi*		SS2
Pallid shiner	*Hybopsis amnis*		SS2
Ribbon shiner	*Lythrurus fumeus*		SS2
Ironcolor shiner	*Notropis chalybaeus*		SS2
Bluehead shiner	*Notropis hubbsi*		SS2
Taillight shiner	*Notropis maculatus*		SS2
Kiamichi shiner	*Notropis ortenburgeri*		SS2
Peppered shiner	*Notropis perpallidus*		SS2
Flathead chub	*Platygobio gracilis*		SS2
Brown bullhead	*Ameiurus nebulosus*		SS2
Mountain madtom	*Noturus eleutherus*		SS2
Stonecat	*Noturus flavus*		SS2
Blue sucker	*Cycleptus elongatus*		SS2
Black buffalo	*Ictiobus niger*		SS2

TABLE 1. (CONTINUED)
Threatened Fishes of Oklahoma with Federal and/or State Conservation Status

COMMON NAME	SCIENTIFIC NAME	STATUS FEDERAL	STATUS STATE
Shorthead redhorse	*Moxostoma macrolepidotum*		SS2
Plains topminnow	*Fundulus sciadicus*		SS2
Chain pickerel	*Esox niger*		SS2
Redbreast sunfish	*Lepomis auritus*		SS2
Spotted bass	*Micropterus punctulatus wichitae*		SS2*
Crystal darter	*Crystallaria asprella*		SS2
Harlequin darter	*Etheostoma histrio*		SS2
Goldstripe darter	*Etheostoma parvipinne*		SS2
River darter	*Percina shumardi*		SS2

Federal Status

E = Listed as Endangered

T = Listed as Threatened

C = Candidate for listing (not presently listed but the U.S. Fish and Wildlife Service has sufficient information on biological status and threats to propose listing under the Endangered Species Act)

State Status

E = Endangered (survival or recruitment in imminent jeopardy)

T = Threatened (not presently in danger of extirpation but likely to become endangered in the absence of special protection efforts)

SS2 = State Special Concern Category 2 (possibly threatened or vulnerable to extirpation but evidence pertinent to status is insufficient)

*We follow Cofer (1995) in concluding *Micropterus punctulatus wichitae* to be an invalid taxon. Specimens of *"M. p. wichitae"* collected historically from the area should be identified as *Micropterus punctulatus* × *M. dolomeiu* or *M. punctulatus*.

Although we have these lists, the true status of a number of these species in the state remains obscure. We would urge an intensive study of these imperiled fishes in Oklahoma, funded by the Oklahoma Department of Wildlife Conservation, to ascertain their current status.

EXOTIC FISHES

Scientists have estimated that approximately 7,000 invasive species of plants and animals are now established in the United States, termed exotics, of which over 80 are fishes established in U.S. waters. An exotic species is defined as one that has been moved by design or accident from its native environment and transported to foreign regions where it is not native. An additional 210 species of North American fishes have been moved and are established beyond their native ranges (Gilbert and Williams 2002). Typically, exotic or nonindigenous species often outcompete native species because they have no competition, diseases, or native enemies in their new environment. If left unchecked, these exotic species can alter entire ecosystems and may drive native species to the point of extinction. Gilbert and Williams (2002) suggested that these invasive nonindigenous species should be treated as biological pollutants. The U.S. Fish and Wildlife Service currently lists more than 100 native fish species as endangered or threatened, and nonindigenous species have contributed to the decline of about half of these. Nonindigenous fishes were a factor in the extinction of 24 of the 30 fish species extinct in the United States (Gilbert and Williams 2002).

In Oklahoma, 13 fish species or 7.3 percent of our total fish fauna are considered exotics (table 2). Some exotics, such as the striped bass, rainbow trout, and brown trout, have acclimated nicely and now generate millions of dollars for the state in revenue from fishermen. Others, such as the rudd and blue tilapia, are more recent invaders and have not been here long enough for us to make determinations about their effects on the native fish fauna of Oklahoma.

How to Use This Book

The most reliable way to identify an unknown fish using this book is through the keys. These are arranged with the key to families preceding the species accounts, and species keys at the beginning of each series of accounts of species belonging to a given family. Until one becomes familiar with the families of fishes, the first step in the identification process is to use the family key to determine the family to which the fish belongs, then use the species keys to determine genus and species (and/or common name). Technical terms for the diagnostic characteristics used in the keys and species descriptions may not be familiar to everyone using this book. Most of these physical characteristics are pictured in figures 3 to 9 at the end of the introduction, and they are defined in the glossary that starts on page 33. Simple equipment such as forceps, proportional dividers, and dissecting needles will generally suffice to manipulate body parts during the identification process, but for most of the smaller species (especially in the larger families such as the Cyprinidae and Percidae) use of a binocular microscope is required.

Proportional measurements are indicated either as fractions of a standard measurement, such as standard length (SL; see fig. 3), or as the number of times one body part measurement fits into that of another (e.g., eye diameter 3.5–4 in head length). Such proportional measurements are best

TABLE 2.
Exotic or Non-native Fish Species Introduced into Oklahoma

COMMON NAME	SCIENTIFIC NAME
Goldfish	*Carassius auratus*
Grass carp	*Ctenopharyngodon idella*
Common carp	*Cyprinus carpio*
Bighead carp	*Hypophthalmichthyes nobilis*
Rudd	*Scardinius erythrophthalmus*
Brown bullhead	*Ameiurus nebulosus*
Northern pike	*Esox lucius*
Rainbow trout	*Oncorhynchus mykiss*
Brown trout	*Salmo trutta*
Striped bass	*Morone saxatilis*
Redbreast sunfish	*Lepomis auritus*
Yellow perch	*Perca flavescens*
Blue tilapia	*Oreochromis aureus*

done with either proportional dividers or calipers. Body parts grow at different rates, however, and their relative sizes may differ at different stages of maturity. Most of the ranges of body part proportions presented represent the fish sizes and ages most commonly encountered during ichthyological collecting trips; thus extremely small or large specimens may occasionally exhibit body proportions outside the ranges given. Unfortunately, such specimens often also show somewhat different color patterns and in some cases different scale counts (especially in the number of pored scales in fishes with incompletely pored lateral lines).

Probably the most critical of the scale counts is the lateral-line count (fig. 3). The most reliable way to determine the limits of the lateral line is as follows: lightly flex the caudal fin; this generally produces a conspicuous fold at the structural base of the caudal fin (hypural plate). Starting with the scale just anterior to the crease, the lateral line extends forward to the scale contacting the bony shoulder girdle. In species with incomplete lateral lines, one should begin counting at the shoulder girdle and work posteriorly, noting both the number of pored scales and the total number of scales in the row that is partially pored (again terminating at the structural base of the caudal fin). Many ichthyologists prefer to count lateral-line scales starting at the anterior end of the fish at all times. In species without a lateral line, the number of scale rows crossing the middle of the side of the body can be counted in the same manner that the lateral-line scales are counted.

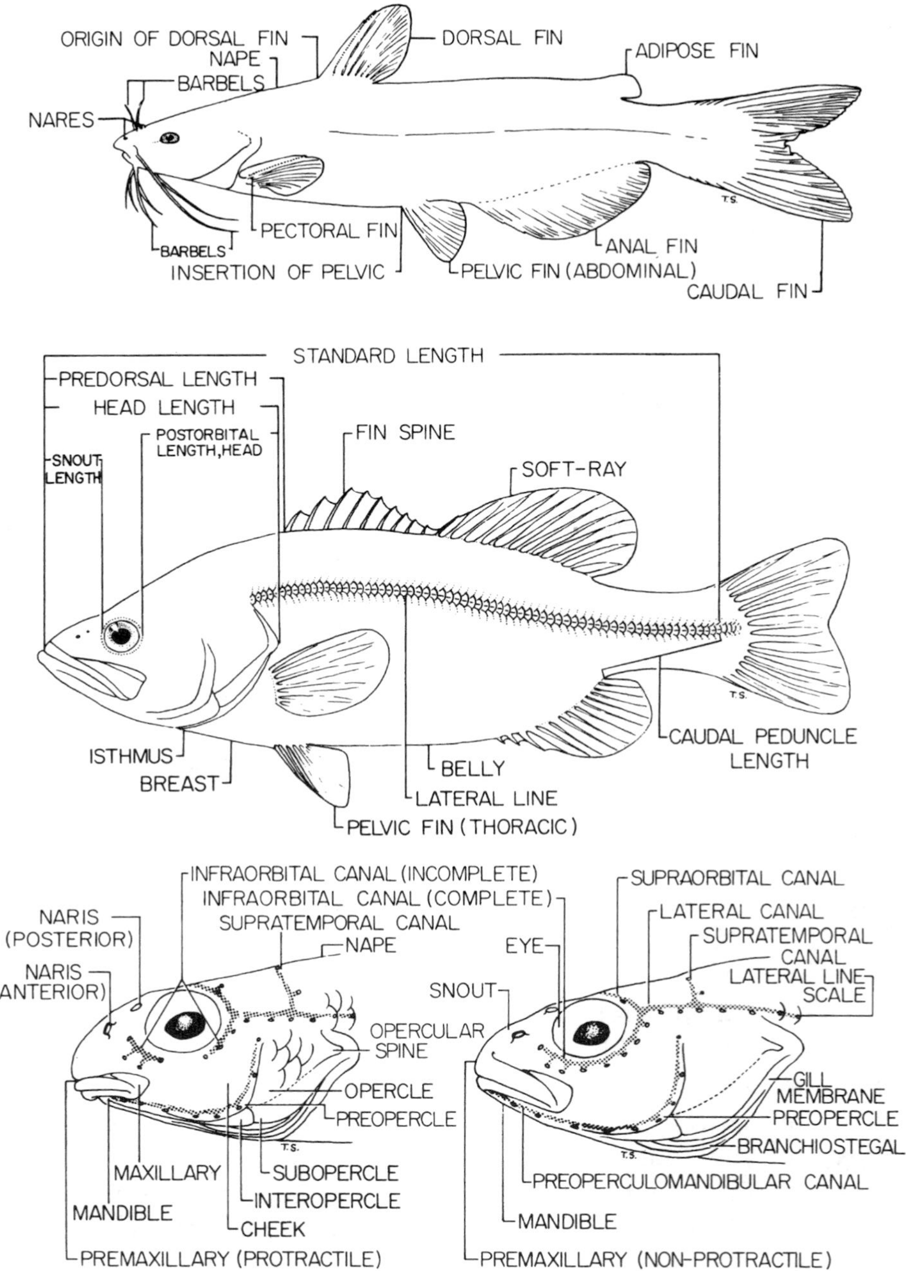

FIGURE 3. Structural features of fishes often used for identification. Species shown are channel catfish *(top)*, largemouth bass *(center)*, johnny darter *(lower left)*, and stippled darter *(lower right)*. (From Cross 1967)

Other counts used here are the number of predorsal scale rows, cheek scale rows, and circumferential scale rows on the body and caudal peduncle. Predorsal scale rows are the total number of scale rows crossing the midline of the back between the occiput (see glossary) and the origin of the dorsal fin. Cheek scale rows are counted along a line from the posteroventral edge of the eye downward and backward to the angle of the preopercle (fig. 3). Body circumference scale rows are counted by starting with the scale just in front of the dorsal fin origin and counting the number of scale rows along a vertical line directly around the entire body, ending with the scale on the opposite side of the body in contact with the initial scale counted. Scales around the caudal peduncle are often counted in a zigzag fashion at its slenderest point, beginning at a dorsal- or ventral-ridge scale or one of the lateral-line scales.

In identifying minnows and suckers it is often important to examine the fifth (pharyngeal) gill arch, which is deeply embedded in fleshy and muscular tissue behind the four gill-bearing arches (fig. 8). The bony pharyngeal arch is not visible because of the overlying tissues and must be loosened from its attachments and cleaned before the teeth can be examined. This can best be done by inserting a sharp instrument such as a fine sharpened dissecting needle, or as Cross (1967) suggests a dissecting needle with the tip formed into a minute hook, along the dorsal arm of the arch and gently tearing the attachment muscles and ligaments loose. After repeating the process on the ventral arm of the arch, the arch and associated tissues can be gently lifted out with fine-tipped forceps and the soft tissue can be cleaned from the arch. The whole process generally requires use of a dissecting microscope, except in the very largest specimens. The manner in which the teeth are counted is illustrated in figure 8. It must be noted that teeth are occasionally missing (during the replacement process) or knocked off during excision and cleaning. Careful examination of the arch usually discloses the presence of scars where teeth have previously been present; such scars must be counted along with the other teeth.

If the descriptions, figures, and glossary definitions given are not clear enough to permit use of a particular characteristic, additional description of methods used for counting and measuring fish characteristics can be found in Cross (1967), Robison and Buchanan (1988), Etnier and Starnes (1993), or Jenkins and Burkhead (1994).

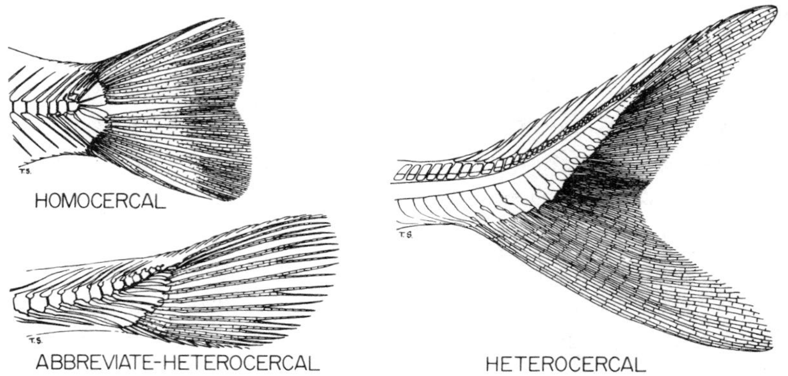

FIGURE 4. Caudal fins in fishes. Homocercal fin is that of the black crappie; abbreviate-heterocercal, shortnose gar; heterocercal, paddlefish. (From Cross 1967)

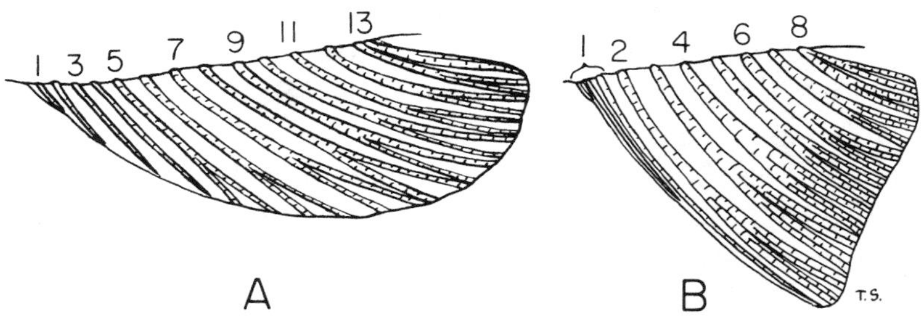

FIGURE 5. Hypothetical anal fins (or, in effect, inverted dorsal fins) showing how fin-rays are counted. (From Cross 1967)

A. Total ray-count, as taken in fins that slope gradually away from the body contour.
B. Principal ray-count, as taken in fins that have a straight leading edge (rudimentary or procurrent rays contiguous anteriorly.

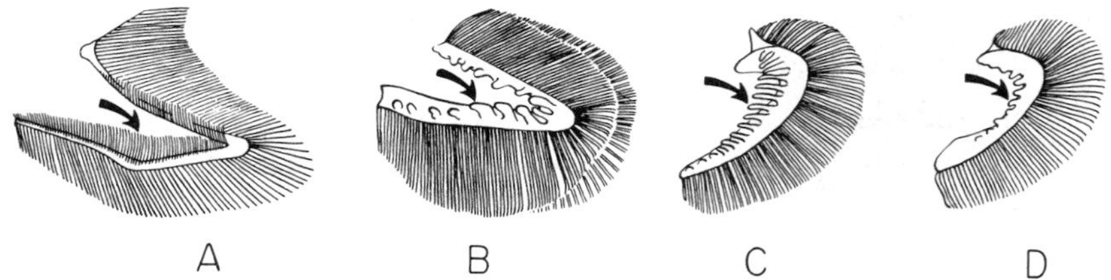

FIGURE 6. First gill arches of four fishes, showing differences in number and shape of gill rakers (on concave side of each arch, see arrows). (From Cross 1967)

A. Rakers numerous and slender, as in Clupeidae. Gizzard shad illustrated.
B. Rakers short and knoblike, as in Hiodontidae. Goldeye illlustrated.
C. Rakers slender, as in species of *Lepomis* other than the longear and the redear. Green Sunfish illustrated.
D. Rakers short and knoblike, as in the longear (illustrated) and the redear.

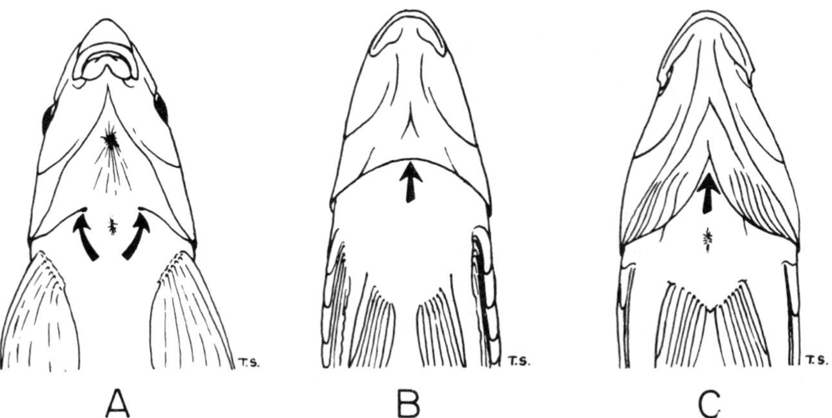

FIGURE 7. Gill membranes of fishes in relation to ventral body wall (note arrows). (From Cross 1967)

A. Right and left membranes bound down to isthmus, as in minnows and suckers (carpsucker illustrated); a needle tip slipped into the gill cleft on one side cannot be moved freely across to the opposite side. Gill membranes free from isthmus in B and C.

B. Gill membranes broadly joined across isthmus, as in banded darter.

C. Gill membranes separate (right and left sides not conjoined), as in stippled darter.

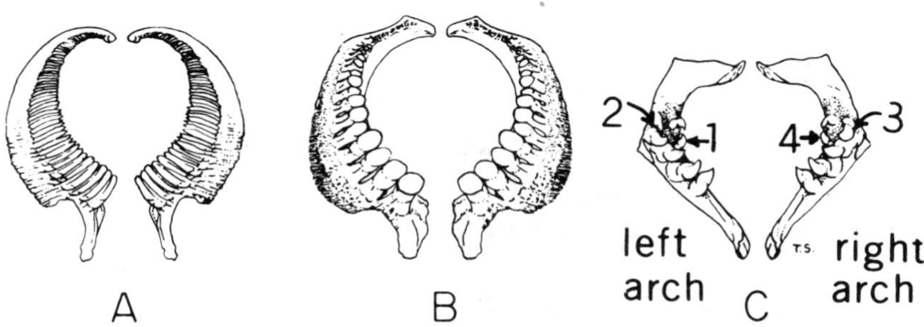

FIGURE 8. Pharyngeal arches of suckers (A and B) and a minnow (C). As shown, arches have been laid on a horizontal surface with teeth projecting upward. (From Cross 1967)

A. Golden redhorse; teeth numerous and slender, in a single row (comblike).

B. River redhorse; lower teeth stumplike or molariform, but numerous and uniserial.

C. Creek chub; teeth few, confined to central part of arch, often hooked (two-rowed in this species). The sequence in which rows are counted is indicated by numerals 1, 2, 3, 4. The count of number of teeth therefore is 2, 5–4, 2.

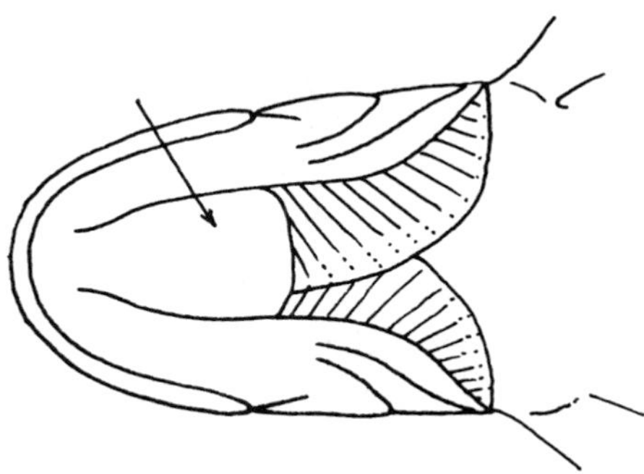

FIGURE 9. Gular plate of *Amia calva* (see arrow).

Use of Keys

The keys constitute pairs (couplets) of alternate statements arranged in a sequence and numbered consecutively along the left margin. Beginning with couplet 1 in the family key, both alternative descriptions (1a and 1b) should be read while examining the specimen—if it has a sucking mouth, lacks paired fins, and has seven gill openings, it is a lamprey, and one should proceed to the key to lampreys. If the specimen has jaws and paired fins, proceed to couplet 2, read the two alternatives (2a and 2b), and decide which one agrees best with the specimen. If the specimen lacks eyes and pigment, it belongs to the family Amblyopsidae (cavefishes) and can be identified by using the key for that family. If the specimen has well-developed eyes and some skin pigment, proceed to couplet 3 and continue through the key until the correct family is located.

The illustrations of representative members of each family should be of some assistance in checking whether the specimen in hand generally resembles a typical member of the family. The same process of systematically proceeding through the consecutive couplets should be used to identify species in each family. When the specimen is tentatively assigned a name as a result of working through the key, it should be compared with the photograph for the species and the brief description presented in the text. If a specimen does not resemble the photograph and description, it may be a member of a different species, a slightly aberrant specimen, or perhaps an individual at a distinctively different development stage. When the resources in this book are exhausted in attempting to identify a fish, an attempt should be made to utilize other references like Moore (1968), or the specimen should be preserved in formalin or alcohol and taken or sent to an ichthyologist at Oklahoma State University or one of the other state institutions where expert taxonomic advice can be solicited.

Most of the fish anatomy terms used in identification keys and species accounts are illustrated in figure 3, with detail about fin and gill structures presented in figures 4 through 9.

KEY TO THE FAMILIES OF FISHES

1a. Jaws absent; mouth a sucking disc; no paired fins; 7 gill openings; without an operculum . . . . PETROMYZONTIDAE

1b. Jaws present; mouth not in shape of sucking disc; paired fins; operculum present 2

2a. Eyes absent or rudimentary; skin without dark pigment . . . . AMBLYOPSIDAE

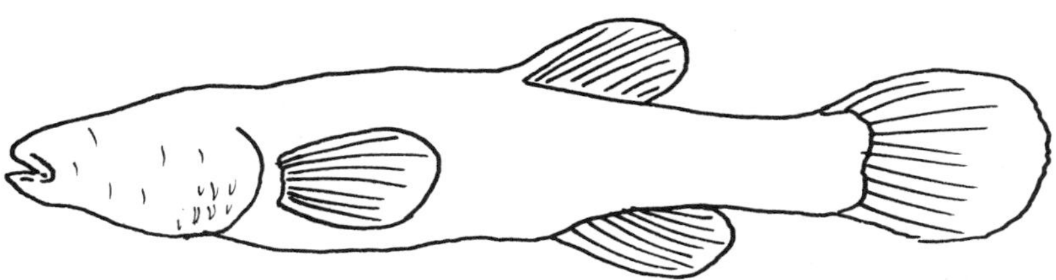

2b. Eyes well developed; skin with at least some pigment 3

3a. Caudal fin typically heterocercal (see fig. 4); body apparently naked or partly plated 4

3b. Caudal fin abbreviate-heterocercal or homocercal; body naked or well scaled 5

4a. Snout paddlelike, many times longer than deep and with 2 minute ventral barbels; body apparently naked . . . . POLYODONTIDAE

4b. Snout flattened and subtriangular with a transverse row of ventral barbels; body with 5 rows of bony plates . . . . ACIPENSERIDAE

5a. Caudal fin abbreviate-heterocercal (see fig 4); scales ganoid or cycloid 6
5b. Caudal fin homocercal; scales, if present, cycloid or ctenoid 7
6a. Snout produced as a long beak; dorsal fin very short, its origin behind anal origin; gular plate absent . . . . LEPISOSTEIDAE

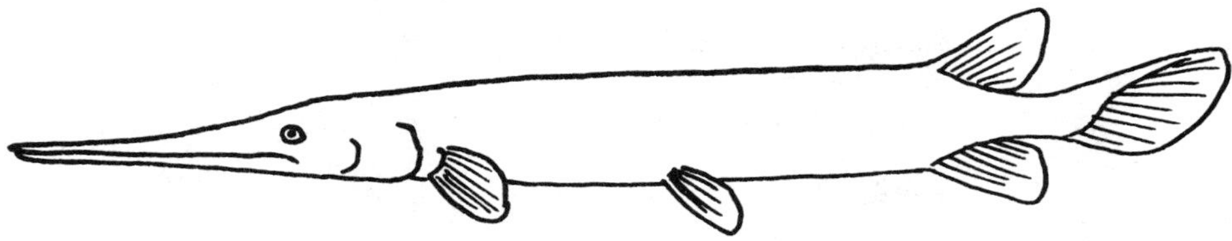

6b. Snout not produced as a long beak; dorsal fin very long, its origin anterior to the pelvic fins; gular plate present (see fig. 9). . . AMIIDAE

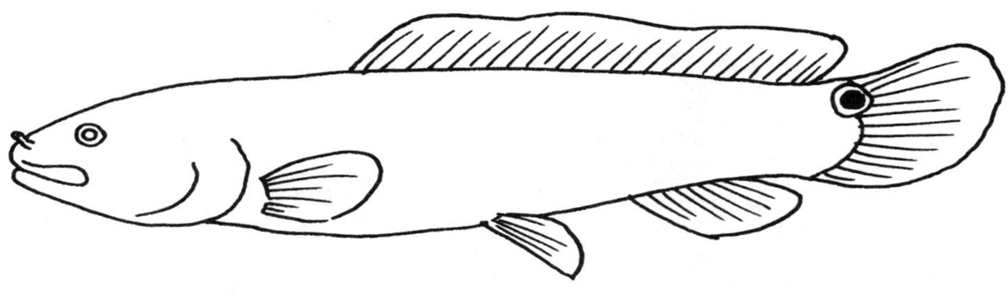

7a. Adipose fin present (see fig. 3) 8
7b. Adipose fin absent. 9
8a. Body naked; pectoral and dorsal fins each with a single spine . . . . ICTALURIDAE

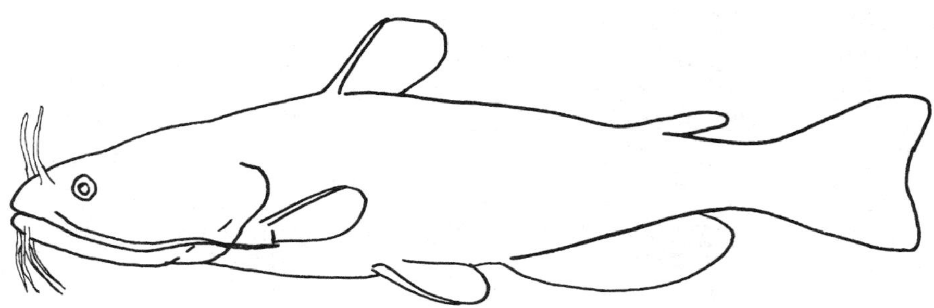

8b. Body scaled; spines absent . . . . SALMONIDAE

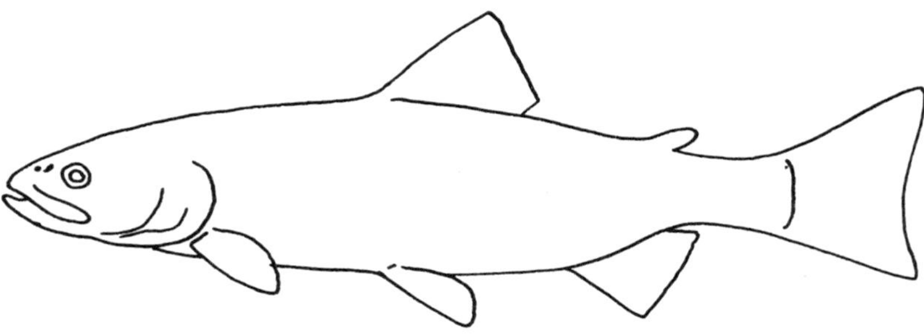

9a. Pelvic fins absent; body very slender (eel-shaped) . . . ANGUILLIDAE

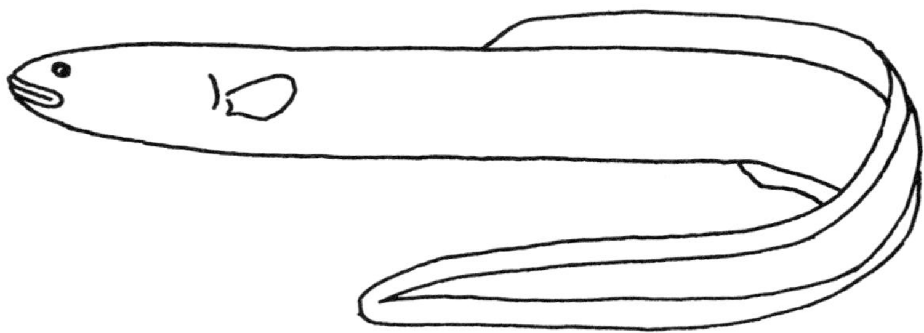

9b. Pelvic fins present; body not slender 10

10a. Snout dorsoventrally flattened into and produced as a ducklike bill . .

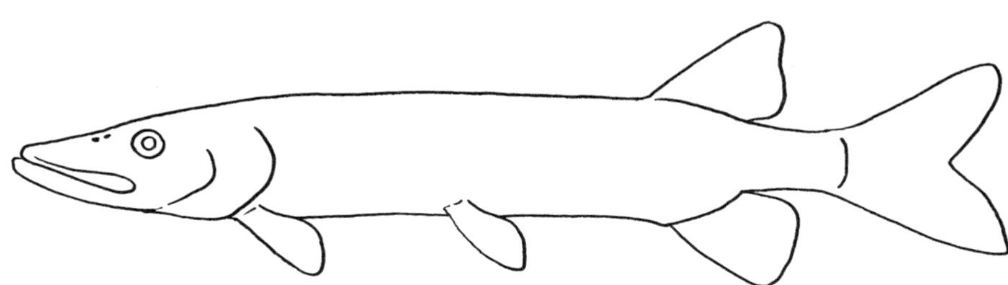

. . . . ESOCIDAE

10b. Snout not produced as a ducklike bill 11

11a. Body naked . . . . COTTIDAE

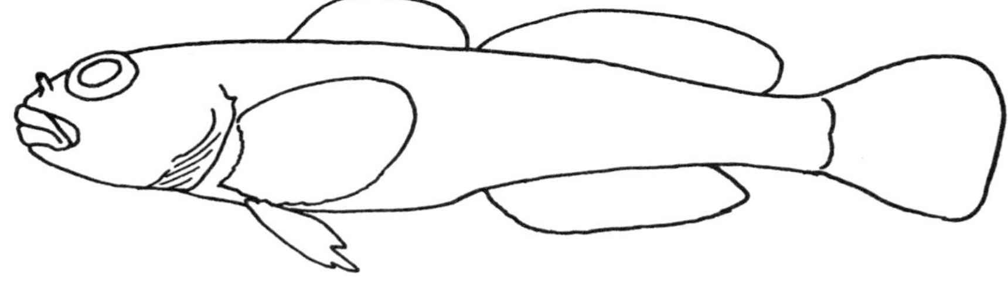

11b. Body well scaled. 12

12a. Gill membranes strongly united with isthmus (see fig. 7). 13

12b. Gill membranes free from, or slightly joined to, the isthmus 14

13a. Dorsal fin with more than 10 rays; distance from origin of anal fin to middle of caudal fin base more than $2^{1}/_{2}$ times that of distance from anal fin origin to snout tip. CATOSTOMIDAE

13b. Dorsal fin short, with fewer than 10 rays (except in *Cyprinus* and *Carassius*); distance from origin of anal fin to middle of caudal fin base less than $2^{1}/_{2}$ times that of distance from anal fin origin to snout tip (except in *Cyprinus* and *Carassius*) . . . . CYPRINIDAE

14a. Spines absent in fins 15

14b. Spines present in fins. 19

15a. Belly keeled 16
15b. Belly not keeled 17
16a. Belly with sharp sawtooth scales; lateral line absent . . . CLUPEIDAE

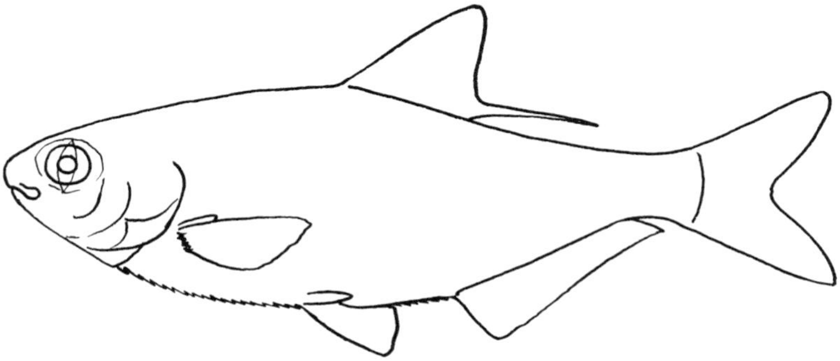

16b. Belly relatively smooth edged; lateral line present . . HIODONTIDAE

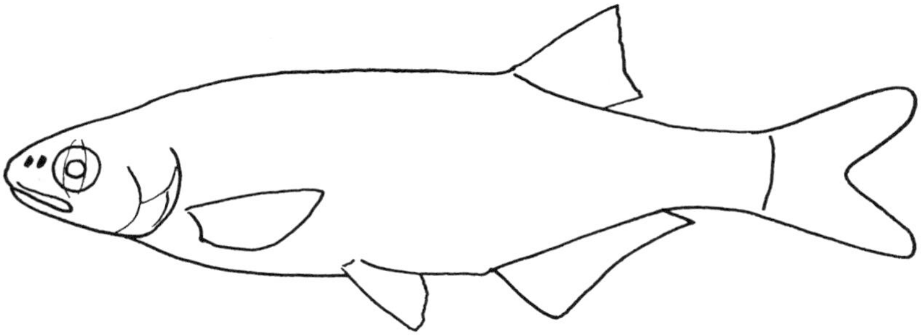

17a. Anal fin of male modified as an intromittent organ; females usually containing developing embryos; 7 or 8 rays in the dorsal fin. . . . . POECILIIDAE

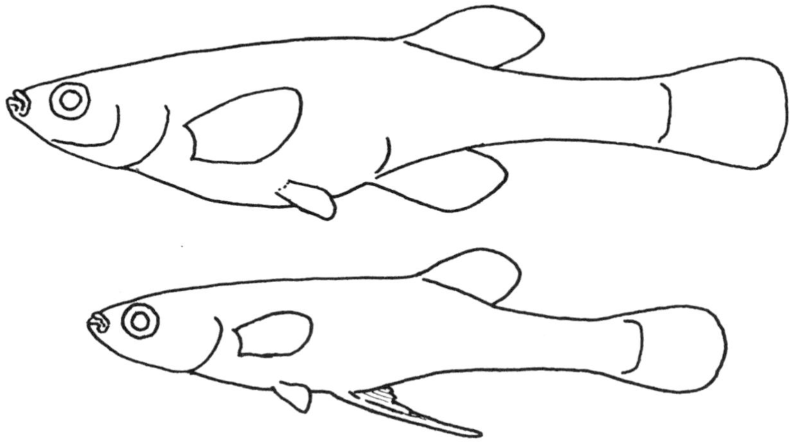

17b. Anal fin of male not modified; females never with internally developing embryos; 9 or more rays in the dorsal fin 18

18a. Deep bodied; deep strongly compressed caudal peduncle; dorsal fin origin about midway between snout tip and hypural; scales in lateral series 24–26; teeth tricuspid, in a single series, incisor-like. . . . . CYPRINODONTIDAE

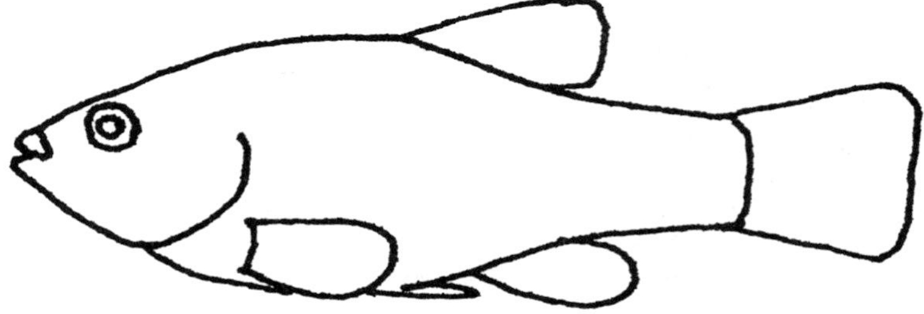

18b. Body more slender; caudal peduncle less compressed; dorsal origin much nearer hypural than snout tip; scales in lateral series smaller, 30 or more; teeth not tricuspid in one or more series, pointed . . . . FUNDULIDAE

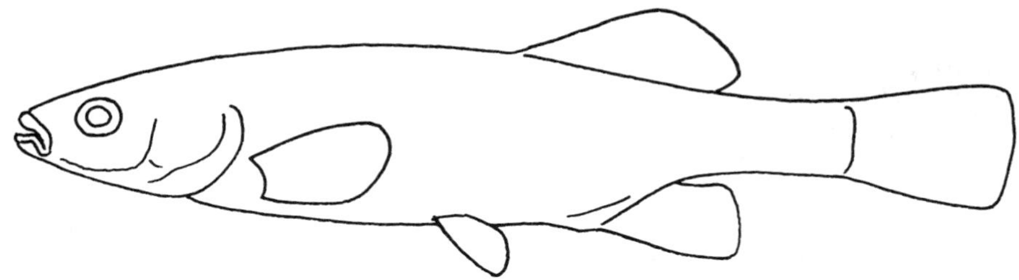

19a. Lateral line extending far onto the caudal fin . . . . SCIAENIDAE

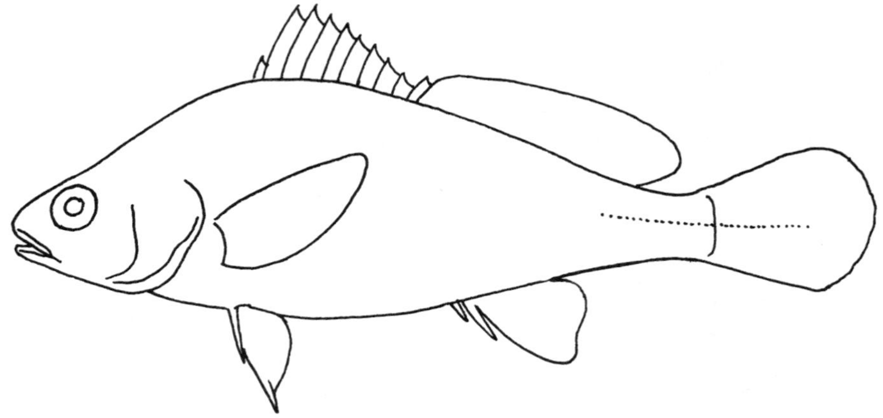

19b. Lateral line, if present, never extending onto caudal fin 20
20a. Anal fin with 1 or 2 spines 21
20b. Anal fin with 3 or more spines 24
21a. Pelvic fins far behind the pectorals 22

21b. Pelvic fins below or only slightly behind the pectorals 23

22a. Anal soft rays 8 or 9; dorsal fin spines stiff .... MUGILIDAE

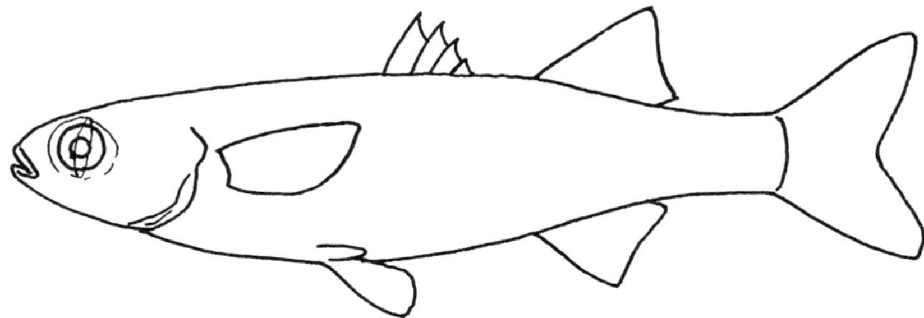

22b. Anal soft rays 14–22; dorsal fin spines flexible .... ATHERINOPSIDAE

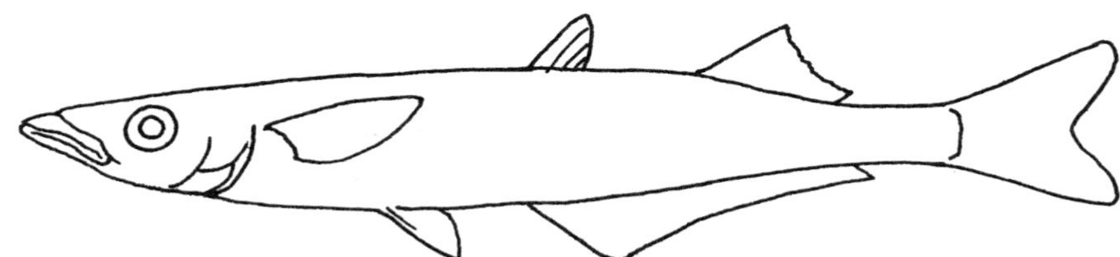

23a. Single dorsal fin; anus anterior to pelvic fins in adults .... APHREDODERIDAE

23b. Two dorsal fins, the spinous portion joined to the soft portion only slightly, if at all .... PERCIDAE

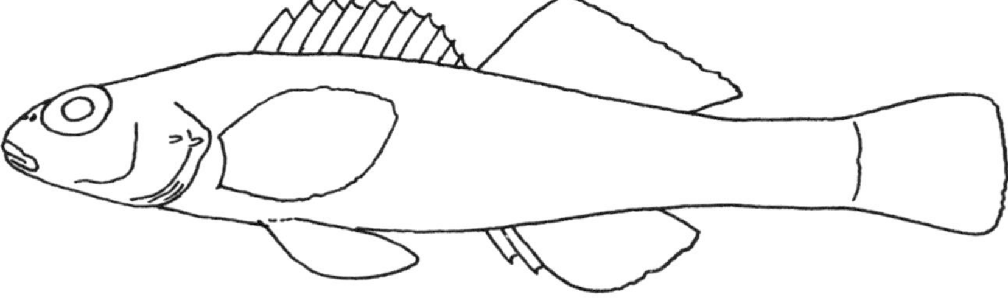

24a. One nostril present on each side of head; lateral line interrupted; in two parts, with the front portion higher on the body than the rear portion . . . . CICHLIDAE

24b. Two nostrils present on each side of head; lateral line present or absent 25

25a. Lateral line absent . . . . ELASSOMATIDAE

25b. Lateral line present, sometimes incomplete 26

26a. Spinous and soft dorsal separate or slightly connected; opercle with a sharp spine; pseudobranchiae well developed . . . . . . MORONIDAE

26b. Spinous and soft dorsal well connected; opercle without sharp spine; pseudobranchiae embedded and inconspicuous . . . CENTRARCHIDAE

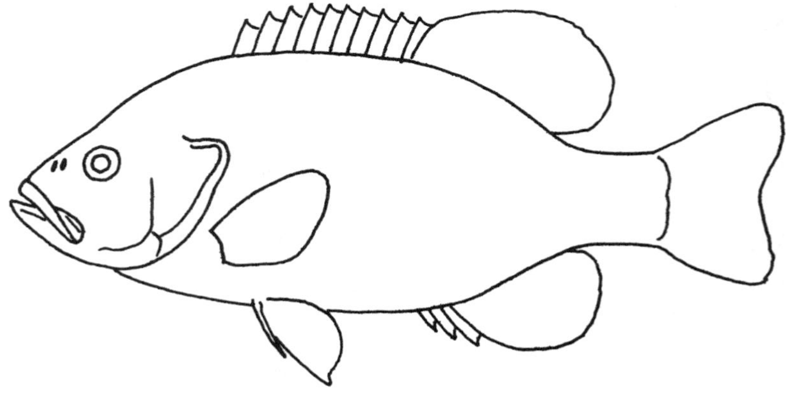

GLOSSARY

Abdominal
Pertaining to the belly; pelvic fins are abdominal when inserted far behind the base of pectoral fins.

Acute
Sharply pointed.

Adipose fin
Fleshy, rayless fin on the midline of the back between the dorsal and caudal fins.

Adnate
Grown together (united).

Air bladder
Membranous, gas-filled sac in the upper part of the body cavity.

Anal fin
Ventral unpaired fin (see fig. 3).

Anteriad
Frontward or in the anterior direction.

Barbel
Slender, flexible process located near the mouth; tactile and gustatory in function (see fig. 3).

Base (of fins)
That line along which a fin is attached to the body.

Basicaudal
Pertaining to the area at the base of the caudal fin.

Basioccipital
Hindmost bone on the underside of the skull. In *Hybognathus*, the basioccipital can be exposed by cutting across the isthmus (throat) and bending the head upward. The posterior process of the basioccipital is then seen as a posterior projection into the anterior part of the body cavity; the bone and its attached muscles pivot downward as the head is bent back.

Belly
Ventral surface posterior to the base of the pelvic fins, anterior to the anal fin.

Bicuspid
Having two points (applicable especially to teeth).

Branchiostegal
One of the bones supporting the gill membranes, ventral to the operculum (see fig. 3).

Breast
Ventral surface anterior to the insertion of the pelvic fins (see fig. 3).

Caducous
Readily shed (e.g., belly scales in genus *Percina*).

Caecum
Blind pouch or other sacklike evagination, especially at the pylorus (junction of stomach and small intestine).

Canine teeth
In fishes, conical teeth in the front part of the jaws; projecting beyond the others.

Caudal fin
Tail fin.

Caudal peduncle
Narrow region of the body in front of the caudal fin (from the posterior end of the base of the anal fin to the base of the caudal fin).

Cheek
Area between the eye and the preopercle bone (see fig. 3).

Circumoral teeth
Horny teeth that surround the esophagus in lampreys.

Circumorbital
Any one of a series of thin dermal bones behind, below, and in front of the eye (preorbital anterior, suborbitals below, postorbitals behind).

Cleithrum
Major bone of the pectoral girdle, extending upward from the fin base and forming the posterior margin of the gill chamber.

Compressed
Narrow from side to side (flattened laterally).

Concave
Curved inward (hollowed).

Convex
Curved outward (arched).

Ctenoid scales
Scales that bear a patch of spinelike prickles on the exposed (posterior) field.

Cycloid scales
More or less rounded scales that bear no ctenii or prickles.

Dentate
Toothlike.

Depressed
Flattened from top to bottom; wider than it is deep.

Distal
Remote from point of attachment (free edge of fins, farthest from their bases).

Dorsal
Pertaining to the back; often used as an abbreviation for dorsal fin.

Dorsal fin
Median unpaired fin (or fins, exclusive of adipose) atop the back (see fig. 3).

Dorsum
The upper part of the body.

Emarginate
Having the distal margin notched.

Entire
Having an edge (as of a spine or bone) that is smooth rather than serrate.

Falcate
Sickle-shaped (with concave margin).

Fimbriate
Fringed at margin.

Fin ray
A bony or cartilaginous rod supporting the fin membrane. Soft rays usually are segmented (cross-striated), often branched, and flexible near their tips, whereas spines are not segmented, are never branched, and usually are stiff to their sharp distal tips.

Fontanelle
Aperture or opening in a bony surface.

Frenum
Ridge or fold of tissue that binds or restrains any part, such as the tissue that binds the upper jaw to the snout.

Fusiform
Spindle-shaped, tapering gradually at both ends.

Ganoid
Pertains to thick, strong scales with a covering of ganoin, as in gars.

Gape
Refers to the mouth; in fishes, width of gape is the transverse distance between the two ends of the mouth cleft, when the mouth is closed; length of gape is the diagonal distance from the anterior (median) end of the lower lip to one end of the mouth cleft.

Genital papilla
Fleshy projection adjacent to anus, as in darters.

Gill filaments
Respiratory structures projecting posteriorly from gill arches.

Gill membranes
Membranes that close the gill cavity ventrolaterally, supported by the branchiostegals.

Gill rakers
Projections (knobby or comblike) from the concave anterior surface of the gill arches (see fig. 6).

Gonopodium
Modified anal fin of *Gambusia* and other poeciliid fishes, used in transfer of sperm to genital pore of female.

Gular fold
Transverse fold of soft tissue across the throat.

Gular plate
Large, median, dermal bone on the throat, as in the bowfin (see fig. 9).

Heterocercal
The caudal fin is heterocercal if the vertebral column turns upward into the dorsal lobe (see fig. 4).

Homocercal
The caudal fin is homocercal if the posterior vertebra (with its hypural plate) is modified to support the entire fin; neither lobe is invaded by the vertebral column (see fig. 4).

Humeral "scale"
Scalelike bone, often dark colored, behind the gill opening and above the base of the pectoral fin (in darters).

Hyaline
Glassy, transparent, or translucent.

Hyoid teeth
Teeth on the tongue.

Hypurals
Expanded last vertebral processes in fishes having a homocercal tail.

Inferior
On the lower side.

Infraorbital canal
Segment of the lateral-line canal that curves beneath the eye and extends forward onto the snout (see fig. 3).

Insertion (of fins)
Anterior end of the bases of the paired fins (see fig. 3).

Intermuscular bones
Fragile, branched bones that are isolated in the connective tissue between body muscles (myomeres).

Interopercle
Small bone of the gill cover situated between the preopercle and the subopercle (see fig. 3).

Interradial membranes
Membranes between fin rays.

Isthmus
Contracted part of the breast that projects forward between (and separates) the gill chambers.

Jugular
Pertaining to the throat; pelvic fins are jugular when inserted in front of bases of pectoral fins.

Keel
A ridge or elevated line.

Lateral line
System of sensory tubules communicating to the body surface by pores; refers most often to a longitudinal row of scales that bear tubules and pores. Incomplete if only the anterior scales have pores; complete if all scales in that row (to base of caudal fins) have pores (see fig. 3).

Lingual lamina
Horny ridge on the "tongue" of a lamprey.

Mandibles
Principal bones of the lower jaw (see fig. 3).

Mandibular pores
Pores along a tube that traverses the underside of each lower jaw (part of the lateral-line system).

Maxilla (maxillary)
Bone of each upper jaw that lies immediately above (or behind) and parallel to the premaxilla (see fig. 3).

Melanophore
Black pigment cell.

Myomere
Muscle segment.

Nape
Dorsal part of the body from the occiput to the origin of the dorsal fin (see fig. 3).

Nares
Nostrils; in fishes, each nostril usually has an anterior and a posterior narial opening, located above and in front of the eyes (see fig. 3).

Nonprotractile
Not protrusible; premaxillaries are nonprotractile if they are not fully separated from the snout by a continuous groove.

Nuchal
Pertaining to the nape.

Nuptial tubercles
Hardened, often thornlike projections from the skin, seen in adult males of many fishes during their breeding season; also called pearl organs.

Obovate
Inversely ovate (narrow end at base).

Occiput
In fishes, the posterior dorsal end of the head, often marked by the line separating scaly and scaleless portions of the skin.

Opercle
Large posterior bone of the gill cover (see fig. 3).

Opercular flap
Posterior extension of the operculum, especially in sunfishes ("ear" flap in *Lepomis* spp.).

Oral valve
Thin membranes, one near the front of each jaw, which function in respiration.

Orbit

Eyesocket; orbital diameter is measured from the anterior to the posterior bony rim of the eyesocket, whereas eye diameter is measured across the cornea only (and is thus slightly less than orbital diameter).

Origin (of fins)

Anterior end of the base of a dorsal fin or anal fin (see fig. 3).

Ovate

Egg-shaped; tapering toward the end.

Palatine teeth

Teeth borne by the paired palatine bones, which lie on the roof of the mouth behind the median vomer and mesial to the upper jaw.

Papilla

In fishes, any small, blunt, soft, and rounded protuberance on the skin.

Papillose

Covered with papillae (as contrasted with plicate, when applied to lips of suckers).

Parietal

Paired dermal bone of the roof of the skull, located between the frontal and occipital.

Pectoral fin

Paired fin on the side, or on the breast, behind the head; corresponding to forelimb of a mammal (see fig. 3).

Pelvic fin

Ventral paired fin, lying below the pectoral fin or between it and the anal fin (see fig. 3).

Peritoneum

Membranous lining of the body cavity.

Pharyngeal teeth

Bony projections from the fifth gill arch, which is nonrespiratory and is embedded in tissues behind the gill-bearing arches, mesial to the cleithrum (see fig. 8).

Plicate

Having parallel folds or soft ridges; grooved lips.

Postcleithrum

One of the bones of the pectoral girdle situated behind the gill cleft.

Posteriad

Backward or in a posterior direction.

Premaxilla (premaxillary)
Paired bone at the front of the upper jaw; the right and left premaxillae join anteriorly and form all or part of the border of the jaw (see fig. 3).

Preopercle
Sickle-shaped bone that lies behind and below the eye.

Preoperculomandibular canal
Branch of the lateral-line system that extends along the preopercle and mandible.

Preorbital
Bone forming the anterior rim of the eyesocket, and extending forward on side of snout; see circumorbital.

Principal rays
Fin rays that extend to the distal margin of median fins, especially if those fins have a straight leading edge; enumerated by counting only one unbranched ray anteriorly, plus subsequent branched rays (see fig. 5).

Procurrent rays
Small, contiguous rays (see fin ray) at the anterior bases of the dorsal, caudal, and anal fins of many fishes; excluded from the count of principal fin rays (see fig. 5).

Protractile
Capable of being thrust out; said of the upper jaw if it is completely separated from the face by a continuous groove (i.e., in the absence of a frenum).

Pseudobranchium
Accessory gill on the inner surface of the operculum.

Punctule
Fine dot.

Ray
See fin ray.

Recurved
Curved upward and inward.

Serrae
Teeth of a sawlike organ or structure.

Serrate
Notched or toothed on the edge, like a saw; as opposed to entire.

Snout
Part of the head anterior to the eye (but not including the lower jaw).

Soft ray
See fin ray.

Spine
See fin ray.

Spiracle
Orifice on the back part of the head (above and behind the eye) in some fishes (paddlefish and some sturgeons), representing a primitive gill cleft.

Standard length
Distance from the tip of the snout to the structural base of the caudal fin (point at which central caudal rays originate, see fig. 3).

Subopercle
Bony plate immediately below the opercle in the gill cover (see fig. 3).

Suborbitals
Thin bones forming the lower part of the orbital rim.

Subterminal mouth
Mouth that opens slightly ventrally, rather than straight forward from the front of the head; lower jaw closing within the upper jaw rather than equal to it in its anterior extent.

Subtriangular
Almost triangular.

Supramaxilla
Small, movable bone adherent to the upper edge of the maxilla near its posterior tip.

Supraorbital canal
Paired branch of the lateral-line system that extends along the top of the head between the eyes and forward onto the snout (see fig. 3).

Supratemporal canal
Branch of the lateral-line system that crosses the top of the head at the occiput, connecting the lateral canals (see fig. 3).

Symphysis
Articulation of two bones in the median plane of the body, especially that of the two halves of the lower jaw (mandibles) at the chin.

Terete
Cylindrical and tapering with circular cross section; having a rounded body form, the width and depth about equal.

Thoracic
Pertaining to the thorax, including especially the chest in fishes; pelvic fins are thoracic when inserted below the pectoral fins.

Tricuspid
Having three points (applicable especially to teeth).

Tuberculate
Having or characterized by a tubercle or tubercles; see nuptial tubercles.

Turgid
Distended; swollen or inflated with fluid.

Species Accounts, with Keys

LAMPREYS

FAMILY PETROMYZONTIDAE

Key

1a. Nonparasitic; expanded disc narrower than head; teeth in posterior field somewhat degenerate; no functional gut in adults; 6 inches maximum size . . . . *Ichthyomyzon gagei*

1b. Parasitic; expanded disc wider than head; teeth in posterior field not degenerate; functional gut present in adults; 14 inches maximum size . . . . *Ichthyomyzon castaneus*

CHESTNUT LAMPREY

Ichthyomyzon castaneus Girard

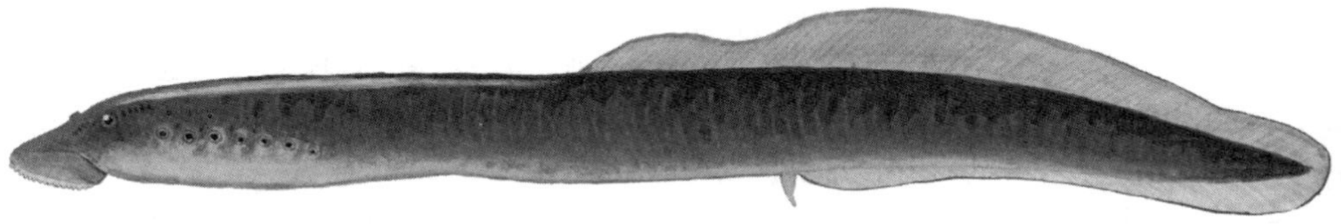

Description:

A grayish, eel-like fish with no jaws, no paired fins, poorly developed eyes, and 7 external gill openings. A single median nostril is present. The cup-shaped mouth is covered with large and well-developed horny teeth. Oral disc is relatively larger (1⁄11 to 1⁄17 of total length) than in *I. gagei*. Myomeres usually 52–56. Adults commonly achieve 10–12 inches in length, with the Oklahoma record about 14 inches. (See also color plate.)

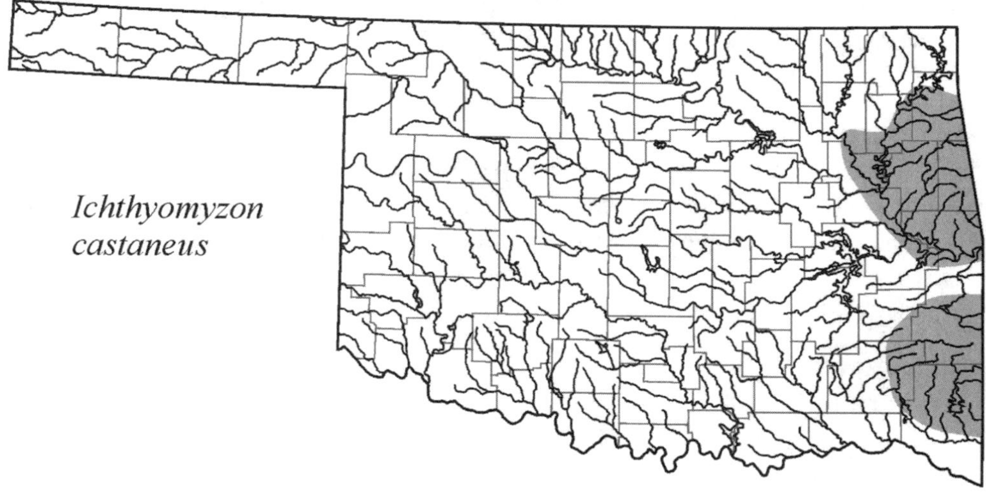

Distribution:

Occurs in a broad band through the center of the country from North Dakota across to Michigan and south through Illinois and the plains states to Texas, Mississippi, and a portion of Georgia. Found in the clear streams of the Arkansas, Poteau, and Little River systems in the eastern third of Oklahoma.

Habitat and Biology:

This parasitic species feeds by using the disclike mouth to attach to the body of larger fish like carp, buffalo, or suckers. The horny tongue is used to rasp a hole in the host while an anti-coagulent keeps the blood and body fluids flowing until the meal is complete. Large fish or victims of smaller lampreys often survive such attacks and may be found occasionally in our eastern streams, particularly during the host's spring spawning run. All lampreys apparently move into small headwater streams to spawn during the spring. They create a depression on a rocky or sandy bottom and the eggs (up to 42,000 in a 284 mm female in Oklahoma) and sperm of many individuals may be shed into it, after which the adults die. Upon hatching, the young lampreys (ammocoetes) drift downstream until they find a soft, silty area or bank in the stream. After burrowing into the bottom, they act as filter feeders, straining microorganisms and other tiny food materials from the water passing by. A year or more later (exact duration not known for this species), the ammocoetes emerge and transform into the definitive adult form. Adults reportedly live about 18 months.

SOUTHERN BROOK LAMPREY

Ichthyomyzon gagei Hubbs and Trautman

Description:

Resembles *I. castaneus*: eel-like, no paired fins, 7 external gill openings, single median nostril, and poorly developed eyes. Differs principally in being smaller (6 inches or less in size at maturity) and in having the posterior disc teeth poorly developed. The oral disc is also smaller (length is 1/16 to 1/30 of total length). Myomeres 52–56. Larvae reach 7 inches (178 mm).

Distribution:

From Florida and the Gulf states to Texas and north to the Arkansas drainage of eastern Oklahoma. Found in the clear streams of the Ozark and Ouachita regions of eastern Oklahoma.

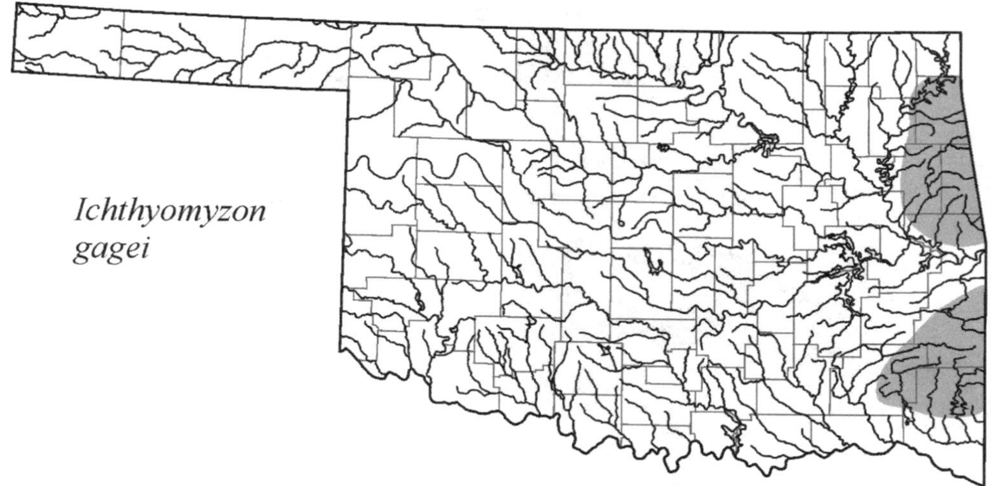

Habitat and Biology:

Most of the differences between this form and the chestnut lamprey are due to the fact that the brook lamprey is not parasitic. Nonparasitic lampreys usually have a longer larval life but shorter adult life because the adult feeding phase is omitted from the life cycle. After metamorphosis the gut degenerates and fewer, less well developed teeth appear in the buccal disc. In spring southern brook lampreys run up small, clear streams to spawn in sand and gravel nests constructed by attaching themselves to stones with the sucking disc and carrying the pebbles upstream or laterally out of the nest pit. From 5 to 20 may be active in a single nest, and nestbuilding and spawning activities appear to be interspersed. After spawning the adults die. The ammocoetes spend a year or more in loose material (detritus, sand, or silt) feeding on minute organic particles and plankton, particularly diatoms, strained from quiet areas at stream margins. Metamorphosis begins in late August or September and requires about six months to complete.

STURGEONS

FAMILY ACIPENSERIDAE

SHOVELNOSE STURGEON

Scaphirhynchus platorynchus (Rafinesque)

Description:

A fairly large, very elongate fish with an unusual appearance. The head is broad and flat with 4 strongly fringed barbels on the underside of the snout. The body has 5 longitudinal rows of bony plates, which converge at the caudal peduncle. The belly has small scales. The tail is strongly heterocercal and

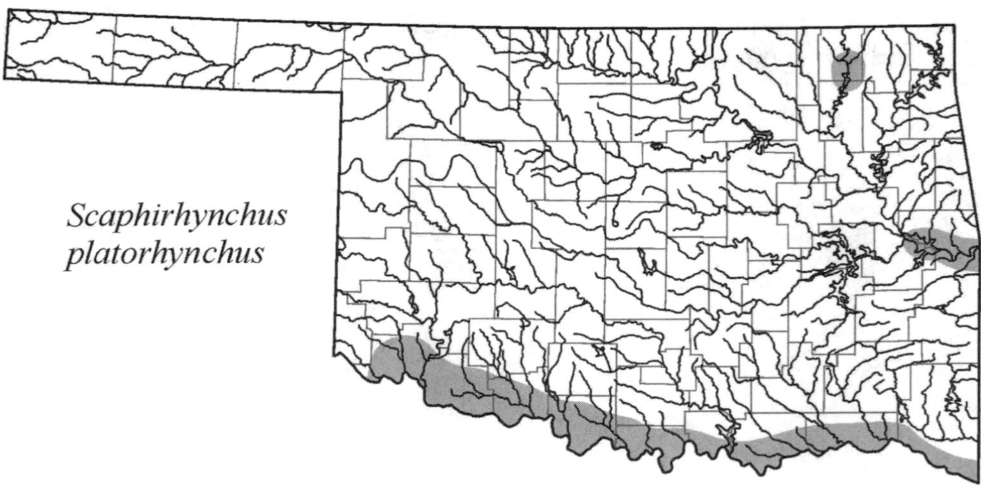

produced into a filament. Color is light brown to grayish above and white below. Maximum size is about 3 feet (914 mm), though individuals rarely reach that size in Oklahoma. State record: 2 lb., 15 oz., 29 in., from the Arkansas River.

Distribution:

The Mississippi Valley south to Mississippi and Texas. Oklahoma records come from the Arkansas, Little, and Red rivers and some of their tributaries. Dams along the eastern portions of the Arkansas and Red rivers may now limit the westward distribution of this species in Oklahoma.

Habitat and Biology:

The shovelnose is one of the smaller sturgeons, rarely exceeding 5 pounds in weight or 30 inches in length. It is a bottom feeder in large rivers, apparently preferring both aquatic and terrestrial insects, molluscs, crustaceans, and worms. In spring (April–June) these sturgeons ascend smaller creeks to spawn, and it is on their spawning runs that they are most often encountered. They have frequently been observed below the dam at Lake Texoma, but recent records are sparse for the Arkansas River and its tributaries. Spawning occurs every two or three years. Males attain sexual maturity at 20 inches (635 mm). Growth is slow, and maturity is reached at about six years and 2 pounds (0.9 kg).

PADDLEFISHES

FAMILY POLYODONTIDAE

PADDLEFISH

Polyodon spathula (Walbaum)

Description:

A large, seemingly scaleless fish easily identified by its extremely long, paddle-shaped snout. The skeleton is almost entirely cartilaginous, and the caudal fin is strongly heterocercal. The large mouth can be opened widely for the intake of voluminous quantities of water and the small organisms on which it feeds. Eyes are small. Two minute barbels are present on the underside of snout. The rear margin of the operculum extends into a long, pointed flap. Numerous gill rakers are extremely long and slender. Maximum length is 60 inches and weight 184 pounds.

Distribution:

Larger bodies of water throughout the Great Lakes and Mississippi drainages. In Oklahoma paddlefish were originally found in most large rivers of the Arkansas system as far west as Great Salt Plains reservoir, the Little

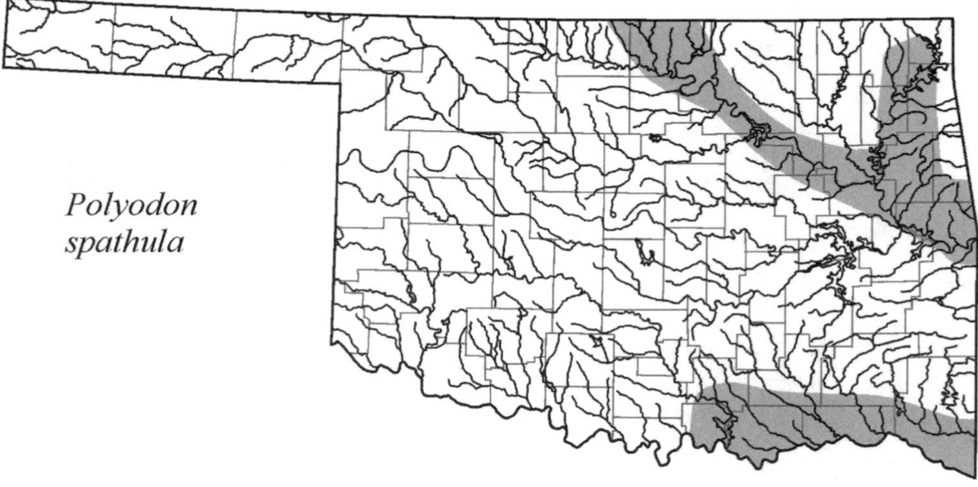

River, and the Red River below Lake Texoma. The species is apparently quite abundant in some large lakes, such as Grand Lake and Fort Gibson Reservoir.

Habitat and Biology:

The paddlefish is a large, primitive, cartilaginous fish that has survived to the present because of its specialized feeding habits and behavior. Plankton and occasionally small fishes are trapped by the hundreds of long gill rakers that filter the stream of water entering the enormous mouth. In spite of the tiny size of the organisms on which they subsist, paddlefish have been shown to grow to 50 inches (1,270 mm) in the first ten years of life (in the Missouri River), after which their growth rate slows down to about 2 inches (51 mm) a year. They spawn in spring when water temperatures reach 60 degrees F (15.7 degrees C) over submerged gravel bars, and the water is fast and turbid, but apparently prefer quieter waters (oxbows, sloughs, lake bottoms), which facilitate their filter-feeding behavior during the rest of the year. Males require approximately seven years to reach sexual maturity, whereas females require nine to ten years. The long snout is well equipped with taste buds and is often waved laterally, apparently to stir up the bottom detritus and food organisms contained therein. Paddlefish are caught mainly in nets, although there is a short season for snagging them in the eastern rivers of the state.

GARS

FAMILY LEPISOSTEIDAE

Key

1a. Snout long and narrow, its length going into head about 1.4 times . . . . . *Lepisosteus osseus*

1b. Snout short and broad, its length going into head about 1.6 times 2

2a. Large upper teeth in 1 row (except in young) 3

2b. Large upper teeth in 2 rows . . . . . *Atractosteus spatula*

3a. Lateral-line scales 59–64; predorsal scales 50–54; head without dark spots and blotches; scale rows from anal plate to middorsal scale 20–23 inclusive . . . . . *Lepisosteus platostomus*

3b. Lateral-line scales 54–58; predorsal scales 46–49; head with large dark spots and blotches; scale rows from anal plate to middorsal scale 17–20 inclusive . . . . . *Lepisosteus oculatus*

ALLIGATOR GAR

Atractosteus spatula (Lacepede)

Description:

A large, heavy-bodied gar (up to a record 9 feet, 8.5 inches, 302 pounds), which differs from all other species in having enlarged teeth on the palatine bones of adults. Teeth in the upper jaw are in two rows. The snout is relatively short and broad, the body is covered with heavy ganoid scales, and the tail is abbreviate-heterocercal. Both dorsal and anal fins are situated far back on the body. Lateral-line scales are 58–62. The body is greenish above and paler below, with no spots evident in adults. Young alligator gar may be distinguished from other species by the presence of a narrow, whitish middorsal stripe bordered by thin, dark lines that run from the snout tip to the dorsal origin. State record: 153 lb., 87 in., from the Red River.

Distribution:

Lower portions of the major rivers of the Mississippi Basin from Illinois and Ohio to the Gulf of Mexico. Known in Oklahoma from Greenleaf Creek,

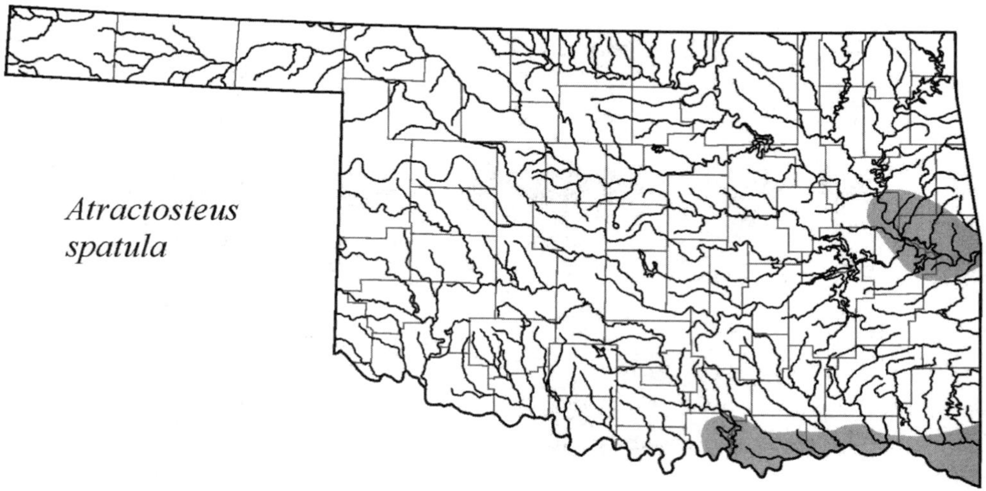

the Poteau, Mountain Fork, and Deep Fork rivers, and the Red River west to Lake Texoma, in which a breeding population is now known to exist (May and Echelle 1968).

Habitat and Biology:

The alligator gar inhabits quiet parts of the large rivers tributary to the Gulf of Mexico and is found in brackish waters from Florida to Mexico. This suggests a preference for warmer waters, which is reflected also by the limited numbers found in more northern parts of its range. It feeds mainly on fishes, although other small vertebrates are consumed. This species probably spawns in early May in Lake Texoma, and its general biology is not known to differ markedly from that of other gars. The large size (up to 7 feet in Oklahoma) has prompted a minor fishing industry for it in some parts of its range, and it apparently is considered a good food fish in Mexico. Generally there has been a consistent decline in numbers of this gar due to impoundments and alteration of navigation channels of the main rivers of Oklahoma.

SPOTTED GAR

Lepisosteus oculatus (Winchell)

Description:

An extremely elongate fish with a prominent snout well equipped with sharp teeth. Snout width is less than in shortnose gar but greater than in longnose gar. The body is almost cylindrical, covered with heavy diamond-shaped scales, and the tail is heterocercal. Dorsal and anal fins are located far back on the body. Lateral-line scales 54–59. Fins, head, and body are typically well covered by large spots. Generally less than 3 feet long, although a maximum size of 36 inches and weight of 6–8 pounds have been recorded.

Distribution:

From the Great Lakes through the Mississippi basin south and west to central Texas and east to western Florida. Found throughout most of eastern Oklahoma; recorded as far west as Optima Reservoir and numerous locations in the North Canadian River system, east as far as Canton Reservoir. Probably located in permanent waters in other parts of western Oklahoma.

Habitat and Biology:

The gars are all inhabitants of relatively clear, sluggish waters, where they feed entirely on small fishes. Some observers have noted that the spotted gar

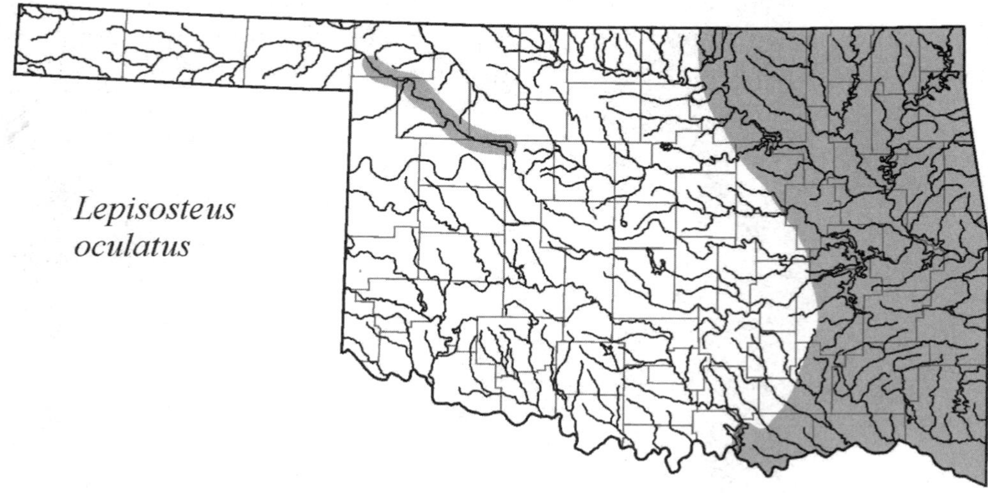

seems to prefer waters that contain much aquatic vegetation, but there seems to be little else in its known ecology to differentiate it from its relatives. As with other gars, feeding behavior consists of a very slow approach to the prey and a quick, darting, lateral movement of the head, which impales the prey on the sharp teeth. The gar spawns in spring, probably in shallow water, where the adhesive eggs are scattered randomly. Gar eggs are poisonous, but the flesh of the fish may be eaten. The gars are all air breathers, with a well-developed lung-like gas bladder. At higher water temperatures, aerial respiration is obligatory.

LONGNOSE GAR

Lepisosteus osseus (Linnaeus)

Description:

As its name suggests, the longnose gar can be distinguished from other gars by its long, narrow snout (length more than 13 times its narrowest width in specimens 50 mm long or larger). General characteristics are similar to those of the spotted gar, but the spots on the body are smaller and generally less well developed. The fins are often tinted with orange, and median fins are conspicuously spotted. Spots on the head are inconspicuous or absent. Lateral-line scales usually 57–63. Generally less than 40 inches long, although maximum length is about 4.5 feet and 35 pounds. State record: 41 lb., 62 in., from the Red River.

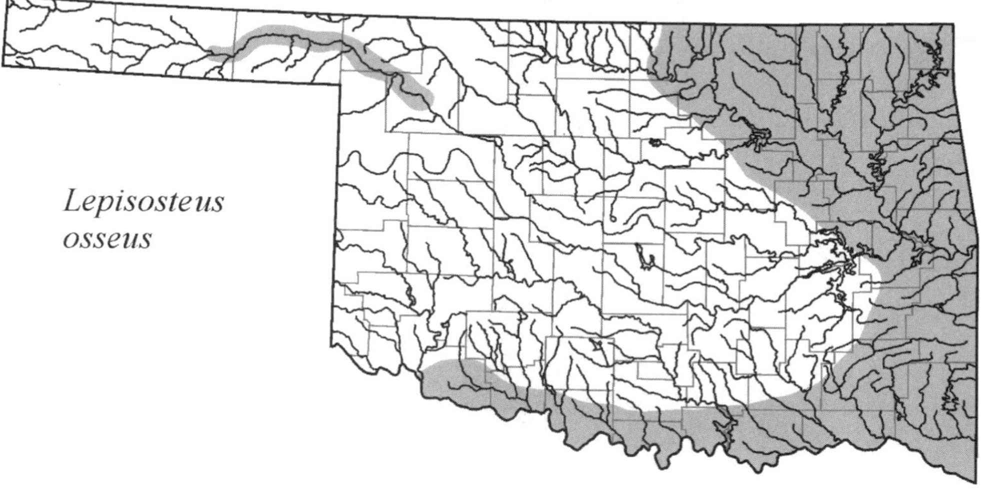

Distribution:

Widely distributed throughout the eastern United States from Quebec through the Great Lakes to the Dakotas, reaching south to West Texas and east to Florida. Fairly well distributed throughout eastern Oklahoma. Pigg and Gibbs (1997) reported this species, as well as shortnose gar, from Lake Optima and the Beaver River in the panhandle and from Lake Fort Supply and the North Canadian River near Woodward. Probably occurs in scattered localities in most of Oklahoma.

Habitat and Biology:

The extremely widespread distribution attests to the success of this predator. The longnose seems to be somewhat more adaptable than some of its relatives. Although it appears to prefer large, sluggish rivers, clear oxbows, and swampy habitats, it can occasionally be found in comparatively small streams and faster water. Like other gars, it spawns in smaller tributaries in April or May, scattering eggs in shallow water. After hatching, the larvae use a specialized organ on the snout for attaching to the substrate during early development. Young fish (less than 25 mm) apparently feed mainly at the surface on small insects, microcrustaceans, and fish, shifting to an almost entirely piscivorous diet as they mature. Males mature at three to four years while females may take six years. Females may live more than 30 years.

SHORTNOSE GAR

Lepisosteus platostomus Rafinesque

Description: An elongate species very similar to the spotted gar in body shape and general appearance. It differs from the longnose gar by its shorter snout and from the spotted gar by its unspotted head and body, though dark spots usually are present on the fins. It also differs from the spotted gar in having more predorsal scales (more than 50 vs. fewer than 50). The shortnose is Oklahoma's smallest gar, generally under 2 feet in length and 5 pounds in weight.

Distribution: Mainstream portions of larger rivers of the Mississippi basin. Found in the larger tributaries and rivers in most of the eastern half of Oklahoma. Pigg and Gibbs (1997) found this species in several areas of the North Canadian River system west to Lake Optima. It will be interesting to

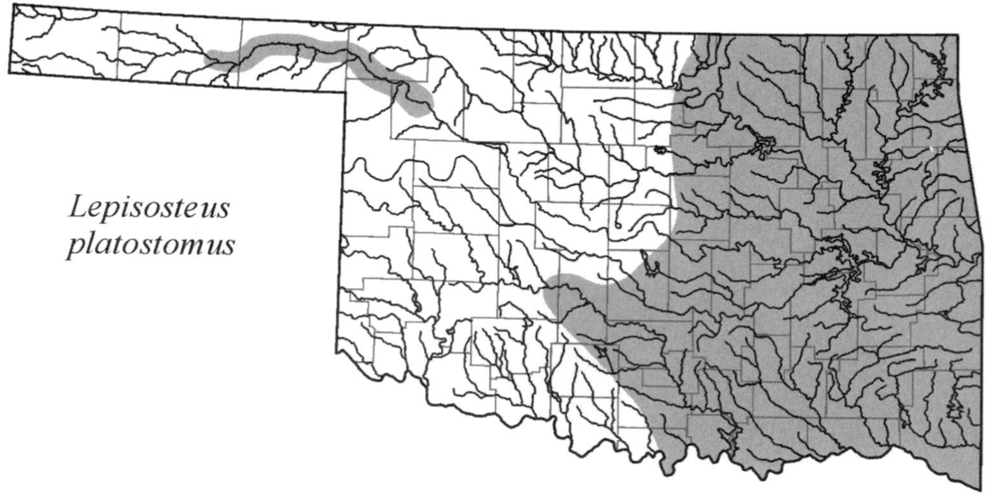

note the distribution changes for this species as more collecting is done in western Oklahoma.

Habitat and Biology:

Although it is commonly found in many lakes, oxbows, and other sluggish habitats, the shortnose gar may be somewhat better adapted for living in the main streams of large, muddy rivers, though it definitely prefers quiet sand- or mud-bottomed pools and backwaters. Feeding patterns and breeding habits appear to be quite similar to those of other gars, although the shortnose is known to feed on insects and crustaceans to a much greater extent than has been shown in other species. Studies in southern Illinois have shown that prior to rain, these fish fed almost entirely on aquatic organisms, whereas following rain they fed mainly on terrestrial forms. Perhaps the more turbid water and greater incidence of floating organisms following a rain produce a shift in feeding behavior. This may explain the apparent ability of this species to do better than other gars in turbid waters. Spawning occurs in shallow backwaters from May to July. Eggs are scattered over vegetation or submerged objects.

THE BOWFIN

FAMILY AMIIDAE

Bowfin
Amia calva

Description:

An elongate, moderately compressed fish with an extremely long, low dorsal fin. The caudal fin is rounded and body scales are cycloid. The mouth is large, and a large bony gular plate is found on the anterior part of the underside of the head. The air bladder is joined to the gut and is lunglike. The bowfin is dark greenish above, lighter below, with dark reticulations on the body and some fins. Males have an orange-edged black ocellus ("eyespot") on the dorsal part of the caudal base. Maximum size attained is about 3 feet (914 mm) and maximum weight is 20 pounds (9.1 kg), but individuals are generally 18–24 inches in length and weigh about 4 pounds or less.

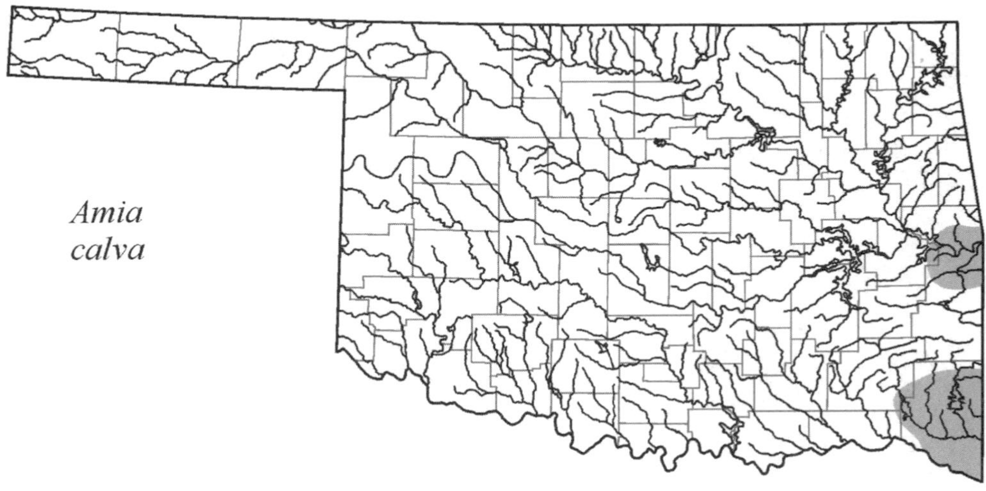

Distribution:

Throughout eastern United States except for the northern Allegheny highlands. Found in Oklahoma only in the southeast; fairly common in McCurtain County.

Habitat and Biology:

The bowfin lives only in relatively clear, quiet waters usually densely supplied with aquatic plants. Thus it often is found in the weedy oxbows and barrow ditches of McCurtain County, where it subsists mainly on a diet of fish and crayfish, although other aquatic animals are eaten. Since it may reach 2 feet in length, it is quite a formidable predator and fights well on hook and line. Spawning occurs in spring (early April into June), when the male clears a nest depression in the weed-choked bottom and may spawn with several females. He defends the adhesive eggs (nests may contain 2,000–5,000 eggs) until they hatch, whereupon the young use an adhesive organ at the tip of the snout to maintain contact with the substrate until they are ready to swim actively in search of food. The male continues to guard the free-swimming fry for a few weeks. Their food-searching forays from the protection of the nest get longer until the young reach about 4 inches in length and depart permanently. Bowfins are interesting fish to watch in aquaria, especially when feeding. Undulations of the long dorsal fin are used to propel the fish slowly toward prey without unduly frightening it; the last few inches are traversed in a flash as the bowfin opens its mouth and engulfs the prey. The procedure resembles the stalking behavior of gars, except that the coup de grace is frontal rather than lateral. Some individuals are reported to have lived for more than 30 years.

MOONEYES

FAMILY HIODONTIDAE

Key

1a. Dorsal origin slightly posterior to origin of anal fin; dorsal fin with 9 or 10 principal rays . . . . *Hiodon alosoides*

1b. Dorsal origin distinctly anterior to origin of anal fin; dorsal fin with 11 or 12 principal rays . . . . *Hiodon tergisus*

GOLDEYE

Hiodon alosoides (Rafinesque)

Description:

A moderately elongate, deep-bodied fish with large forward-placed eyes and rounded snout, superficially resembling the shads or herrings. It differs in having well-developed canine teeth on the jaws and tongue and a fleshy belly keel extending from the anus to beneath the pectoral fins. The dorsal fin inserts behind the origin of the anal fin and has 9 to 10 rays. Dorsum is nearly straight from occiput to dorsal fin origin. Anal fin is long with 30–32 rays. Gill rakers are short and knoblike. Lateral line is complete with 57–62 scales. The back is blue to greenish, grading to silvery sides and a white belly. The fins may contain yellow to pink color. The iris is yellow to gold and an adipose eyelid is present. Up to 18 inches in length and nearly 3 pounds in weight. State record: 2 lb., 8 oz., 18⅝ in., from the Arkansas River.

Distribution:

From the Mississippi drainage of the central United States south to Alabama and north to the Hudson Bay drainage. Known from many tributaries of the Arkansas and Red rivers in the eastern half of Oklahoma and west to the North Fork of the Red River near Tipton in Tillman County (Pigg and Tyler 1990) and in the Washita to Fort Cobb Reservoir.

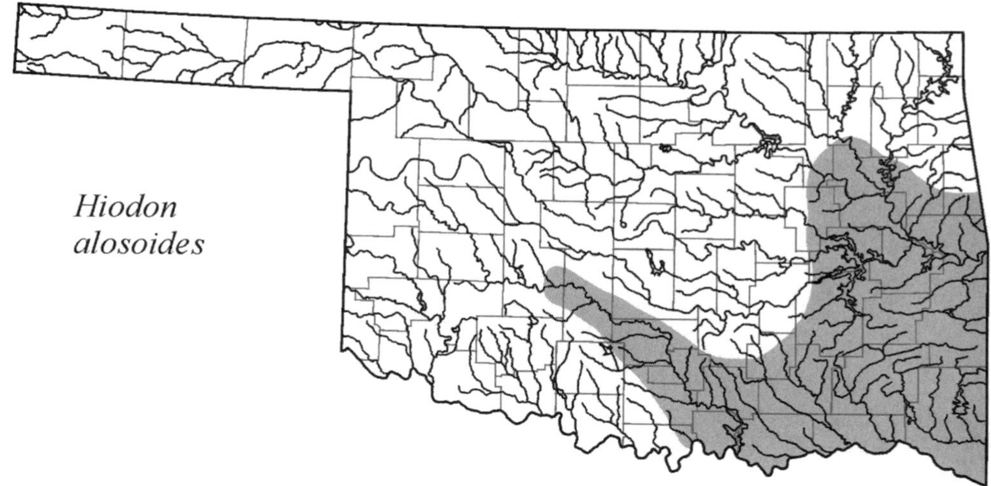

Habitat and Biology:

The goldeye seems to inhabit larger rivers and lakes, where it forms schools, particularly during the annual spawning run. It is known to feed on fish in most parts of its range, and studies in Lake Texoma have shown that locally it often feeds primarily on small insects. Goldeyes succumb readily to spinners and other artificial lures as well as a variety of live baits. Spawning occurs in the early spring (April) over shallow gravelly areas, either in flowing water or lakes at water temperatures of 50–55 degrees F, and no parental care is provided. Males are distinguished from females by the curvature of the anal fin margin, which is strongly sigmoid (S-shaped) in males and concave or straight in females. Maximum life span is 14 years.

Mooneye

Hiodon tergisus Lesueur

Description:

Resembles the goldeye in many respects but may be distinguished by the following characteristics: the fleshy belly keel extends forward only to the base of the pelvic fins; the dorsal fin origin is slightly in front of the anal fin origin, and there are 11 or 12 dorsal rays; the body is somewhat deeper and the dorsal body outline is gently curved rather than straight; the eye is somewhat larger with no yellow pigment; and the body is more silvery in appearance. Lateral line is complete with 52–57 scales. Anal rays 26–29. Usually about 12 inches long and ranging from 12 ounces to 2 pounds in weight.

Distribution:

From the tributaries of Hudson Bay south through the lower Great Lakes to Oklahoma and Tennessee and east to the St. Lawrence River. Present in Oklahoma only in the Mountain Fork and Little River.

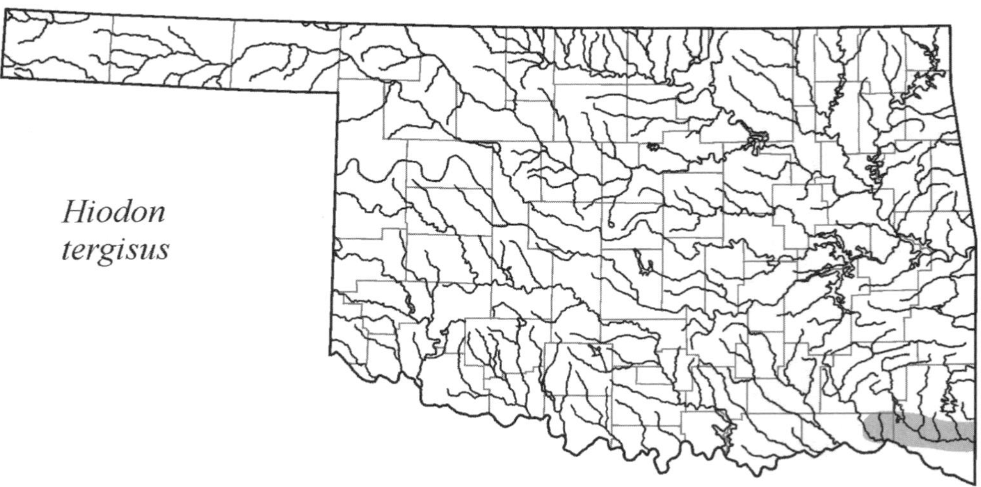

Habitat and Biology:

The mooneye seems to prefer large, clear streams, rivers, and lakes. It appears to be less tolerant of turbid waters than the goldeye, and this may be one reason for its limited distribution in Oklahoma. It occurs most often in current over a firm substrate. It feeds on insects, molluscs, crayfish, and small fish and can be caught on artificial lures. On hook and line, the mooneye is an active fighter, but it is not usually eaten because of the great number of tiny bones in the flesh. Spawning occurs in spring, with fish often ascending tributary streams to spawn over shoal areas. Females may produce 10,000 to 20,000 eggs. Sexes reach maturity in the third or fourth year of life, but may take six to seven years to reach a size of 13 inches. Maximum life span is about ten years. Not significant as a game or food fish in Oklahoma.

EELS

FAMILY ANGUILLIDAE

AMERICAN EEL

Anguilla rostrata (Lesueur)

Description:

An extremely long, slightly compressed fish with no pelvic fins and a continuous median fin consisting of united dorsal, caudal, and anal fins. The gill opening is a small slit just anterior to the pectoral fins. There are well-developed teeth in the jaws. Scales in the slimy skin are so small and embedded that they are visible only on close inspection. Color is yellowish to brown above and yellowish to white below. Generally between 15 and 30 inches long, under 3 pounds in weight. State record: 5 lb., 7 oz., 39½ in., from the lower Illinois River.

Distribution:

Most of eastern United States through the plains states. Found throughout much of the eastern half of Oklahoma but quite sporadic in occurrence.

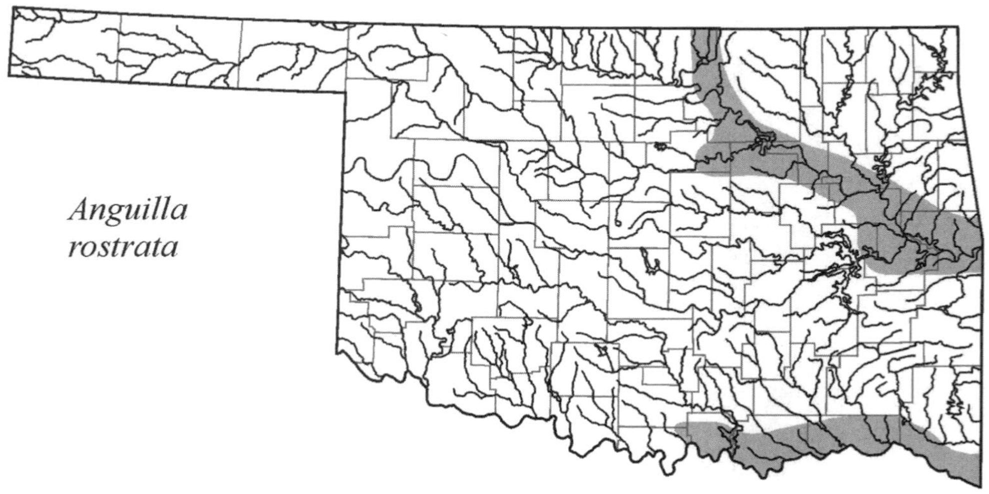

Habitat and Biology:

The eel seems to prefer moderately large streams and rivers, where it feeds mainly on living and dead fish, crustaceans, and other organisms. Much of the eel's juvenile phase and nearly all its adult life is spent in such streams and in some lakes and ponds close to flowing waters. At maturity eels move downstream to the sea in one of the classic migrations known in the fishes. Swimming to breeding grounds south of Bermuda, the adults spawn, then die, leaving the young to find their own ways back to the mainland and the rivers they will inhabit for several years. Females seem to penetrate farthest upstream. The construction of dams on nearly all larger rivers has drastically reduced the number of eels in Oklahoma. Anglers may occasionally catch eels using live baits, but they are generally not eaten.

SHADS

FAMILY CLUPEIDAE

Key

1a. Dorsal fin with 12–13 rays with last ray greatly elongated; dorsal origin behind or over pelvic insertion; mouth small, terminal or subterminal 2

1b. Dorsal fin with 16–18 rays with last ray not elongated; dorsal origin in front of pelvic insertion; mouth large 3

2a. Lateral series with more than 50 scales; anal rays usually 29–35; ventral scutes 17–19 and 10–12; mouth subterminal or inferior . . . . *Dorosoma cepedianum*

2b. Lateral series with fewer than 50 scales; anal rays usually 20–27; ventral scutes 16 and 11 or 12; mouth terminal . . . . *Dorosoma petenense*

3a. Hyoid teeth in 2 or 4 longitudinal rows; lower jaw with dark pigment only anteriorly near tip; gill rakers on lower limb of first arch about 23 . . . . *Alosa chrysochloris*

3b. Hyoid teeth in a single longitudinal row; lower jaw with dark pigment along most of its length; gill rakers on lower limb of first gill arch more numerous, 30–40 . . . . *Alosa alabamae*

ALABAMA SHAD

Alosa alabamae Jordan and Evermann

Description:

A slab-sided, herringlike fish similar to *Alosa chrysochloris* but differing in several respects. The upper and lower jaws are almost equal in length (the lower jaw projects well past the upper in the skipjack); the mandible is pigmented over more of its length, and there are more than 30 gill rakers on the lower limb of the first arch. Teeth on tongue are in a single median row. Lateral line absent. Dorsal rays 17–18; anal rays 18 or fewer. Color is silvery as in most herrings. Up to 18 inches in length and 3 pounds in weight.

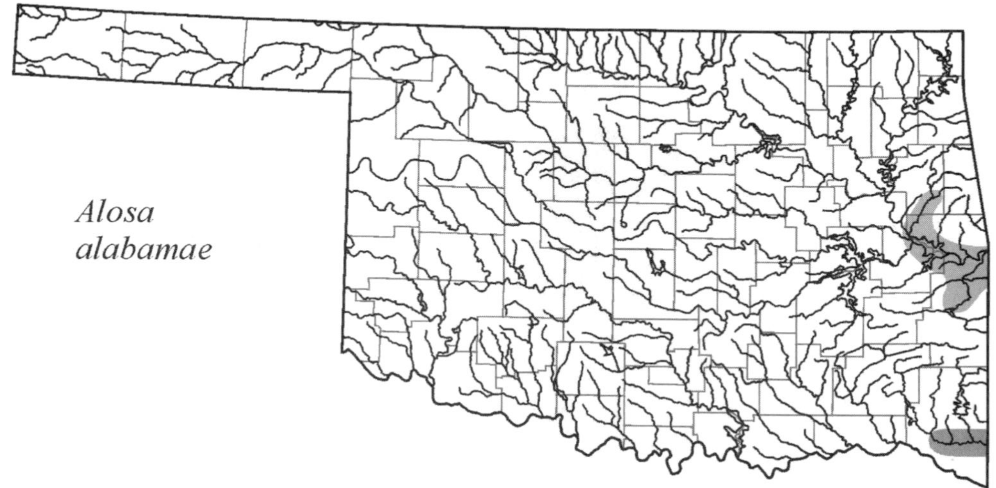

Distribution:

From the lower Ohio River Valley through the Mississippi basin to Oklahoma and Tennessee. Rare in most parts of its former range. Oklahoma has only a handful of specimens and records from the Poteau and Illinois river drainages and from the Little River in McCurtain County.

Habitat and Biology:

The Alabama shad is an anadromous species that migrates inland in the spring to spawn. Spawning occurs at water temperatures of 19–22 degrees C in moderate current over gravel and sandy substrates; females scatter thousands of eggs. Adults then return to the marine environment. Young 4-5 inches long feed on small fish and aquatic insects before migrating downriver in the fall to the sea. If the Alabama shad still inhabits Oklahoma waters, it is probably to be found in the mainstream portions of larger clear streams of the Ozark/Ouachita region.

SKIPJACK HERRING

Alosa chrysochloris (Rafinesque)

Description:

A fairly typical herringlike fish with compressed, thin body, deeply forked tail, thin cycloid scales, and sharp scutes on the midline of the belly. An adipose eyelid (clear) covers anterior and posterior portions of the eye. The terminal mouth is large, but jaws are weakly toothed. Teeth on the tongue are in 2–4 rows. The lower jaw projects well beyond the upper, with black pigment on lower jaw confined to the tip. Fewer than 30 gill rakers (about 23) on the lower part of the first gill arch. Color is bluish silver above and silvery below with occasional dark spots showing on dorsolateral parts of the body. Adults are usually less than 15 inches long and half a pound in weight, with a maximum length of 21 inches and 3.5 pounds. State record: 3 lb., 6 oz., 19 in., from Eufaula tailwaters.

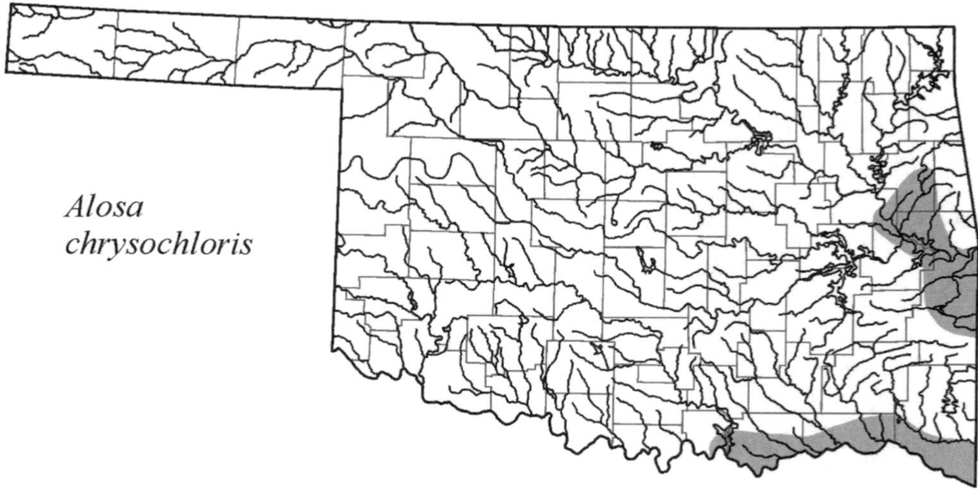

Distribution:

Mississippi Valley from Minnesota to Texas and from Ohio to Florida. Found in the clear upland streams and rivers along the eastern edge of Oklahoma and in the Red River and its tributaries west to Lake Texoma.

Habitat and Biology:

Little is known of the biology of the skipjack in Oklahoma, perhaps because it is encountered so infrequently by biologists. The skipjack is a predator on invertebrates and fishes and received its common name from its habit of schooling behind minnow schools and forcing them to crowd to the surface, whereupon the skipjack darts among them, snapping up the prey as they leap into the air (Trautman 1957). It inhabits backwater areas of large rivers, although it seems to prefer clear water. This species is probably not significant as a contributor to the biota of most Oklahoma waters.

Gizzard Shad

Dorosoma cepedianum (Lesueur)

Description:

A very deep-bodied, highly compressed herringlike fish with a long, filamentous posterior dorsal fin ray. The snout is blunt, and the relatively small mouth is subterminal to inferior and toothless in adults. Gill rakers are long and comblike. Anterior and posterior adipose eyelids present. Scales in lateral series 59–67. The anal fin is long, usually with 29–35 rays. The midline of the belly has 17–19 sharp scutes in front of the pelvic fins and 10–12 behind. Color is bluish to greenish above and silvery or white laterally. A dusky spot above the upper angle of the gill cover is usually prominent. Adults usually less than a foot in length but recorded up to 19 inches and 3 pounds.

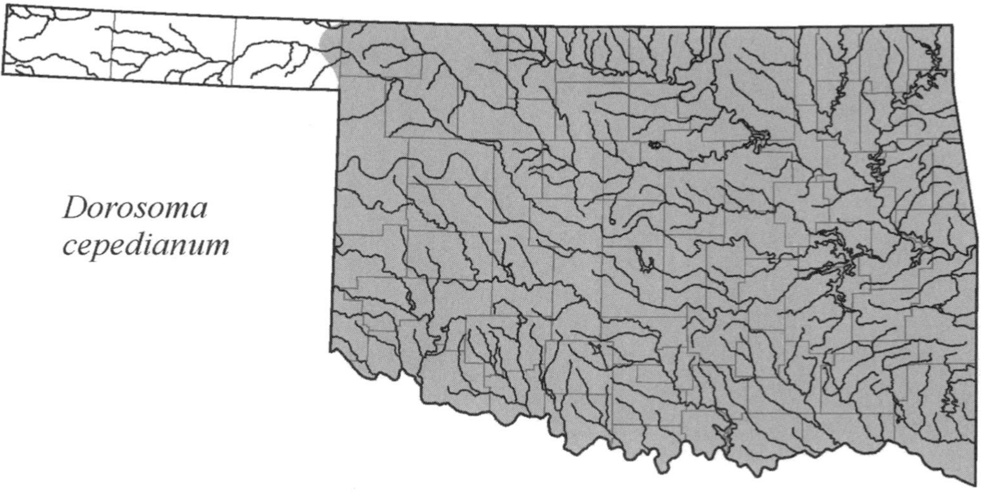

Distribution:

Throughout the eastern United States from the Dakotas to Quebec, south to Florida, and southwest to Texas and northeastern Mexico. Found throughout Oklahoma.

Habitat and Biology:

The gizzard shad is one of Oklahoma's most ubiquitous fishes, successful in both stream and lake habitats. Where present in newly created impoundments, it often proliferates to the point of dominating the fish fauna. Gizzard shad are filter feeders, using their fine gill rakers to strain detritus from the bottom and plankton from the water. Usually traveling in large schools, they are occasionally foul-hooked by fishermen but rarely caught by means other than nets. They are not desirable food fish. Although young shad provide forage for the larger predators in lakes, the fact that most of the mass of shad is made up of adults mainly unavailable as food has caused biologists to question their value in the sport fishery. They generally spawn in schools at night in late April to May, scattering their eggs and sperm randomly. Adhesive eggs sink to the bottom, where they attach to anything with which they come in contact.

THREADFIN SHAD
Dorosoma petenense (Gunther)

Description:

In overall appearance the smaller threadfin shad closely resembles the gizzard shad: a silvery clupeid with a thin, deeply compressed body, moderately blunt snout, long dorsal filament, and deeply forked tail. It differs in having a terminal mouth, scales in the lateral series 42–48, a shorter anal fin (20–27 rays), and fewer than 17 ventral scutes before the pelvic fins. The caudal fin and back are also more yellowish than in the gizzard shad. In most northern waters threadfin shad rarely exceed 2–4 inches in length, though in Louisiana they reach 8 inches.

Distribution:

Tributaries of the Gulf of Mexico from Florida to Texas, extending north in the Mississippi drainage to Oklahoma and Tennessee. In Oklahoma it

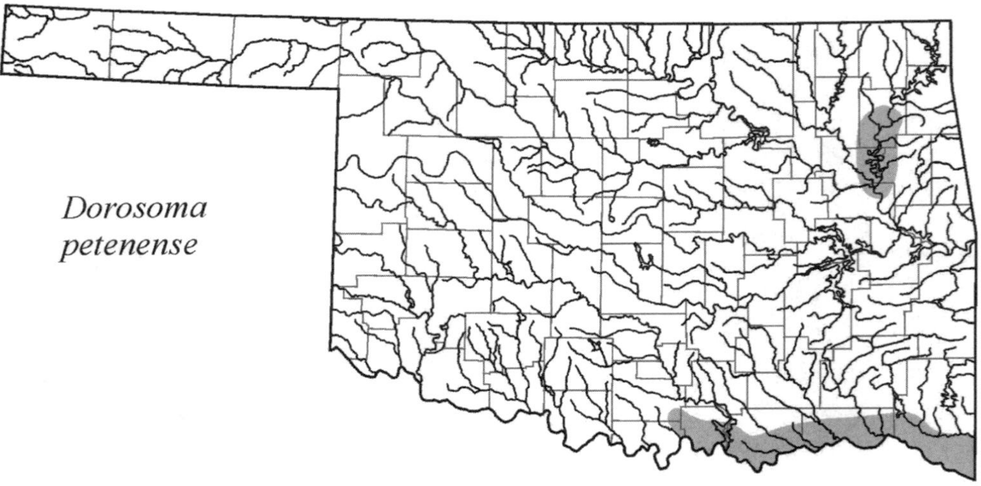

occurs naturally in the Red River and some of its tributaries and possibly in some parts of the Arkansas River drainage in Mayes and Wagoner counties. Introduced as a forage species in various lakes around the state.

Habitat and Biology:

The threadfin differs somewhat from the gizzard shad in being essentially a pelagic, planktivorous fish. Studies in Arkansas, however, have shown that they may also feed on larger particulate foods and may have a more diversified ecological niche than has so far been attributed to them. Since they are smaller than gizzard shad, they are more desirable forage fish for impoundments. Because it is essentially a southern species, the threadfin cannot tolerate water temperatures below the low 50s and will thus prove of little use in northern Oklahoma. A well-adapted breeding population exists in Lake Texoma. Spawning takes place in the spring near shore when water temperatures reach 70 degrees F and continues for several months. Adhesive eggs are scattered over submerged plants and other objects and hatch in about three days. Sexual maturity is reached at about one to two years of age.

MINNOWS

FAMILY CYPRINIDAE

Key

1a. Dorsal fin elongate and having more than 11 soft rays; a strong hardened serrate ray at origin of dorsal and anal fins 2
1b. Dorsal fin of fewer than 11 soft rays; no hardened rays 3
2a. Two pairs of barbels present at corners of mouth. . . . . . *Cyprinus carpio*
2b. Barbels absent . . . . *Carassius auratus*
3a. Anal fin situated far to the rear; distance from anal fin origin to caudal base into distance between tip of snout and anal fin origin more than 2.5 times; pharyngeal teeth with prominent parallel grooves; size large; often exceeding 15 inches . . . . *Ctenopharyngodon idella* (grass carp; see Exotic Species in introduction)
3b. Anal fin situated in normal position, distance from anal fin origin to caudal base into distance between tip of snout and anal fin origin fewer than 2.5 times; pharyngeal teeth lacking grooves; small, seldom exceeding 12 inches. 4
4a. Lateral line complete, with 85 or more scales (if 85 or more and lateral line incomplete, 2 dark lateral bands present, and a ventral keel absent between vent and pelvic fin, then go to couplet 5) . . . . *Hypophthalmichthys nobilis* (bighead carp; see Exotic Species in introduction)
4b. Lateral line complete or incomplete, but with fewer than 85 scales . . . 5
5a. Barbels present (at posterior angle of the jaw or placed forward from the angle of the jaw on the maxilla) 6
5b. Barbels absent 13
6a. Barbel minute, flat and concealed in groove above the maxilla; barbel not terminal (see fig. 10). . . . . *Semotilus atromaculatus*

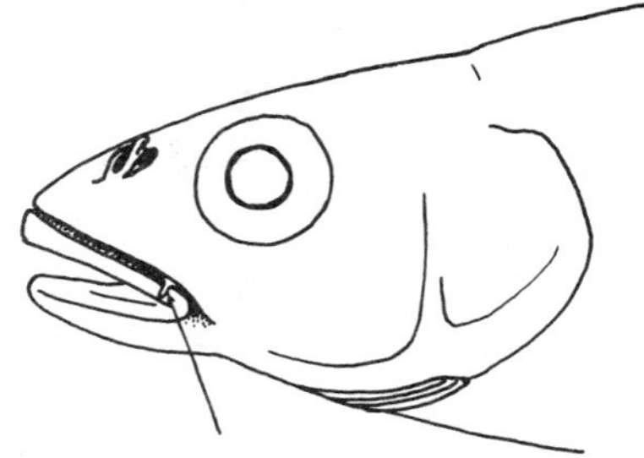

FIGURE 10. Small, flat barbel of *Semotilus atromaculatus*; note position anterior to end of maxillary (see arrow).

6b. Barbel larger and terminal (at angle of jaws). 7

7a. Distance from dorsal origin to caudal base less than distance from dorsal origin to snout tip; mouth terminal; snout barely projecting beyond upper lip (see fig. 11) . . . . *Nocomis asper*

7b. Distance from dorsal origin to caudal base is equal to or greater than distance from dorsal origin to snout tip; mouth subterminal or inferior; snout projecting beyond upper lip (see fig. 11) 8

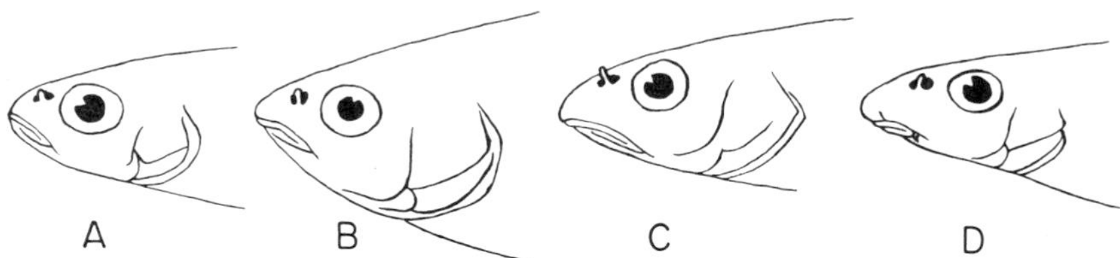

FIGURE 11. Characteristics of mouths of minnows (lateral views). (From Cross 1967)

A. Mouth terminal and oblique, upper and lower jaws equal. *Notropis boops* illustrated.

B. Mouth nearly terminal, oblique, but lower jaw included (shorter than upper jaw, closing within it). *Cyprinella camura* illustrated.

C. Mouth subterminal, scarcely oblique, lower jaw included (shorter than upper jaw, closing within it). *Notropis dorsalis* illustrated.

D. Mouth ventral and nearly horizontal. Note also barbel projecting from groove at corner of mouth (barbel absent in A, B, and C). *Erimystax x-punctatus* illustrated.

8a. Body with scattered black spots or dark X-shaped markings; pharyngeal teeth 4-4 9

8b. Body without scattered black spots or dark X-shaped markings; pharyngeal teeth 2, 4-4, 2 or 1, 4-4, 1 11

9a. Body with X-shaped markings; barbels much shorter than the eye diameter; scales in lateral line usually more than 40 . . *Erimystax x-punctatus*

9b. Body without X-shaped markings but with scattered black spots; barbels longer than eye diameter; scales in lateral line usually less than 40 10

10a. One or two pairs of barbels present, posterior barbels usually less than orbit length, anterior barbels absent or less than 50 percent of orbit length; pectoral fin tuberculation of breeding males uniserial, with 1–2 rows of tubercles at midsection of rays; lips not as fleshy or greatly expanded posteriorly . . . . *Macrhybopsis hyostoma*

10b. Two prominent pairs of barbels present, posterior barbels usually greater than orbit length, anterior barbels usually greater than 50 percent of orbit length; pectoral fin tuberculation of nuptial males usually biserial or primary branches, with 3–4 rows of tubercles at midsection of rays; lips fleshy and greatly expanded posteriorly. . . . . *Macrhybopsis australis*

11a. Lateral-line scales usually more than 42; pharyngeal teeth 2, 4-4, 2; head conspicuously flattened dorsoventrally; eye small . . . *Platygobio gracilis*

11b. Lateral-line scales usually less than 42; pharyngeal teeth 1, 4-4, 2; head not conspicuously flattened dorsoventrally; eye large. 12

12a. Caudal fin uniformly colored; lateral band dark; distance from dorsal origin to caudal base about equal to distance from dorsal origin to snout tip . . . . *Hybopsis amblops*

12b. Caudal fin lower lobe margined with white; lateral band indistinct; distance from dorsal origin to caudal base greater than distance from dorsal origin to snout tip. . . . . *Macrhybopsis storeriana*

13a. Lower jaw with hardened inner cartilaginous ridge; intestine coiled spirally around the air bladder 14

13b. Lower jaw without hardened inner cartilaginous ridge; intestine not coiled spirally round the air bladder. 15

14a. Scale rows around the body just anterior to dorsal fin usually 40–55; breeding males with black pigment in anal fin and with 1–3 tubercles beside each nostril; least width of skull between eyes generally less than the distance from back of eye to upper end of gill opening . . . . *Campostoma anomalum*

14b. Scale rows around body just anterior to dorsal fin usually 32–39; breeding males without black pigment in anal fin and without tubercles beside each nostril; least width of skull between eyes about equal to distance from back of eye to upper end of gill opening . . . . *Campostoma oligolepis*

15a. Belly between pelvic fins and anal fin with a sharp, scaleless keel; anal rays 10 or more . . . . *Notemigonus crysoleucas*

15b. Belly between pelvic fins and anal fin without a sharp, scaleless keel; anal rays usually less than 10 16

16a. Second unbranched ray of dorsal fin usually thickened, short, and separated from the third ray by a membrane (first ray extremely small, usually overlooked without dissection); anterior dorsal rays sometimes blackened, producing an appreciable spot; predorsal scales small, crowded (*Pimephales*) 17

16b. Second unbranched ray of dorsal fin slender and closely joined to the third ray; predorsal area not broad or flattened, with scales about same size as those on upper sides; anterior dorsal rays usually not blackened 20

17a. Body stout, greatest body depth contained about 3.2 to 4.0 times in standard length; lateral line usually incomplete; basicaudal spot absent or indistinct; breeding males with 3 rows of tubercles on snout . . . . *Pimephales promelas*

17b. Body slender, greatest body depth contained about 3.9 to 5.1 times in standard length; lateral line complete; basicaudal spot distinct; breeding males with 1 to 3 rows of tubercles on snout. 18

18a. Peritoneum black; mouth more ventral, upper lip overhung by a fleshy snout; intestine with several loops . . . . *Pimephales notatus*

18b. Peritoneum silvery; mouth terminal, upper lip not overhung with fleshy snout; intestine with a single S-shaped loop 19

19a. Basicaudal spot vertically elongate; well-defined lateral stripe; body slender, body depth contained 4.5 to 5.1 times in standard length; cross hatching distinct (pigment concentrated along scale margins); nuptial tubercles 11–13, in 3 rows; no black pigment in dorsal fin crotches . . . . *Pimephales tenellus*

19b. Basicaudal spot wedge-shaped; lateral stripe indistinct or absent; body stouter, body depth contained 3.9 to 4.3 times in standard length; cross hatching indistinct (pigment dispersed on scales); nuptial tubercles 9, in 2 rows; black pigment in dorsal fin crotches. . . . . *Pimephales vigilax*

20a. Intestine long, with several coils that are transverse or spiraled (see fig. 12); peritoneum black; pharyngeal teeth in 1 row. 21

20b. Intestine short, with 1 or 2 loops; peritoneum various (see fig. 12); pharyngeal teeth in 1 or 2 rows. 25

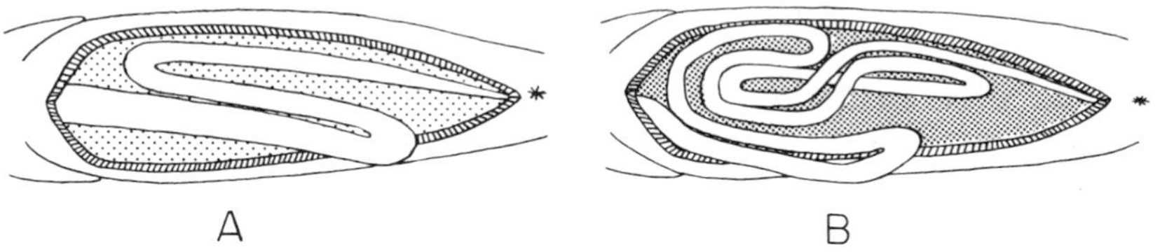

FIGURE 12. Ventral views (diagrammatic) of body cavities in minnows, as they would appear if lower body wall were cut away. (From Cross 1967)

A. Intestine short, with a single S-shaped loop; peritoneum silvery.

B. Intestine long, looped across body cavity; peritoneum dark (usually black).

21a. Scales small, more than 70 in lateral series; pharyngeal teeth 5-5 . . . . *Phoxinus erythrogaster*

21b. Scales large, less than 70 in lateral series; pharyngeal teeth 4-4 22

22a. Lateral line marked with 2 rows of spots; pharyngeal teeth hooked; eye diameter going into head length less than 4 times, equal to or greater than length of snout . . . . *Dionda nubila*

22b. Lateral line without rows of spots; pharyngeal teeth not hooked; eye diameter going into head length 4 to 6 times, less than length of snout (*Hybognathus*) 23

23a. Eye diameter greater than snout length; snout rounded, not easily seen from below; tip of upper lip about level with middle of eye; edges of scales on forward part of side prominently dark-edged, forming a distinct diamond-shaped pattern . . . . *Hybognathus hayi*

23b. Eye diameter less than snout length; snout more pointed, extending noticeably beyond mouth; upper lip tip below middle of eye; edges of scales on forward part of side evenly pigmented, not prominently dark-edged, not forming a distinct diamond-shaped pattern 24

24a. Eye large, its diameter going into head length about 4 times; posterior process of the basioccipital bone thin and expanded (see fig. 13); scale rows below lateral line fewer than 15 . . . . *Hybognathus nuchalis*

24b. Eye smaller, its diameter going into head length about 5 to 6 times; posterior process of the basioccipital bone rodlike, not expanded (see fig. 13); scale rows below lateral line 15 or more . . . . *Hybognathus placitus*

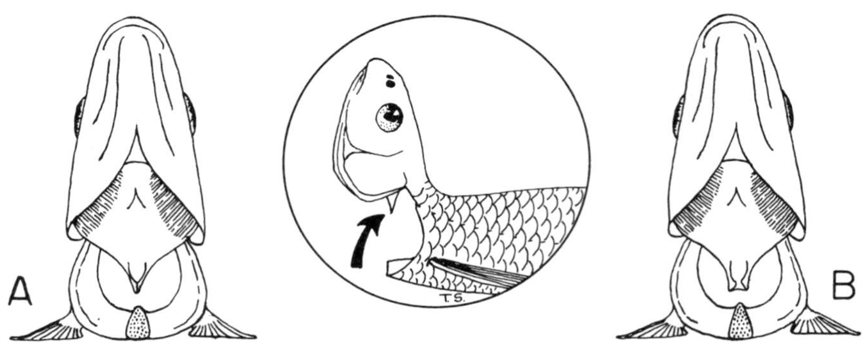

FIGURE 13. Basioccipital bones in two species of *Hybognathus*. The three figures demonstrate a method of revealing the structure, by cutting across the isthmus and bending the head backward. (From Cross 1967)

A. *Hybognathus placitus*: Posterior process of basioccipital rodlike, with contiguous muscle attachments at tip.

B. *Hybognathus nuchalis*: Posterior process of basioccipital expanded, with widely separated muscle attachments at tip.

25a. Lower lip developed as a fleshy lobe; mouth suckerlike; pharyngeal teeth 4-4. . . . . *Phenacobius mirabilis*

25b. Lower lip normally formed; mouth not suckerlike; pharyngeal teeth 2, 4-4, 2; 1, 4-4, 0; or 5-5 26

26a. Dorsal fin rays 9 or 10 27

26b. Dorsal fin rays 8 28

27a. Anal fin rays 8; body terete; lateral line present; pharyngeal teeth 5-5 . . . . *Opsopoeodus emiliae*

27b. Anal fin rays 9 or 10; body slab-sided; lateral line absent; pharyngeal teeth 4-4 . . . . *Notropis hubbsi*

28a. Caudal fin base with a distinct round or wedge-shaped spot very clearly set off from the lateral band 29

28b. Caudal fin base without distinct round or wedge-shaped spot, or if present, spot appears as a rectangular extension of the lateral band or as an indiscrete splash 31

29a. Basicaudal spot wedge-shaped and small; anal rays usually 8; fins in breeding males not highly colored . . . . *Notropis greenei*

29b. Basicaudal spot large and round; fins in breeding males yellow or reddish 30

30a. Basicaudal spot with a small black triangle at upper and lower edge of caudal base; anal rays 7; posterior interradial membranes of dorsal not blackened . . . . *Notropis maculatus*

30b. Basicaudal spot without small triangle at upper and lower edge of caudal base; anal rays 8; posterior interradial membranes of dorsal somewhat blackened . . . . *Cyprinella venusta*

31a. Black pigment on interradial membranes of dorsal fins most prominent on the posterior portion (see fig. 14); anal rays 8 or 9. 32

31b. Black pigment on interradial membranes of dorsal fin, if present, not confined to posterior interradial dorsal membranes (except sometimes in *C. lutrensis* (see fig. 14); anal rays 7–12 34

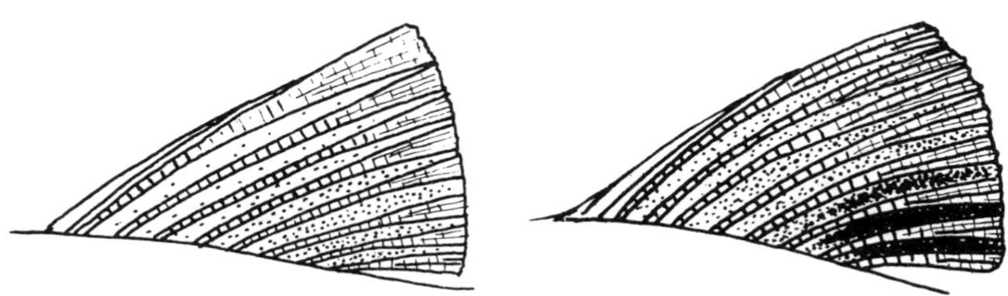

FIGURE 14. Black pigment on interradial membranes of dorsal fin of *Cyprinella lutrensis (left)* and *C. whipplei (right)*.

32a. Anal rays usually 8; dark lateral stripe of caudal peduncle narrow, prominent, and centered below pores of lateral line . . . . . *Cyprinella spiloptera*

32b. Anal rays usually 9; dark lateral stripe on caudal peduncle broad, faint, and centered on pores of lateral line. 33

33a. Caudal fin base with a narrow milky white patch; snout blunt and head outline sharply decurved; lateral-line scales 35–37 . . . *Cyprinella camura*

33b. Caudal fin base without milky white patch; snout sharply pointed and head outline not decurved; lateral-line scales 37–39 . . . . *Cyprinella whipplei*

34a. Upper lip distinctly swollen posteriorly (see fig. 15); lower lip thickened medially; mouth large; pharyngeal teeth 2, 4-4, 2 . . . . . . *Notropis potteri*

34b. Upper and lower lip thin, and little thickened (see fig. 15) 35

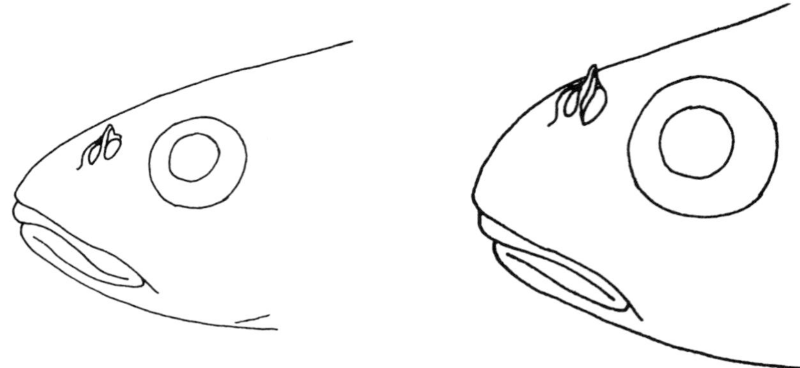

FIGURE 15. Shape of the mouth and lips in *Notropis potteri (left)* and *N. blennius (right)*. Note the swollen posterior portion of the upper lip and the thickened medial portion of the lower lip.

35a. Pharyngeal teeth 4-4 (occasionally 1, 4-4, 1 in *Cyprinella lutrensis*, which has 9 and sometimes 10 anal rays) 36

35b. Pharyngeal teeth 1 or 2, 4-4, 2 or 1 43

36a. Anal rays usually 7 (sometimes 8) 37

36b. Anal rays 8–10 39

37a. Lateral band conspicuous, ending in a rectangular caudal spot joined with and as wide as lateral band; in young there may be a narrow clear hiatus between the lateral band and the caudal spot .... *Notropis atrocaudalis*

37b. Lateral band not as conspicuous and not ending in a rectangular caudal spot; if spot present, it appears as an indiscrete splash on the basal portion of the middle caudal rays 38

38a. Nape fully scaled; mouth horizontal or nearly so; pectorals rounded, not falcate .... *Notropis stramineus*

38b. Nape often naked or partly so; mouth more oblique, often about 45 degrees from the horizontal; pectoral fins long, pointed and falcate (especially in males) .... *Notropis bairdi*

39a. Anal rays 8 40

39b. Anal rays 9–10 (rarely 8) 42

40a. Lateral-line scales not conspicuously elevated anteriorly; exposed surfaces about as long as high (see fig. 16) .... *Notropis girardi*

40b. Lateral-line scales conspicuously elevated; exposed surfaces much higher than long (see fig. 16) 41

FIGURE 16. Head and anterior lateral-line scales of *Notropis volucellus (left)* and *N. girardi (right)*. Note the conspicuous elevation of the lateral-line scales in *N. volucellus.*

41a. Infraorbital canals complete (see fig. 17); pigmentation of scale borders intense near middorsal line and present though diminishing downward on entire dorsum . . . . *Notropis volucellus*
41b. Infraorbital canals incomplete (see fig. 17); pigmentation of scale borders less intense and often absent just above lateral line . . . . *Notropis buchanani*

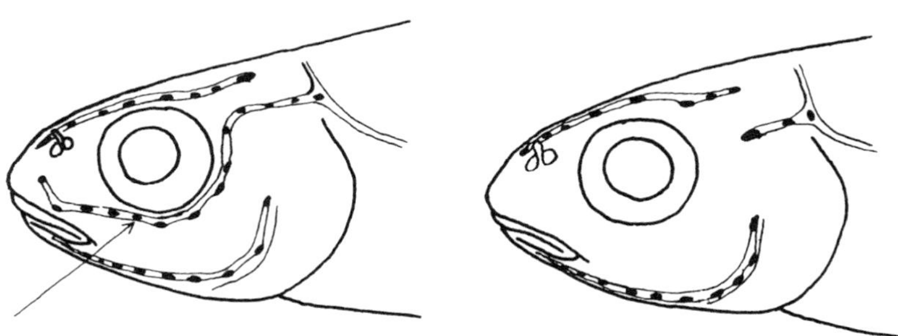

FIGURE 17. Cephalic lateral-line system in *Notropis volucellus (left)* and *N. buchanani (right)*, showing the presence of the complete infraorbital canal (arrow) in *N. volucellus*. (After Reno 1966)

42a. Lateral band well developed anteriorly and the row of scales above it largely without pigment; mouth extremely oblique, more than 45 degrees from the horizontal, and the chin strongly convex in profile . . . . *Notropis ortenburgeri*
42b. Lateral band poorly developed anteriorly and the row of scales above it well pigmented, presenting a diamond-shaped appearance . . . . *Cyprinella lutrensis*
43a. Origin of dorsal fin placed well behind pelvic base (see fig. 18). 44
43b. Origin of dorsal fin not definitely behind pelvic base but sometimes near the end of the pelvic base. 47

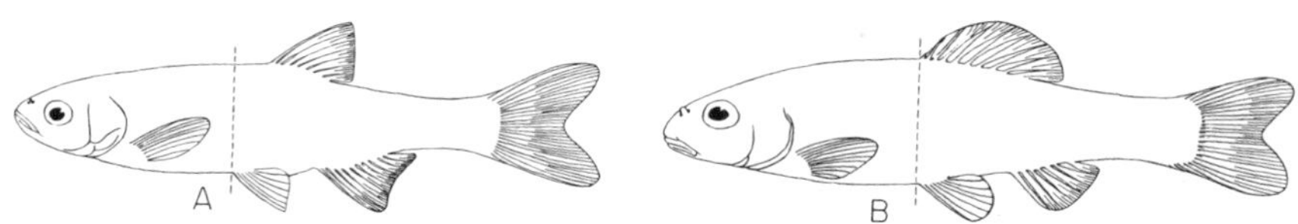

FIGURE 18. Differences in position and shape of dorsal fins of minnows. (From Cross 1967)

A. Origin of dorsal fin posterior to insertion of pelvic fins, as indicated by vertical dashed line. Also, the dorsal fin is triangular (pointed at the tip), and its anterior rays would extend to or beyond the tips of the posterior rays if the fin were folded downward against the body.

B. Origin of dorsal fin approximately over insertion of pelvic fins. Also, the dorsal fin is rounded, and its anterior rays would not extend to the tips of the posterior rays if the fin were folded downward against the body.

44a. Predorsal scales large (12–20) 45

44b. Predorsal scales small, more crowded (about 25) 54

45a. Lateral-line pores marked with melanophores at least anteriorly; chin not sprinkled with dark pigment; anal rays 9 or l0; dorsal fin rounded (fig. 18) 46

45b. Lateral-line pores marked by melanophores for short distance or not at all; chin sprinkled with dark pigment; anal rays 10–13; dorsal fin pointed (fig. 18) . . . . *Notropis atherinoides*

46a. Body slender, narrower at dorsal fin and caudal peduncle; lateral line usually straight or only slightly decurved 1–2 scale rows; lip pigmentation light, gular region clear or with scattered melanophores; lateral stripe variable, always thicker caudally than anteriorly; lateral line well outlined by melanophores for at least half of its length; Ozark Mountain region . . . . *Notropis percobromus*

46b. Body more robust, deeper at dorsal fin and caudal peduncle; lateral line deeply decurved 5–6 scale rows; lip pigmentation intense, always some pigment on gular region, typically a dense median patch present; lateral line not outlined by melanophores but often continuous with lateral band; lateral stripe thick, nearly equal from caudal base to opercular cleft; Red River drainage . . . . *Notropis suttkusi*

47a. Peritoneum with intense black pigment overlying the silver 48

47b. Peritoneum never with intense black pigment but silvery and with or without scattered melanophores. 50

48a. Anal rays 8; pharyngeal teeth 1, 4-4, 1 (occasionally lacking lesser row on either side) . . . . *Notropis boops*

48b. Anal rays 9 (occasionally 8); pharyngeal teeth 2, 4-4, 2. 49

49a. Lateral band indistinct, not extending forward on head to snout tip, without a narrow stripe above and running parallel to it; body deep and compressed . . . . *Luxilus chrysocephalus*

49b. Lateral band prominent, extending forward on head to snout tip, with narrow stripe above and running parallel to the lateral band; body slender and not compressed . . . . *Luxilus cardinalis*

50a. Interior of mouth heavily pigmented with black; sides with an intense black lateral band . . . . *Notropis chalybaeus*

50b. Interior of mouth without black pigmentation 51

51a. Anal rays 9–11; pigment of dorsum forming no regular pattern but with scattered, stellate melanophores . . . . *Notropis perpallidus*

51b. Anal rays 7–9; pigment of dorsum in a regular pattern without stellate melanophores 52

52a. Anal rays usually 8; maxillary bone (see fig. 19) extending far behind the angle of the mouth; snout very blunt and overhanging the upper lip . . . . *Hybopsis amnis*

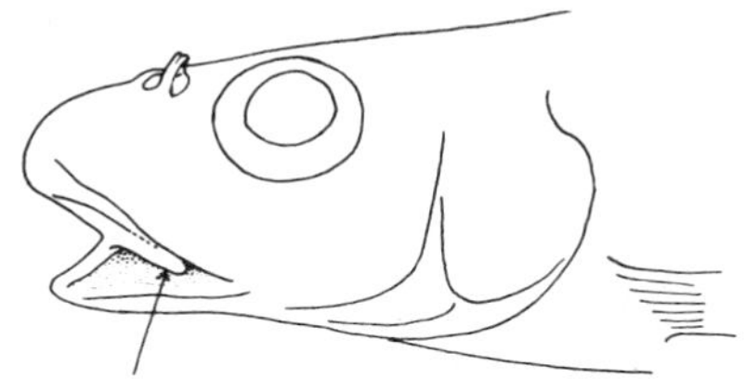

FIGURE 19. Extension of the maxillary bone behind the angle of the mouth in *Hybopsis amnis* (see arrow).

52b. Anal rays usually 7–9; maxillary bone not extending far behind the angle of the mouth; snout not especially blunt nor overhanging the upper lip 53

53a. Anal rays usually 7; dorsal fin short and blunt, the length of longest rays contained more than twice in predorsal length . . . . . . *Notropis blennius*

53b. Anal rays 8 or 9; dorsal fin long and pointed, the length of longest ray contained twice or less in predorsal length . . . . *Notropis shumardi*

54a. Concentration of black pigment at dorsal fin origin; body of adult deep, its greatest depth going into standard length fewer than 4 times; dorsum usually with chevronlike markings, most evident in adults; lateral band poorly developed . . . . *Lythrurus umbratilis*

54b. No concentration of black pigment at dorsal fin origin; body of adult slender, its greatest depth going 4 or more times into standard length; dorsum without chevronlike markings; lateral band better developed, extending onto snout 55

55a. Anal fin rays usually 10 (9–11); body slender; terete; breeding colors red on head; confined to Little River system . . . . *Lythrurus snelsoni*

55b. Anal fin rays usually 11–12 (10–13); body deep, compressed; breeding colors yellowish on fins . . . . *Lythrurus fumeus*

CENTRAL STONEROLLER

Campostoma anomalum (Rafinesque)

Description:

A large, heavy-bodied, terete minnow with a markedly inferior mouth. The lower jaw is equipped with a prominent cartilaginous ridge, and the mouth is overhung by the bulbous snout. Pharyngeal tooth count is usually 4-4, and there are 8 dorsal, 7 anal, and 8 pelvic rays. The intestine of this herbivorous cyprinid is extremely long and wound around the air bladder. Peritoneum lining is black. Scales are small, generally 49–57 in the lateral line. Scales around the body 39–46. Color is dark olivaceous above grading to whitish on the underside. The sides of most adults are marked by randomly scattered, small, dark spots, which represent regenerated scales. Fins are colorless except in breeding males, which develop bright orange and black markings on all but the pectoral fins. Breeding males have well-developed tubercles on the

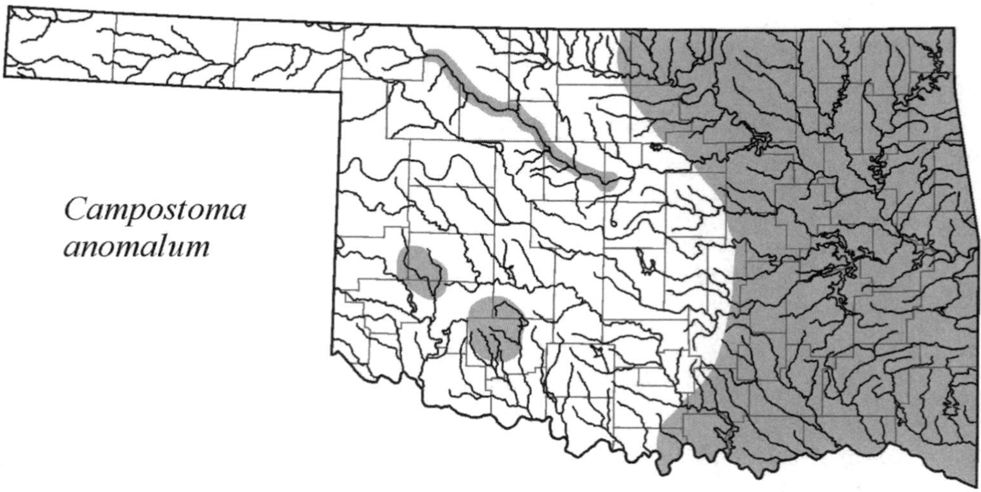

head and upper body and along some rays of the dorsal, caudal, and pectoral fins. Maximum size is 8 inches but usually less than 5 inches. (See also color plate.)

Distribution:

Found over most of the eastern United States west to the Rockies except for the southern Atlantic coastal states. Occurs statewide in Oklahoma.

Habitat and Biology:

Stonerollers are usually inhabitants of clear streams with gravel, rubble, or bedrock bottoms. Using the exposed cartilaginous ridge of the lower jaw, they feed on the soft diatomaceous and algal mats coating the rocky bottoms of pools and slow raceways. Spawning occurs in the spring when water temperatures exceed 58 degrees F, with the brightly colored tuberculate males digging and defending shallow pits in the gravel bottom. Stones are both pushed and carried by mouth out of the pits. Ripe females swim into the pits, and a flurry of activity ensues when adjacent males crowd in with the resident male and the spawning female. The eggs fall into the interstices of the pit bottom, where they develop to hatching. The young are usually found among vegetation at the sides of the stream and in quiet water.

LARGESCALE STONEROLLER

Campostoma oligolepis Hubbs and Greene

Description:

A large, terete minnow with markedly inferior mouth. This species is sympatric over its entire range in Oklahoma with the similar and more common central stoneroller. Like the latter, it has a large, bulbous snout that overhangs the ventral U-shaped mouth. It also shares with the stoneroller the cartilaginous ridge on the lower lip and the extremely long intestine coiled around the gas bladder. Pharyngeal teeth usually 4-4. Predorsal scales 16–20. Lateral line scales usually 43–47 (versus 49–57 in *C. anomalum*). Fins are small and rounded, with 8 dorsal and 7 anal rays, and are clear except for a dark crescent on the dorsal fin of adults. Breeding tubercles are as in *anomalum,* except that tubercles are generally absent along inner margin of nostrils. Body color is olivaceous or dark tan grading to whitish on the belly, the sides with scattered dark scales. Young are lighter in color, often with a dark midlateral

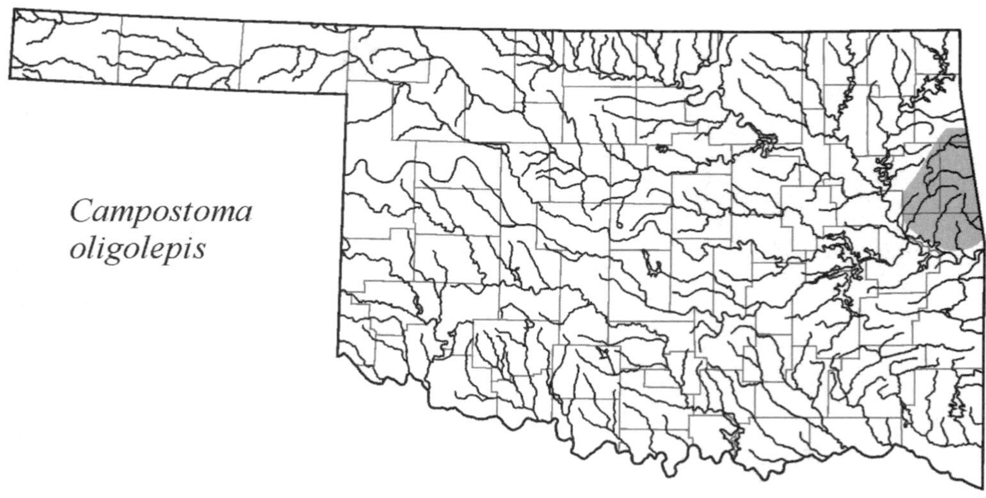

stripe. Breeding males develop black and pink-red colors and a reddish caste on pelvic and anal fins and ventral area; the anal fin has no black medial band. Maximum size 8 inches.

Distribution:

A midwestern species found in clean, clear streams from Wisconsin south to Oklahoma and east to Tennessee and Mississippi. In Oklahoma, found in the Illinois River system in Adair and Cherokee counties and in eastern streams south to Sallisaw Creek.

Habitat and Biology:

Numerous authors, including Burr and Smith (1976), have noted that *C. oligolepis* is less tolerant of turbidity, reduced flow, and silt than is *C. anomalum*, preferring faster water and larger riffles and therefore less common in smaller streams. It feeds primarily on diatoms, green and blue-green algae, and detritus in swifter riffle sections than *C. anomalum*. Thus there appears to be some habitat segregation between the two very similar species. Spawning has been observed in May in Missouri, and appears to be similar to that of *anomalum*.

Goldfish

Carassius auratus (Linnaeus)

Description:

A stout, somewhat compressed fish similar to the carp: the body shape, long dorsal fin, and hard, serrated spinous rays at the dorsal and anal origins are common to both species. The goldfish, however, has a shorter dorsal fin (18–19 rays), no barbels on the lips, fewer lateral-line scales (26–30), and no small dark spots at the bases of the scales. There are 6 or 7 anal rays. Color varies widely. In areas where goldfish have been wild for some time, they seem to revert to their original natural coloration, olivaceous above with lighter bronze sides and olivaceous to transparent fins. Recent introductions may retain the bright orange or occasional blacks and reds of pet store varieties. Adults may reach 15 inches and 2.5 pounds but are usually smaller.

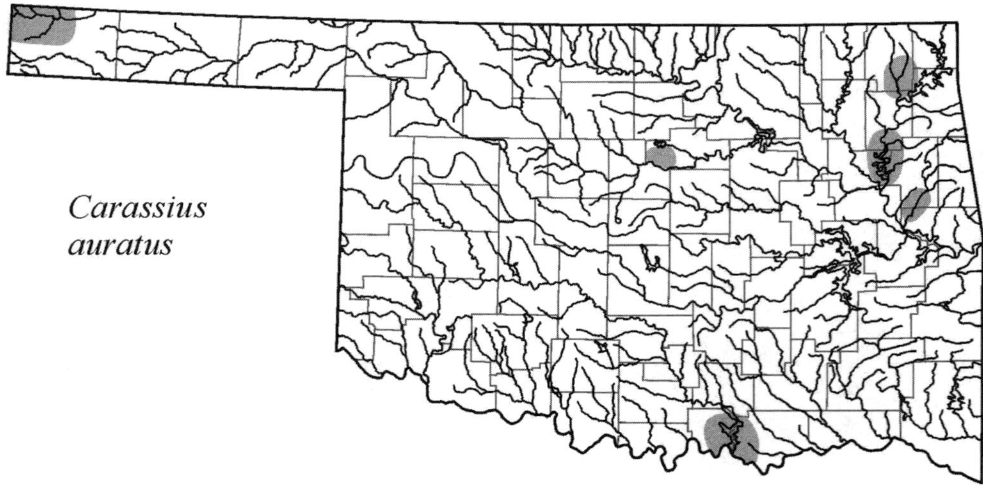

Distribution:

Well-established large breeding populations are most common in the northeastern states, but scattered ponds and lakes throughout the country harbor high densities of goldfish. In Oklahoma they are scattered across the state, though some limited areas (such as South Carizzo Creek, Cimarron County) have had large populations. Most records result from release of aquarium inhabitants.

Habitat and Biology:

Generally similar to the carp but seems to be more specifically adapted to shallow, warm ponds and streams and apparently prefers even denser vegetation than does the carp. Basically a plant and detritus feeder, the goldfish also eats small bottom invertebrates. Similar to that of the carp, spawning is in shallow weedy areas in spring or early summer. In Ohio and a few other areas goldfish-carp hybrids have been found fairly commonly, and such hybrids may occasionally be encountered in Oklahoma; none has been recorded to date, perhaps because established goldfish populations in the state are few. This species is of little consequence as a game or food fish.

BLUNTFACE SHINER

Cyprinella camura (Jordan and Meek)

Description:

A compressed, deep-bodied shiner (greatest depth 3–4 into SL), with large, deep scales and a relatively blunt snout. The mouth is slightly subterminal and oblique, and the eye is moderately small. The bluntface shiner is most similar to *Cyprinella venusta*, *C. spiloptera*, *C. lutrensis*, and *C. whipplei*. It can be distinguished from the first three by its 9 anal rays (usually 8 in the others except *C. lutrensis*) and from all four others by the broad pigmentless vertical band at the base of the caudal fin, milky white in life. Adult *C. whipplei* also tend to have a much more pointed snout, and breeding males have a single row of tubercles on each side of the chin (vs. two rows in *C. camura*). Lateral-line scales 36–37. Pharyngeal teeth 1, 4-4, 1. Breeding males develop fairly prominent head tubercles and bluish color on the body, dorsal fin, and posterior portion of the caudal fin. Lower fins develop pink to orange color. Generally less than 4.5 inches long.

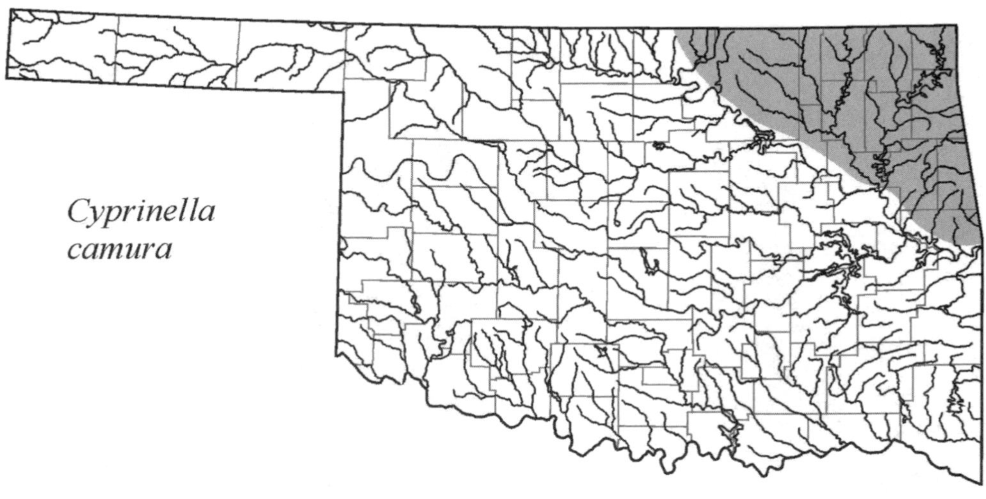

Distribution:

Tributaries to the Arkansas and lower Mississippi rivers from Oklahoma and Kansas to Mississippi and Tennessee. Occurs in the northeastern corner of Oklahoma west to Kay County.

Habitat and Biology:

An inhabitant of moderate-sized clear streams, the bluntface shiner seems to prefer areas with fairly high gradient and gravel bottom. In Oklahoma it seems to spawn in summer, and males in good breeding condition have been captured as late as August 13 in the Illinois River.

RED SHINER

Cyprinella lutrensis (Baird and Girard)

Description:

A highly compressed, deep-bodied minnow (body depth usually 3.2–3.6 into SL) of moderate size, reaching about 2.5 inches. It shares with our four other species of *Cyprinella* the characteristic spindle-shaped body outline, the diamond-shaped scales (higher than they are wide) outlined in black on the dorsum and sides, and the tendency for large males to develop a sharply pointed snout that overhangs the mouth. The red shiner can be separated from all other *Cyprinella* species by the absence of intense black pigment on the posterior membranes of the dorsal fin (see fig. 14 in key) and the absence of a large, conspicuous black blotch at the caudal base. It also differs in usually having a pharyngeal tooth formula of 4-4 (vs. 1, 4-4, 1 in the others). The mouth is terminal and oblique—subterminal in large males—and the eye is of average size (about 4 in head length). There are 8 dorsal and pelvic rays,

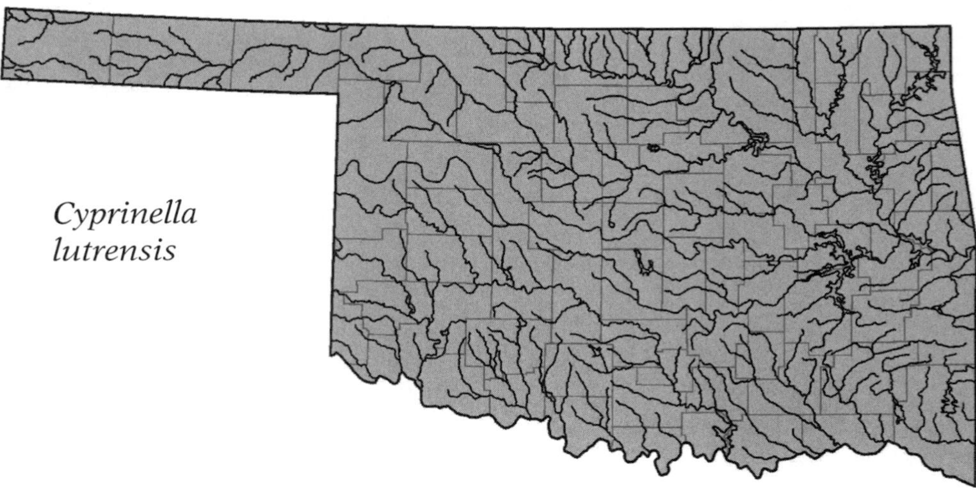

generally 9 (8–10) anal rays, and 34–36 scales in the lateral line, which is sharply decurved. Color is sandy to light olivaceous above, silvery laterally, and white below. Breeding males have all fins but the dorsal bright red-orange, the sides iridescent blue except for a light purple crescent above the pectoral fin, and the top of the head red, with prominent tubercles. (See also color plate.)

Distribution:

West of the Mississippi River from Wyoming and Minnesota south to Texas and introduced elsewhere in the western states. Found throughout Oklahoma except in high-gradient streams of the Ozarks and Ouachitas.

Habitat and Biology:

The red shiner is probably the most common and widespread of all Oklahoma shiners. It can survive in a wide variety of habitats but seems to do best in small streams, even those with intermittent flow, with a wide variety of bottom types, from clay or sand to gravel. Matthews and Hill (1977) documented the fairly broad ecological tolerances of this shiner in Oklahoma, reporting a tolerance of pH between 5 and 10, salinity up to 10 parts per thousand, dissolved oxygen as low as 1.5 parts per million, and thermal shock of T + 10 to T −21 degrees C. Red shiners are least common in the permanently clear, gravel-bottomed, high-gradient streams of eastern Oklahoma. Cross (1967) found that they are most abundant during drought periods when other species often show marked decline. Foods eaten consist of algae, insects, and aquatic invertebrates. In Oklahoma, spawning occurs from April to September (Farringer et al. 1979) in the nests of a variety of sunfishes as well as over beds of aquatic vegetation or other submerged structures. Marsh-Matthews et al. (2003) showed that red shiners hatched in May can successfully spawn by late August. Hybridization between the red shiner and blacktail shiner has been reported.

Spotfin Shiner

Cyprinella spiloptera (Cope)

Description:

A moderately deep-bodied, somewhat compressed shiner, which shares with other members of the genus *Cyprinella* the diamond-shaped pigment outlines on the body scales and the pointed snout with slightly subterminal, oblique mouth. It differs from *C. whipplei*, *C. camura*, and *C. lutrensis* in having 8 anal rays (not 9) and from *C. venusta* in lacking a prominent black basicaudal spot. Color is olivaceous above grading to a silvery or whitish underside. Fins are colorless except for dark slashes on the posterior membranes of the dorsal fin. Breeding males become bluish and develop a fairly prominent dark lateral stripe posteriorly. The dorsal fin does not become longer or posteriorly convex, though all fins develop milky white depositions distally. Lower fins and snout are yellow, and prominent breeding tubercles develop on the head and snout and to a lesser extent on the nape. Rarely larger than 3 inches.

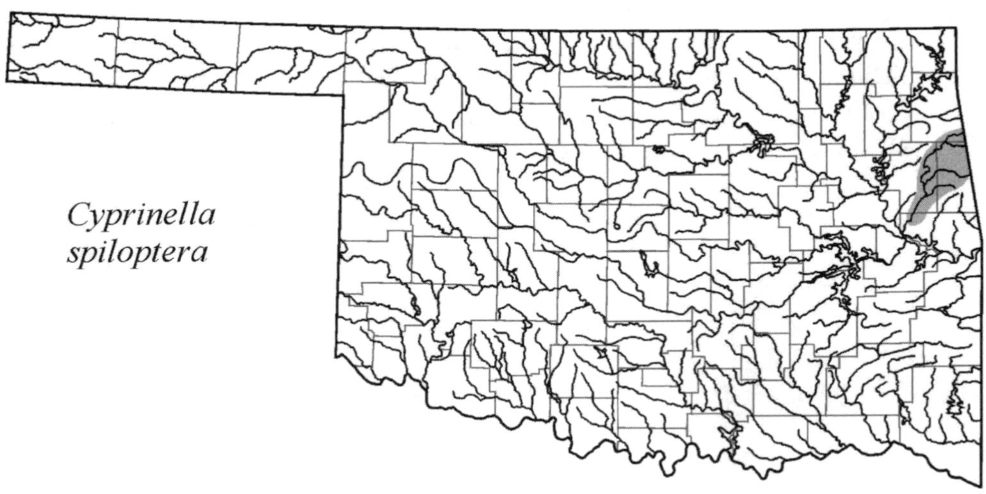

Distribution:

Northeastern and north-central United States from New York to the Dakotas in the north and Oklahoma to Alabama in the south. Apparently present in Oklahoma only in the Illinois River and some tributaries.

Habitat and Biology:

The spotfin shiner is generally found over clear gravel or sandy areas in the Illinois River, primarily in moderate currents. It is more tolerant of turbidity, siltation, and pollution than *C. whipplei*. The spotfin spawns in late spring and summer, and its breeding habits in Ohio apparently are similar to those of *whipplei* (Pflieger 1965). Males make sounds during courtship and defend territories that include one or more spawning crevices in a rocky substrate (Gale and Gale 1977). Eggs are deposited in rocky crevices longer than 0.8 inches or on logs having loose bark. Spotfins are fractional spawners, spawning up to 12 times at intervals of one to seven days.

Blacktail shiner

Cyprinella venusta Girard

Description:

A fairly deep-bodied, compressed *Cyprinella* with the large, diamond-shaped scales outlined in black, the small head and pointed snout, and the slightly subterminal mouth common to many species of the genus. There are 8 rays in the dorsal, anal, and pelvic fins and 37–41 scales in the slightly decurved lateral line. Posterior dorsal fin membranes are dusky. This species can be distinguished from the other *Cyprinella* species by the prominent black basicaudal spot, which is larger than in any other Oklahoma minnow. A dark band extends forward from the caudal spot to under the anterior part of the dorsal fin. Breeding males develop numerous tubercles on the head, and median fins become yellow with a milky deposition also present. Usually 4 inches or less in length. (See also color plate.)

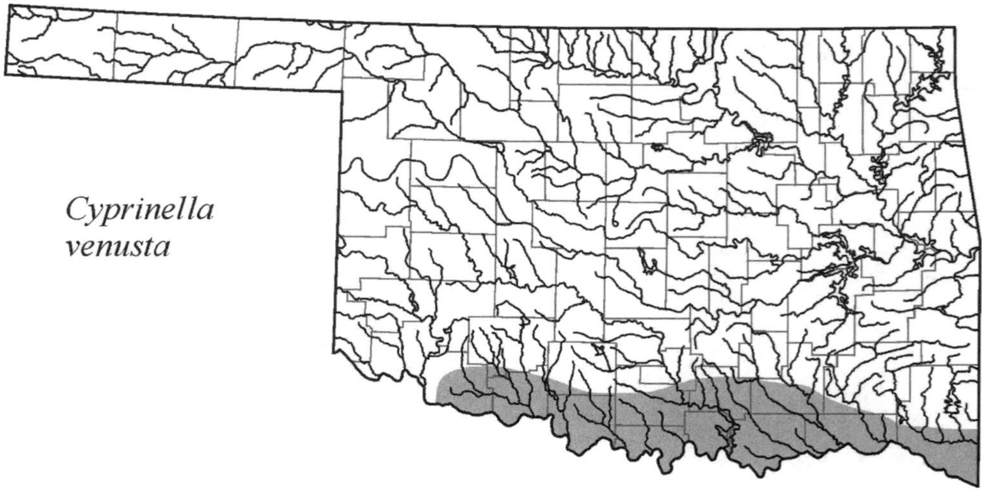

Distribution:

Southern United States from Texas and Oklahoma north to Missouri and Illinois and east to Georgia and Florida. Found throughout most of the Red River basin in Oklahoma.

Habitat and Biology:

The blacktail shiner generally prefers clear water. In eastern Oklahoma, we have found it most commonly in small to medium-sized streams with gravel bottoms and good flow, but Riggs and Bonn (1959) found it common in sandy or rocky areas of Lake Texoma, generally in the clearer part of the lake. Nevertheless, this species appears to be quite tolerant of turbidity and varied bottom types. Its diet consists primarily of terrestrial insects and plant materials. In Missouri, this species spawns from June to August with eggs deposited in crevices of submerged objects (Pflieger 1997). It readily hybridizes with *C. lutrensis* wherever the two species occur together.

Steelcolor Shiner

Cyprinella whipplei Girard

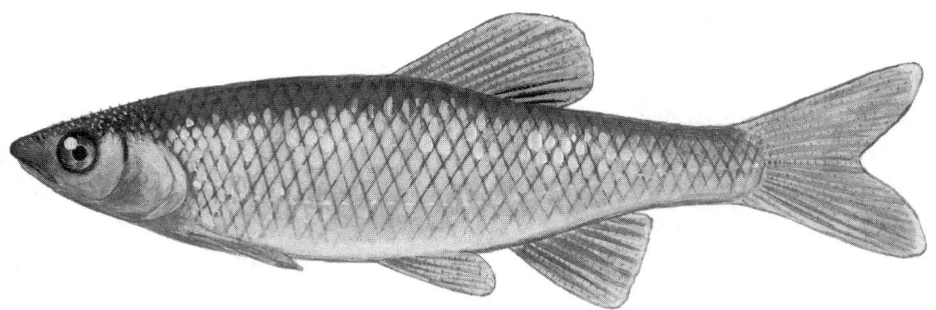

Description:

A fairly typical representative of the genus *Cyprinella*, this shiner exhibits the characteristic large diamond-shaped and pigment-outlined scales, pointed snout with a subterminal mouth, and conspicuous dark slashes in the last two interradial membranes of the dorsal fin. Lateral line scales number 37–39 and pharyngeal teeth are 1, 4-4, 1. A rather compressed and deep-bodied fish (body depth 3.7–4.3 into SL), it most closely resembles *C. spiloptera* but differs in having 9 anal rays, not 8. It differs from *C. lutrensis* in having black dorsal fin slashes, from *C. venusta* in lacking a discrete basicaudal spot and in anal ray count, and from *C. camura* in lacking the clear white band at the caudal base. Breeding males develop fine tubercles on the head and snout and extremely tiny ones on the nape. The fins become yellow and the snout turns reddish. The dorsal fin enlarges and its distal edge becomes convex. Generally less that 4.5 inches long. (See also color plate.)

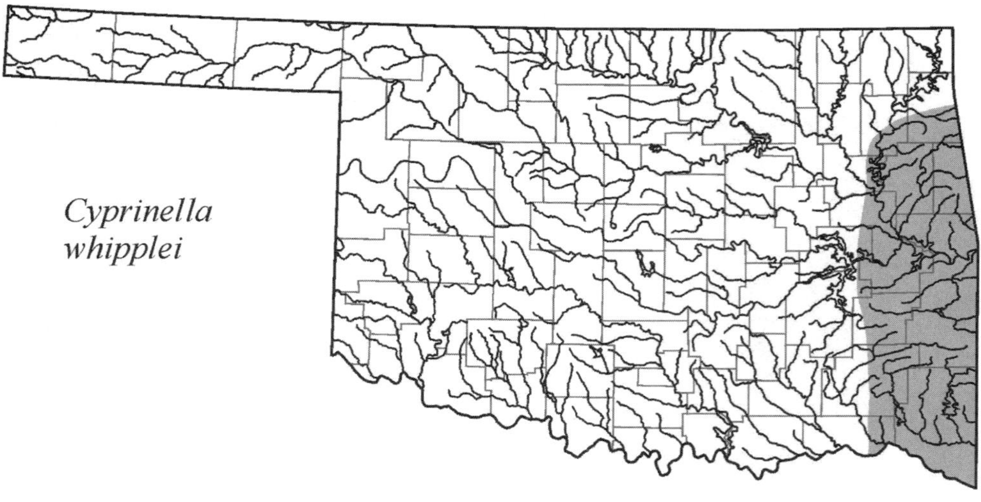

Distribution:

From Ohio through the lower Mississippi basin to Louisiana. Occurs in about the southeastern fifth of the state with occasional more westerly records probably the result of bait-bucket introductions.

Habitat and Biology:

The steelcolor shiner is most common in large to medium-sized streams with clear water and gravel bottom. Spawning occurs during late spring and summer, when the eggs are deposited under loose bark or in crevices of logs or tree roots (Pflieger 1965). The food of this species consists mainly of insects, primarily terrestrial. It hybridizes with *C. camura* in Greenleaf Creek, the only place the two species are known to occur together.

Carp

Cyprinus carpio Linnaeus

Description:

A deep-bodied, compressed fish with a strongly arched back and very long dorsal fin (18–21 rays). The first ray of both the dorsal and anal fins is large, hard, and serrated; anal fin ray count is 6. The head and eye are relatively small. The mouth is thin and nearly terminal with thin lips and two pairs of barbels, the posterior pair typically the larger. Scales are moderate in size with about 32–37 in the lateral line. Occasionally partly scaled (mirror) or scaleless (leather) carp are encountered, but these are rare in Oklahoma. Color is dark olive to slate above grading quickly to bronze or golden sides and yellowish

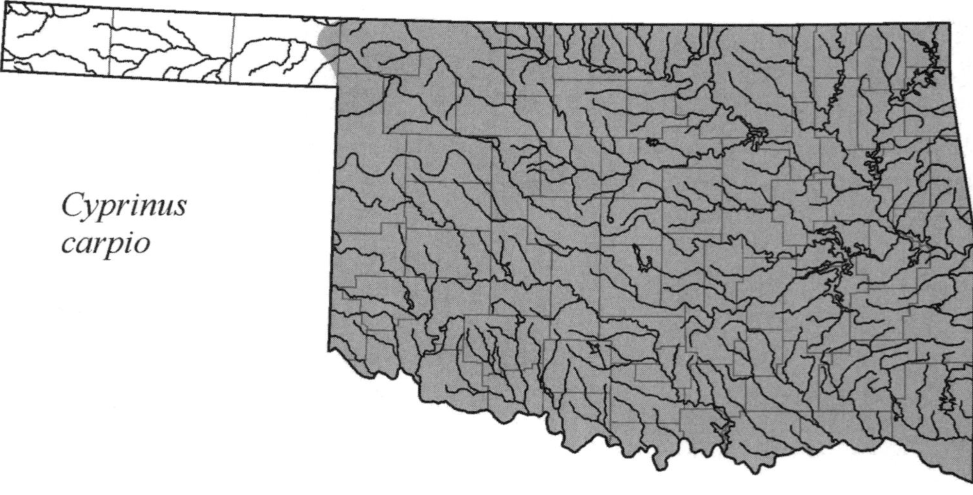

white below. Fins are golden, orange, or light olive. Usually up to 30 inches and 20 pounds. State record: 35 lb., 37½ in., from Spavinaw Lake.

Distribution:

The carp is a Eurasian fish that was first brought to this country in 1877. Since that time it has been introduced or has spread to virtually the entire country. It probably occurs throughout Oklahoma, though dense populations are fairly localized.

Habitat and Biology:

The carp is probably the most adaptable fish found in the state. Although it seems to prefer quiet, shallow waters of rivers and impoundments, it can survive almost anywhere it can find organic detritus, plants, insect larvae, crustaceans, or other kinds of organisms it can engulf for food. In shallow weedy areas in spring, the splashing of great carp bodies during spawning can create a conspicuous commotion. Although used little except as bait in Oklahoma, fish from clean, unpolluted waters are satisfactory table fare and can be tasty if care is taken in their preparation. Carp often provide sport for bow hunters in the spring, when they move into shallows to spawn, and for skin-divers in some of our clearer lakes. On light tackle, the carp is a tough, unyielding fighter.

OZARK MINNOW

Dionda nubila (Forbes)

Description:

A slim, terete minnow with relatively small head (about 4 into SL), large eye (3.2 into head length), and snout about as long as the postorbital head. The eye is large (3.2 into head length). The mouth is subterminal, small, and only slightly oblique, and both lips are pigmented. Dorsal, anal, and pelvic fins are low, and all have 8 rays. The pharyngeal tooth count is 4-4. Lateral line is complete with 33–37 scales. The most distinctive characteristics of this species are the long coiled intestine and black peritoneum, which are found in no other fish with the general appearance of the Ozark minnow. Pigmentation features are also fairly distinctive: the lateral line is margined above and below for its entire length with dark spots or dashes; a dark lateral band may be more or less prominent from snout to caudal peduncle, sometimes obscuring the lateral-line etchings; and the dorsolateral scales are outlined in

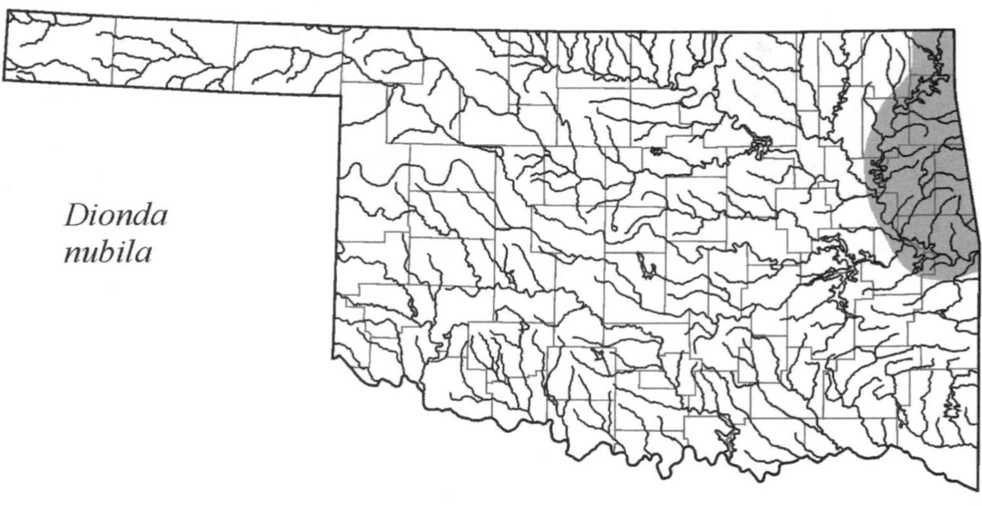

and sometimes sprinkled with black pigment. A black caudal chevron is usually present. Breeding males tuberculate and develop pink to reddish or orange colors on the head and underside, and the fins become yellowish. Up to 3 inches long. (See also color plate.)

Distribution:

From Minnesota and Wisconsin south to Oklahoma and Arkansas. Found in the Ozark region of northeastern Oklahoma and possibly present elsewhere as a result of bait-bucket introductions.

Habitat and Biology:

The Ozark minnow is limited to the clear, high-gradient streams of the Ozark region. It seems most common in pools of small to medium-sized streams with gravel or rubble bottom. Spawning occurs in spring with the date probably determined in part by water temperatures. This species is known to hybridize with *Luxilus cardinalis*.

Note:

Although Swift (1970) allied *Dionda nubila* with members of *Notropis* under the subgenus *Hydrophlox*, observations by Fowler and colleagues (1984) on the similarity between the Ozark minnow and *Dionda episcopa* in spawning activity, egg characteristics, and gut morphology suggest that these species are more closely related to each other than either is to *Notropis*. Also, the pharyngeal teeth are definitely not *Notropis*-like. We therefore use the name *Dionda nubila* in preference to *Notropis nubilus* for the Ozark minnow.

Gravel chub

Erimystax x-punctatus (Hubbs and Crowe)

Description:

A slim, terete, beautifully streamlined, barbeled minnow with a moderately large head (nearly 4 into SL) and large eye (about 3.5 into head length). The snout is long, has numerous taste buds, and protrudes considerably beyond the inferior mouth. Scales are of medium size, 39–42 in the lateral line. The dorsal and anal fins are slightly falcate, with 8 and 7 rays respectively. The gut is short and the peritoneum pigmented. Color is light olivaceous above, with silvery sides and a white underside. Dark X- or W-shaped markings are scattered along the upper half of the body, but there is little or no pigment on the fins. Up to 3.5 inches.

Distribution:

The Ohio River basin east to Pennsylvania and the Mississippi basin from Minnesota south to Oklahoma and Arkansas. Found in Oklahoma only in the Ozark region.

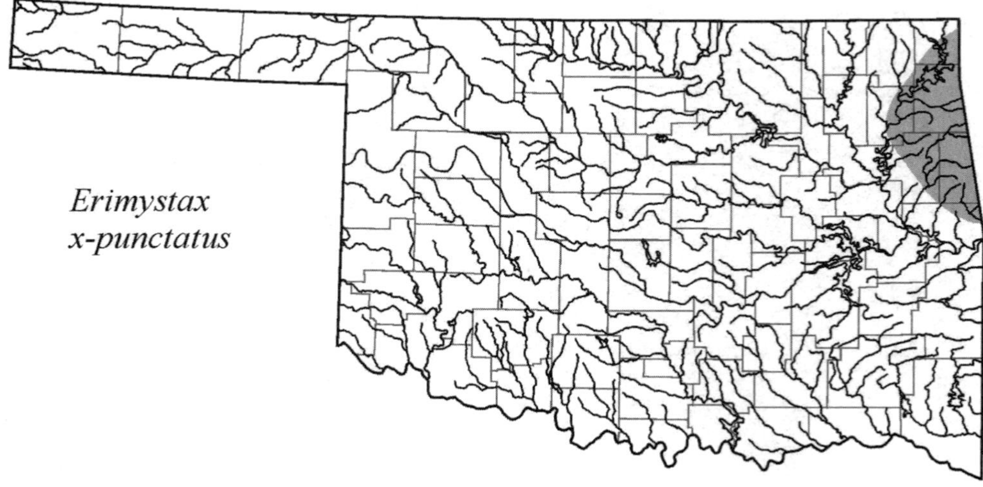

Habitat and Biology:

This species is highly specialized as a deep riffle and raceway inhabitant. It lives in clear water streams and rivers with medium to large size gravel. Judging from its sensory equipment, Davis and Miller (1967) suggested that it uses its long, sensitive snout to probe the interstices of the gravel for food. The curved dorsal surface and pectoral fin would serve to keep the fish on or near the bottom of fast water whenever it leaves sheltered areas. Food consists of periphyton (diatoms, detritus, and bacteria), aquatic insect larvae, small gastropods, and plant material (Harris 1986). Spawning occurs from March to early May at the head of riffles over a clean substrate of small to medium-sized gravel.

Cypress Minnow

Hybognathus hayi Jordan

Description:

The smallest of the three species of *Hybognathus* in our state, with a maximum size of 3.5 inches. This species looks much like a smaller version of the silvery minnow, with a fairly slab-sided body and oblique terminal mouth. However, the tip of the upper lip is above the middle of the eye, whereas it is below the eye in the silvery minnow. The snout is broadly rounded, scarcely visible from below. Eye diameter is fairly large and roughly equal to snout length (about 3.4 to 3.8 into head length). The head is short (4–4.5 times into SL). Body color is tan to olive above, with silvery sides and a white belly. This species and the silvery minnow resemble members of the genus *Notropis* in external appearance, but the flat, grinding pharyngeal teeth and elongate gut separate them from most species of *Notropis*, which have hooked teeth and a short gut. Scales are moderate in size, 35–41 in the lateral line, and there are 8 rays in the dorsal, anal, and pelvic fins. The cypress minnow can be distinguished from the other species of *Hybognathus* by the more densely pig-

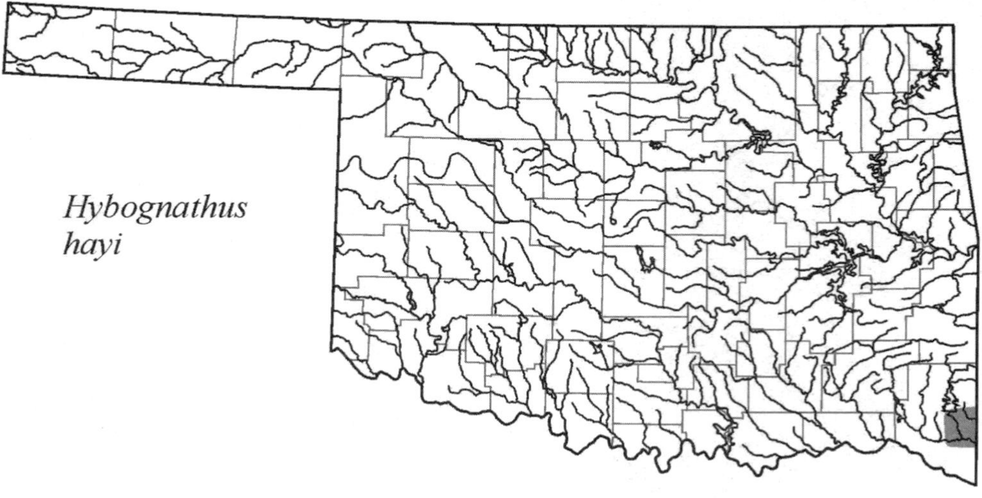

mented outlines of the scales on the dorsum, the absence of a lateral stripe anteriorly, and the oblique mouth and broadly rounded snout.

Distribution:

The cypress minnow is a lowland form extending from Florida west to Arkansas and the southeastern tip of Oklahoma and north in the Mississippi basin to Missouri, Illinois, and Indiana. Miller and an ichthyology class collected a small series of this species in the lower Mountain Fork River in 1972. One can expect to encounter the species occasionally in the Mountain Fork and other streams in McCurtain County.

Habitat and Biology:

Fingerman and Suttkus (1961) reported that the cypress minnow tended to occur in the quiet, soft-bottomed backwaters of rivers while the silvery minnow seemed to prefer the main stream with slow to moderate current and harder bottom. Robison and Buchanan (1988) found them in cypress-lined oxbows over mud and detritus in Arkansas. While almost nothing is known of their behavior and feeding habits, one can infer from the long gut and grinding pharyngeal teeth that they are largely plant eaters, perhaps scraping algae and diatoms from the roots of cypress and other submerged vegetation.

SILVERY MINNOW
Hybognathus nuchalis Agassiz

Description:

The silvery minnow is a large, streamlined minnow of up to 5.5 inches, with a small head, small subterminal mouth, and generally silvery coloration. It shares with *H. placitus* (but not with other silvery colored minnows in the genus *Notropis*) a small knob just inside the tip of the lower jaw. There are no barbels, and eye diameter is relatively larger than in *H. placitus* (about 3.5–4 into head length). Pharyngeal teeth are 4-4. The fins are moderate in size and unpigmented. Body color is tan to brown above with silvery sides and a white belly. Scales are moderate in size, usually 34–40 in the lateral line, and there are 8 rays in the dorsal, anal, and pelvic fins. The gut is long and coiled, and peritoneum is black. Basioccipital process is wider than it is long and distinctly concave posteriorly.

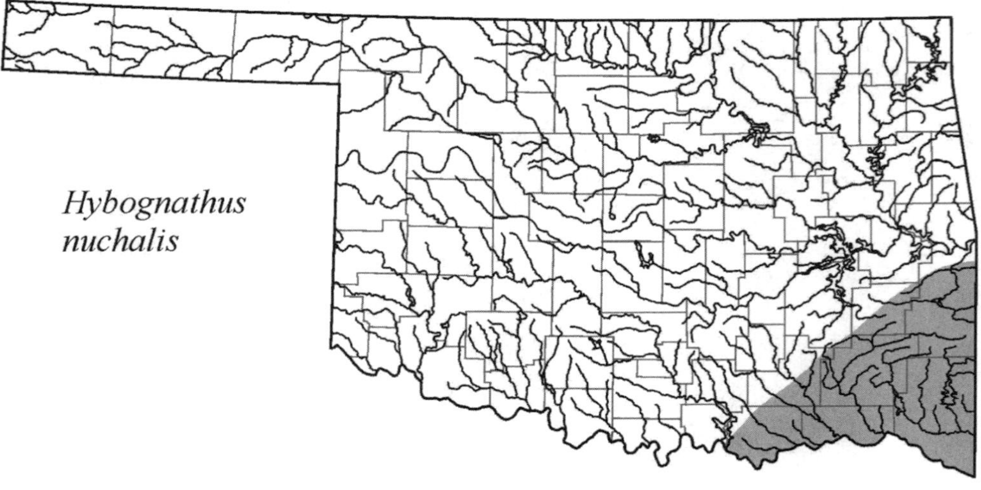

Distribution:

Occurs in the central Mississippi Valley from Minnesota and Ohio south to Texas and Alabama. An eastern subspecies inhabits most of the East Coast north to the St. Lawrence River. In Oklahoma this minnow is found in the Red River and its tributaries west to Lake Texoma.

Habitat and Biology:

The silvery minnow definitely prefers quiet water in pools and backwaters of the large streams and rivers of the Red River basin. It seems to feed mainly on diatoms, algae, and other plant materials that form a surface layer over the soft bottoms with which it is associated. Spawning occurs in the spring and summer, probably over soft bottoms, but spawning habits have not yet been observed. The eastern subspecies is known not to exhibit parental care. It may be used as a bait fish but is not very hardy.

Plains minnow

Hybognathus placitus Girard

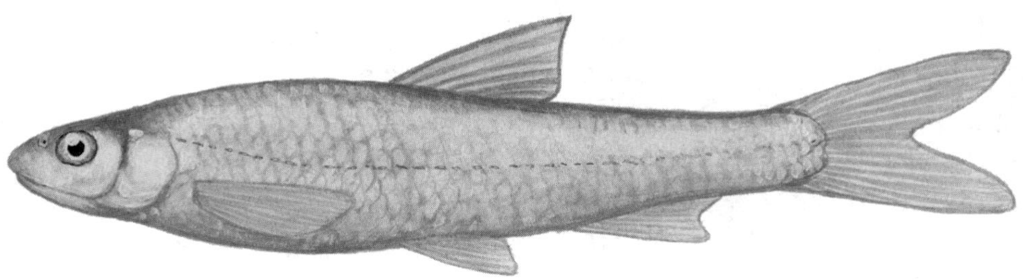

Description:

Resembles the silvery minnow in most respects: a large, silvery, terete minnow with a small head, small subterminal mouth, and small knob on the inside tip of the lower jaw. It differs in having a much smaller eye and wider head, and *H. placitus* tends to have 15 or more scale rows below the lateral line compared to fewer than 15 in *H. nuchalis*. Pharyngeal teeth 4-4. Lateral-line scales 36–39. The intestine is long and coiled. Color is tan to brown or olive above with silvery sides and a white belly; fins are colorless. Ostrand and colleagues (2001) have described sexual dimorphism in this species, the most prominent difference being the longer dorsal fin of males. *Hybognathus placitus* is generally less than 5 inches long. (See also color plate.)

Distribution:

The plains states from Montana and North Dakota south to Texas. Found throughout Oklahoma but rarely in uplands of the Ozarks or Ouachitas.

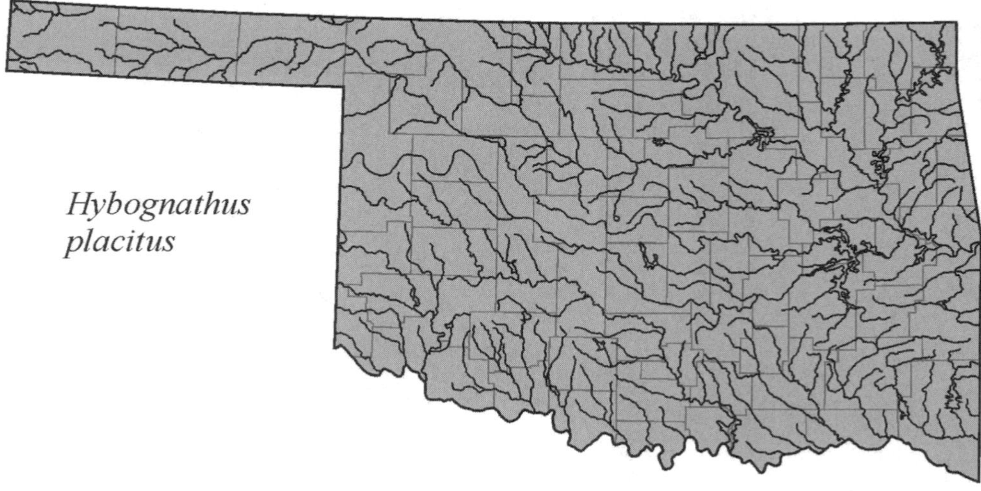

Recent declines of this species in the large rivers of Oklahoma are the cause of some concern (W. J. Matthews, pers. comm., 2003).

Habitat and Biology:

The plains minnow is one of Oklahoma's ubiquitous species. It seems most abundant in the turbid silt- or sand-bottomed streams of the western part of the state. Like the silvery minnow, it tends to prefer backwaters and quieter parts of streams, where it probably feeds on bottom microflora (algae, diatoms, etc.). Spawning occurs in spring and summer. The eggs of *H. placitus* have been collected in the Cimarron River from April to August, with a major peak in May and June and a secondary peak in midsummer (Taylor and Miller 1990). Spawning coincides with high or receding flows. Eggs are slightly demersal and nonadhesive, and gently bounce along the bottom during most of their development. Spawning may be similar to that found in *Hybognathus regius* (Girard), except that it must occur in moving water rather than in coves or backwaters as described by Raney (1939) for the latter species. Variation was studied by Al-Rawi and Cross (1964) but no subspecies were recognized.

BIGEYE CHUB

Hybopsis amblops (Rafinesque)

Description:

A small silvery minnow usually less than 3 inches long, with a large eye and conspicuous dark stripe down the length of the body. The mouth is small and inferior with a tiny barbel at the posterior tip of the jaw. The 8-rayed dorsal and anal fins are high and moderately falcate. Scales are moderately large, 36–38 in the lateral line. Pharyngeal teeth 1, 4-4, 1. The peritoneum is silvery. Color is olivaceous to tan above, silvery below, with the black lateral band varying in intensity. Fins are colorless. Maximum size 4 inches.

Distribution:

From Lake Ontario through the Ohio Valley west to Kansas and Oklahoma and south through Tennessee to Alabama and Louisiana. In Oklahoma it is found mainly in the clear streams of the eastern edge of the state, with a few scattered occurrences elsewhere.

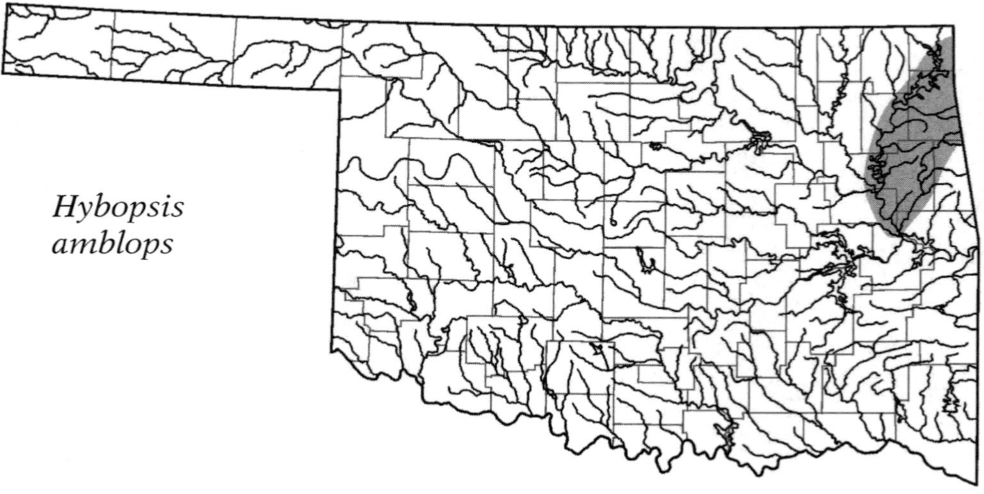

Habitat and Biology:

Little is known of the biology of the bigeye chub in Oklahoma. It prefers the clear medium to large streams with moderate gradients found in the Ozark region. It is often associated with aquatic vegetation. Numerous authors have suggested that the species cannot survive where siltation is heavy, and Davis and Miller (1967) suggest that it also cannot survive in high-gradient areas cleanly scoured by water action. *H. amblops* is a visual feeder eating midge larvae, mayfly and stonefly nymphs, and caddisfly larvae over clean sandy and gravel bottoms. It is a spring spawner, but its breeding habits have not yet been described.

Note:

We follow Jenkins and Burkhead (1994; see their cogent discussion, p. 345) in retaining the monophyletic *amblops* group in the genus *Hybopsis*, hence our use of *Hybopsis amblops* and *H. amnis* for the Oklahoma members of this group.

PALLID SHINER

Hybopsis amnis (Hubbs and Greene)

Description:

We include the pallid shiner in the *amblops* group of *Hybopsis* and thus recognize *Hybopsis amnis* as the correct scientific name (see note in *H. amblops* account). A relatively slim, slightly compressed shiner with a moderate-sized head (3.7 into SL). The eye is fairly large (3.2 into head length). The snout is long (2.8 into head length) and rounded and projects considerably over the inferior mouth. When closed, the mouth appears to be quite small. When the mouth is opened, however, nearly a third of the upper jaw is hidden by the suborbital bone, which can be seen to extend beyond the angle of the mouth (see fig. 19 in key). This character is unique, serving to identify the species conclusively. Fins are moderately high with 8 rays in the dorsal, anal, and pelvic fins. Body scales are fairly large with about 36–37 in the lateral line. Scales above the sometimes prominent dark lateral band are outlined with melanophores, while the underside is relatively clear but for a sprinkling of tiny melanophores above the anal and pelvic fins and on the underside of the caudal peduncle. Generally under 2.5 inches long.

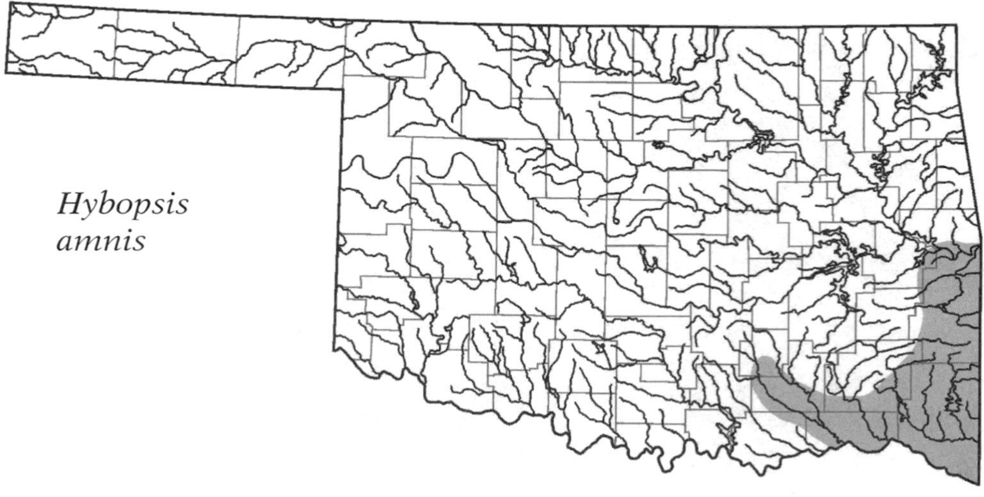

Distribution:

The Mississippi River drainage from Wisconsin and Indiana south to the Gulf Coast. Occurs in Oklahoma in the Poteau River, Lee Creek, and the Red River system west to Clear Boggy River.

Habitat and Biology:

The pallid shiner seems to prefer large to medium-sized clear streams and rivers, where it is generally found over sand and mud substrates and away from swift currents. Breeding occurs in late winter and early spring in the southern portion of its range; ripe adults have been collected in Arkansas in March. Pflieger (1997) reported that this shiner is intolerant of excessive siltation associated with changing land practices. Little else seems to be known of its biology.

CARDINAL SHINER

Luxilus cardinalis (Mayden)

Description:

A large (up to 4 inches), moderately deep-bodied, slightly compressed shiner with large fins and distinctive coloration. The head is moderate in size (about 4 into SL). The terminal mouth is large and oblique, and the eye is also large (about 3.5 into head length).Dorsal and pelvic fins have 8 rays, while the anal fin usually has 9. The lateral line is slightly decurved anteriorly with 39–43 scales. Pharyngeal teeth 2, 4-4, 2. Color is olivaceous above and silvery or whitish below with a broad and conspicuous dark middorsal stripe and a dusky lateral stripe extending the length of the body. A narrow dark line is usually visible just above the lateral band and separated from it by a lighter line. Breeding males develop brilliant deep red on the underside of the head and body and on all the fins. At the same time the lateral band becomes intensely black and broader than usual. Prominent breeding tubercles also appear on the head.

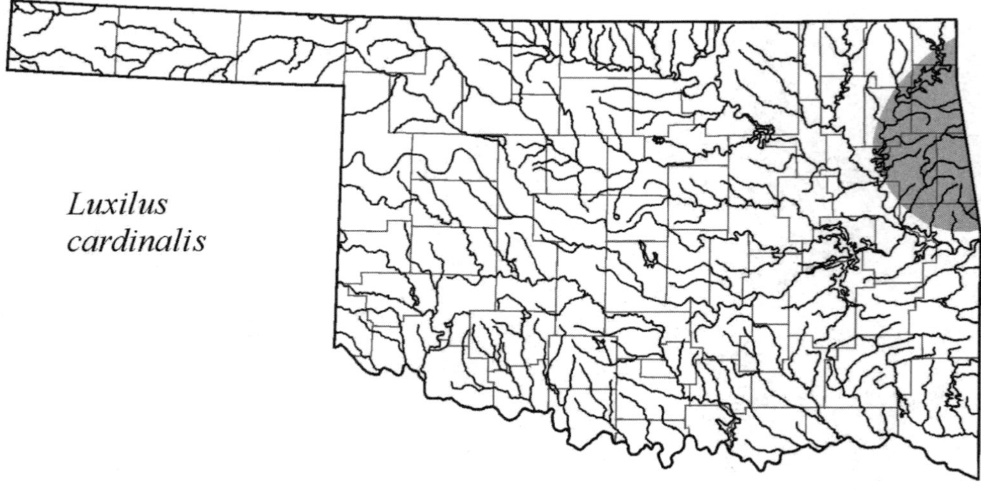

Distribution:

Middle and lower Arkansas River drainage of Kansas, Missouri, Arkansas, and Oklahoma. Common in the Ozarks in northeastern Oklahoma and historically known from a few areas farther up the Arkansas River and in the Red River basin, probably as a result of bait introductions.

Habitat and Biology:

The cardinal shiner is an inhabitant of the clear, gravel-bottomed streams of the Ozark region. Large specimens are most common in deep, flowing pools, where they feed on a variety of invertebrates carried by the water. Spawning occurs in shallow riffles and over the nests of other cyprinids in spring, usually in May, though the precise timing probably depends on water temperatures (Miller 1967).

STRIPED SHINER
Luxilus chrysocephalus Rafinesque

Description:

The striped shiner is a heavy-bodied, compressed fish with a moderate-sized head (3.6–4 into SL). It has a large terminal and oblique mouth and large eye (3.2–4 into head length). Fins are moderately high, with 8 rays in the dorsal and pelvic fins and 8–10 (usually 9) rays in the anal fin. Body scales are large and deep, with 37–41 scales in the decurved lateral line. The most prominent external features of the two forms of *L. chrysocephalus* in Oklahoma are a broad dark lateral band and three dark horizontal lines running from behind the upper head to the prominent middorsal stripe. The lines are rather uneven in *L. c. chrysocephalus* but smooth in *L. c. isolepis*. Breeding males develop reddish pigment on head, body, and fins and tubercles on the snout, head, and pectoral fins. Up to 7 inches in length.

Distribution:

From New Brunswick to Saskatchewan in the north through the Great Lakes and Mississippi basin to Oklahoma, Louisiana, and Alabama. In Oklahoma *L. c. chrysocephalus* occurs in the Ozark region, while *L. c. isolepis* occurs in the Red River basin west at least to the Blue River, where a population may be distinct enough to warrant designation as a separate species (W. J. Matthews, pers. comm., 2003).

Habitat and Biology:

Both forms occur mainly in small to moderate-sized streams with clear water and gravel bottom. They are infrequently found in riffles, except at spawning time, and generally are most common in raceways or nonstagnant pools. Spawning occurs over clear gravel in late spring or early summer at water temperatures above 60 degrees F. Food consists mainly of terrestrial insects, filamentous and unicellular algae, and other aquatic invertebrates, especially mayfly nymphs.

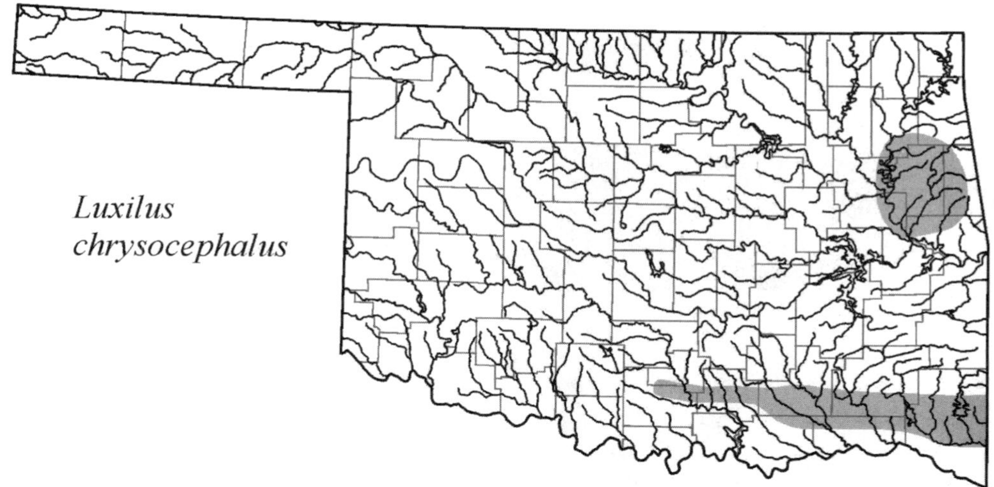

Note:

Gilbert (1964) elevated to species status the "central common shiner," an Ozark-inhabiting form that we formerly considered *Notropis cornutus chrysocephalus,* and he reassigned the Red River tributary form that we formerly considered *N. c. isolepis* as a subspecies of the striped shiner, *Notropis chrysocephalus* (Rafinesque). Most authors have now elevated the subgenus *Luxilus* to the genus level. Although we still have some reservations about this arrangement, we have decided to follow the majority of ichthyologists in referring to the two forms in Oklahoma as subspecies: *Luxilis chrysocephalus chrysocephalus* inhabiting the Ozark area and *L. c. isolepis* in the Red River drainage. See Etnier and Starnes (1993) for discussion of this knotty taxonomic problem.

Ribbon shiner

Lythrurus fumeus (Evermann)

Description:

Maximum size of this shiner is about 2.5 inches. The mouth is large and oblique, the pointed snout shorter than the eye, and the head small (about 4 into SL). Pharyngeal teeth are 2, 4-4, 2. The sharply decurved lateral line has 39–41 scales. A well-developed dark lateral band is the most conspicuous pigmentary characteristic, the band growing narrower but more intense posteriorly. The ribbon shiner is most similar to *Lythrurus snelsoni* but differs in having 11–12 anal rays rather than 10; green tuberculation and yellowish rather than red breeding colors; and a stouter body than that of the more elongate *snelsoni*. It can be distinguished from *L. umbratilis* by absence of a prominent spot at the origin of the dorsal fin and of the dark dorsolateral chevrons characterizing that species; also separating the two are the ribbon shiner's higher anal ray count, more posteriorly located dorsal fin, and relatively clear band of nonoutlined scales above the lateral band. It differs from *Notropis percobromus, N. suttkusi,* and *N. atherinoides* in having smaller

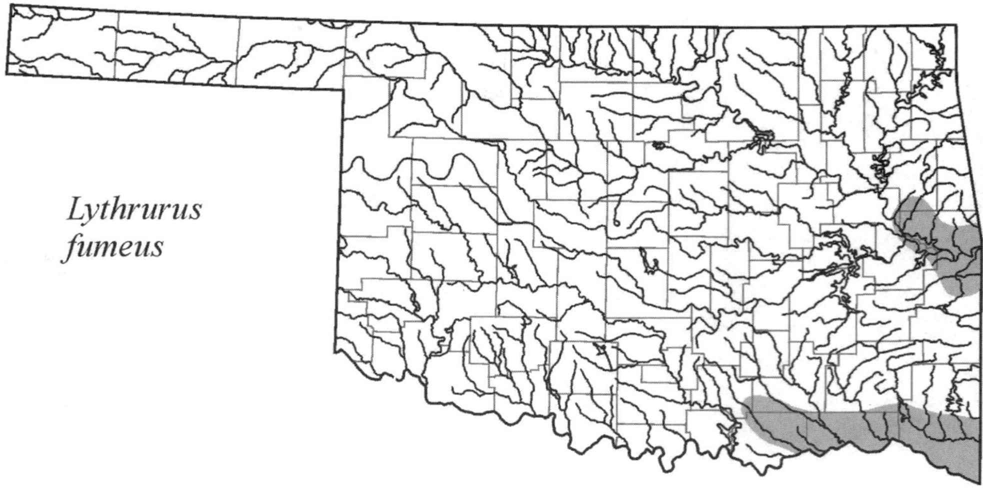

scales in front of the dorsal fin (more than 25), a lower and more diffuse lateral band, and a decurved lateral line. (See also color plate.)

Distribution:

From the Tennessee River basin west to Oklahoma and Texas. Found in tributaries of the Red River in southeastern Oklahoma and in the Illinois and Poteau rivers.

Habitat and Biology:

The ribbon shiner appears to be most common in clear low-gradient streams of the Red River basin. It favors tannin-stained waters and substrates of sand, firm mud, clay silt, or detritus, with quiet pools and backwater areas its preferred microhabitat. This schooling midwater shiner feeds from the surface. Males in yellowish breeding color have been collected in May in Arkansas and females with eggs have been taken in mid-July in Missouri.

Ouachita Mountain Shiner
Lythrurus snelsoni (Robison)

Description:

A diminutive, slender, terete silvery shiner with a bluntly rounded snout, large eye, and terminal, slightly oblique mouth. Anal rays usually 10. Front of the dorsal fin base is closer to caudal fin base than to tip of snout. Lateral line is decurved slightly with 38–45 scales. Pharyngeal teeth are 2, 4-4, 2. Breeding males have red coloration on the dorsal part of the head to the occiput area and on the chin and anterior third of the gular area. The Ouachita Mountain shiner can be distinguished from *Lythrurus fumeus* by its 10 anal rays rather than 11 or 12, red breeding color rather than yellow, and slimmer, more elongate body. *Lythrurus snelsoni* differs from *L. umbratilis* in having a slender body, no prominent spot at the dorsal origin, and no dorsolateral chevrons. It typically (modally) has 10 anal rays vs. modally 11 in *L. umbratilis*. Head tubercles are small in *snelsoni* and large and erect in *umbratilis*. Maximum size is about 2.5 inches. (See also color plate.)

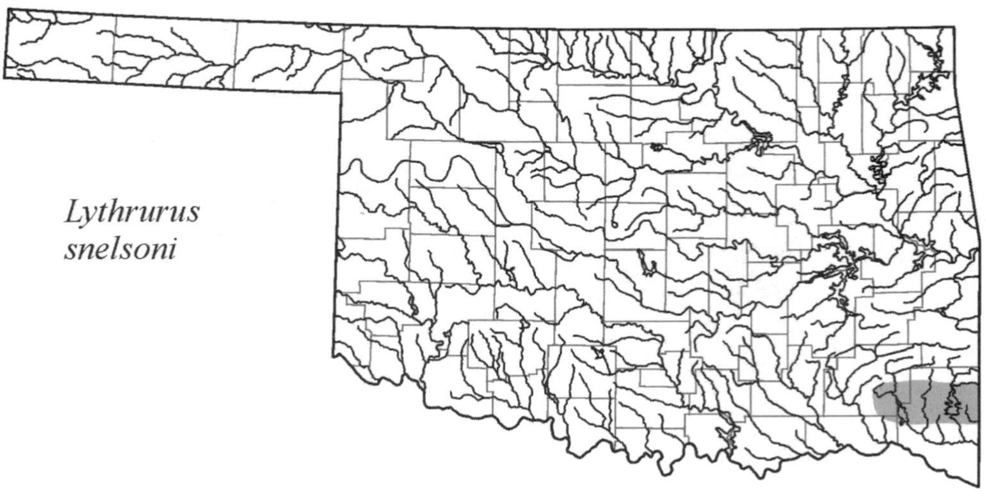

Distribution:

Ouachita Mountain portion of the Little River system of southeastern Oklahoma and southwestern Arkansas. This shiner is found in the upper portions of the Little River tributaries draining the Ouachita Mountains.

Habitat and Biology:

The Ouachita Mountain shiner inhabits pool regions of clear, medium to large high-gradient streams and rivers, where it schools at stream margins lined with water willow. Taylor and Lienesch (1995) found this shiner strongly associated with high elevation streams with boulder substrates. In Oklahoma, this shiner has been collected in the upper part of Broken Bow Reservoir on the Mountain Fork River (W. J. Matthews, pers. comm.). Diet includes simuliids, chironomids, and mayfly larvae. Reproduction occurs from late May to mid-July. Robison and Buchanan (1988) provide a description of the spawning behavior of *L. snelsoni* as witnessed by G. A. Moore and F. B. Cross on May 30, 1948, below the dam on Mountain Fork River. Because of its restricted distribution, this shiner is vulnerable to large-scale watershed disturbances such as clear-cutting and reservoir construction.

REDFIN SHINER
Lythrurus umbratilis (Girard)

Description:

Two forms occur in Oklahoma, *Lythrurus umbratilis cyanocephalus* in the Red River basin and *L. u. umbratilis* in the Arkansas basin. Although the two forms may eventually be elevated to species level, we consider both to be representatives of a single species, and the characters described apply to both forms. The redfin shiner is a deep-bodied, compressed fish with a small head (4.2 into SL). It has a rounded snout, terminal and oblique mouth, and fairly large eye (3.2–3.8 into head length). The species can be identified using the following complex of characteristics: anterior dorsolateral scales are small and crowded (more than 25 predorsal rows); the markedly decurved lateral line has 38–43 scales; at the dorsal fin origin is a conspicuous black spot; and adults have dark, chevronlike markings on the anterior dorsolateral part of the body. There are 9–11 anal rays and 8 dorsal and pelvic rays. Breeding

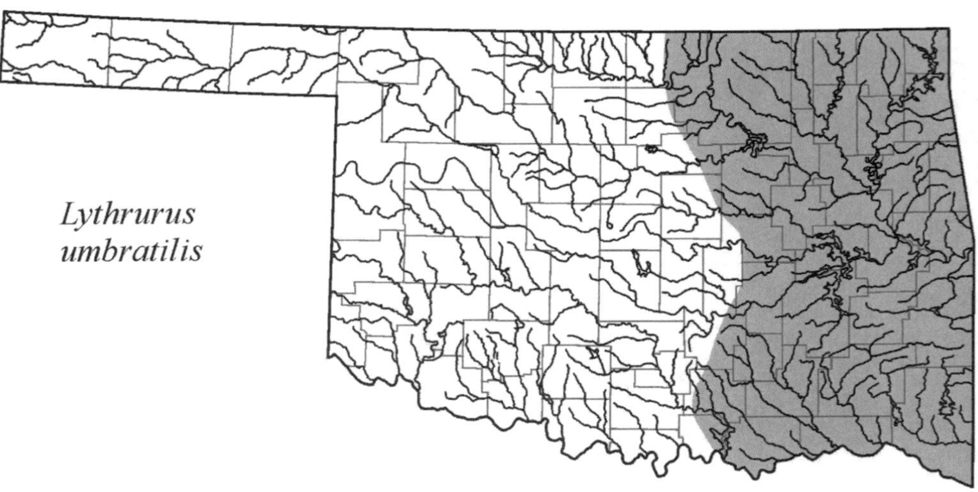

males develop an iridescent blue color and at least some red pigment in the dorsal, anal, and caudal fins, though black pigment predominates in the median fins of both forms. Up to 3 inches long. (See also color plate.)

Distribution:

From Minnesota and Pennsylvania south to Texas and Mississippi. Occurs in about the eastern third of Oklahoma.

Habitat and Biology:

The redfin shiner occurs in a wide variety of stream types in Oklahoma, and while it is abundant in some of the more sluggish plains streams, it is rarely encountered in streams lacking some gravel riffles. It tends to avoid swift currents and is often found in deep sluggish pools. A surface feeder, the redfin shiner primarily takes aquatic and terrestrial insects, but it occasionally consumes bits of filamentous algae and other plant material. Spawning occurs in late spring and summer over the nests of longear, orangespotted, and green sunfish. This species matures at one year and has a maximum age of two years.

PRAIRIE CHUB

Macrhybopsis australis (Hubbs and Ortenburger)

Description:

The small, barbeled chubs previously known as *Hybopsis aestivalis* have undergone changes in classification in recent years (see Note). The prairie chub is a streamlined, terete fish adapted for life on the bottom of flowing waters. Its body is fairly deep at the dorsal origin, tapering rapidly to a conical head and moderately slender caudal peduncle. Dorsal and anal fins are slightly falcate, usually with 7 anal rays. Pelvic fins are pointed; pectoral fins in males are long and falcate, reaching past pelvic bases. The mouth is inferior and horizontal with a bulbous snout overhanging it, and lips are greatly thickened posteriorly. This chub has two pairs of well-developed barbels, the anterior pair longer than orbit length and the posterior pair greater than 50 percent of orbit length. Pharyngeal teeth 4-4. Eyes are small and the head is conical with a relatively pointed snout. Lateral line scales 36–42, caudal

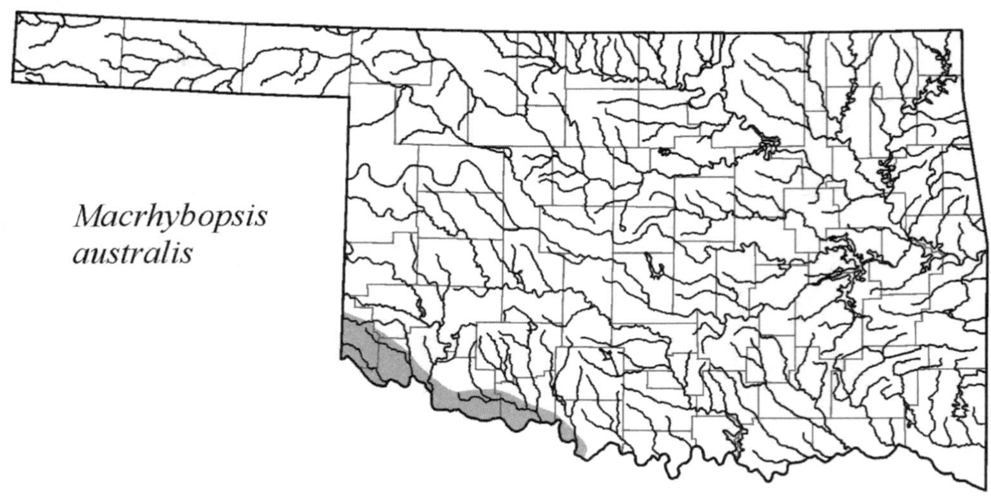

peduncle scales 12–16. Color is tan to creamy above, with a silvery lateral stripe, white belly, and randomly scattered small black spots on the upper half of the body. The belly anterior to pelvic fin base is usually naked. Nuptial males show biserial pectoral fin tuberculation, and the lateral stripe centered one scale row above lateral line may be absent or weakly expressed. *M. australis* and *M. hyostoma* both occur in the middle section of the Red River mainstem (Eisenhour, in press). *M. australis* can be distinguished by the combination of two pairs of well-developed barbels and 7 anal rays. (See also color plate.)

Distribution:

Endemic to the upper Red River basin from about Jefferson County, Oklahoma, to its upper reaches. Apparently extirpated from the Washita River, where it was known from only two specimens collected in 1926 in Roger Mills County, Oklahoma (Eisenhour, in press). Winston and colleagues (1981) considered it extirpated from the upper North Fork of the Red River as a result of reservoir construction.

Habitat and Biology:

The prairie chub is an inhabitant of the shallow main streams of the Red River basin. It is typically found over clean sand or gravel bottoms, rarely in areas with silt accumulation. Although little is known about the biology of this species, it is probably a flood-pulse spawner like its close relative *M. tetranema* (Bottrell et al. 1964).

Note:

Eisenhour (1997; 1999) has shown that the *Hybopsis aestivalis* complex now placed in the genus *Macrhybopsis*, which was formerly considered a subgenus, actually represents five species, of which three formerly occurred in Oklahoma: *M. australis* in the upper Red River; in the upper Arkansas River drainage *M. tetranema*, a species now extirpated from Oklahoma; and the more widespread *M. hyostoma* known from the Arkansas and Red River drainages. *M. australis* was originally treated as a subspecies of *Extrarius aestivalis* by Moore (1950), but its distribution was unclear because the number of barbels varied in populations in the lower and middle Red River (Davis and Miller 1967; Miller and Robison 1973; Douglas 1974; Robison and Buchanan 1988). Miller and Robison (1973) suggested that two species or subspecies might be present due to the polymorphic nature of the Red River populations. Eisenhour (1997) studied the entire *aestivalis* complex and elevated *M. australis* to species status (Eisenhour 1999).

SHOAL CHUB

Macrhybopsis hyostoma (Gilbert)

Description:

The shoal chub is a fusiform fish adapted for bottom life in swift water. It tapers anteriorly from the dorsal fin origin to a moderately rounded head and posteriorly to a moderately thick caudal peduncle. Dorsal and anal fins vary from bluntly pointed to slightly falcate, usually with 8 anal fin rays; pelvic fins vary from rounded to pointed. Pectoral fins are variable in shape and short, not reaching pelvic bases in adult males. The mouth is inferior and horizontal with moderately fleshy lips that are not thickened posteriorly. Pharyngeal teeth 4-4. This chub has one or two pairs of well-developed maxillary barbels, the posterior pair usually shorter than orbit length and anterior barbels absent or less than 50 percent of orbit length. The eye is relatively large and oval. Head and snout are moderately rounded and moderately flattened ventrally. Body color is pale green to gray dorsally with a broad silvery lateral stripe and a silvery white belly. Small black spots are randomly scattered on the upper half of the body. Lateral line scales usually 35–38, caudal

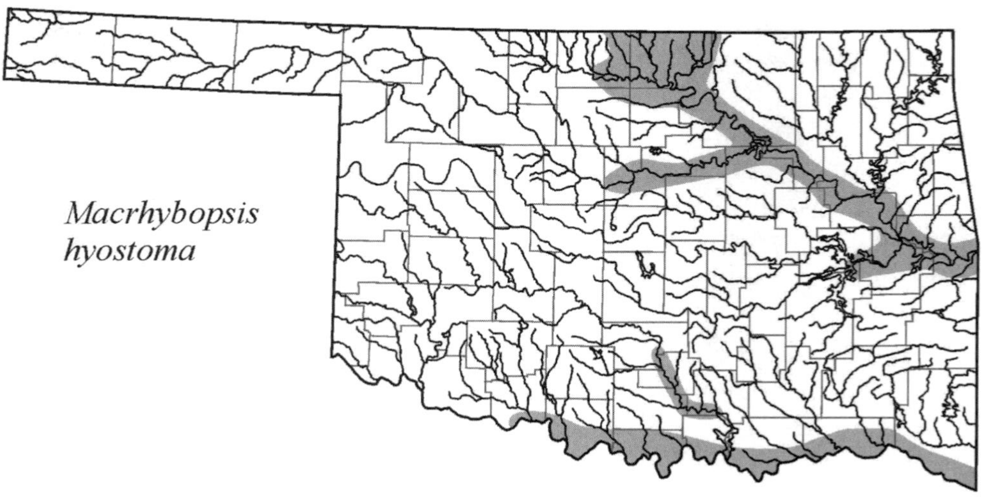

peduncle scales usually 12. Tubercles on nuptial males are usually arranged uniserially on the first primary branches of pectoral fin rays. Where *M. hyostoma* and *M. australis* both occur in the middle section of the Red River mainstem, *hyostoma* can be distinguished by usually having 8 anal rays (not 7); posterior barbels shorter than orbit length and anterior barbels less than half orbit length; a rounded rather than conical head; pectoral fins not reaching pelvic fin bases in adult males; and uniserial (not biserial) pectoral fin tuberculation in breeding males. See *M. australis* account for a brief summary of the taxonomic history of this and related species.

Distribution:

Lower part of the Red River basin downstream from Cotton County, Oklahoma, including the lower Washita River. Also known in the Arkansas River mainstem and the lower portion of its major tributaries, including the Canadian, Salt Fork, and Cimarron. Alteration of flow patterns has eliminated this chub from some of its former range. Luttrell and colleagues (1999) estimate that the species has been extirpated from approximately 55 percent of its historic range.

Habitat and Biology:

The shoal chub is a large-river form that inhabits shallow main streams. It seems to prefer coarse, clean sand or gravel raceways with strong current (Eisenhour, in press). Davis and Miller (1967) observed feeding behavior in captivity that strongly suggests this chub swims over the bottom with barbels in contact with the substrate until the taste buds on body, fins, and barbels are stimulated by substances emanating from food. In aquaria individuals feed on a variety of animal foods and animal detritus and may ingest plant materials. This chub is probably a flood-pulse spawner like *M. tetranema* (Bottrell et al. 1964). Little else is known about its biology.

Silver Chub

Macrhybopsis storeriana (Kirtland)

Description:

The silver chub is a moderately large (to 5.5 inches), silvery fish that is slightly compressed but well streamlined. The head is fairly short, the snout rounded, and the mouth small. Barbels are rather small but visible with the mouth closed. The fins are fairly high and falcate, and the scales are moderately large, about 40–42 in the lateral line. As in most *Macrhybopsis*, the gut is short and the peritoneum silvery. Color is light olivaceous above, silvery on the sides, and white on the belly. Fins are colorless except for dark pigment on the lower lobe of the caudal fin and the adjacent white lower rays. This white edge next to the dark fin rays constitutes a good field recognition character. Maximum length is 9.1 inches. (See also color plate.)

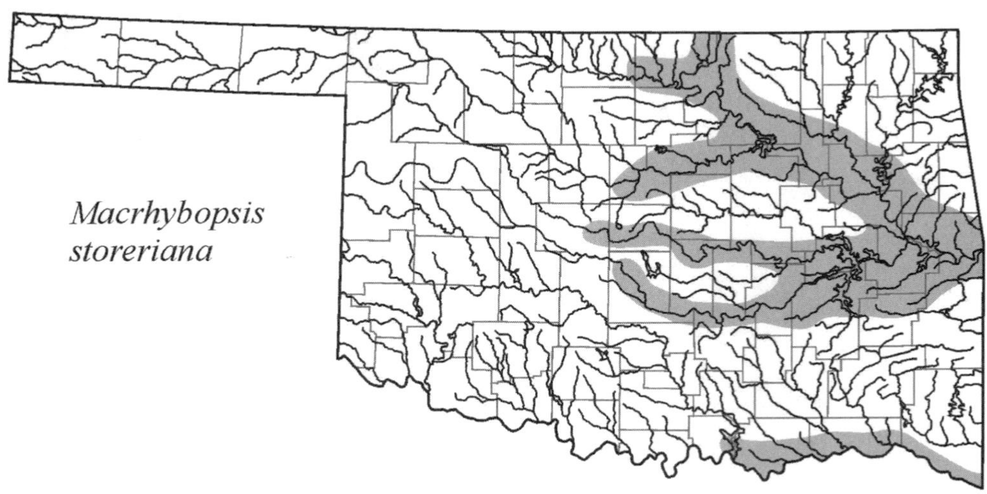

Distribution:

From Lake Ontario through the Ohio River drainage and the Mississippi basin from Wyoming south to Texas, Louisiana, and Alabama. Occurs in about the eastern three-quarters of Oklahoma.

Habitat and Biology:

The silver chub inhabits larger, sandy-bottomed rivers and streams and is quite tolerant of the silt found in western waters. It inhabits deep water with moderate to swift current during the day but moves shoreward into shallow water (20–40 inches) at dark to feed on aquatic insects, small crustaceans, and small molluscs. Spawning occurs in spring (April–May), but the spawning behavior has not been described. In Oklahoma this species is common in Lake Texoma (W. J. Matthews, pers. comm.).

Redspot chub

Nocomis asper Lachner and Jenkins

Description:

The head is large and compressed with a fairly large eye and large, nearly terminal mouth. The barbel often is not visible unless the mouth is opened. The small, rounded fins have 8 dorsal and pelvic rays and 7 anal rays. Scales are somewhat smaller anteriorly than posteriorly, 40–44 in the lateral line. The redspot is more greenish than any of the barbeled chubs in Oklahoma. It has an olivaceous back, lighter olive sides, and a white belly. The fins are orange, and adults have a red spot behind the eye. Young fish have a dark lateral band and conspicuous black caudal spot. Breeding males have large tubercles on top of the head and smaller tubercles on the pectoral fins. Size to 10 inches.

Distribution:

The Arkansas River basin from Arkansas to Kansas; common in the Ozarks but in the Red River basin in Oklahoma it is known only from the

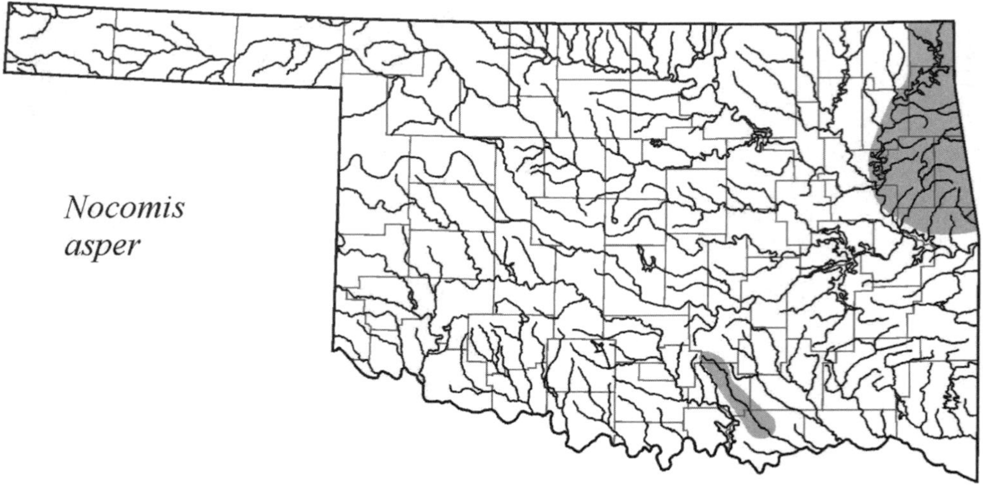

Blue River. May be found in a few places in the center of the state as a result of bait-bucket introductions.

Habitat and Biology:

The redspot is strictly an inhabitant of clear eastern and southern streams with gravel bottoms and low silt load. It is largely a sight-feeding fish, which can move to the surface to secure food as easily as it can feed on the bottom. In aquaria the redspot chub seems to prefer surface or midwater feeding (Davis and Miller 1967). It feeds on a variety of insect larvae and adults, crustaceans, and other invertebrates and sometimes ingests plant material. It is a spring spawner, with peak activity usually in May. A breeding male constructs a large pile of stones, which is used for spawning and which attracts several other cyprinid species that also spawn over it (Miller 1964; 1967).

Golden Shiner

Notemigonus crysoleucas (Mitchill)

Description:

A fairly large, compressed, deep-bodied minnow with a small head and small, nearly superior, oblique mouth. Pharyngeal tooth formula 0, 5-5, 0. The most striking characteristics are the sharply decurved lateral line (46–54 scales), the long and falcate anal fin with 11–14 rays, and the fleshy, naked keel extending from between the pelvic fins to the anus. The dorsal fin has 8 rays, the pelvic 9, and the pectoral about 15. Color is golden to olivaceous above, golden to silvery on the sides, and yellowish to silvery on the underside. Young often have a dark lateral band. Fins are usually colorless, but breeding males have yellow to orange fins. Most specimens are less than 6 inches long but individuals may reach 12 inches.

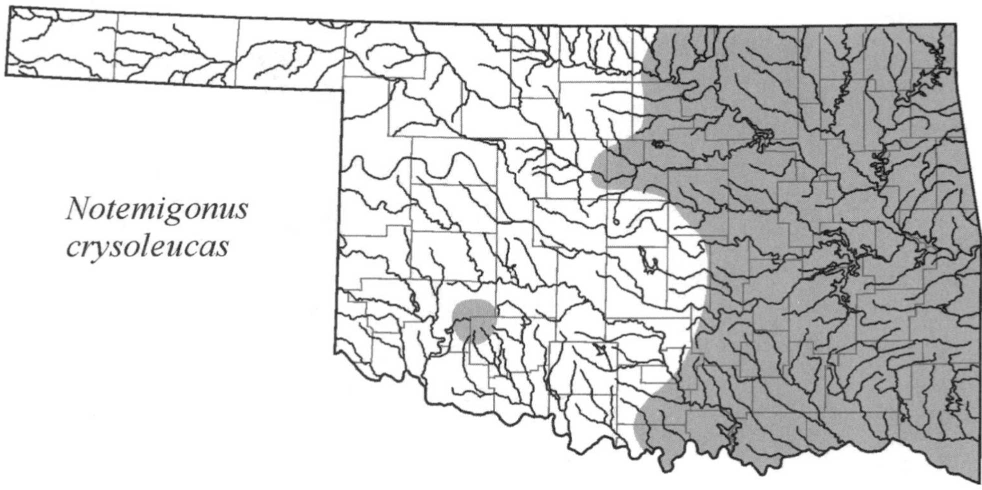

Distribution:

Throughout most of the United States east of the Rockies and widely introduced in the West. In Oklahoma this shiner is most common in the eastern two-thirds of the state and probably sporadic in the west.

Habitat and Biology:

Basically an inhabitant of quiet waters, the golden shiner is common in most larger impoundments, large natural lakes, and the quieter pools of more sluggish streams. It prefers clear waters with much vegetation but can withstand moderate siltation. It feeds mainly on zooplankton, insects and their larvae, and occasionally algae. Spawning occurs from spring through early summer in vegetation, where the adhesive eggs attach to the plants. The golden shiner is one of the most universally popular bait fishes and has been readily cultured in farm ponds. Its major drawback as a bait fish is that it is not as hardy as some other minnow species.

EMERALD SHINER

Notropis atherinoides Rafinesque

Description:

A slender and compressed shiner with a short, rounded snout and moderate-sized head (4 into SL). The eye is medium-sized (3 into head length). The dorsal fin is slightly falcate with 8 rays and situated well behind the pelvic fin base. Scales in front of the dorsal number 18–21. It has 10 or 11 anal fin rays, 35–38 lateral-line scales, and 2, 4-4, 2 pharyngeal teeth. The chin is sprinkled with dark pigment. Breeding males have tiny tubercles on pectoral rays 2–10. *N. atherinoides* is most similar to *N. percobromus* (see that species account for differences) and *L. umbratilis*, from which it differs in having fewer than 25 predorsal scales and in lacking a distinct spot at the origin of the dorsal fin. Generally less than 3 inches long.

Distribution:

From northwestern and central Canada through the plains states and Great Lakes region to the Mississippi basin and south to the Gulf of Mexico. Occurs throughout Oklahoma.

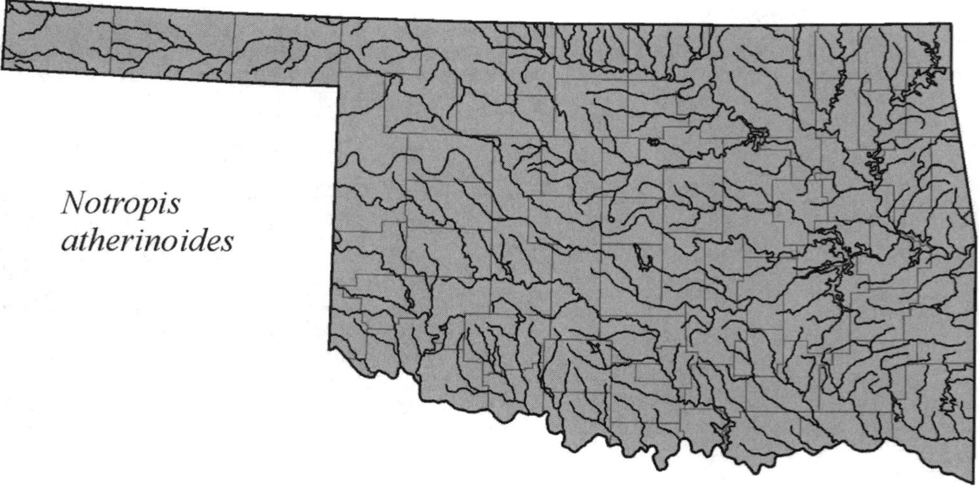

Habitat and Biology:

Although eastern forms seem most common in clear streams with gravel bottoms, western forms typically inhabit sandy-bottomed rivers and streams that are sometimes turbid. Spawning occurs in late spring and summer, and food consists mainly of zooplankton and insects.

BLACKSPOT SHINER

Notropis atrocaudalis Evermann

Description:

A thick-bodied, slightly compressed shiner with a small head (4 into SL). The snout is blunt and shorter than the fairly large eye (3.2 into head length). The slightly subterminal mouth is rather small and somewhat oblique. Pharyngeal teeth are 4-4 and the anal ray count is 7. The most distinctive external feature is the prominent dark lateral band, about as wide as the pupil of the eye, extending from the snout to the end of the caudal peduncle, where it terminates in a conspicuous rectangular black spot of about the same depth as the lateral band. In some young specimens there may be a narrow clear hiatus

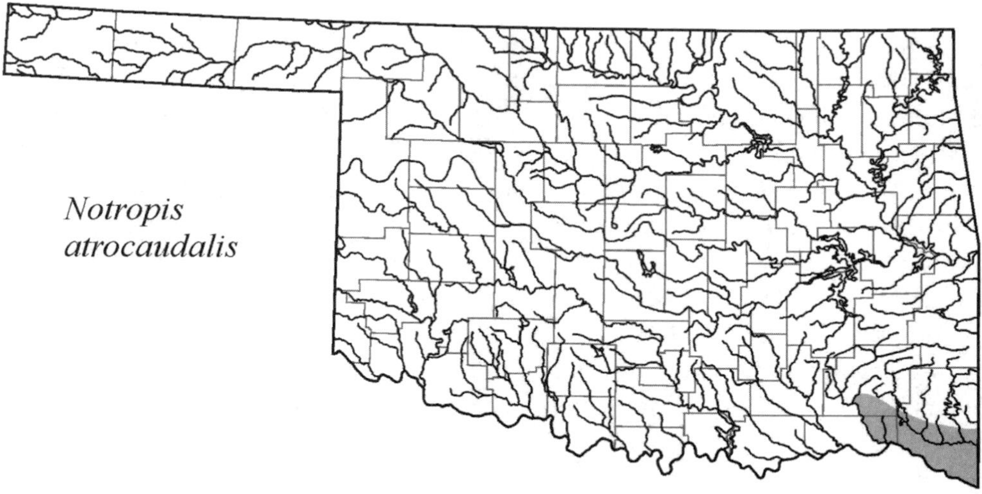

between the lateral band and the caudal spot. Dark spots above and below the lateral-line pores are prominent and are visible even when the lateral line runs within the lateral band. Scales above the lateral band are outlined with dark pigment and scales on the dorsum are usually darker than those just above the lateral band. The underside is clear. Size to about 2.7 inches.

Distribution:

Eastern Texas, western Louisiana, and Little River tributaries in McCurtain and Choctaw counties in Oklahoma, west to lowland eastern tributaries of the Kiamichi River.

Habitat and Biology:

The blackspot shiner occurs rarely in the lower reaches of the Little River in sandy and rocky runs and pools of small, clear, sand-bottomed streams. Virtually nothing is known of its biology or ecological relationships.

RED RIVER SHINER

Notropis bairdi Hubbs and Ortenburger

Description:

A husky, somewhat deep-bodied, slightly compressed shiner with a broad head, conical snout, and large mouth (upper jaw about 1.5 times as large as eye diameter). The caudal peduncle is deeper than in most of the other pale-colored riverine shiners. An anal ray count of 7 separates this species from *N. girardi*, *N. volucellus*, and *N. buchanani*, and the 0, 4-4, 0 pharyngeal tooth count separates it from *N. blennius* and *N. potteri*, which have two rows of pharyngeal teeth. It differs from *N. stramineus* in having a much larger mouth, deeper body, smaller eye, lack of pigmented dashes above and below the pores on the lateral-line scales, and much more crowded scales before the dorsal fin. Most specimens have a small area on the anterior nape devoid of scales. Color is generally pale, made somewhat grayish above by the pigment outlining the dorsolateral scales. The lower half of the body tends to be silvery. Generally less than 2.5 inches long.

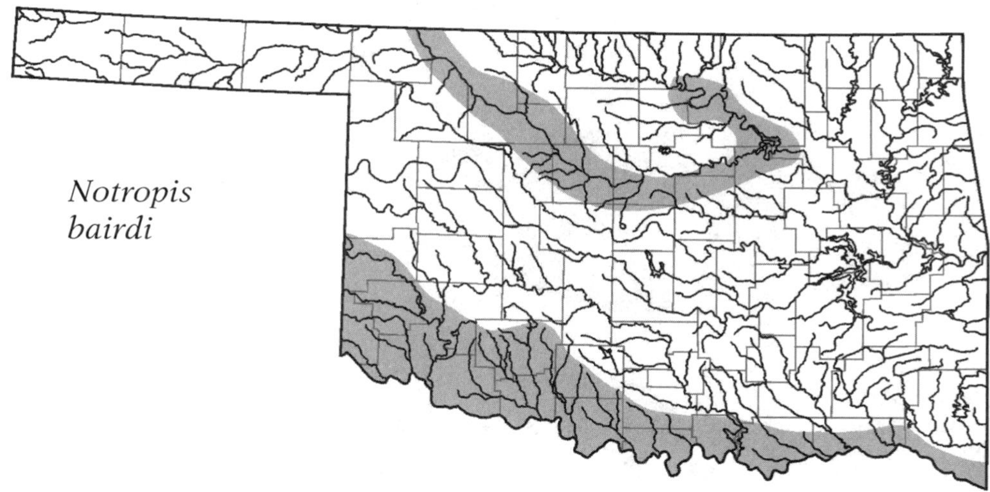

Distribution:

The Red River and principal tributaries in Oklahoma, Arkansas, and Texas. Luttrell and colleagues (1995) indicate that this species is now widespread in the Cimarron River and that specimens have been taken from the Arkansas, Salt Fork, and North and South Canadian rivers. While we indicate its presence in the Cimarron on our map, persistent populations in the other rivers await verification in the future.

Habitat and Biology:

The Red River shiner is an endemic inhabitant of the larger rivers and streams of the Red River basin. It was apparently introduced in the Cimarron between 1964 and 1972 (Luttrell et al. 1995) but has become firmly established since that time. It is thus mainly associated with broad, turbid, sandy-bottomed channels over silt and shifting sand substrates. Nothing else is known of the biology of this species. Spawning probably occurs in summer with the eggs drifting downstream during development.

RIVER SHINER

Notropis blennius (Girard)

Description:

A moderately deep-bodied, slightly compressed pale-colored minnow, the river shiner differs from other pale river shiners in having a larger mouth (upper jaw usually longer than the eye diameter) and smaller fins. It can be separated from *N. girardi*, *N. volucellus*, and *N. buchanani* by its 7 anal rays (not 8) and from *N. bairdi* and *N. stramineus* by its two rows of pharyngeal teeth (l or 2, 4-4, 2 or 1 vs. 0, 4-4, 0 in the other two species). It is most similar to *N. potteri* (see key for characteristics). Lateral-line scales are not enlarged and number about 34–36. Coloration is tan above and whitish below with a silvery lateral stripe. A well-developed middorsal stripe is present and is not interrupted at the base of the dorsal fin. In some specimens the dorsolateral scales are faintly outlined in dark pigment. The slightly decurved lateral line is sometimes lightly marked anteriorly by small melanophores, and a faint dark lateral band may be visible below the silvery lateral stripe. Usually less than 3 inches long.

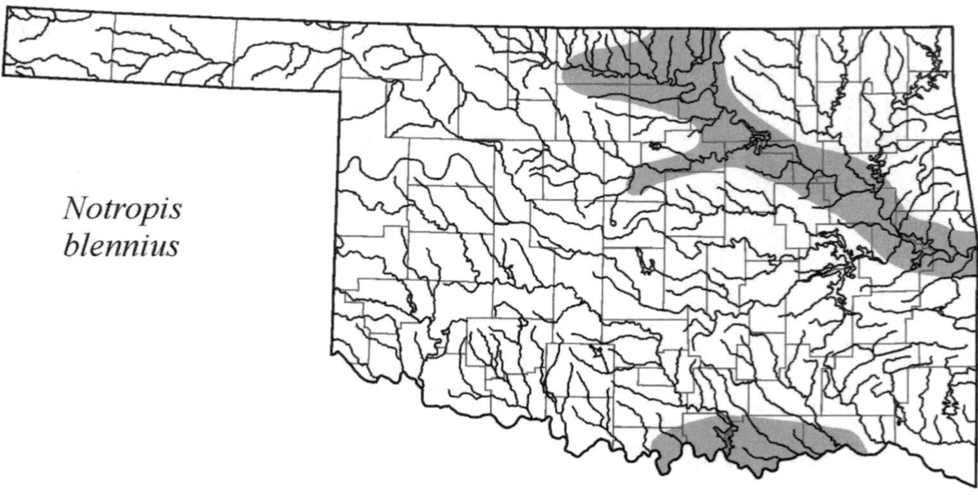

Distribution:

From Alberta and Manitoba through the northern plains states to the Ohio River basin and south through the Mississippi basin to Texas and Louisiana. Found in both the Red and Arkansas basins in Oklahoma.

Habitat and Biology:

The river shiner is not an extremely common fish anywhere in Oklahoma, though it occurs in both clear and turbid streams. It is usually found in larger rivers and streams and seems to prefer sand or gravel bottoms. Foods consist of aquatic insects, algae, and other plant matter. It spawns during much of the summer over such bottoms, but little is known of its ecology or behavior. Trautman (1957) noted that the river shiner occupies deeper water during the daylight hours and moves into shallow areas at night.

BIGEYE SHINER
Notropis boops Gilbert

Description:

A slim to moderately deep-bodied, slightly compressed shiner with an unusually large eye (2.2–2.8 into head length). It has a large, oblique, nearly terminal mouth and a moderately small head (about 4 in SL). The fins are clear, and median fins are slightly falcate with anterior dorsal rays of the folded dorsal fin extending past the tips of posterior rays. The dorsal origin is directly above the pelvic insertion. Dorsal, anal, and pelvic fins all have 8 rays. Body scales are fairly large, with the lateral-line scales (35 or 36) etched with a pair of small black dashes, curving slightly below the dark lateral band anteriorly. The intestine is short and the peritoneum is black. Color is greenish to olive above with silvery sides and silvery to white below. A dark lateral stripe extends from the lips through the eye posteriorly to the end of the caudal peduncle. A clear band, slightly wider than the lateral band, runs the

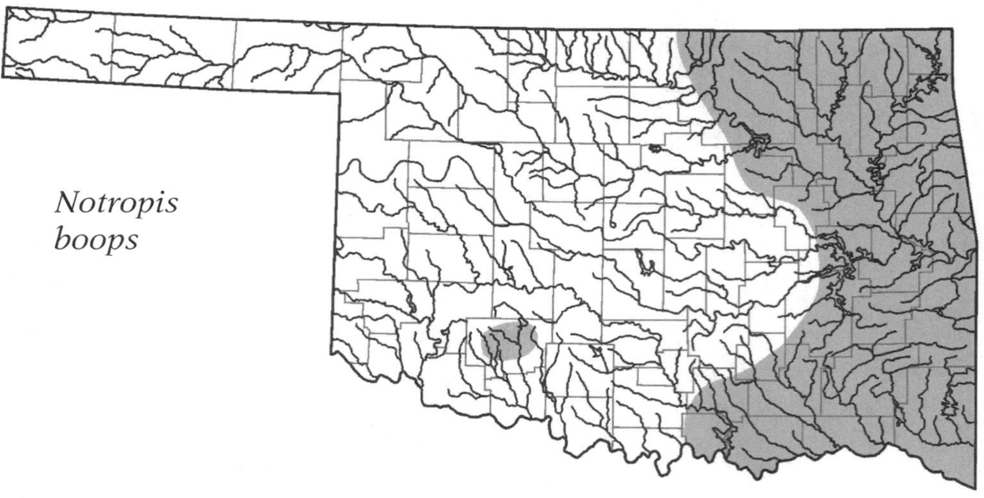

length of the body just above the lateral band. Scales above this clear band are outlined in black. Breeding males have fine tubercles on the head, upper body (anteriorly), and anterior rays of dorsal, anal, and pectoral fins. About 2 inches long.

Distribution:

The lower Ohio River basin to Tennessee in the south and through the central Mississippi drainage to Kansas and Oklahoma. This shiner is found in both the Arkansas and Red River drainages in the eastern half of Oklahoma and is known as far west as Kay County in the north and Comanche County in the south.

Habitat and Biology:

The bigeye shiner is one of our most common eastern shiners, generally most abundant in moderate-sized streams with fairly high gradients and gravel or clean sand bottoms. It can withstand sporadic siltation but is not found in streams that do not have clear water most of the time. It feeds primarily on surface insects. Spawning occurs from late April into August in Oklahoma (Lehtinen and Echelle 1979), but its breeding habits have not been described.

GHOST SHINER
Notropis buchanani Meek

Description:

This small, pale shiner, usually about 1 inch long, is most similar to *N. volucellus*. It differs in having a deeper body (about 3.5 into SL, vs. 4–4.5 in *volucellus*); in having little pigment on the dorsal scales—almost none is visible in many specimens; and in lacking an infraorbital lateral-line canal. The snout is rounded, and the mouth is small and moderately oblique. There are 8 rays in the dorsal, anal, and pelvic fins and about 32–35 scales in the lateral line. Lateral-line scales are much deeper than they are long, conspicuously more so than contiguous scales. Color is very pale with some pigment on the head and some faintly outlining dorsal scales. A faint lateral band is barely visible in some specimens.

Distribution.

The Mississippi basin from Iowa and Ohio southward to Alabama in the east and Mexico in the west. Found in about the eastern half to two-thirds of Oklahoma with a few scattered records in the west.

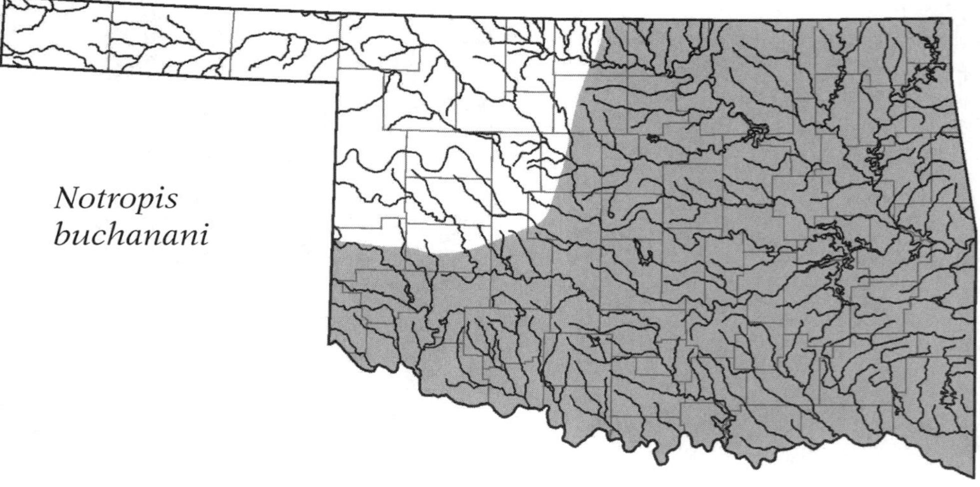

Habitat and Biology:

Relatively little is known of the biology of the ghost shiner. Although it is found throughout the eastern part of the state, it is generally most abundant in the sluggish streams of the plains region, where it inhabits backwaters, eddies, and other similar habitats away from strong currents. Spawning occurs from late spring through August in Oklahoma. In Missouri this species spawns over sluggish riffles composed of sand and fine gravel.

IRONCOLOR SHINER

Notropis chalybaeus (Cope)

Description:

Rarely longer than 2 inches, this small, compressed shiner has a moderately small head (about 4 into SL), very large eye (about 2.7 into head length), and short, pointed snout. The mouth is terminal, moderately large, and oblique. Fins are fairly large and unpigmented with 8 rays in the dorsal, anal, and pelvic fins. Both dorsal and anal fins are slightly falcate. Body

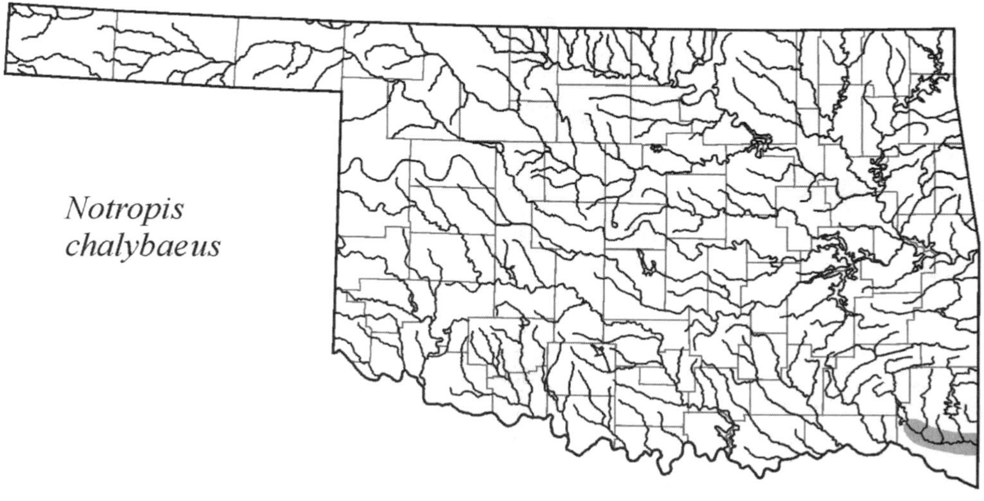

scales are fairly large with 31–34 in the lateral line, which may be incomplete in young fish. Characteristic features of this species are the prominent dark lateral band extending forward from a somewhat distinct caudal spot across the head and around the snout on both lips; the abundance of dark pigment on both the floor and roof of the mouth just inside the lips; and dark pigment outlining the anal fin and extending posteriorly, but less intensely, along the ventral edge of the caudal peduncle. Dorsolateral scales are outlined with melanophores, and a thin, dark middorsal stripe is present anterior to the dorsal fin. A light line separates the dark dorsolateral scales from the lateral band. Breeding males develop a bright orange underside and have tubercles on the head.

Distribution:

Coastal streams from New York to Texas and up the Mississippi basin to Iowa. Found in Oklahoma only in the lower Mountain Fork and Little River drainages.

Habitat and Biology:

The ironcolor shiner is a schooling fish found in sluggish lowland streams and rivers. It is most abundant in pools with aquatic vegetation or along the edges of rivers where currents are reduced. Feeding is by sight on aquatic insects and copepods. Spawning occurs from late spring through late summer in other parts of the range with females scattering eggs in pools over sand substrates, but little is known of the biology of this rare species, which has been collected only four times in Oklahoma (Williams and Echelle 1998).

ARKANSAS RIVER SHINER

Notropis girardi Hubbs and Ortenburger

Description:

A small, heavy-bodied shiner, only slightly compressed and usually less than 2 inches long. It is separable from *N. stramineus*, *N. blennius*, and *N. bairdi* in having 8 anal rays (vs. 7) and from *N. volucellus* and *N. buchanani* in having the exposed portions of the lateral-line scales about the same size

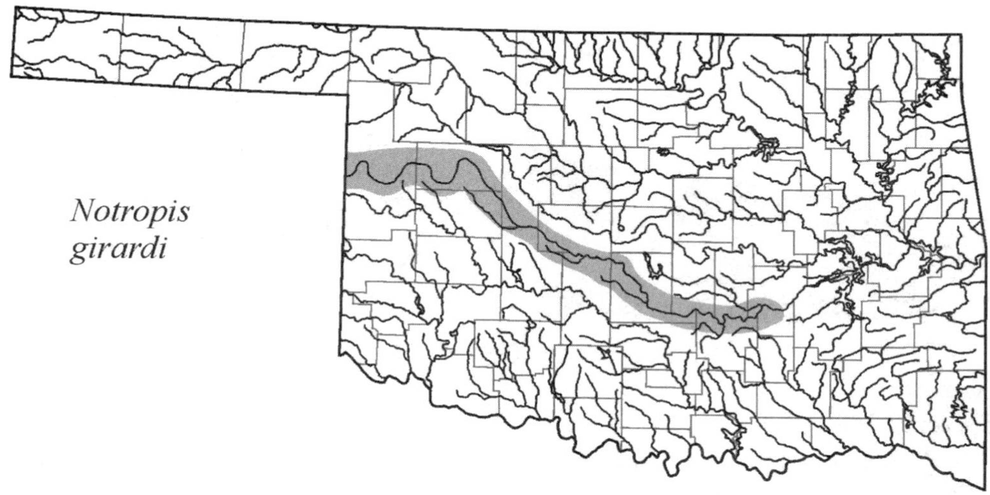

and shape as adjacent scales. The head is thick and small (about 4.3 into SL). The snout is rounded, and the mouth is small (about as long as the eye diameter). There are 8 rays in the dorsal and pelvic fins and 33–37 lateral-line scales. Color is sandy above and silver laterally, with dorsal scales lightly outlined with dark pigment. Anterior lateral-line pores are scarcely outlined by tiny melanophores, and a small black chevron is usually visible at the caudal base. Maximum length about 2 inches. (See also color plate.)

Distribution:

Originally found in the Arkansas River basin in Kansas, Oklahoma, Arkansas, Texas, and New Mexico, this shiner has been extirpated from three-fourths of its former range in Oklahoma and Kansas. It occurs in the South Canadian River of south-central Oklahoma, with small numbers present in the North Canadian River and the Arkansas River (Pigg 1991; 1999). Several records from the Red River drainage exist (Cross 1970; Pigg 1991).

Habitat and Biology:

This shiner is found in the turbid main channels of large, shallow, sandy-bottomed rivers and streams over silt and sandy substrates. Cross (1967) notes that Arkansas River shiners lie on the "lee" side of large transverse sand ridges in these channels, where they feed on small aquatic organisms washed downstream or exposed by sand movement. Spawning is in July in mainstream channels, usually following heavy rains, the eggs drifting with the current and developing as they go (Moore 1944). This species is currently threatened with extinction in Oklahoma, as numbers in the South Canadian River are dwindling due to low flows, pollution, and possibly competition.

Wedgespot Shiner

Notropis greenei Hubbs and Ortenburger

Description:

A relatively slim, slightly compressed shiner with a moderately large head (3.8 into SL), large eye (2.8 into head length), and large, subterminal, and slightly oblique mouth. This shiner shares overall color pattern and body conformation with *Notropis boops* and *N. ortenburgeri* but can be distinguished from the latter by its anal ray count of 8 (vs. 9, 10) and from both species by the absence of pigment on the lower lip and chin and by the presence of a conspicuous black wedge-shaped spot at the base of the caudal fin. Although a few other cyprinid species in the state occasionally show traces of such a spot, it is always much smaller and fainter than that of *N. greenei*. The scales are fairly large (35–38 in the lateral line) and the anterior pores of the lateral line are edged with black. Pharyngeal tooth count is 2, 4-4, 2, and dorsal and pelvic fins have 8 rays. Size is generally less than 2.5 inches. (See also color plate.)

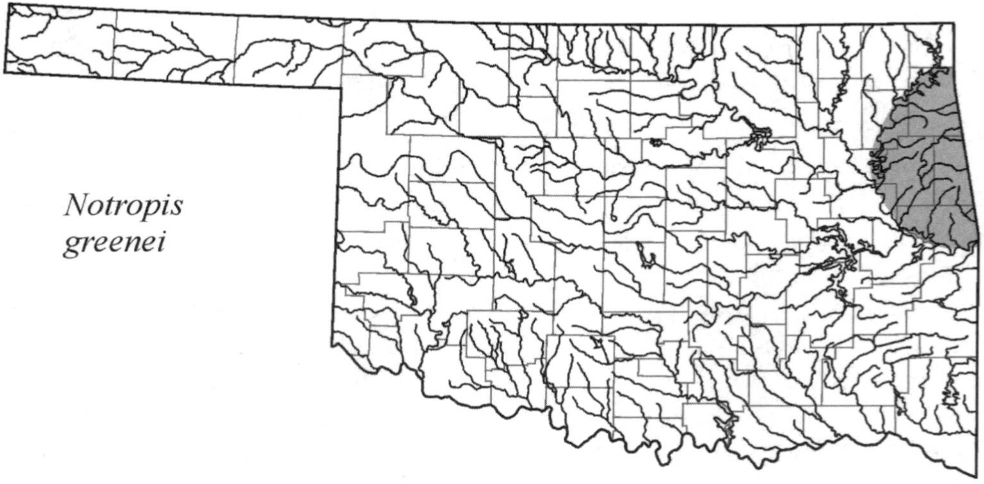

Distribution:

The Ozark region of Oklahoma, Missouri, and Arkansas. Limited in Oklahoma to the streams of the Ozark upland.

Habitat and Biology:

The wedgespot shiner inhabits the clear, hard-bottomed streams of the Ozark region, where it seems to prefer deep, fast-water channels. Moore and Paden (1950) reported individuals in spawning condition on August 15 in Oklahoma and hypothesized that they have a long summer breeding period. In Missouri, adults in spawning condition have been collected from late May to late August, with spawning occurring over gravel riffles in swift current (Pflieger 1997). Although this shiner probably resembles many stream minnows in feeding habits, its life history is little known.

Bluehead Shiner

Notropis hubbsi Bailey and Robison

Description:

A distinctive slab-sided species with 9 or 10 dorsal fin rays and a broad black lateral stripe extending from the tip of the snout to the caudal base, terminating in a deep caudal spot that extends onto the caudal fin. Pharyngeal teeth 4-4. The mouth is terminal and sharply upturned, the snout projecting slightly beyond the upper lip, and the eye is moderate. Lateral line is incomplete with 2–9 pored scales; 34–36 scales in lateral series. The dorsal fin origin is behind the pelvic insertion and closer to the caudal base than to the snout tip. Anal rays number 9–11. The dorsal and anal fins of males are large and rounded, with the middle dorsal rays longest. Body is dusky above with a broad black lateral stripe from chin to caudal base expanding onto caudal fin; underside is white. Breeding fish have a reddish orange dorsolateral surface above the lateral stripes, and rays of the basal half of caudal and dorsal

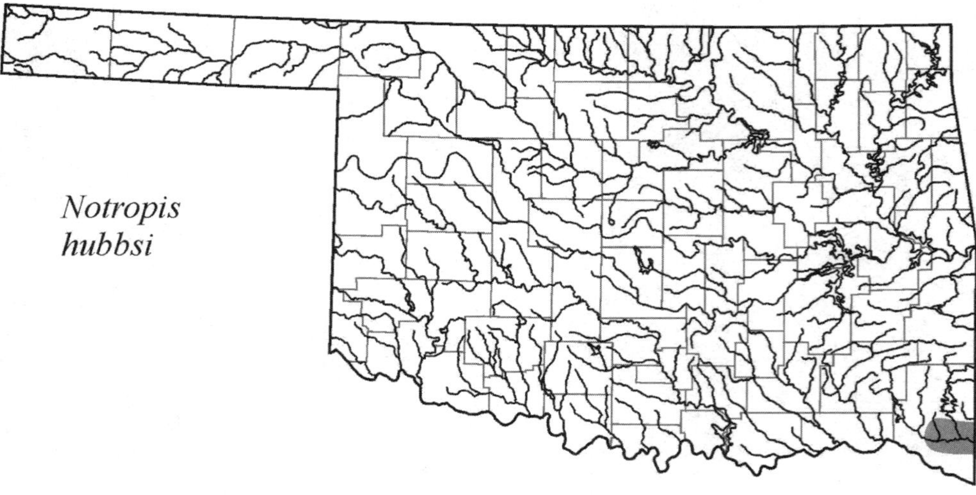

fins also show reddish orange. Males have yellow on the anal fin membranes but not rays. Larger males have iridescent greenish blue on dorsal fin membranes. Pelvic fins of breeding males have a blue-green wash. Small breeding tubercles are well-developed in males on the head, opercle, body, and fins, and the top of the head becomes deep azure blue with green iridescence. Maximum size 2.5 inches. (See also color plate.)

Distribution:

A resident of the Ouachita and Little River systems of Arkansas, Louisiana, and Oklahoma. In Oklahoma it is known from streams and swamps of southeastern McCurtain County.

Habitat and Biology:

This beautiful minnow has only recently been discovered in Oklahoma (Miller 1984). It inhabits quiet backwater areas of small to medium-sized streams and oxbow lakes. Swampy, tannin-stained water, often heavily vegetated, with substrates of mud or sand and mud seem to be preferred. Hanging in midwater near vegetation, schools of bluehead shiners can dart into protective plant masses when disturbed. Tuberculated males have been collected from early May to July, and young of the year have been collected in early June. The species may be migratory, as breeding adults have been found in the prime habitats only during spring. Fletcher and Burr (1992) described two morphologically distinct classes of males and noted that the larger, more aggressive "terminal" males developed more expansive dorsal, anal, and pelvic fins. They also defended breeding territories over sunfish nests, while the secondary males may act as "sneakers," stealing fertilizations. There is some speculation that large adult breeders may die after spawning (Robison and Buchanan 1988).

Note:

Bailey and Robison (1978) described *Notropis hubbsi* and noted it was allied to *N. welaka* but differed significantly from that species. Later Dimmick (1987), Mayden (1989), and Amemiya and Gold (1990) placed *N. hubbsi* within the elevated subgenus *Pteronotropis*. Coburn and Cavender (1992) retained *Pteronotropis* as a subgenus, placing *N. hubbsi* within it. We concur with Suttkus and Mettee (2001), who analyzed the subgenus *Pteronotropis* and consider *N. hubbsi* and *N. welaka* sufficiently different to warrant subgeneric placement. Hence we retain the name *Notropis hubbsi* for the bluehead shiner.

TAILLIGHT SHINER

Notropis maculatus (Hay)

Description:

A slim, moderately compressed shiner reaching 2.3 inches, with a small head (about 4 into SL). The eye is fairly large (about 3.5 into head length). The rounded snout is about the same length as the eye and has a definite depigmented area on its tip in preserved specimens. The mouth is nearly terminal and only slightly oblique. Pharyngeal teeth are 4-4 and there are 8 rays in the anal fin. Scales are moderately large with about 35–37 in the incomplete lateral line. The most striking identification characteristics are pigmentary. A dark lateral band extends from the snout to the caudal peduncle, terminating in a large black basicaudal spot. Immediately above and below the spot are clear areas and then smaller dark triangles on the margins of the caudal fin adjacent to the end of the caudal peduncle. In overall aspect these give the appearance of 3 spots at the caudal base. Dorsolateral scales are lightly outlined with melanophores and the underside is clear. Breeding

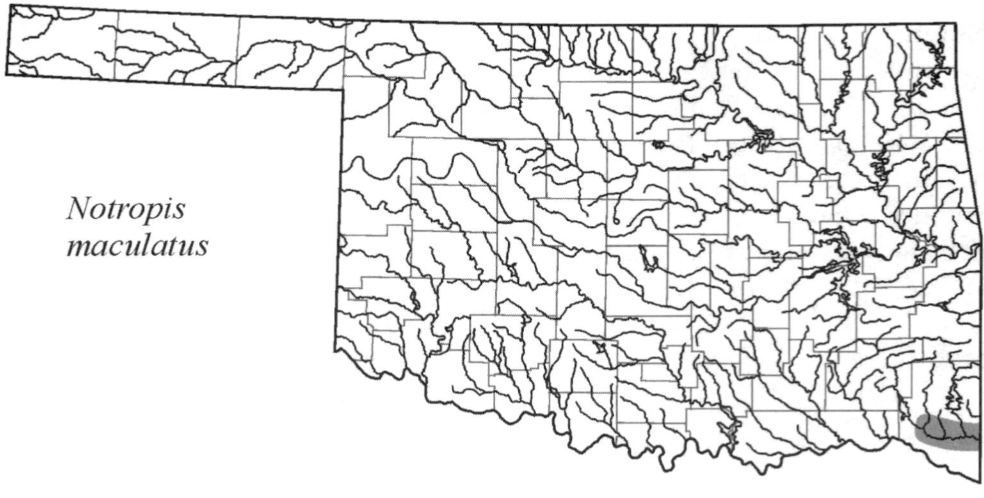

males are pink with red pigment on the snout and iris. Median and pelvic fins are red with clear tips and bases. (See also color plate.)

Distribution:

From Missouri and Oklahoma to the Gulf Coast, east to Florida, and north along the Atlantic Coast to North Carolina. Occurs in the lower Little River drainage of Oklahoma.

Habitat and Biology:

The taillight shiner occupies quieter areas of low-gradient streams and rivers and is commonly found in sloughs, oxbows, swamps, and lakes. Apparently this species avoids high-gradient streams and has been collected only in the lakes and lowland streams of McCurtain County. This midwater schooling shiner is often found associated with dense aquatic vegetation. Foods include algae, microcrustaceans, and insects. Breeding males have been taken from April to mid-June in Arkansas. Life span is less than two years.

KIAMICHI SHINER

Notropis ortenburgeri Hubbs

Description:

A slim, terete minnow with a large eye, extremely oblique mouth, and small head (4–4.3 into SL). Lateral line scales number 32–37; peritoneum is silvery. In general body shape, size, and coloration it is similar to *N. boops* but can be distinguished by its pharyngeal tooth count of 4-4 (1, 4-4, 1 in *boops*) and the anal ray count of 9 or 10 (8 in *boops*). Useful characteristics for separating the two in the field are the markedly more oblique mouth of *N. ortenburgeri* and the clearly visible black patch on the tip of the chin (absent in *N. boops*). In *N. boops*, the preorbital dark band extends around the snout, whereas dark pigment is present only on the lips of *N. ortenburgeri*. The dark lateral band of the Kiamichi shiner also becomes perceptibly wider at its terminus on the caudal peduncle, whereas it remains narrow all the way to the slightly separated caudal spot of *N. boops*. Otherwise, general coloration is

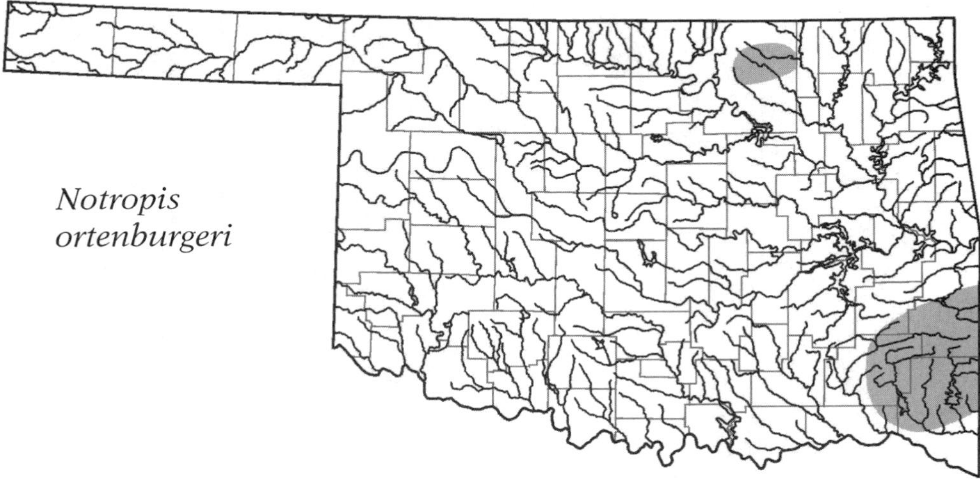

similar to that described in the account of *N. boops*. Maximum size about 2.3 inches. (See also color plate.)

Distribution:

Found in the Osage Hills streams tributary to the Arkansas River in Oklahoma, the Poteau River, and streams of the Ouachita Mountains in southeastern Oklahoma and south-central and southwestern Arkansas.

Habitat and Biology:

The biology of the Kiamichi shiner is almost unknown. It is rarely collected in great numbers in Oklahoma but is almost always found in relatively small to moderate-sized clear upland streams of moderate gradient, in pools over gravel, cobble-sized, or boulder substrates. We have collected it in relatively quiet water in pools and among large boulders. It avoids swifter stream sections and riffles.

Carmine Shiner
Notropis percobromus (Cope)

Description:

A slender, slightly compressed shiner with a moderately long head (3.7 into SL). The mouth is terminal and oblique. There are 8 dorsal rays, 10 (occasionally 9) anal rays, 8 pelvic rays, and 36–38 lateral-line scales. Pharyngeal teeth are 2, 4-4, 2, the gut is short, and the peritoneum is silvery. This species is most similar to *Lythrurus umbratilis*, *Notropis atherinoides*, and *N. suttkusi:* all four have the dorsal fin origin posterior to the pelvic fin insertion and closer to the caudal base than to the snout tip. The carmine shiner can be distinguished from *L. umbratilis* by larger anterodorsal scales and absence of a dark spot at the origin of the dorsal fin. It can be distinguished from *N. atherinoides* by a darker lateral stripe, the black edging of the lateral-line pores extending past the middle of the body, and the greater scattering of pigment on dorsolateral scales (vs. concentration on scale margins in *atherinoides*). The snout of Oklahoma *N. percobromus* is not appreciably longer than that of

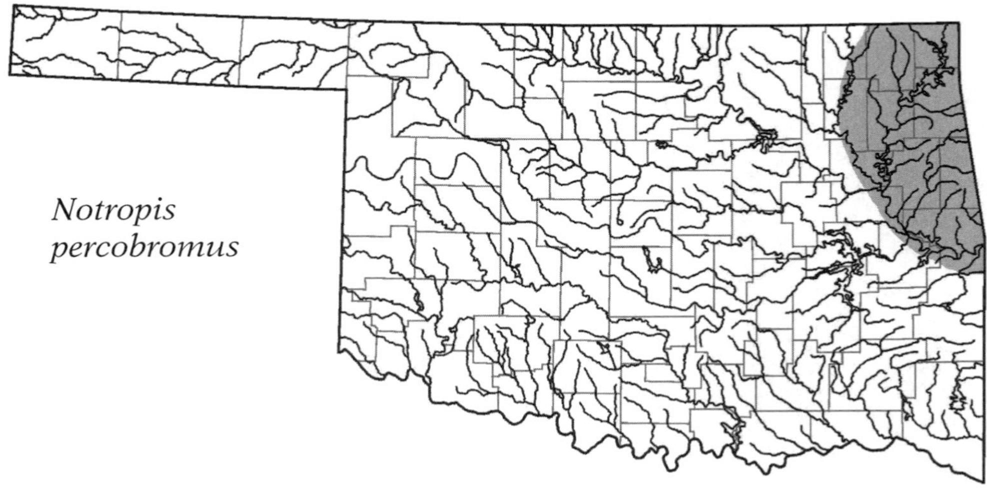

some *N. atherinoides* and is not a useful character here. From *N. suttkusi, N. percobromus* differs in having a larger snout and upper jaw; a slimmer body; less dense pigmentation on scales, lips, and gular region; lateral-line pigment outlined by melanophores rather than continuous with the lateral band; and the lateral line straight or decurved 1–2 scale rows (decurved 5–6 scale rows in *suttkusi*). Breeding male carmine shiners develop bright red or orange pigment on the head and underside. (See also color plate.)

Distribution:

North-central United States from North Dakota to Illinois, south to Oklahoma and Arkansas. It occurs in Ozark upland streams and rivers tributary to the Arkansas River in eastern Oklahoma.

Habitat and Biology:

The carmine shiner definitely prefers clear streams with gravel and limestone bottoms and rather high gradient. It spawns in spring over clean gravel in shallow riffles and utilizes the cleared gravel nests of other cyprinids when these are available. Food consists mainly of insects and other small invertebrates.

Note:

This form has been known for many years as *Notropis rubellus* (Agassiz). Wood and colleagues (2002) have recently shown, based on allozyme data, that the old polytypic *N. rubellus* is best considered as four distinct species and that Humphries and Cashner's *N. suttkusi* (1994) constitutes the fifth species of this complex. We have followed these designations.

Peppered shiner

Notropis perpallidus Hubbs and Black

Description:

A small, slim, pale shiner with a small head (about 4 into SL). The pointed snout is shorter than the large eye (about 2.8 into head length). There are 8 rays in the dorsal and pelvic fins and 9–11 rays in the anal fin. Scales are large, with 32–35 in the decurved lateral line. Pharyngeal teeth number 2, 4-4, 2 or 1, 4-4, 1. Peritoneum is silvery. The peppered shiner has distinctive pigmentation. Scales on the dorsum and upper parts of the sides are faintly outlined with tiny melanophores, and aggregations of melanophores tend to form a diffuse mid-dorsal stripe, darkest just before the dorsal fin and at the base of the posterior dorsal rays. Large, round melanophores are sparsely and randomly distributed on the dorsum and dorsolateral region and in the very diffuse lateral band. Concentrations of melanophores also occur on top of the head and on the snout, lips, and chin. Maximum size 2.7 inches.

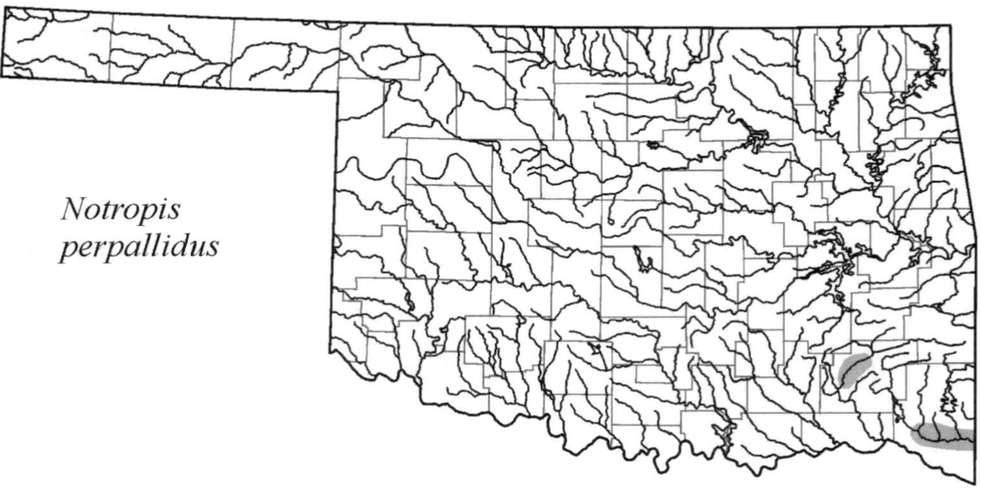

Distribution:

Found in the Little River system of southeastern Oklahoma and southwestern Arkansas. Pigg and Hill (1974) reported two collections from the Kiamichi River near Stanley.

Habitat and Biology:

The peppered shiner is a relatively rare species that inhabits pool regions 2–4 feet deep in moderate-sized, warm, clear rivers with current speeds of less than 0.01 feet per second. It avoids smaller streams. This shiner is often collected in association with water willow or in the lee of islands away from the main current. Foods eaten include aquatic and terrestrial insects, primarily dipterans, thus indicating feeding on benthic, midwater, and surface organisms (Snelson and Jenkins 1973). Sexually mature adults in spawning condition have been collected in Arkansas from late May to early August (Robison and Buchanan 1988). Life span is about four years.

Chub shiner

Notropis potteri Hubbs and Bonham

Description:

The chub shiner is a fairly large, husky shiner reaching 3.5 inches, not very deep-bodied and only slightly compressed. The head is broad and the eye small (about 4.2 into head length). The mouth is large (about 2.5 into head length). Distinctive characteristics are the swollen posterior portion of the upper lip and the medially thickened lower lip. With an anal ray count of 7, this species is most similar to *N. bairdi*, *N. stramineus*, and *N. blennius*. It is distinguished from the first two in having 2 rows of teeth in the pharyngeal arch (2, 4-4, 2 vs. 0, 4-4, 0) and in lacking a dark streak in the middle of the caudal base. Distinguishing it from *N. blennius* are its swollen lips (see fig. 15 in key) and slimmer body (body depth about 4.4 into SL vs. about 4 in *blennius*). Coloration is slightly dusky above and silvery below with a faint

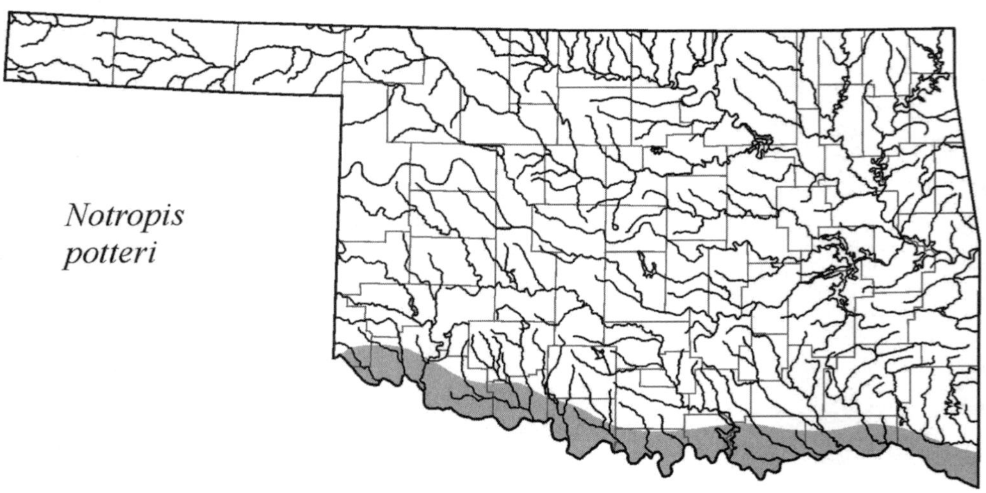

dark lateral band underlying the silvery band. A faint, diffuse basicaudal spot is sometimes evident.

Distribution:

Red River and some tributaries in Texas and Oklahoma and the Brazos and Colorado rivers in Texas.

Habitat and Biology:

The chub shiner seems to be an adaptable fish. It appears to do well in both silt-laden and relatively clear streams and is a fairly common resident of Lake Texoma. Nothing is known of its biology in Oklahoma.

Silverband Shiner

Notropis shumardi (Girard)

Description:

The silverband shiner is a moderately deep-bodied, compressed fish with a relatively small head (4.2 into SL). The snout is short and rounded and the eye large (3.2–3.4 into head length).This species is superficially similar to the deeper-bodied form of *N. atherinoides* but has the dorsal origin just above the pelvic insertion rather than far behind it. The most conspicuous features of the species are the narrow silvery lateral band (in life) and the high, pointed dorsal fin with anterior rays about as long as the head. Red River populations have 8 anal rays (rarely 9 or 10), while Arkansas River fish have 9 anal rays (rarely 8). The lateral line has 34–37 scales, and the pharyngeal teeth number 2, 4-4, 2. Color is light dusky above and whitish below. Rarely more than 2.5 inches long.

Distribution:

Channels of the principal rivers of the Mississippi basin from South Dakota and Illinois to Louisiana and Gulf Coast rivers to Texas and Alabama.

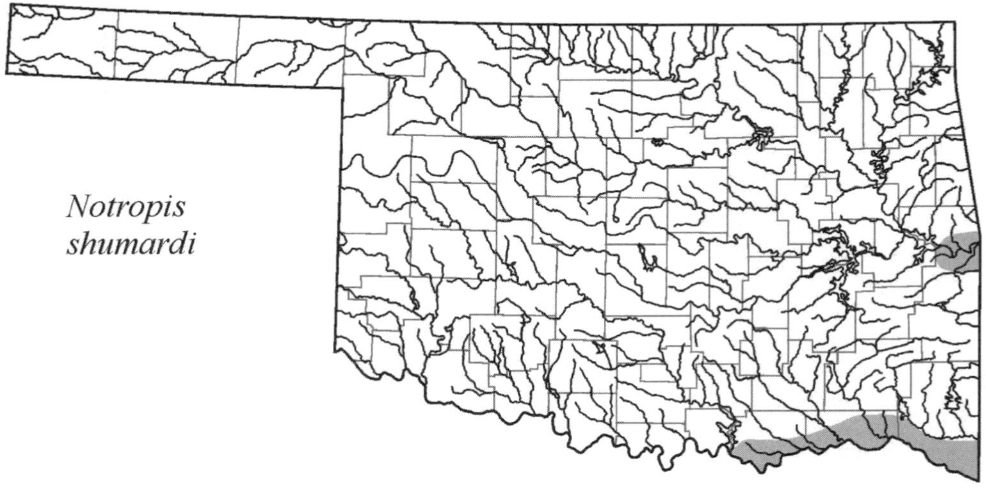

Found in the Arkansas and Poteau rivers in eastern Oklahoma, and in the Red River to Lake Texoma.

Habitat and Biology:

The silverband shiner is known only from the main streams of the major rivers within its distribution. Fish in breeding condition have been captured in late May in Illinois, mid-August in Missouri, and June to early August in Louisiana, indicating a summer spawning season; however, nuptial individuals have been taken in the Red River as early as April 23. Breeding aggregations have been observed over substrates ranging from hard sand to fine gravel in water 3–6 feet deep in strong current (Suttkus 1980).

Note:

Gilbert and Bailey (1962) changed the name of this shiner from *N. illecebrosus* to *N. shumardi* and synonymized *N. brazosensis* with the latter.

SAND SHINER

Notropis stramineus (Cope)

Description:

A fairly robust, slightly compressed minnow that rarely exceeds 2.5 inches in length. It has a moderately small eye, slightly subterminal, oblique mouth, and short head (3.5–4 into SL). This rather pallid fish is similar in overall appearance to a small group of minnows common in many of our plains streams but can be distinguished from most of them by its 7 anal rays; *N. girardi*, *N. volucellus*, and *N. buchanani* have 8. It differs from *N. blennius* in having a black dash in the center of the dorsal fin base and only a single row of pharyngeal teeth, 0, 4-4, 0 (1 or 2, 4-4, 2 or 1 in *blennius*). There are 8 dorsal and pelvic rays and usually 33–37 lateral-line scales, which do not differ in height from adjacent scales. Scales on the upper part of the body are outlined with dark pigment, and the lateral-line pores have small clusters of tiny melanophores above and below them. The sides are silvery, but a faint, dark lateral band is visible posteriorly in some specimens, as is a small basicaudal wedge or spot.

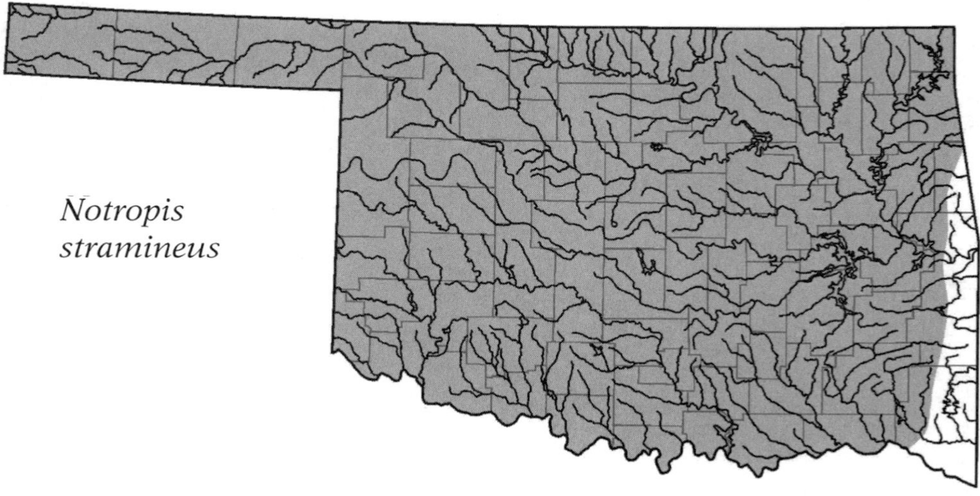

Distribution:

From the St. Lawrence drainage to Montana in the north and through the Mississippi basin south to Texas, also occurring in Gulf streams to Mexico. The species is common in the plains tributaries to both the Red and Arkansas systems but relatively rare in the higher sections of eastern Oklahoma.

Habitat and Biology:

The sand shiner is an extremely common fish in most sandy-bottomed streams and rivers of central Oklahoma but can be found in turbid, mud-bottomed streams and gravel-bottomed creeks as well. It breeds from May through August, scattering eggs over clean gravel and sand. Food consists principally of both terrestrial and aquatic insects and detritus.

ROCKY SHINER

Notropis suttkusi Humphries and Cashner

Description:

A slender, slightly compressed shiner with a moderately long head (3.7 into SL). The mouth is terminal and oblique. There are 8 dorsal rays, 9–10 (occasionally 11) anal rays, 8 pelvic rays, and a deeply decurved lateral-line usually with 34–37 scales. Pharyngeal teeth are 2, 4-4, 2. The gut is short, and the peritoneum is silvery. *Notropis suttkusi* is most similar to *Lythrurus umbratilis*, *N. atherinoides*, and *N. percobromus*, all four having the dorsal fin origin posterior to the pelvic fin insertion, and closer to the caudal base than to the snout tip. The rocky shiner can be distinguished from *L. umbratilis* by its larger anterodorsal scales and the absence of a dark spot at the origin of the dorsal fin. It differs from *N. atherinoides* in its darker and wider lateral stripe, the black edging of the lateral-line pores extending past the middle of the body, and the greater scattering of pigment on dorsolateral scales (vs. concentration on scale margins in *atherinoides*). From *N. percobromus*, *N.*

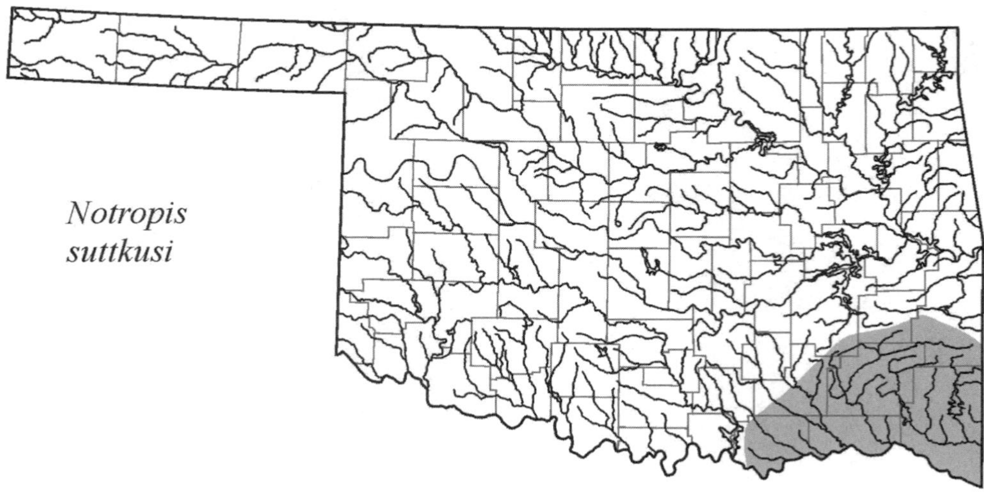

suttkusi differs in having a shorter snout and upper jaw; a deeper, more robust body; denser pigmentation on scales, lower lip, and gular region; lateral-line pigment not outlined by melanophores but often continuous with lateral band; and lateral line decurved 5–6 scale rows (straight or decurved 1–2 scale rows in *percobromus*). Breeding males develop a raspberry or lilac caste over much of the body surface.

Distribution:

Endemic to the tributaries of the Red River draining the Ouachita Mountains in southeastern Oklahoma and southwestern Arkansas, including the Blue, Kiamichi, Muddy Boggy, and Little rivers.

Habitat and Biology:

The rocky shiner inhabits clear rivers and streams of moderate to high gradient with gravel and rubble substrates (Humphries and Cashner 1994). Pratt (2000) studied the reproductive season, size at first reproduction, and seasonal gonad development in the Blue River and Kiamichi River populations. Reproductive season begins in late March and ends in early August, although some variation occurred between the two populations.

Mimic shiner

Notropis volucellus (Cope)

Description:

A small minnow reaching about 1.5 inches, with a slim and only slightly compressed body. The head is fairly small (about 4 into SL). The snout is rounded, the mouth small and moderately oblique, and the eye moderate (about 3–3.5 into head length). There are 8 rays in the dorsal, anal, and pelvic fins, which are average size. Lateral-line scales are higher than they are long (exposed surfaces) and higher than adjacent scales; generally 32–34 in the nearly straight lateral line. The infraorbital lateral-line canal is present (absent in *N. buchanani*; see fig. 17 in key). Coloration is generally pale with silver sides. Scales on the dorsum are conspicuously outlined with dark pigment, which gradually decreases in intensity down the sides. Little pigment is present on the scales just above the dark lateral band, which is rather prominent in some specimens. Tiny dark spots are found above and below the lateral-line pores.

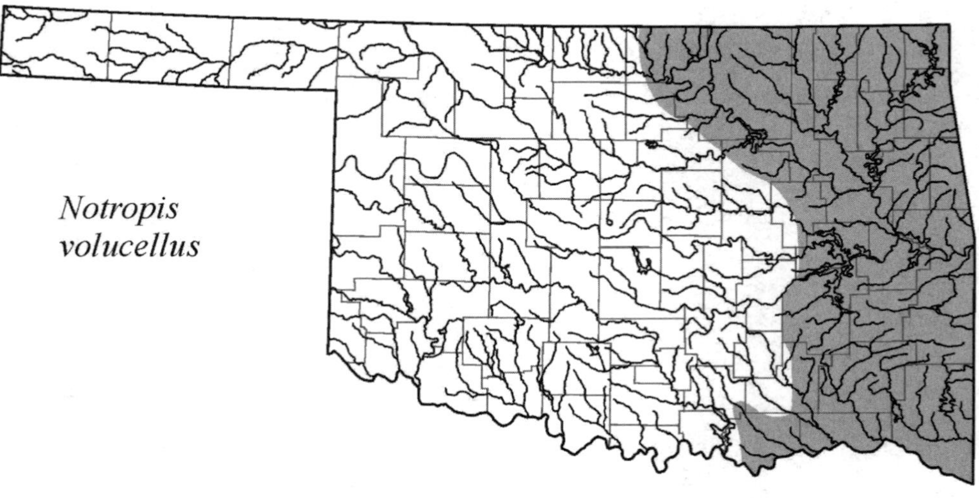

Distribution:

From southern Canada through the St. Lawrence and Great Lakes region south to North Carolina and throughout the Mississippi basin to Texas and Mississippi. Also occurs in Gulf Coast rivers to Mexico. Found in both Red and Arkansas basins in about the eastern half of Oklahoma.

Habitat and Biology:

The mimic shiner generally occurs in flowing rivers and larger streams and apparently prefers to live over gravel or hard bottom in the main stream. It can withstand periodic turbidity but generally is not found in heavily silted or mud-bottomed streams. In Indiana it is known to feed on copepods, various insect larvae, and algae. Spawning occurs from early June to late July in Missouri, indicating an early summer breeding season (Pflieger 1997); however, details of reproductive activities are unknown.

Pugnose minnow
Opsopoeodus emiliae Hay

Description:

The pugnose minnow is a very distinctive fish, unlikely to be confused with any other cyprinid in Oklahoma. It is elongate and moderately compressed with a short blunt snout and short head (4.3–4.7 into SL). The eye is moderately large (about 3 into head length). This species is distinguishable from all other minnows and shiners in the state by its very small, nearly vertical mouth and 9 dorsal rays. All other minnows and shiners have 8 dorsal rays except *Notropis hubbsi*, which has 9–10; however, anal rays separate the two, numbering 9 in *N. hubbsi* but 8 in *O. emiliae*). There are 8 rays in the anal and pelvic fins, and the pharyngeal tooth count is 5-5. Scales are moderate in size with 37–40 in the lateral line. Scales on the upper 75 percent of the body are outlined with melanophores, and a narrow, dark lateral band may be more or less prominent. The bases of three or four caudal rays at the terminus of the lateral band are often moderately to heavily pigmented. Males

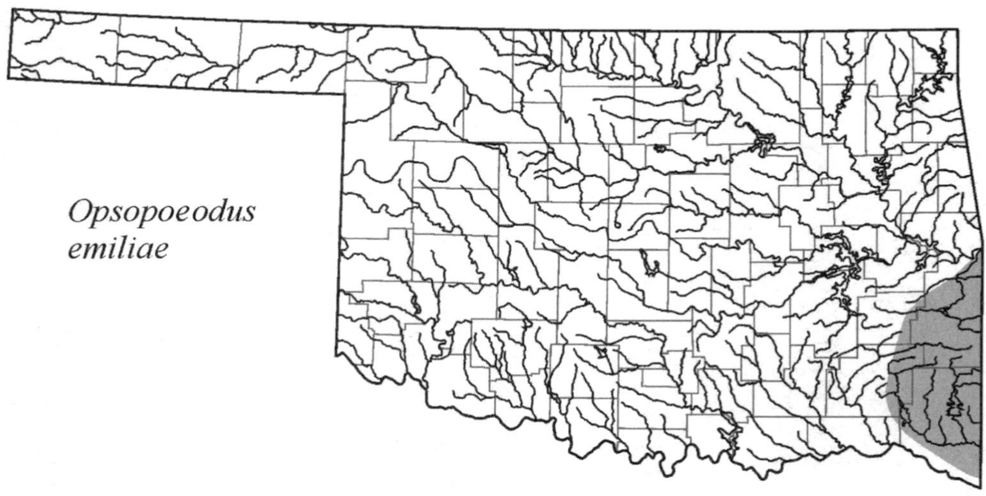

have the membranes of the four anterior and three posterior dorsal rays dusky, with membranes in the middle of the fin whitish to clear. Usually less than 2 inches long.

Distribution:

From the lower Great Lakes drainage through the Mississippi River system to the Gulf of Mexico. On the Gulf Coast from Florida to Mexico. Occurs in the southeastern corner of Oklahoma.

Habitat and Biology:

The pugnose minnow is an inhabitant of clear lowland streams and lakes and of upland streams with relatively low gradients. Often it occurs over sandy areas with vegetation present. Food consists largely of insect larvae, filamentous algae, and microcrustaceans taken from the surface or midwater areas. Based on tuberculate males collected, spawning probably occurs in late spring or early summer in Oklahoma. Eggs are deposited on the underside of a flat object by the female, and the eggs and nest are subsequently defended by the male (Johnston and Page 1988).

Note:

We retain the genus *Opsopoeodus* as distinct based on a combination of characters, including 9 dorsal rays, 5-5 pharyngeal teeth, vertical mouth, specialized *Pimephales*-like reproductive behavior, and diploid chromosome count of 50. See Etnier and Starnes (1993) for a complete discussion of this taxonomic problem.

SUCKERMOUTH MINNOW

Phenacobius mirabilis (Girard)

Description:

A fairly large, terete minnow with a long snout (about twice the eye diameter) and inferior mouth. It is most similar to *Campostoma* spp. but can be distinguished by using the following characteristics: the entire upper lip and lateral portions of the lower lip in the suckermouth minnow are fleshy and expanded, and there is no cartilaginous ridge inside the lower lip; a dusky band about the width of the eye extends from the head to the end of the caudal peduncle, with a conspicuous horizontally elongate black blotch forming its terminus; the dorsal fin origin is anterior to the point of pelvic insertion (posterior to it in *Campostoma*); and the number of lateral-line scales is usually less than 50 (usually more than 50 in *Campostoma*). There are 8 dorsal and pelvic rays and usually 7 anal rays. The peritoneum is silvery, and the gut is short. Color is olivaceous above and whitish below. Silvery sides may obscure the lateral band in life. Maximum size is about 4 inches. (See also color plate.)

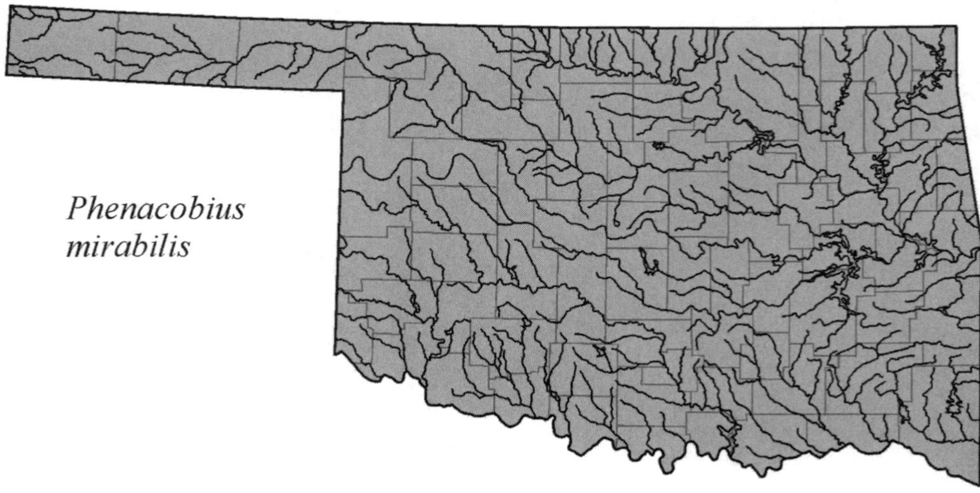

Distribution:

The Mississippi basin from Wyoming and Colorado to Ohio and south to Louisiana and Texas. Occurs throughout Oklahoma.

Habitat and Biology:

The suckermouth minnow is an inhabitant of riffles, particularly those with gravel or sand and gravel bottoms, in streams with moderate gradients. It is less sensitive to turbidity than many riffle fishes and is therefore distributed much more widely than most. It feeds mainly on aquatic insect larvae, especially midges, and detritus and plant matter. Breeding occurs from late March or April when water temperatures reach 57.2–77 degrees F and continues through June or July.

SOUTHERN REDBELLY DACE
Phoxinus erythrogaster (Rafinesque)

Description:

A conspicuously marked, terete little minnow with a relatively small head, large eye, and small, terminal mouth. It is distinguishable from all other minnows in Oklahoma by the following combination of features: very small scales with more than 65 in the lateral line and its continuation scale row (the lateral line is incomplete); intestine long with several loops; black peritoneum; pharyngeal teeth 5-5; two dark bands extending the length of the body, a broad one just below the midline of the side, and a narrower one a short distance above it; dorsal, anal, and pelvic rays usually 8. Color is olivaceous above, with scattered dark spots above the upper black stripe, and creamy between the stripes and below the lower stripe. Breeding fish have bright red undersides and bright yellow fins. Usually up to 2.5 inches long. (See also color plate.)

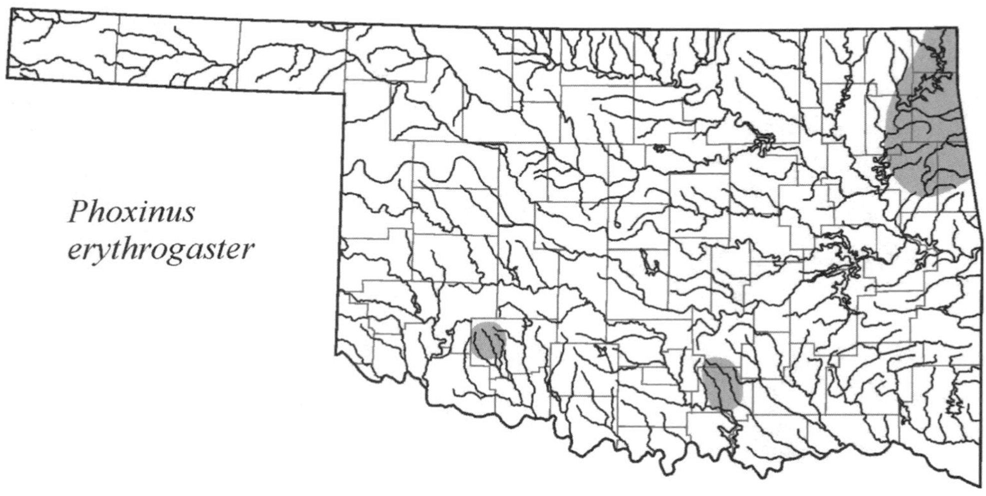

Distribution:

The central Mississippi Valley from Wisconsin to Pennsylvania south to Oklahoma and northern Alabama. Found in spring creeks of the Ozark, Arbuckle, and Wichita mountains and at times in the Blue River main stream.

Habitat and Biology:

This species is occasionally abundant in the clear, spring-fed creeks of the areas noted. It is most abundant in quiet pools but can sometimes be found in fairly large schools in faster flowing water. This species feeds largely on diatoms, algae, and organic detritus scraped or picked from the bottom and occasionally on aquatic insects. Breeding occurs mostly in April and May in swift, shallow riffle areas. One or two males press against the female using their breeding tubercles to help hold themselves against her. In areas where they occur with *Nocomis* spp., they often utilize chub nests for spawning, as do several other cyprinid species. Consequently several hybrid combinations may be produced accidentally.

Bluntnose minnow

Pimephales notatus (Rafinesque)

Description:

A fairly slim, nearly terete minnow with a blunt, rounded snout that overhangs the inferior mouth and with the predorsal scales conspicuously smaller and more crowded than adjacent scales on the sides. The top of the head is flat, the mouth is small, and the intestine is fairly long and coiled with at least one transverse loop. This species differs from other *Pimephales* in combining a slim body (fewer than 32 scale rows around the body) with a black peritoneum and an upper lip of uniform width. Color is bluish or olivaceous above, creamy white below. A narrow but typically conspicuous dusky band extends from the snout to the end of the caudal peduncle, terminating in a more intensely black spot at the caudal base. Most specimens 3 inches or smaller.

Distribution:

Mississippi Valley and Great Lakes drainages from the Dakotas to New England and south to Georgia, Louisiana, and Oklahoma. Found in about the eastern half of Oklahoma.

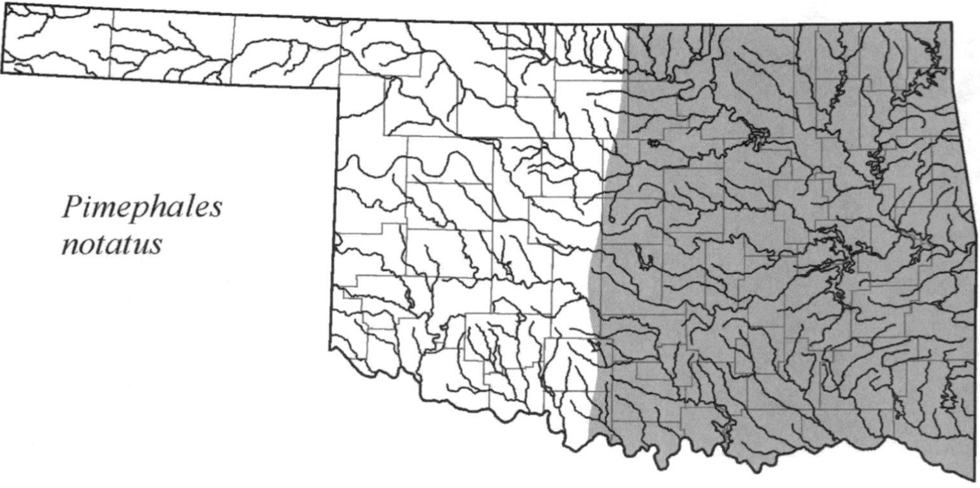

Habitat and Biology:

Although bluntnose minnows are adaptable enough to be found in a wide variety of stream and lake habitats and are resistant to pollution and siltation, they seem to do best in relatively clear streams with gravel bottoms in the eastern part of the state. They typically are found in the slower pools and backwaters, where they feed on plankton, algae, and insect larvae. They spawn from May to August, under stones, in tin cans, and under boards or other objects, when highly territorial males excavate nests on the stream bottom. Breeding tubercles and the swollen dorsal pad are used to clean the roof of the nest after it has been excavated by sweeping movements of the body and caudal fin. The female deposits her adhesive eggs on the undersides of such solid objects, and the male defends the eggs until they hatch. Sometimes multiple females may spawn in the same nest. The bluntnose minnow is an excellent bait fish but is not raised in ponds as easily as the fathead minnow and is therefore not used as commonly.

FATHEAD MINNOW
Pimephales promelas Rafinesque

Description:

The fathead minnow has a terminal mouth, small head, moderately deep, robust body, and typically incomplete lateral line. It resembles other *Pimephales* in having small, crowded scales in front of the dorsal fin. There are usually more than 39 scale rows around the body, the intestine is long and generally coiled more than once, and the peritoneum is black. Color is olivaceous above, grading to tan or creamy white below. A dark lateral band is sometimes present but rarely conspicuous. A faint, dark blotch may be present at the anterior base of the dorsal fin. Breeding males become very dark with the head a more intense black except for light-colored cheeks. Two lighter bands appear on the body, one just behind the head, the other extending down from the anterior base of the dorsal fin. Three rows of breeding tubercles are present on the snout. Maximum size is about 3 inches.

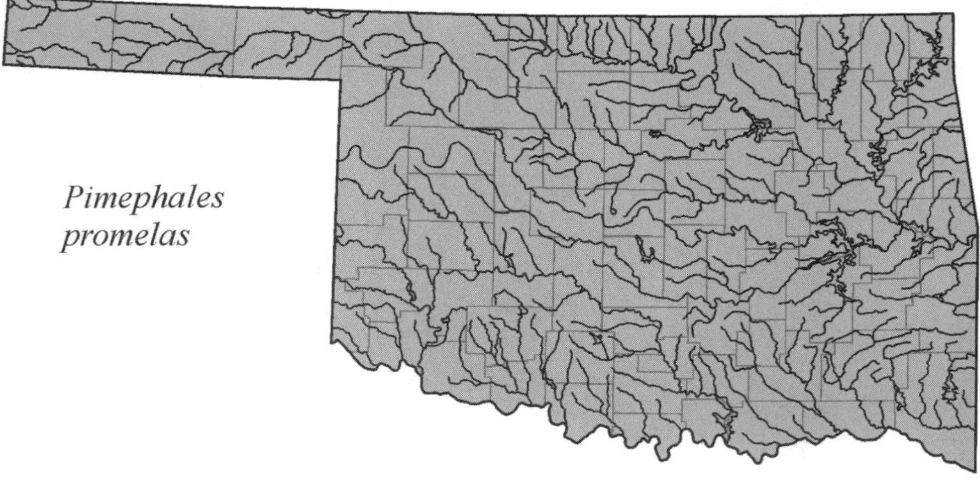

Distribution:

Throughout central North America west of the Appalachians and south into Mexico. Not native in coastal drainages of the southeastern United States but widely introduced throughout the country. May be found anywhere in Oklahoma, often as a result of bait fish release.

Habitat and Biology:

The fathead is a most adaptable minnow and is found in both clear and turbid waters throughout the state. Although it seems to occur most commonly in small streams, it thrives in small ponds and is cultured extensively as a bait fish. Breeding occurs from April until July in the typical *Pimephales* fashion. Males darken and develop numerous tubercles and a thick, fatty dorsal pad in front of the dorsal fin. This pad secretes mucus, which is deposited on the spawning surface during contact by the male. Eggs are deposited on the underside of hard objects in the stream, and males fertilize them and defend the nest site until hatching. This species is considered a fractional spawner (Gale and Buynak 1982) with intervals between spawning sessions ranging from 2 to 16 days. The fathead feeds on plankton, insect larvae, and some plant materials. It is one of Oklahoma's most common bait species.

Slim minnow

Pimephales tenellus (Girard)

Description:

The slim minnow is aptly named—it is the smallest and slimmest member of the genus *Pimephales* and is characterized by a terete body (28–30 scale rows around the body), complete lateral line, silvery peritoneum, and relatively short intestine. Perhaps the most useful feature for identification is the narrow black line that marks the end of the caudal peduncle and extends above and below the distinct basicaudal spot. Color is olivaceous above and creamy white below. A dark lateral band extends the length of the body to the caudal spot. A small dark spot is present near the anterior edge of the dorsal fin. Breeding males become much darker and acquire nearly black heads and dark and white markings on the fins. This is the smallest of the *Pimephales*, rarely exceeding 2 inches in length. (See also color plate.)

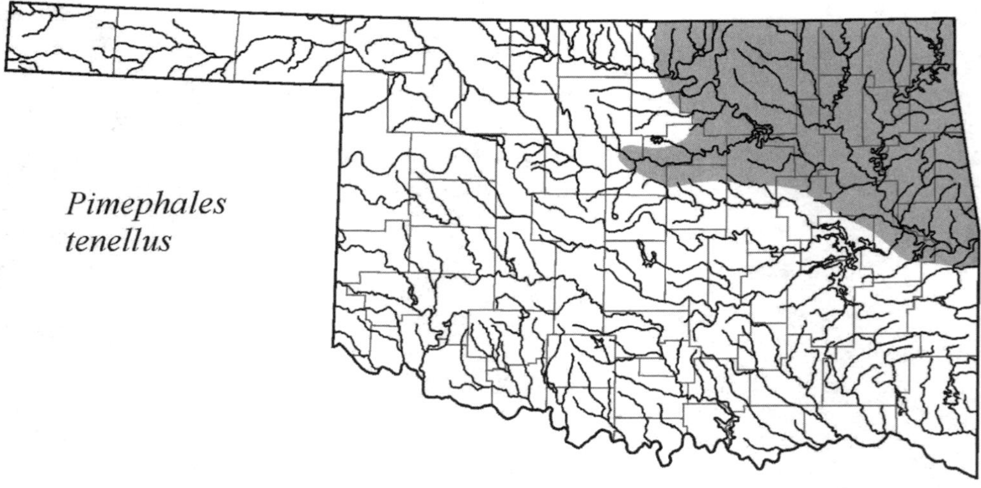

Distribution:

Found mainly in the Ozarks and adjacent regions of Oklahoma, Kansas, Missouri, and Arkansas. In Oklahoma it is most common in the northeastern part of the state, but records exist from the Red River drainage as far west as Jackson County.

Habitat and Biology:

We have rarely encountered this species except in small, clear, gravel-bottomed streams in the Arkansas basin. It seems to prefer streams with relatively high gradient, and unlike other species in the genus it can often be found actively swimming in the current. Breeding occurs in late spring and early summer, but breeding activities have not yet been documented. Food habits also are unknown, but this species probably feeds on small aquatic invertebrates.

BULLHEAD MINNOW

Pimephales vigilax (Baird and Girard)

Description:

In body shape and stoutness, the bullhead minnow falls between *P. notatus* and *P. promelas*. It resembles *P. tenellus* in having a large, conspicuous black spot at the anterior edge of the dorsal fin and in having a large wedge-shaped caudal spot, but it has no narrow dark lines extending above and below the spot. Furthermore, the bullhead minnow rarely exhibits a lateral stripe, and the edges of the dorsal scales are usually not heavily pigmented as in *P. tenellus*. Color is light olive to tan above with lighter or silvery sides. A black dash is present on the upper lip at each corner of the mouth. As in other *Pimephales*, breeding males become dark on the body and fins and the head becomes nearly black. About 9 breeding tubercles also develop on the snout (in 2 rows). May reach 3 inches or more in length.

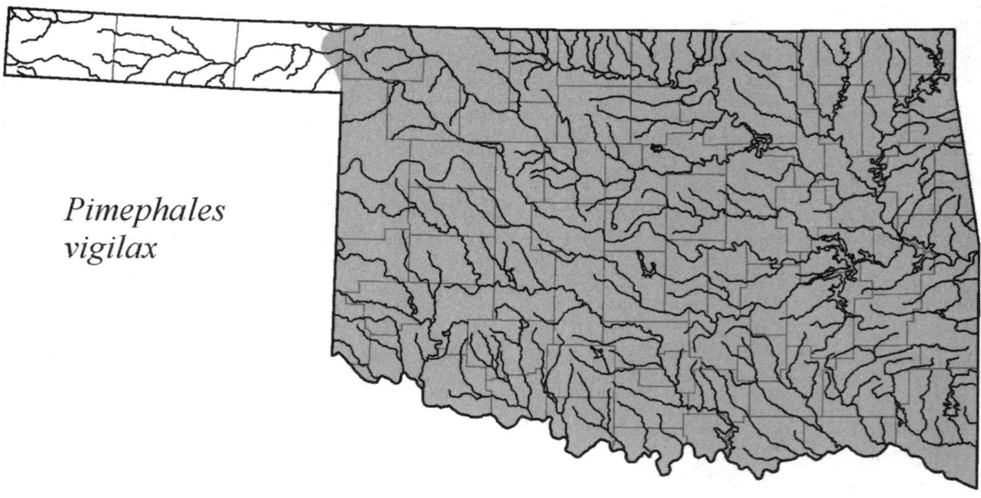

Distribution:

In the Mississippi basin from Minnesota and Pennsylvania in the north reaching southward west of the Appalachians to Georgia and Texas. Found throughout most of Oklahoma.

Habitat and Biology:

The bullhead minnow lives mainly in pools and backwaters of sluggish streams and rivers. It is quite resistant to turbidity and typically is found over sand or silt bottoms. Omnivorous in feeding habits, this minnow seems to eat a variety of plant and animal food. Breeding, similar to that of other *Pimephales*, occurs in late spring and early summer, and territorial males guard clutches of eggs attached to the undersides of stones and other solid objects on the bottom. Eggs hatch in four to six days at water temperatures of 79–83 degrees F.

FLATHEAD CHUB
Platygobio gracilis (Richardson)

Description:

A large, terete, barbeled chub with a flat head, small eye, and pointed snout. At a maximum size of about 12 inches, it is one of the largest cyprinids in the state. The mouth is quite large and subterminal, and the barbels are of moderate size. Scales are moderate in size, about 44–50 in the lateral line, and the fins are fairly high and falcate. The pectoral fin is extremely long, extending beyond the dorsal origin. Pharyngeal teeth 2, 4-4, 2. Basically a silvery fish, the flathead is tan to brown above and has some pigment on the lower lobe of the caudal fin.

Distribution:

From the Mackenzie River in Canada south through the plains states to Arkansas and New Mexico. Known from the South Canadian River and western portions of the Cimarron River in Oklahoma.

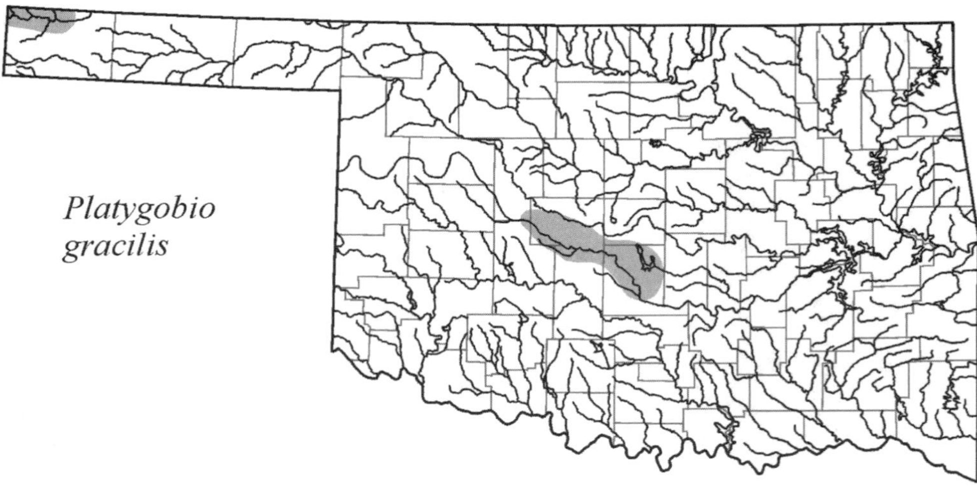

Habitat and Biology:

A fairly distinct form (*P. gracilis gulonella*) is found in the southern part of the species range including Oklahoma. Olund and Cross (1961) suggested that this form, while found principally in the main streams of large, turbid rivers, is less highly specialized for living in the strong currents of these rivers than is the northern form (*P. g. gracilis*). Davis and Miller (1967) found that sensory systems are not highly specialized in this form and suggest that it is an opportunistic feeder utilizing whatever senses are required to find food. Food consists mainly of aquatic and terrestrial insects and crustaceans. Although the breeding behavior is unknown, the flathead chub spawns from mid-July to mid-August.

Creek Chub
Semotilus atromaculatus (Mitchill)

Description:

A large, terete minnow with a large head and mouth and a conspicuous brown or black spot at the anterior base of the dorsal fin. The creek chub's most distinctive characteristic is a small, flaplike barbel (sometimes inconspicuous or absent) located in the groove above the upper lip, just anterior to the end of the upper jaw (see fig. 10 in key). Scales are small, 52–63 in the lateral line, with anterior body scales smaller than posterior ones. Pharyngeal tooth formula is 2, 5-4, 2, and there are 8 rays in the dorsal, anal, and pelvic fins. Color is grayish to olivaceous above grading to whitish below. A dark lateral stripe may run the length of the sides, terminating in a dark spot at the caudal base. Breeding males have well-developed tubercles on the snout and head and smaller tubercles on the pectoral rays. May reach 12 inches in length.

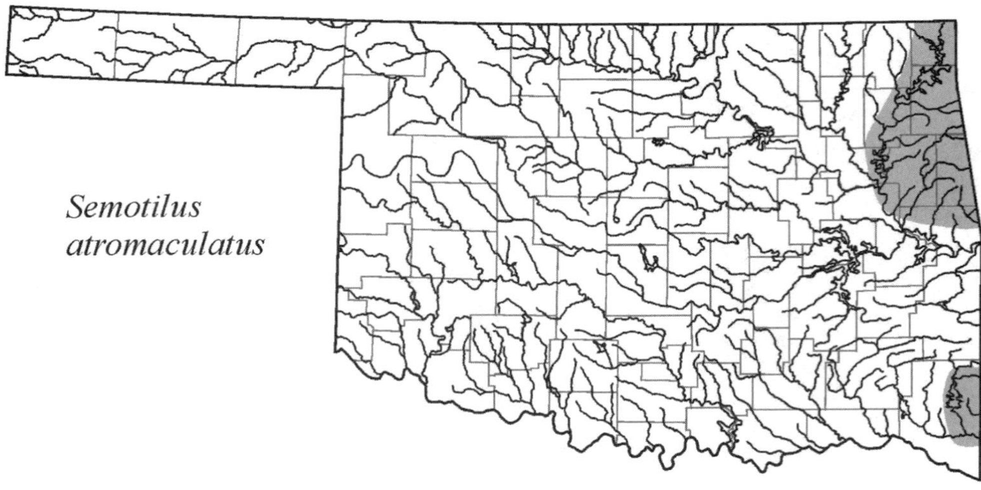

Distribution:

Occurs throughout most of the United States east of the Rockies but is absent from much of the Southwest. In Oklahoma it is most common in the northeast, with some records from tributaries of the Red River and the Mountain Fork River.

Habitat and Biology:

This species is well named, since it clearly prefers small, gravel-bottomed, clear-water creeks. It feeds mainly on small aquatic animals, including fish, crayfish, worms, and a variety of other bottom invertebrates. Breeding occurs in early spring (usually April), when the males build conspicuous nests, each consisting of a small pit with a pile of stones upstream. After females spawn in the nest, continual male digging in the downstream portion and depositing of pebbles in the upstream portion often produces a long gravel ridge upstream from the nest pit. Deep within the ridge, of course, are the developing eggs that were deposited in successive spawnings. Large creek chub provide much sport on light tackle, and while they are not usually eaten, Trautman (1957, p. 318) quoted Kirtland, who considered them excellent pan fish.

SUCKERS

FAMILY CATOSTOMIDAE

Key

1a. Dorsal fin long, with 24–50 rays; air bladder divided into 2 chambers. . . 2

1b. Dorsal fin shorter, with fewer than 20 rays; air bladder divided into 2 or 3 chambers 8

2a. Head abruptly more slender than body; lateral-line scales tiny, 50 or more; eye in rear portion of head; body long and slender; lips papillose . . . . *Cycleptus elongatus*

2b. Head not abruptly slenderized; lateral-line scales fewer than 50; eye near middle of head; body deep and compressed; lips weakly plicate 3

3a. Subopercle semicircular (see fig. 20); mouth large, nearly terminal; body coloration grayish or blackish; arrangement of intestines linear or S-shaped (*Ictiobus*). 4

3b. Subopercle subtriangular (see fig. 20); mouth small, inferior; body coloration silvery; arrangement of intestines circular or coiled (*Carpiodes*) 6

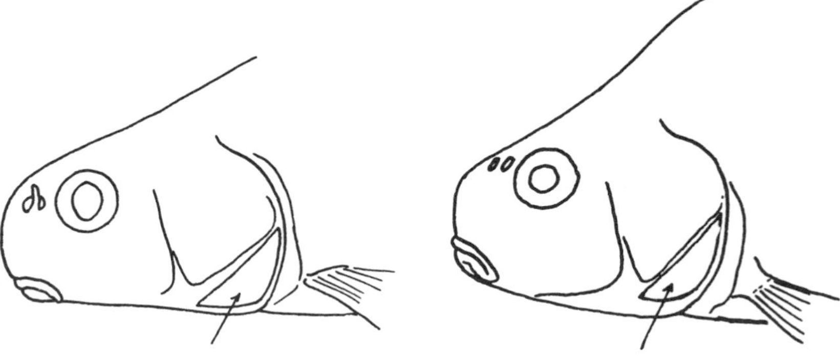

FIGURE 20. Diagrammatic views of the heads of *Carpiodes carpio (left)* and *Ictiobus cyprinellus (right)*, showing the subtriangular shape of the subopercle bone of *Carpiodes* (see arrow) and the semicircular shape of the subopercle bone of *Ictiobus*.

4a. Upper lip on level with lower margin of eye; upper jaw length about as long as snout length; lower pharyngeal arch thin and teeth weak; body and anal fin light-colored; mouth large and oblique . . . . *Ictiobus cyprinellus*

4b. Upper lip far below margin of eye; upper jaw length shorter than snout length; lower pharyngeal arch thick and teeth strong; body dark or light and anal fin dark; mouth small and ventral or horizontal 5

5a. Body depth 2.2 to 2.8 into standard length; back elevated and sharpened; eye large, about equal to snout length; mouth small and inferior . . . . *Ictiobus bubalus*

5b. Body depth 2.6 to 3.2 into standard length (except in young smaller than 80 mm); back less elevated and sharpened; eye smaller, not equal to snout length; mouth large and less inferior. . . . . *Ictiobus niger*

6a. Middle of lower jaw without a small, nipplelike knob at tip; lateral-line scales 37–41; dorsal fin rays 27 or more; upper jaw not extending backward beyond front of eye . . . . *Carpiodes cyprinus*

6b. Middle of upper jaw with a small, nipplelike knob at tip (not well developed in young); lateral-line scales 33–37; dorsal fin rays 27 or fewer; upper jaw extending backward beyond front of eye 7

7a. Distance from tip of snout to anterior nostril contained more than 3 times in postorbital length; longest dorsal ray shorter than dorsal base; body more slender and less compressed . . . . *Carpiodes carpio*

7b. Distance from tip of snout to anterior nostril contained fewer than 3 times in postorbital length; longest dorsal ray nearly as long as or longer than dorsal base (somewhat shorter in adults); body deep and markedly compressed . . . . *Carpiodes velifer*

8a. Lateral line absent or poorly developed in adult 9

8b. Lateral line present, well developed in adult 11

9a. Lateral line poorly developed; mouth inferior, horizontal; each scale usually with black spot, forming parallel lines on sides; lips plicate . . . . *Minytrema melanops*

9b. Lateral line absent; mouth slightly oblique; scales without dark spots, but vertical bars, blotched or plain in adults; in young, body with horizontal lateral stripe 10

10a. Lateral scale rows 34–37; dorsal fin rays 11 or 12; head pointed; eye diameter into snout length twice or less . . . . *Erimyzon sucetta*

10b. Lateral scale rows 39–43; dorsal fin rays 9 or 10 (occasionally 11); head bluntly rounded; eye diameter into snout length more than twice . . . . *Erimyzon oblongus*

11a. Lips papillose (see fig. 21); air bladder with 2 chambers 12

11b. Lips plicate (see fig. 21); air bladder with 3 chambers (*Moxostoma*) . . . 13

12a. Lateral-line scales more than 50; head between eyes convex; eye near middle of head in adults; no conspicuous markings . . . . *Catostomus commersonii*

12b. Lateral-line scales fewer than 50; head between eyes broad and strongly concave; eye far behind middle of head in adult; body with conspicuous oblique bars. . . . . *Hypentelium nigricans*

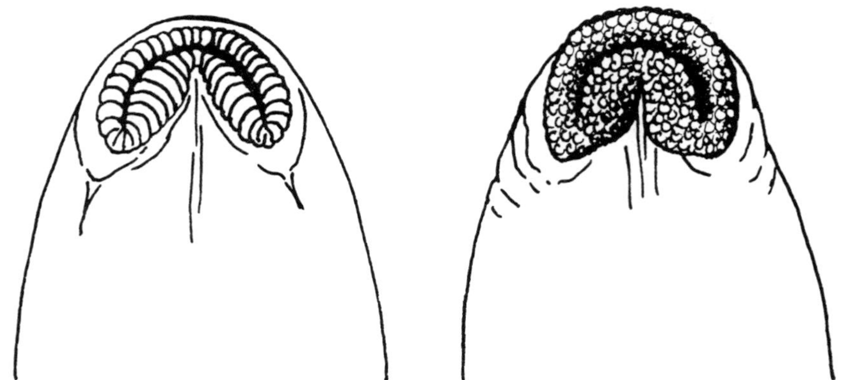

FIGURE 21. Characteristics of the lips of some suckers: at left the fleshy, plicate lips of *Erimyzon oblongus*; at right the fleshy, papillose lips of *Hypentelium nigricans*.

13a. Lower pharyngeal arch very heavy, subtriangular in cross section; teeth on lower half of arch greatly enlarged and molarlike; last caudal scales in posterior margins outlined with melanophores forming sharp points extending backward on the fin rays; mouth slightly oblique; lips very thick . . . . *Moxostoma carinatum*

13b. Lower pharyngeal arch only moderately heavy, in cross section distinctly narrower than it is high; teeth on lower half of arch not enlarged but compressed to form a comblike series; last caudal scales without conspicuous dentate black borders; mouth inferior, horizontal; lips thinner . . . 14

14a. Posterior margin of lower lip presenting almost a straight line; lower lip broad with plicae divided by grooves forming papillae; center of upper lip thickened, plicae obliterated at least in half-grown individuals and adults; head short; caudal fin bright red . . . . *Moxostoma macrolepidotum*

14b. Posterior margin of lower lip not presenting a straight line, but a rather distinct V-shaped angle; lower lip relatively narrow and plicate, plicae not divided by transverse grooves forming papillae; head longer; caudal fin not red 15

15a. Lateral-line scales 44–48; pelvic rays usually 10 (often 9, rarely 8 or 11); body more slender; caudal peduncle long and slender, its least depth contained about 1.5 times in its length; eye smaller; tubercles of nuptial males present on anal and caudal fins but not on snout . . . . *Moxostoma duquesnei*

15b. Lateral-line scales 39–45; pelvic rays usually 9 (often 8, rarely 7 or 10); body stouter; caudal peduncle shorter, its least depth more than ⅔ its length; eye larger; tubercles of nuptial males present on snout and anal and caudal fins . . . . *Moxostoma erythrurum*

River carpsucker

Carpiodes carpio (Rafinesque)

Description:

A large, deep-bodied, compressed fish with a scarcely curved ventral outline and a highly arched back. The dorsal fin is long and falcate, but the anterior dorsal rays are shorter than the length of the dorsal fin base. The mouth is inferior and small, the lower lip is thin, and a small knob is present on the tip of the lower jaw. The snout may be rounded or pointed and its length is about equal to or greater than the eye diameter. Bronze to greenish above with sides silvery to white. Fins colorless or tinted with pink or orange. Usually less than 20 inches long. State record: 7 lb., 11 oz., 24 in., from a Canadian County pond.

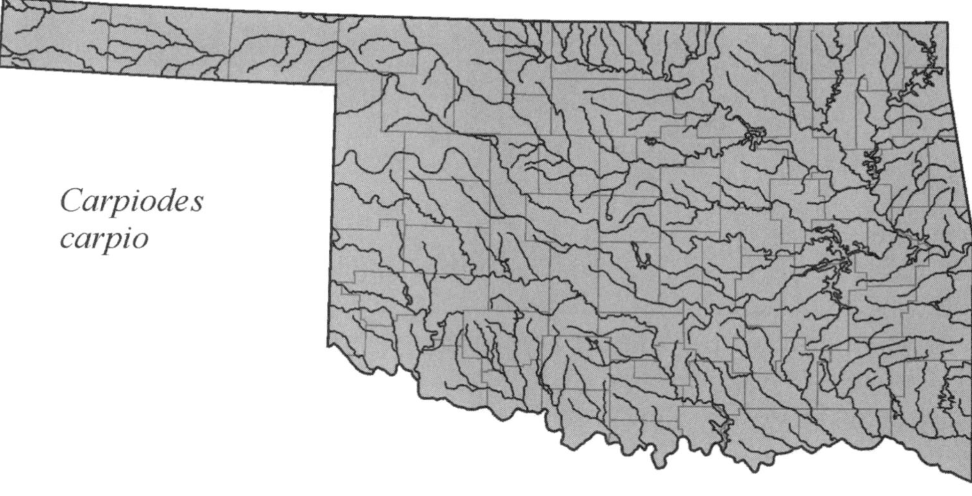

Distribution:

The Great Plains from Montana to Texas through the Mississippi drainage northeast to Ohio. Occurs throughout Oklahoma.

Habitat and Biology:

The river carpsucker is probably the most ubiquitous of our suckers, occurring in streams and rivers of every size and physical-chemical constitution. It also seems to be doing well in many reservoirs. All three species of carpsucker are essentially bottom feeders, ingesting a wide variety of small planktonic plants and animals found in quiet pools and backwaters of most rivers and streams and at the mouths of streams entering lakes. This species seems more tolerant of turbid waters than are other carpsuckers. It has fine gill rakers and a highly efficient gustatory system in the buccal epithelium. Breeding occurs in late May and June. In Oklahoma, spawning was observed after dark over a firm sand bottom in shallow water (1–3 feet deep). Adhesive eggs were broadcast loose in the water over the substrate (Walberg and Nelson 1966).

QUILLBACK

Carpiodes cyprinus (Lesueur)

Description:

A large, compressed, deep-bodied fish with a long dorsal with high anterior rays. The caudal is large and falcate. The inferior mouth is positioned far forward on the head, the upper jaw not extending past the front of the eye. This species can be distinguished from the other two carpsuckers by the larger scales (36–42 in the lateral line) and from the river carpsucker by the elongate anterior dorsal rays, as long as the dorsal base. It differs from the highfin carpsucker in lacking a nipplelike mandibular knob at the tip of the lower jaw. The head is small and the body is more slender than in the other

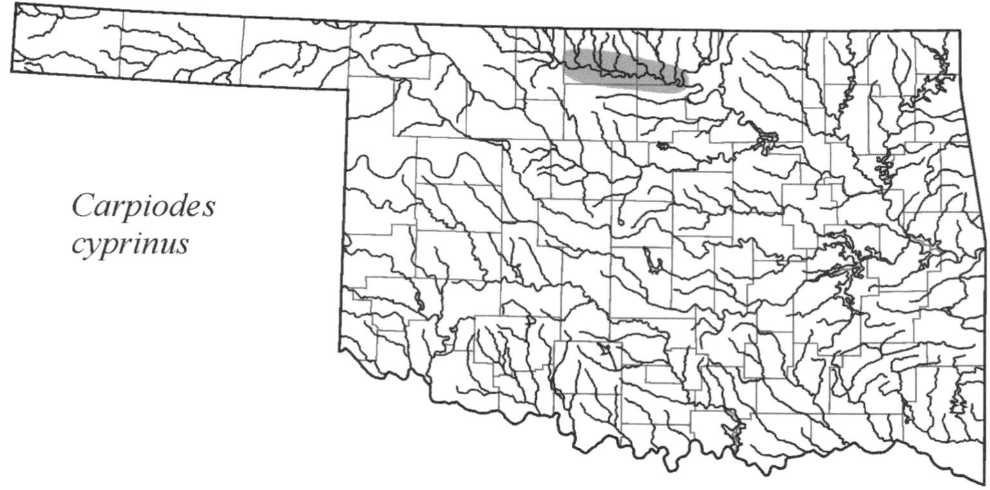

carpsuckers, and the snout is blunter. Dorsal rays 22–30, anal rays 7 or 8. Color is silvery olivaceous to greenish above, grading to yellow or white below. Grows to 8 pounds and 24 inches, though most Oklahoma specimens are considerably smaller.

Distribution:

From southern Canada through the Great Lakes to the St. Lawrence River system, south to Florida and west to the Great Plains states. Relatively rare in Oklahoma, but has been collected in the Salt Fork of the Arkansas River and possibly some of the eastern reservoirs. The carpsuckers exhibit considerable variation, with spurious distribution records not uncommon.

Habitat and Biology:

Pflieger (1997) found quillbacks in fairly clear, highly productive streams with large permanent pools and stable gravel bottoms. They feed on a variety of organic detritus, insect larvae, and plants. Miller and Evans (1965) found that the carpsuckers have extremely well-developed gustatory reception in the buccal cavity and on the gill rakers, suggesting that they ingest bottom materials indiscriminately, then sort out food matter using the pharyngeal pad and gill rakers. Spawning apparently occurs in the lower ends of deep riffles in Missouri (Pflieger 1997), probably in May or early summer. Little is known of their biology in Oklahoma waters.

HIGHFIN CARPSUCKER
Carpiodes velifer (Rafinesque)

Description:

Generally similar to the river carpsucker but with a much deeper body and longer dorsal rays. Body depth is contained 2.5 times or less in the standard length of adults (vs. 2.7 or more in *C. carpio*). The longest dorsal ray is as long as or longer than the length of the dorsal fin base. The snout is blunter than in *C. carpio* and shorter than the eye diameter. Most of the fin ray and scale counts overlap with those of *C. carpio*, so morphometric characters are the only useful ones for adults. Young less than 3 or 4 inches long are almost impossible to distinguish. *Carpiodes velifer* rarely exceeds 12 inches in length or 1.5 pounds in weight.

Distribution:

The greater Mississippi basin from Nebraska and Ohio in the north to Oklahoma and western Florida in the south. Found sporadically in the

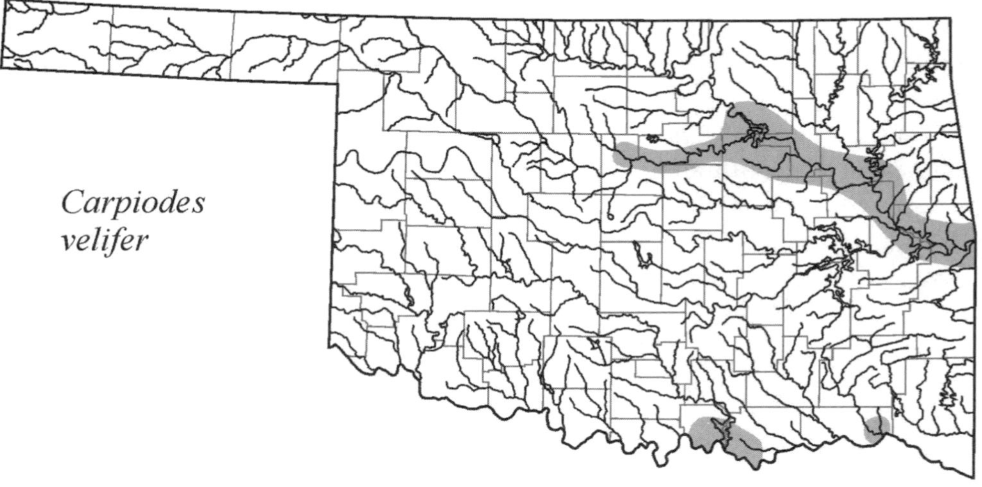

clearer rivers tributary to the Arkansas and Red rivers (Poteau, Illinois, and others).

Habitat and Biology:

Little is known of the biology of this smallest and infrequently encountered carpsucker. Distribution in Oklahoma suggests that it prefers clearer streams and rivers, but some observations elsewhere contradict this. The overall morphology of the sensory systems and the locomotor organization are quite similar to those of the river carpsucker, suggesting similar feeding habits and a predilection for remaining out of the current. Perhaps this species is simply more sensitive to high turbidity than is the river carpsucker. In Oklahoma, spawning probably occurs in late spring or early summer. Adults in breeding condition were collected in Missouri in late July over deep, gravelly riffles (Pflieger 1997) and in Ohio spawning occurred from late June through September (Woodward and Wissing 1976).

WHITE SUCKER

Catostomus commersoni (Lacépède)

Description:

A slim-bodied, terete fish with gracefully curved dorsal outline. The head is small and convex between the eyes, which in lateral view are near the middle of the head. Lips are large, fleshy, and papillose. The lateral line has 55–58 scales, dorsal fin 11–13 rays, and anal fin 7–8 rays. Color is grayish above with lighter sides and whitish belly. Young have 3 dark spots on each side. Breeding males develop a reddish band on the side and large breeding tubercles on the rays of the anal fin and lower caudal fin and on scales on the underside of the caudal peduncle. Tiny tubercles also are present on the head, body, and other fins. Length is usually less than 18 inches.

Distribution:

Throughout North America east of the Rocky Mountains from Hudson Bay in the north to Oklahoma, northern Mississippi, and northern Georgia in the south. Found in the clear Ozark streams of northeastern Oklahoma.

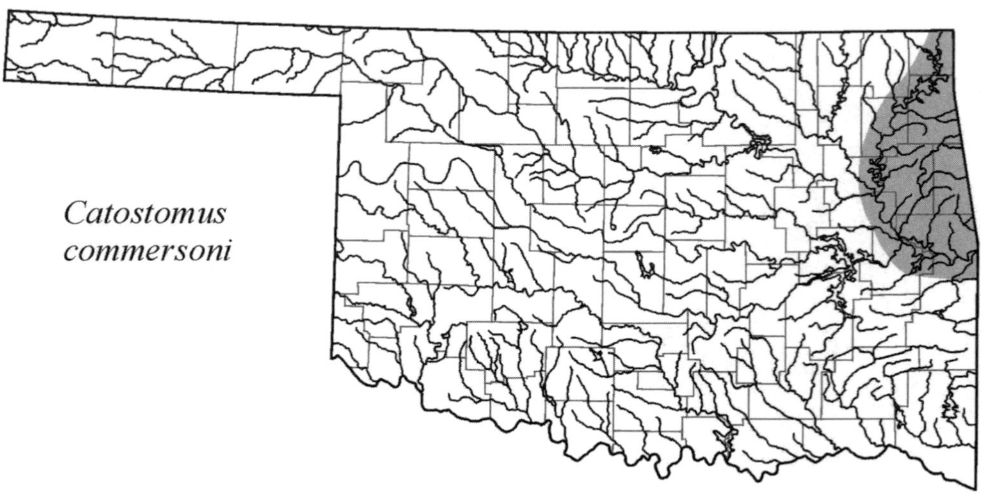

Habitat and Biology:

The white sucker is an extremely successful inhabitant of clear northern rivers and streams; in Oklahoma it is at the southern edge of its range. Although Trautman (1957) found the white sucker to be a most hardy species, tolerant of siltation and other pollutants, its distribution in Oklahoma and Kansas suggests that some combination of factors in Great Plains streams inhibits maintenance of the species through most of the region. Since it spawns in spring (March–April), over clean gravel bottoms, the critical factor may be absence of appropriate spawning habitat throughout most of the state. Although individuals can grow to a large size (over 20 inches) in the north, we have rarely seen specimens much over 12 inches long in Oklahoma. They feed on a variety of terrestrial and immature aquatic insects. A desirable food fish on its spawning runs in northern waters, the white sucker is of little significance to Oklahoma anglers.

Blue sucker

Cycleptus elongatus (Lesueur)

Description:

This beautifully streamlined fish is the only slim-bodied sucker possessing a long dorsal fin with as many as 28–35 rays. The head is small and slender, and the mouth is inferior with large papillose lips. The dorsal fin is falcate and the pectoral moderately so (16–17 rays). Scales are tiny, with 50 or more in the lateral line. The eye is small. Sides and dorsum are blue-black to dark gray, males becoming more intensely colored during the breeding season. In juveniles, the lower lobe of the caudal fin is darkened. May reach 40 inches and 15 pounds in some areas; most local specimens below 30 inches in length. (See also color plate.)

Distribution:

Limited to the larger rivers and impoundments of the lower Mississippi basin from Minnesota and Ohio south to Texas. Found in Lake Texoma and Grand Lake and their tailwaters and in the Poteau River below Lake Wister.

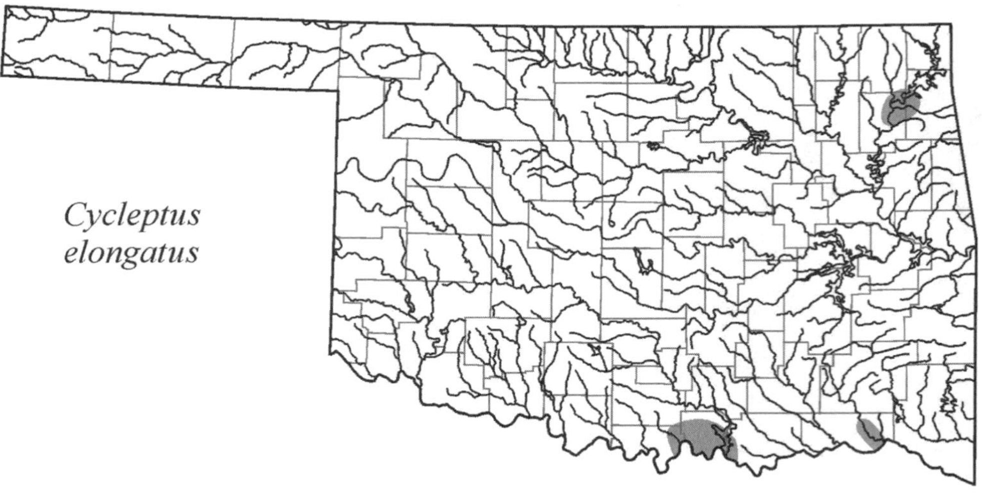

Habitat and Biology:

The blue sucker is morphologically well-adapted for life on the bottom in deep, fast-moving rivers and also lives in the channels of deep lakes. Spawning occurs in late April or May. In Kansas individuals move in May into deep riffle areas with cobble and bedrock substrates to spawn. Blue suckers are rather rare throughout much of their range, with sporadic records indicating brief periods of local abundance, especially when adults migrate to spawning habitats. Foods consist of aquatic insects, particularly caddisfly larvae and pupae, and a variety of small invertebrates (hellgrammites and fingernail clams) from the bottom. This is apparently an excellent food fish but is unlikely to be of much importance in Oklahoma, except perhaps on a local and seasonal basis.

CREEK CHUBSUCKER

Erimyzon oblongus (Mitchill)

Description:

A moderately deep-bodied sucker with relatively large fins and an oblique mouth that is less inferior than in most suckers. The distal edge of the dorsal fin is convex, in contrast to the concave edges found in most other species. The lateral line is absent, and there are about 40 lateral scale rows. Color is dark bronze above shading to golden yellow on the sides and yellowish white below. A series of 5 to 8 darker bars mark the side. In younger specimens the bars are broken into lateral blotches with dorsal saddle-bands above them. Very young individuals are minnowlike with a dark lateral band and nearly terminal mouth. Breeding males have three tubercles on each side of the snout, and their anal fins become more falcate. Maximum size is 9 inches, although most adults are 4–7 inches in length.

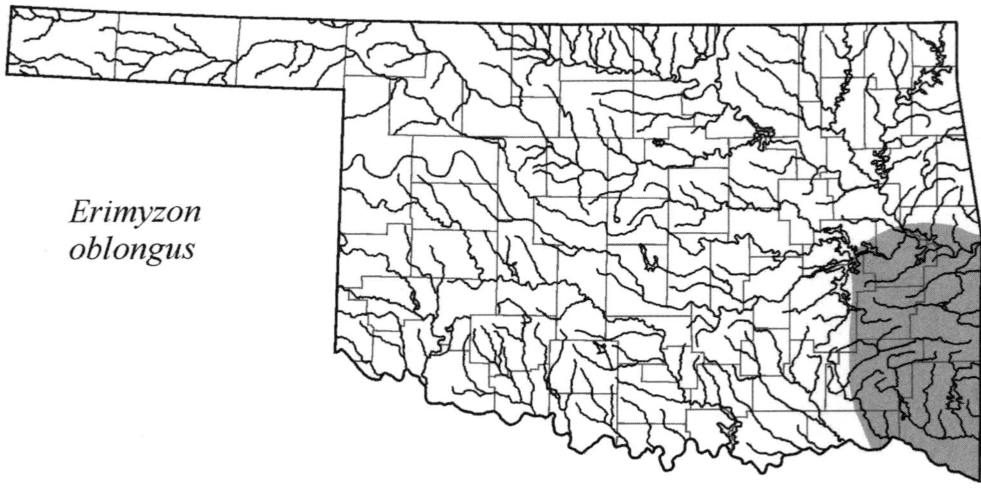

Distribution:

Eastern United States from New Brunswick to Florida and west to Texas and Iowa. Common in eastern and southeastern Oklahoma from Cherokee County southward in the Arkansas and Red River systems.

Habitat and Biology:

The creek chubsucker is well adapted for life in relatively small creeks and rivers of moderate gradient. Usually found in sandy or gravel-bottomed streams, it is not very tolerant of heavy silt loads in the water. Adults feed on small organisms (Entomostraca, rotifers, small insects, and algae) in the detritus deposited in quiet pools and backwaters, though the nearly terminal mouth may permit some feeding above the stream bottom. W. J. Matthews (pers. comm.) has observed young of the year feeding on algae. Spawning occurs in spring. Because it rarely exceeds 6 inches in length, the chubsucker is of little interest to anglers.

Lake Chubsucker

Erimyzon sucetta (Lacepede)

Description:

A small, relatively deep-bodied fish quite similar to the creek chubsucker. The olivaceous upper body, large, expansive fins, and small head with nearly terminal, slightly oblique mouth are good characteristics for both species. Neither has lateral-line pores. The dorsal fin in *E. sucetta* is short and rounded with 10–13 rays; the anal fin has 7. Scales in lateral series usually 35–37 (vs. 40–45 in *E. oblongus*). Lower lips are plicate, forming a V-shaped angle at the rear margins. Breeding males have 3 large tubercles on each side of the snout. Anal fin is distinctly bilobed. Body olive to gold above, grading to white on the belly. Young with prominent black lateral band, which breaks into blotches and gradually disappears as the young mature. Size to 10 inches and less than a pound.

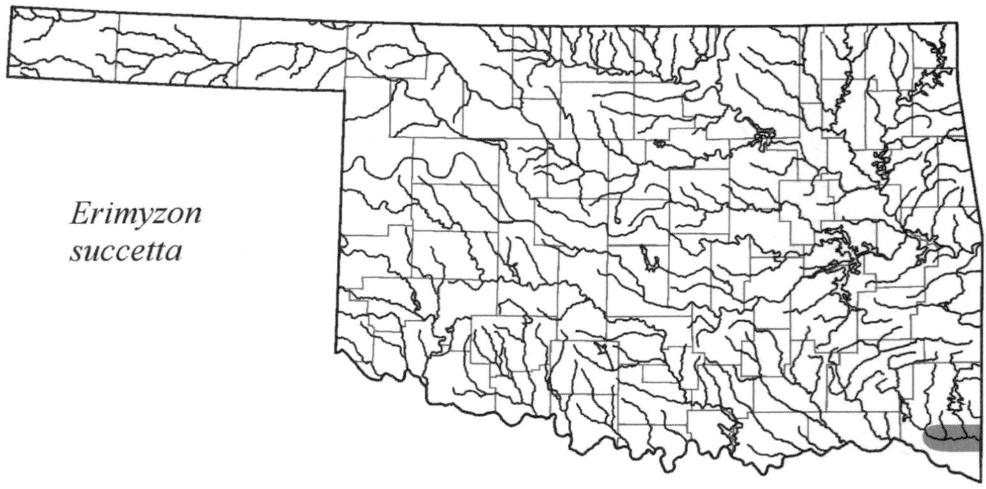

Distribution:

From the Great Lakes through the Mississippi Valley to eastern Texas and east along the coastal plain to Florida and New York. Rutherford and Echelle (1985) collected this species from four localities in the Little River system in McCurtain County and considered it widespread in the lower reaches of the drainage in Oklahoma.

Habitat and Biology:

Throughout its range, the lake chubsucker is an inhabitant of sluggish lowland streams and heavily vegetated oxbow lakes with varying clarity and substrates of mud, sand, and organic detritus. It is often found in dense vegetation around cypress trees. It feeds on *Daphnia* and other small crustaceans, insect larvae, and occasionally filamentous algae. Pflieger (1997) has reported May spawning in Missouri in ponds over submerged vegetation. The species is of no interest to anglers because of its small size.

Northern Hog Sucker

Hypentelium nigricans (Lesueur)

Description:

A large-headed, slender, terete fish with large, fleshy, papillose lips (see fig. 21 in key). The small eye is located far back on the head, which is concave between the eyes. The lateral line is well developed with fewer than 50 scales. Breeding males have tubercles on the anal, pelvic, and caudal fins. Dark bronze to olive above, sides more yellowish, and belly usually white. Body with 4–6 dark olivaceous saddles extending obliquely down the sides. Generally less than 15 inches long. (See also color plate.)

Distribution:

Eastern United States excluding southern Georgia, Florida, and Alabama. Found in the Ozark upland region of northeastern Oklahoma.

Habitat and Biology:

Hog suckers are adapted for feeding on small aquatic insects and snails living on and under stones in streams with clear gravel riffles. Individuals are

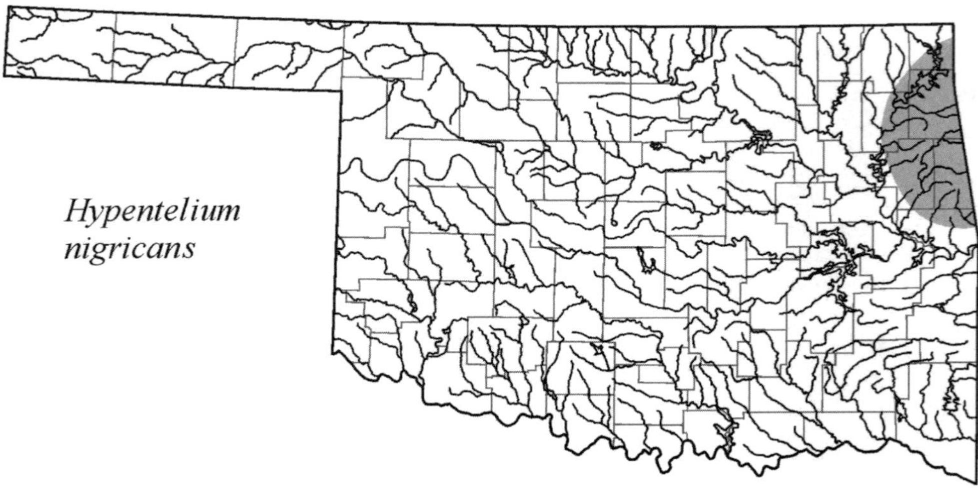

most often encountered in moderately deep riffles and raceways or the pools below these. Their mottled coloration makes them almost impossible to see when at rest on the bottom, and many a wader has been startled to see the bottom suddenly burst into action just inches away as a foot-long fish darts off. Hog suckers breed in April in relatively shallow riffle areas that are cleaned of deposited silt by the movements of fish over the substrate. During winter they may retire to quieter, deeper waters downstream. They seem to be intolerant of pollution and silty water, however, which probably limits them to the headwaters of most stream systems.

Smallmouth Buffalo

Ictiobus bubalus (Rafinesque)

Description:

A deep-bodied, highly compressed fish with a straight ventral contour and highly arched back. The dorsal fin is long (26–31 rays) and falcate. The mouth is small, nearly horizontal, and subterminal, with the anterior tip of the upper lip far below the lower edge of the eye. The lips are plicate. The eye is moderately large, its diameter equal to or longer than the upper jaw. Fewer than 60 gill rakers are present on the first gill arch. Dark golden to olive in color above, silvery with a golden cast on the sides, and whitish ventrally. Up to 25 inches long and 15 pounds in weight, though most are much smaller. State record: 34 lb., 8 oz., 39½ in., from Lake Texoma.

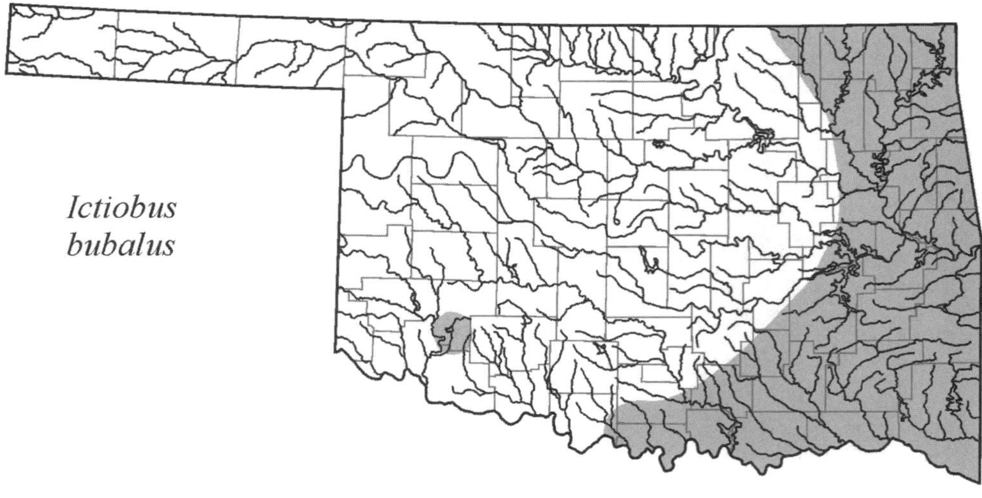

Distribution:

The Mississippi basin from the Gulf states north to Ohio and the Dakotas. Found in roughly the eastern half of Oklahoma.

Habitat and Biology:

The smallmouth buffalo seems to be an inhabitant of deeper, somewhat less turbid waters than the bigmouth and seems to be more common than the latter in some areas. It does not grow as large as the bigmouth, and can sometimes be found in smaller streams. Adults are mainly opportunistic bottom feeders, eating a variety of small aquatic benthic (bottom-living) animals and some attached algae. Young feed on microcrustaceans. The smallmouth spawns from April through June in quiet, shallow backwaters or flooded riparian areas during periods of high water. It is a valuable commercial species in Oklahoma and a good table fish.

Bigmouth Buffalo

Ictiobus cyprinellus (Valenciennes)

Description:

A large, heavy, deep-bodied sucker with an oblique, nearly terminal mouth and long and falcate dorsal fin (23–30 rays). The head is large, the eye small (smaller than snout or upper jaw), and the tip of the upper lip is about even with the lower edge of the eye. There are more than 60 gill rakers on the first gill arch. The lips are thin and the mouth is large, with upper jaw and snout about equal in length. Brownish or olive above becoming more yellowish on the sides and whitish below. Maximum size 80 pounds, more usually up to 3 feet and 30–40 pounds. State record: 59 lb., 15 oz., 43¾ in., from Greenleaf Lake.

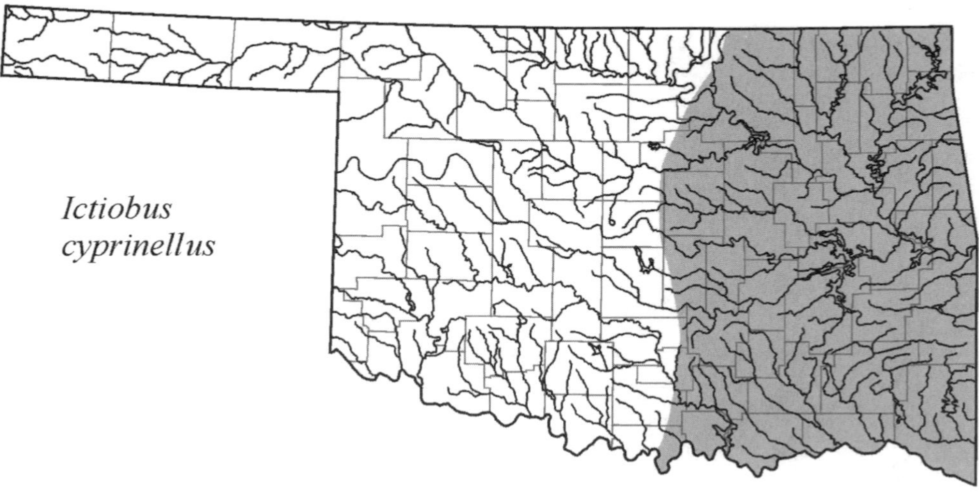

Distribution:

The greater Mississippi Valley from Minnesota and Ohio in the north to Alabama and Texas in the south. Found throughout the eastern half of Oklahoma.

Habitat and Biology:

The bigmouth is a fairly common inhabitant of deep pool regions of larger rivers and lakes in eastern Oklahoma. It seems to prefer quieter waters than the other two species of buffalo, and this contributes to its success as a lake inhabitant. It is more tolerant of higher turbidity than the other two *Ictiobus* species. Foods are a variety of small organisms, primarily Cladocera and cyclopoid copepods, midge larvae, and a considerable amount of algae and diatoms. The large terminal mouth and many fine gill rakers permit this species to operate as a filter feeder, utilizing the swarms of plankton found in quiet areas of larger rivers and lakes. The extent to which this sort of behavior prevails over the bottom-grubbing activities of a mud feeder is not known. Spawning seems to be triggered by floodwaters in April and May, when water temperatures reach 60–65 degrees F. Spawning is accomplished as several males accompany a single female with eggs scattered in shallow, weedy areas.

Black buffalo

Ictiobus niger (Rafinesque)

Description:

A large, heavy-bodied fish similar to the other buffalos but not as deep-bodied and with a less arched dorsal contour. The mouth is subterminal and slightly oblique, and its anterior tip is far below the lower edge of the eye. The eye is small, its diameter fitting more than twice into snout length. Anterior dorsal rays are shorter than in *I. bubalus* (1.3–1.8 in head length vs. 0.8–1.4 for *bubalus*). Fewer than 60 gill rakers in the first arch. Blue-gray to dark brown above, light brown laterally, and yellowish white below. Young less than 12 inches long are difficult to distinguish from *I. bubalus*. To 35 lb. State record: 7 lb., 7 oz., from the lower Illinois River.

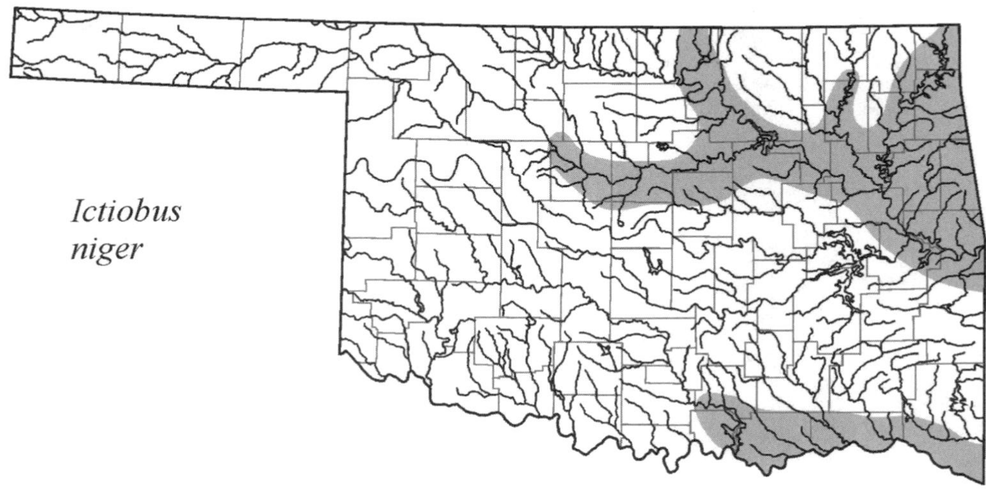

Distribution:

Mississippi basin from Nebraska to Ohio and south to Alabama and Texas. Located throughout most of eastern and central Oklahoma.

Habitat and Biology:

Like the smallmouth buffalo, this species seems to favor flowing waters more than does the bigmouth. Its feeding habits and activities also seem to be more similar to those of the smallmouth, and Moore (1968) pointed out that *I. bubalus* and *I. niger* hybridize in some of the impoundments in our region, producing offspring impossible to identify. Adults feed mainly on benthic macroinvertebrates with molluscs and aquatic insects being most important. Minckley and colleagues (1970) reported that the introduced clam *Corbicula* was the principal food with small amounts of algae, diatoms, and crustaceans also eaten. Along the margin of a flooded swamp in the Mississippi River, Yeager (1936) documented an April spawning in which several hundred adults participated. This buffalo seems to be somewhat less abundant than the other two forms, though it may be locally common.

Spotted sucker

Minytrema melanops (Rafinesque)

Description:

A slim-bodied, nearly terete sucker similar in body shape to the redhorses. It is distinctive, however, in having the lateral line incomplete or absent, a two-chambered air bladder, and a conspicuous black spot at the base of each scale. These spots form longitudinal stripes on the sides, which are clearly evident except in young fish. The lips are fairly thin and plicate. The head may be covered with well-developed tubercles in breeding males. Color is olivaceous to dusky brown above with the sides bronze to silvery. Adults about 12 inches long, 1 pound in weight.

Distribution:

Throughout most of the eastern United States west to eastern portions of the plains states and north to Minnesota. Found in about the eastern half of Oklahoma.

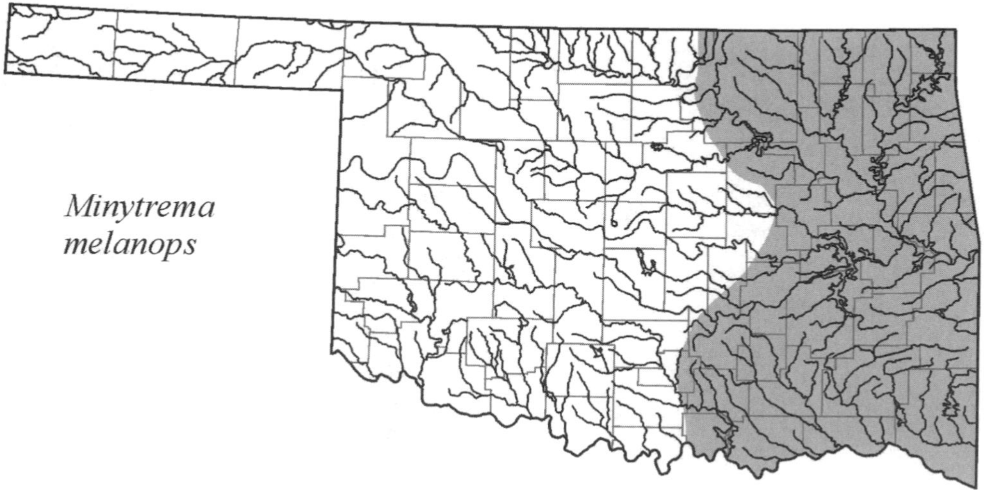

Habitat and Biology:

Apparently best adapted for life in the slow-moving waters of creeks and small rivers, this species is more tolerant of silt (especially if only intermittently high) than are suckers like *Hypentelium* but less tolerant than carpsuckers. It may be locally quite common but is not widely abundant because it seems to require hard-bottomed streams (Cross 1967). Spotted suckers also do well in some eastern Oklahoma lakes. They feed on detritus and zooplankton, with bottom organisms such as molluscs and other invertebrates also consumed. Cross (1967) suggested that spotted suckers spawn in summer in Kansas, but tuberculate specimens were captured in early June in Ohio (Trautman 1957). In Alabama, spawning occurs as early as mid-March, and McSwain and Gennings (1972) detailed spawning behavior similar to that of other suckers: males establish loosely defined territories, which they defend against intruding males. Spawning is accomplished when a female and two males settle to the bottom, one on either side of her and all facing upstream. After vigorous vibrations, eggs and milt are shed. The adhesive, demersal eggs drift downstream below the spawning sites. In Oklahoma, spotted suckers measured at the end of their first through fifth growth seasons reached total lengths of 155, 287, 338, 410, and 440 mm; they were sexually mature at three years. Not a significant food or game fish in Oklahoma.

River redhorse

Moxostoma carinatum (Cope)

Description:

A fairly typical heavy-bodied redhorse similar to *M. erythrurum* but distinctive in having a red tail and a well-developed pharyngeal arch with large molariform teeth. The mouth is large and lips are plicate. The head is moderate or small in juveniles but large in adults (4.3 or less into SL). Pelvic fins usually number 9, lateral line scales 43–47, and the air bladder has 3 chambers. Color is brownish or olive above, yellowish laterally, and whitish below. Dorsal, caudal, and anal fins are reddish; paired fins are orange. Bases of scales show dark crescents. Mostly 15 inches or less in length, 1.5 pounds in weight.

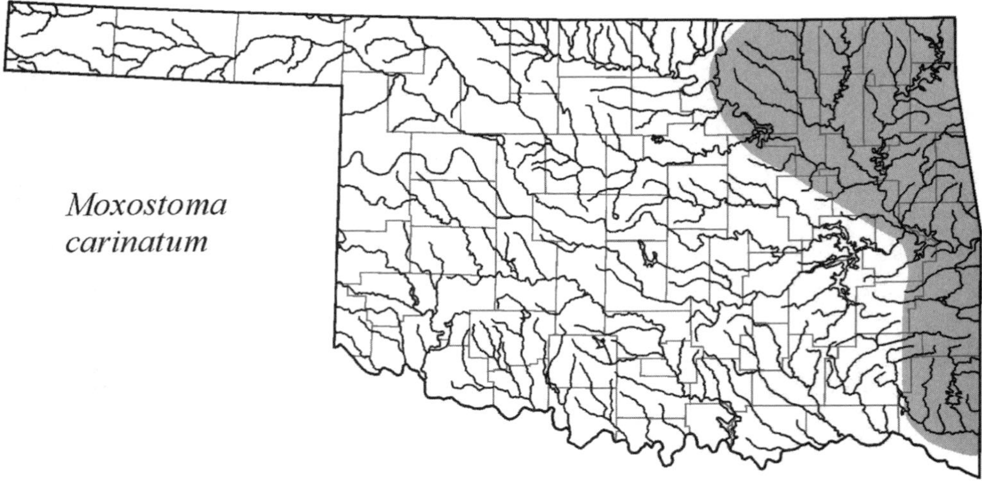

Distribution:

Mississippi Valley from Iowa to Minnesota and Pennsylvania in the north, including the southern Great Lakes and Ottawa and St. Lawrence drainages, south to western Florida, Louisiana, and Oklahoma. Found mainly in the eastern rivers of Oklahoma, such as the Illinois, Poteau, and Mountain Fork.

Habitat and Biology:

Little is known of the biology of this species in Oklahoma. The strong molariform teeth of the pharyngeal arch are used to crush the shells of the small bivalve molluscs that make up much of this redhorse's diet; benthic insect larvae are also consumed, often in major amounts. The species is known to prefer the main channels of clear rivers, apparently being sensitive to pollution. We have captured specimens below the low-water dam at Beaver's Bend State Park in late April that gave indications of being on a spring spawning run. Hackney and colleagues (1970) detailed spawning during mid-April at water temperatures of 71–76 degrees F in Alabama. Males move into runs where they maintain territories prior to spawning (Ross 2001). R. E. Jenkins (pers. comm.) reports that males do not actually excavate nests or show well-developed courtship behavior. Spawning fish create depressions ("nests") in the gravel by substrate agitation; however, males do not seem to guard these depressions, although they do seem to maintain their position in the stream. This redhorse is considered a tasty food fish.

Black redhorse

Moxostoma duquesnei (Lesueur)

Description:

A relatively slender-bodied redhorse without distinct dark crescents on the scale bases and with gray or olive dorsal and caudal fins (rather than red). Body depth usually goes into standard length more than four times. The mouth is of moderate size and lips are plicate, the bulbous snout of adults (not juveniles) overhanging the upper lip. The air bladder is 3-chambered, pelvic rays usually number 10, and there are 44–48 lateral-line scales. Color is grayish, olive, or brownish above, with the sides more silvery and the belly white. Breeding males develop large tubercles on the anal and caudal fins. Generally less than 15 inches long and 1 pound in weight.

Distribution:

The Mississippi and Great Lakes drainages from the St. Lawrence River west to Iowa, south to Oklahoma, and across the northern portions of the Gulf states to Georgia. Located in the clearer tributaries of the Arkansas and Red rivers in the eastern half of Oklahoma.

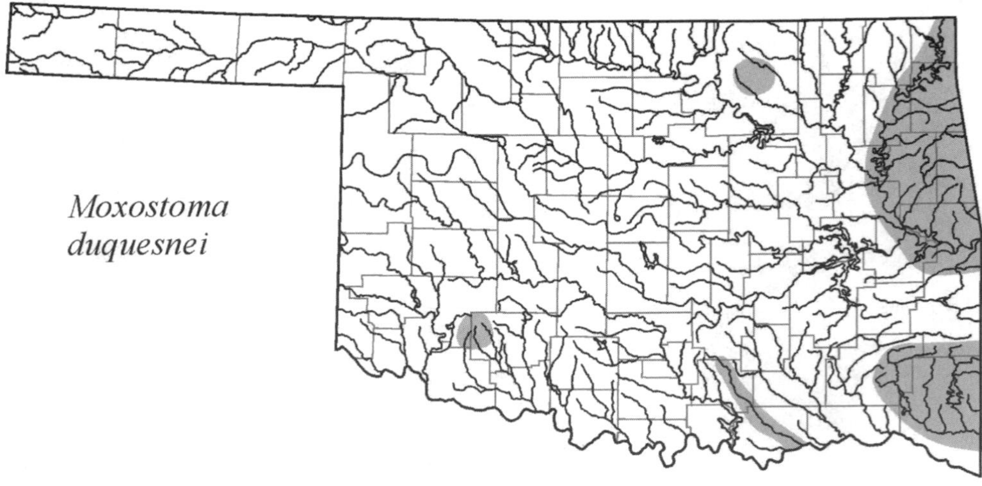

Habitat and Biology:

The black redhorse feeds mainly on insect larvae, crustaceans, and aquatic worms in medium-sized clear streams. This sucker prefers short, rocky pools with current. It is not very tolerant of turbidity and pollutants but seems to have a wider tolerance than some other redhorses. In Missouri it is known to spawn in April over shoals; males occasionally jostle each other for individual space. Spawning occurs with a male on each side of the ripe female. This species is probably also an April spawner in Oklahoma. It is often described as an excellent food fish.

Golden Redhorse

Moxostoma erythrurum (Rafinesque)

Description:

Similar to the black redhorse in having grayish or olive dorsal and caudal fins but differs in having a slightly stouter body, larger lateral-line scales (39–45) and usually 9 pelvic rays. The lips are fairly large and plicate with the posterior edges of the lips forming a distinct angle. Color is olivaceous above, usually brassy on the sides, and white below. Paired fins usually have an orange cast. Breeding males have well-developed tubercles on the snout, anal fin, and caudal fin. Usually less than 15 inches long. (See also color plate.)

Distribution:

Lower Great Lakes drainage through the Mississippi basin to Oklahoma and Mississippi in the south. This is the common redhorse of eastern and southern Oklahoma.

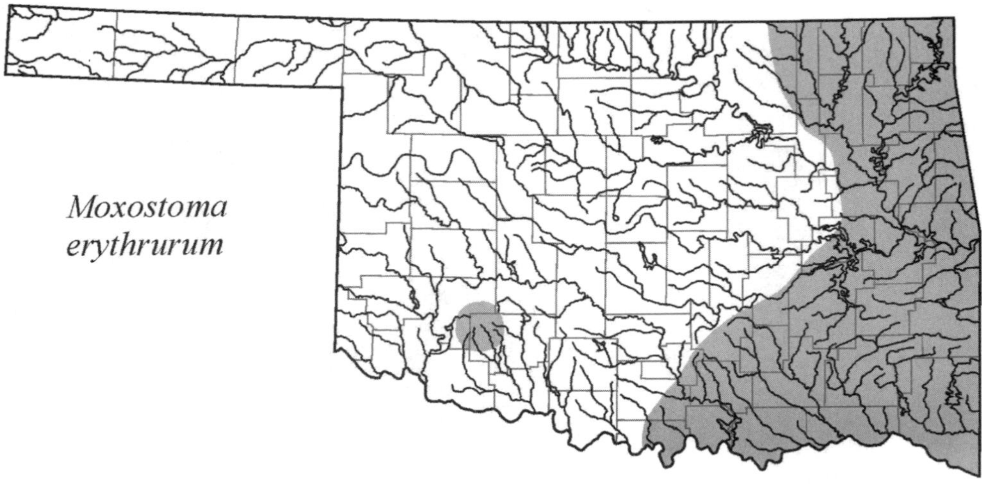

Habitat and Biology:

The golden redhorse is a fairly common inhabitant of many hard-bottomed rivers and streams in eastern Oklahoma. It seems to prefer pools and slower raceways of moderate-sized streams. It feeds on insect larvae and small molluscs and spawns in shallow riffles during April and May, in groups of from three to five up to 100 (R. E. Jenkins, pers. com.). This is probably the most abundant of Oklahoma redhorses where it occurs and perhaps has the widest distribution because it is more tolerant of silt turbidity than are most other *Moxostoma*. A tasty food fish, it could be utilized more than it is in many parts of the state.

SHORTHEAD REDHORSE

Moxostoma macrolepidotum (Lesueur)

Description:

Like most redhorses, this species has a rather slender body, reddish or red-orange tail, and dark crescents at the bases of scales on the sides. The mouth is small, but the lips are well developed with the posterior edge of the lower lip forming a straight line or very obtuse angle. There is a pealike thickening at the "tip" of the upper lip (adults have a knob over the medial ¼ or ⅓ of the upper lip). The head is short (more than 4 into SL), and the pharyngeal teeth are very thin. Air bladder 3-chambered, pelvic rays 9, and lateral-line scales 39–46. Color is olive yellow above with golden to silvery sides and white below. All fins are yellow to reddish with the anal and caudal usually brightest. Some adults reach 20 or 25 inches, but most are 15 inches or less.

Distribution:

From central Canada east to the St. Lawrence region, south through the Great Lakes and much of the Mississippi basin, with the southernmost

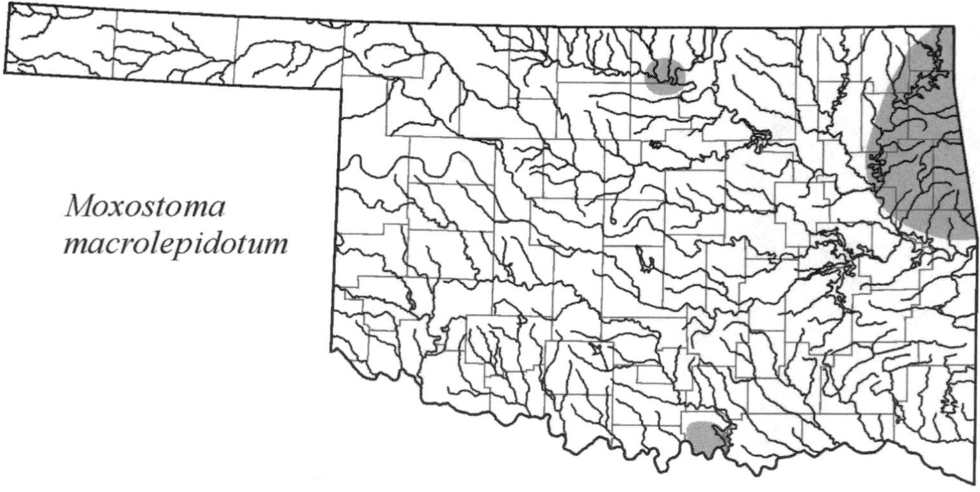

records in Oklahoma. Found in about the northeastern third of Oklahoma; one record from the Red River drainage.

Habitat and Biology:

Usually found in clear, gravel-bottomed large streams and rivers, often in riffle areas, where it feeds mainly on insect larvae and other bottom invertebrates. The shorthead redhorse is probably quite sensitive to siltation and pollution and is encountered in numbers only during spawning runs in April and May. Spawning commences on gravelly riffles and raceways (Sule and Skelly 1985). In Illinois, Burr and Morris (1977) observed spawning of over 100 individuals near the edge of a sandbar on a shallow riffle during the day in mid-May. They reported no overt territoriality or aggressive displays. As groups of three to seven individuals quiver during the spawning activity, shallow troughs and circular depressions are created in the sand and gravel by apparently incidental disturbances of substrate. The flesh of these fish is quite tasty, especially in early spring.

CATFISHES

FAMILY ICTALURIDAE

Key

1a. Adipose fin free posteriorly, separate from caudal fin. 2

1b. Adipose fin adnate, continuous with the caudal fin 7

2a. Caudal fin deeply forked 3

2b. Caudal fin not forked, but emarginate or rounded 4

3a. Anal fin with curved outer margin; anal rays 24–30; back not conspicuously humped at dorsal origin; body typically with dark spots . . . . *Ictalurus punctatus*

3b. Anal fin with straight outer margin; anal rays 30–35; back conspicuously humped at dorsal origin; body without dark spots . . . *Ictalurus furcatus*

4a. Premaxillary band of teeth with backward processes; head conspicuously flattened between eyes; caudal fin with upper tip light in color . . . . *Pylodictis olivaris*

4b. Premaxillary band of teeth without backward processes; head not conspicuously flattened between eyes; caudal fin without upper tip light in color 5

5a. Anal fin long with about 25 rays; anal base length going less than 3.8 times into standard length; distal margin of caudal fin straight or slightly rounded (convex); chin barbels white . . . . *Ameiurus natalis*

5b. Anal fin shorter with 17–24 rays; anal base length going more than 3.8 times into standard length; distal margin of caudal fin slightly notched; chin barbels black 6

6a. Anal rays 17–21; body not heavily mottled; teeth on rear margin of pectoral fin spine weakly developed or absent . . . . *Ameiurus melas*

6b. Anal rays usually 21–24; body heavily mottled; teeth on rear margin of pectoral fin spine well developed . . . . *Ameiurus nebulosus*

7a. Premaxillary band of teeth with a conspicuous backward extension on each side. . . . . *Noturus flavus*

7b. Premaxillary band of teeth without a conspicuous backward extension on each side 8

8a. Pectoral fin spines with conspicuous sharp teeth on posterior margin . . . 9

8b. Pectoral fin spines without conspicuous sharp teeth on posterior margin 12

9a. Body unicolored (except for faint predorsal blotch), olive yellow or brownish; pectoral spines moderate . . . . *Noturus exilis*

9b. Body mottled or punctulate with black or brown; pectoral spines very strong with barbs recurved 10

10a. Dark bar on adipose fin extending to the margin; without midcaudal dark bar; dorsal fin with dark black blotch distally .... *Noturus miurus*

10b. Dark bar on adipose fin not extending to the margin; with midcaudal dark bar; dorsal with dusky but never dark black blotch distally 11

11a. Adipose nearly free from caudal fin, forming a free posterior flap; body color is a dull brown; caudal peduncle narrow; caudal rays 39–52, usually fewer than 49; anterior serrae of pectoral spine rather well developed .... *Noturus eleutherus*

11b. Adipose well connected with caudal fin; body color is moderately mottled; caudal peduncle moderately deep and heavy; caudal rays 50–59, usually 52–58; anterior serrae of pectoral spine poorly developed .... *Noturus placidus*

12a. Upper jaw equal to lower; median fins are uniformly colored; abdomen without scattered melanophores .... *Noturus gyrinus*

12b. Upper jaw longer than lower jaw (snout projecting beyond mouth); median fins with pigment basally; abdomen with scattered melanophores .... *Noturus nocturnus*

Black bullhead

Ameiurus melas (Rafinesque)

Description:

The bullheads are heavy-bodied catfishes with generally dark coloration and only a slightly notched caudal fin. They grow to a smaller size (12–16 inches, usually 1–2 pounds) than the blue and channel cats and tend to stunt more readily in small ponds. The black bullhead has gray chin barbels and pectoral spines without well-developed serrae (teeth). Young are black, and adults are brownish or olivaceous to black above and yellowish to white below. Membranes of the anal fin are dark with the fin rays light. The anal fin has 17–21 rays. Generally less than a pound in weight. State record: 6 lb., 13 oz., 18⅝ in., from a Jackson County pond.

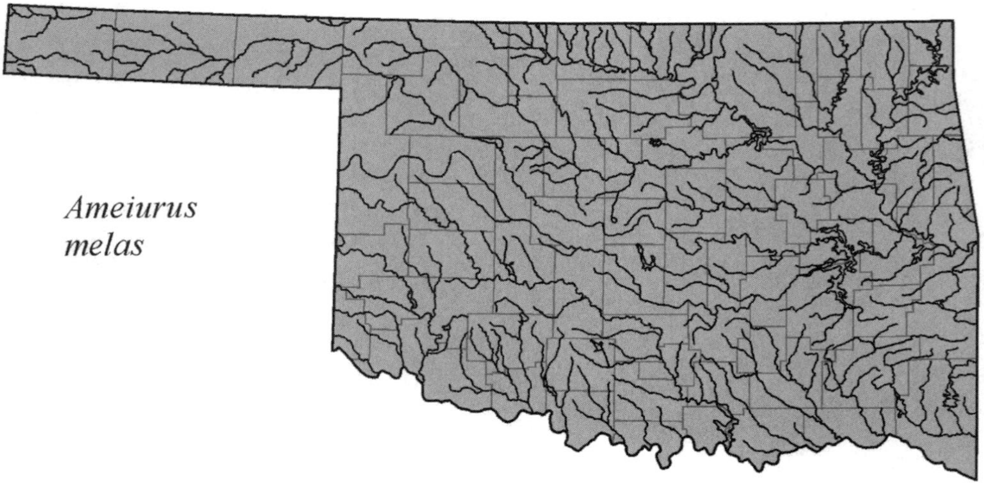

Distribution:

Most of the central United States east of the Rockies except for the eastern coastal states. Found throughout Oklahoma.

Habitat and Biology:

Black bullheads are inhabitants of quieter, soft-bottomed backwaters, oxbows, and pools of smaller streams across the state. They are also common in many lakes and ponds, especially smaller, more turbid ones. They feed on nearly any animal food they can engulf and may occasionally ingest plant material as well. Specialized for night feeding, they have well-developed tactile, gustatory, and olfactory systems and use these senses to locate decaying animals and other organic materials in the mud. They nest in cleared holes under dense vegetation or other types of cover in May or June. Reproductive behavior has been described by Wallace (1967). Nests are guarded by both parents. When the young leave the nests, they form dense schools, which may be accompanied by one or more adults.

Yellow bullhead

Ameiurus natalis (Lesueur)

Description:

A heavy-bodied catfish similar to the black bullhead. It is readily distinguished from the latter by having white chin barbels, a longer anal fin (about 26 rays), and sharp serrations on posterior edges of the pectoral spines of all but the largest specimens. The caudal fin is only slightly emarginate or rounded, as it is in other bullheads. The body is somewhat more slender than in the other two species. Young are black, adults yellowish to brown or black above with the belly white. Rarely more than 12 inches in length and one pound in weight. (See also color plate.)

Distribution:

Throughout the eastern United States west to the eastern Great Plains, including most of Oklahoma.

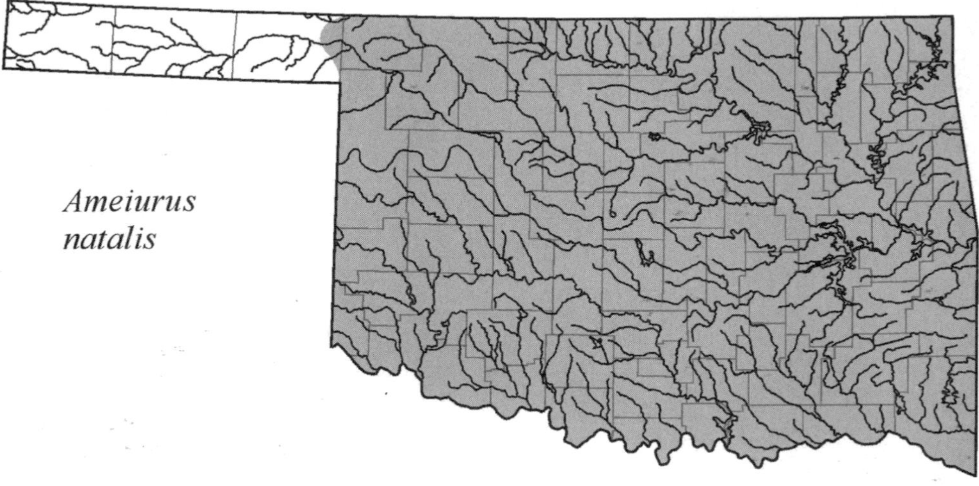

Habitat and Biology:

The yellow bullhead, while found almost everywhere in Oklahoma, may be more of a clear-water inhabitant than the black bullhead. It seems to do better in streams, usually preferring those with some aquatic vegetation, and is not as successful in soft, muddy-bottomed ponds. Feeding habits may be somewhat more specialized than in the other bullheads, with insect larvae, molluscs, crustaceans, and small fish preferred. Spawning occurs in late spring and early summer, when a saucer-shaped nest is excavated at a depth of 1.5–4 feet next to a log, tree root, or the bank (Becker 1983). Eggs, larvae, and juveniles are guarded by parents until they reach 2 inches long. Bullheads are highly edible, as are all catfish, but are eaten less than some, perhaps because of the unattractive habitats they often utilize.

Brown bullhead

Ameiurus nebulosus (Lesueur)

Description:

A stout-bodied catfish similar to the black bullhead. It can be distinguished from both other species on the basis of its anal ray count (21–24), which is intermediate between those of the other two. The chin barbels are pigmented (unlike in *A. natalis*), and the posterior edge of the pectoral spines is sharply serrate (unlike in *A. melas*). Olivaceous to dark gray above, sometimes with darker mottlings evident. The sides are typically mottled with brown to yellowish blotches, and the belly is white to yellow. Young are black. Adults usually a pound or so in weight.

Distribution:

Found from North Dakota to Arkansas in the west throughout the eastern United States north to Maine. In Oklahoma it is known only from McCurtain County.

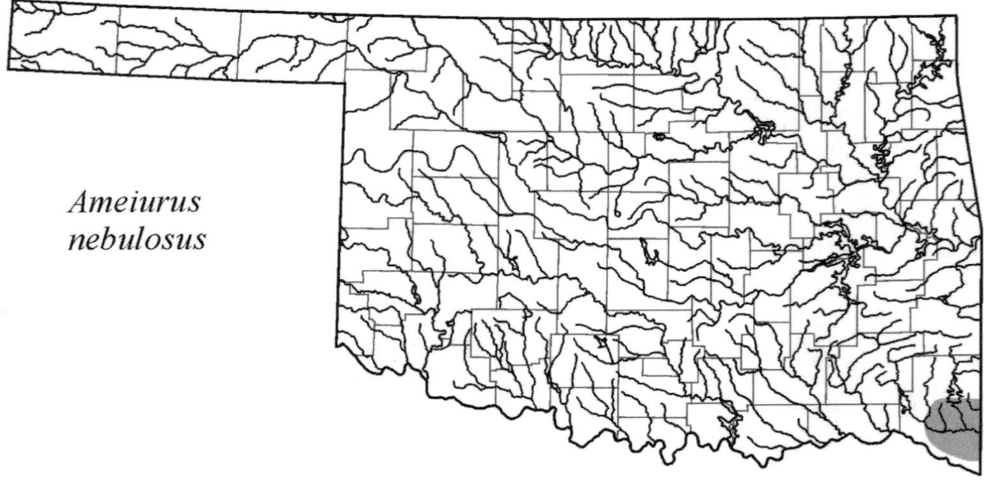

Habitat and Biology:

Accounts of the biology of this species elsewhere suggest that it is somewhat intermediate between the other two forms in most of its needs and habitat preferences, though seemingly somewhat closer to the black bullhead. It is apparently not as tolerant of silty water as the black but is less often associated with dense vegetation than the yellow. In Arkansas and Illinois, this species has been found to occur in clear, well-vegetated lakes. Nesting and breeding habits are similar to those of other bullheads, with a cleared shallow depression serving as an egg deposition site. Spawning occurs from April through June. Eggs and young are defended by both parents, and the young form the typical dense bullhead schools, which are accompanied by a parent for a few weeks. Feeding is about as universal as in the black bullhead: almost any small living or dead creature on the bottom.

Blue catfish

Ictalurus furcatus (Lesueur)

Description:

A large, heavy-bodied catfish with a deeply forked tail. The blue catfish is most similar to the channel catfish but differs in having the body conspicuously humped in front of the dorsal fin; a longer anal fin (30–35 rays) with a straight margin, and in having a relatively small eye. Color is bluish to pale gray above grading to white on the sides and belly. Breeding males are darker with the head and dorsum bluish black. There are no dark spots on the body. Up to 40 inches and 40 pounds in size and weight, but specimens larger than 20 pounds are rare. The record for this species is well over 100 pounds. Oklahoma record is 85 lb., 54¼ in. from Lake Texoma, though specimens up to 118 lb. have been caught on jug lines.

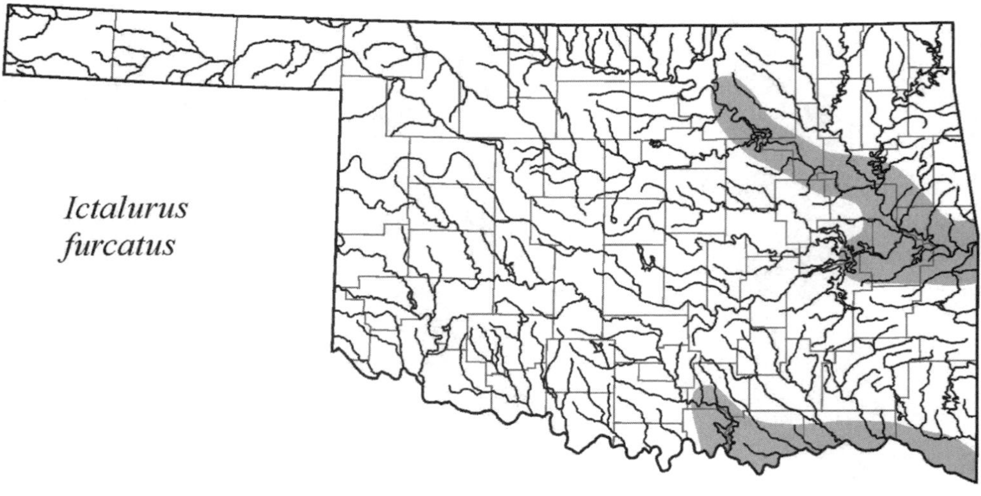

Distribution:

In the main channels of rivers in the Mississippi basin south into Mexico and introduced in large impoundments and lakes elsewhere. Native in Oklahoma in the Red River and possibly some tributaries of the lower Arkansas; planted in several large impoundments across the state.

Habitat and Biology:

Blue catfish primarily inhabit large lakes and the deeper portions of major rivers with swift waters. They are omnivorous, feeding on a variety of living or dead animals. Recently, blue catfish have been reported to feed on the introduced clam *Corbicula* and the zebra mussel. They breed in late spring and early summer, apparently in a manner similar to that of the channel catfish. This species is caught commonly in Lake Texoma and the Red and Washita rivers. A favorite of jug-line fishermen.

CHANNEL CATFISH

Ictalurus punctatus (Rafinesque)

Description:

An elongate, fairly slender catfish with a deeply forked tail. There is no distinct hump in front of the dorsal fin. The head is small, eyes are moderate and fairly dorsal in position, and the upper jaw protrudes conspicuously over the lower. The anal fin is rounded with 24–29 rays. Body color is gray-blue above grading gradually to a whitish underside. Small dark spots are randomly scattered on the sides of all but the largest specimens. Breeding males may develop blue-black heads and darker color dorsally. Adults up to 30 inches and 15 pounds, occasionally larger. State record: 30 lb., 39½ in., from the Washita River. (See also color plate.)

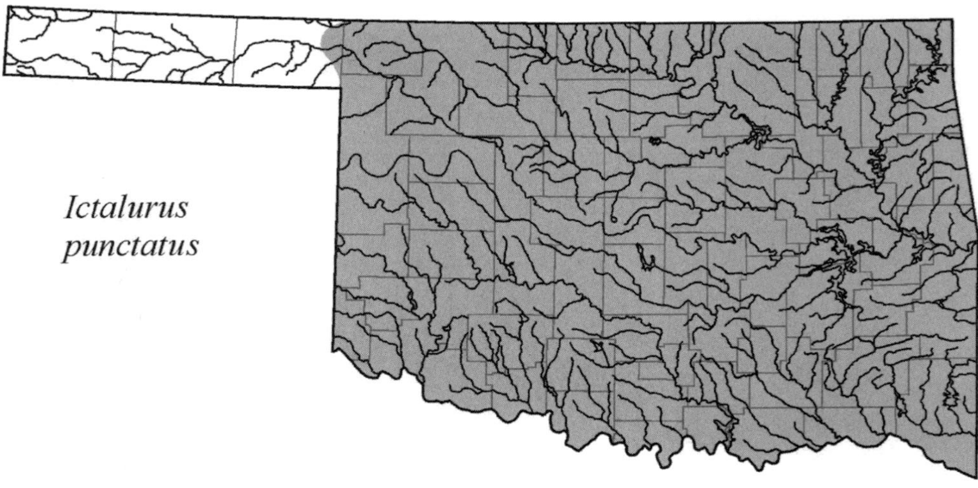

Distribution:

The entire east-central United States from the Rocky Mountains to just west of the Appalachians and widely introduced throughout the entire country. Found everywhere in Oklahoma.

Habitat and Biology:

Channel catfish seem to do equally well in streams, rivers, lakes, and ponds. In streams and rivers they often spend the days in deep pools, under logs and other cover, or in holes in stream banks, venturing out to feed in shallower water at night, though they can be caught on live bait in deep water during the day. They feed on almost any organic materials, dead or alive, and differ from most other catfish in occasionally taking artificial lures. Spawning occurs in May or June when the male cleans out a hole in a bank or under some suitable permanent cover. The female deposits her eggs in the hole, and the male guards them and the young until they leave the nest a few days after hatching. The young school for several weeks before breaking up, but adults seem not to stay with them. Edds and colleagues (2002) have shown that where channel and blue catfish occur together, as in Lake Texoma, channel cats tend to occur primarily in shallower portions of the lake while blues occur in deeper sections, whereas channel cats inhabiting lakes without blue cats are found in all habitats.

MOUNTAIN MADTOM

Noturus eleutherus Jordan

Description:

Like all madtoms, the mountain madtom is a small, flat-headed catfish, usually less than 4 inches long, with an adnate adipose fin (see glossary). Color is brownish to yellowish brown with conspicuous mottling and fine dots on the sides. The adipose fin is nearly free from the caudal, and the dark blotch on the adipose does not extend to the dorsal edge of the fin. The adipose notch is closer to the tip of the caudal fin than to the tip of the depressed dorsal. Dark saddles on the back are usually not conspicuous. Each pectoral spine has 4–11 serrae. The caudal fin has a subterminal dark band, which is separated from a basal brownish blotch by a clear area. Maximum length 5 inches.

Distribution:

Tributaries of the Ohio and Tennessee rivers, the Ouachita River system of Arkansas, and the Mountain Fork and Little River of Oklahoma.

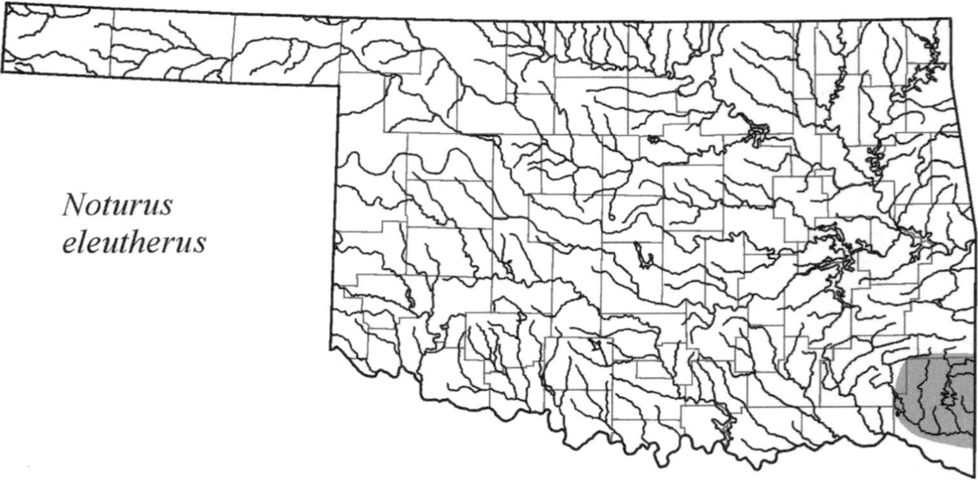

Habitat and Biology:

The mountain madtom is mainly found in clear, large, moderate- to swift-flowing rivers and streams. It generally occurs among larger stones, rubble, and gravel but has been associated in the Mountain Fork with dense vegetation in relatively gentle riffles. Like most madtoms, it hides under stones during the day and moves out to feed at night on aquatic insect larvae, particularly mayflies. Starnes and Starnes (1985) studied the biology of this species in Tennessee. Spawning occurred in June with nests constructed under flat rocks and guarded by males.

SLENDER MADTOM

Noturus exilis Nelson

Description:

A fairly slender, unicolored madtom with conspicuous barbs on the pectoral spines. The adipose fin is long, low, and scarcely notched at the origin of the caudal fin. There are 17–22 anal rays and 9 or 10 pelvic rays. Color is brownish to olive yellow above grading to a whitish underside. Fins are not blotched or spotted, but some specimens have dark distal edges to the dorsal, caudal, and anal fins. Usually 3 inches or less in size with a maximum of about 4 inches. (See also color plate.)

Distribution:

Mainly the Ozark and Tennessee highlands, extending north to Iowa and Minnesota. Found in most of the Ozark region of Oklahoma and in McCurtain County.

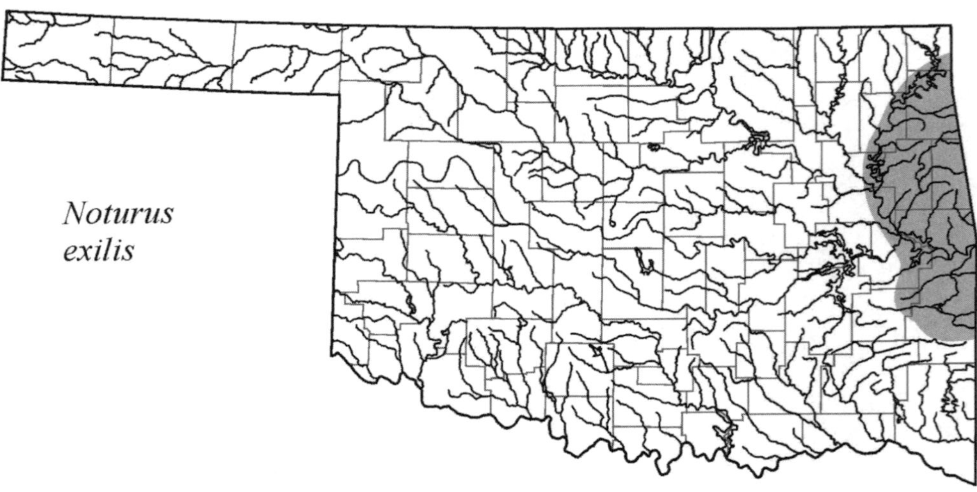

Habitat and Biology:

The slender madtom is abundant in eastern Ozark streams, especially in clear, shallow gravel riffles. It often seems to occur in shallow riffles with a fairly heavy supply of epiphytes (algae, etc.). In Oklahoma Vives (1987) found 90 percent of specimens at depths of less than 12 inches. Like other madtoms, it hides under stones and in weeds during the day, venturing forth after dark to feed on aquatic insect larvae, crustaceans, nematodes, and gastropods. Breeding occurs in April to early June in riffle areas. Nests are found in cavities constructed by adult males in riffles or pools beneath large rocks and are guarded by a male or both parents.

Stonecat

Noturus flavus Rafinesque

Description:

A slender, unicolored madtom that is distinguished from other Oklahoma madtoms by the posterior extensions on either side of the premaxillary tooth patch. The upper jaw protrudes beyond the lower, and the pectoral spines are nearly smooth. The adipose fin notch is easily visible but not deep. Coloration is brownish to yellowish above with lighter sides and whitish belly. Faint dark saddles are sometimes evident on the anterior part of the body. A darker band of pigment runs through the caudal fin, with upper and lower rays lighter. Other fins are light. Although specimens up to a foot long are known from Ohio, most local specimens are less than 6 inches long.

Distribution:

Most of the north-central United States from Montana to New York and south to Oklahoma and northern Alabama. Found in the northeastern corner of Oklahoma.

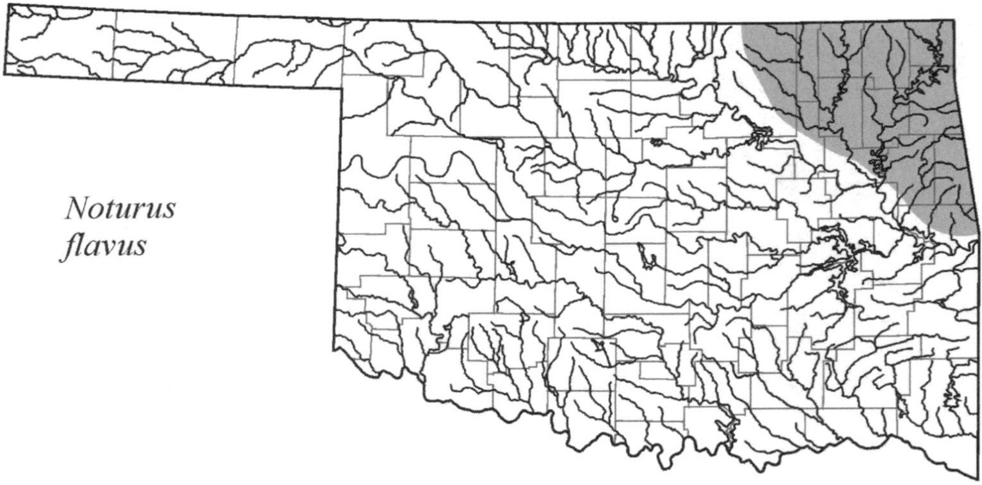

Habitat and Biology:

While it seems to be found in clear, gravel-bottomed, moderate-sized streams and rivers, inhabiting riffle areas and other habitats with significant cover, Cross (1967) suggested that this form is probably one of the most adaptable of the madtoms. Its feeding habits are also less specialized than in other species, since it feeds on a wide variety of aquatic insect larvae, small crustaceans, and crayfish and on occasion small fish. It spawns from April to July at a water temperature of 77 degrees F. Nests are constructed beneath flat stones and guarded by one of the parents.

Tadpole madtom

Noturus gyrinus (Mitchill)

Description:

A deep-bodied madtom shaped somewhat like a tadpole, with smooth pectoral spines and uniform coloration. There are no posterior premaxillary extensions, and upper and lower jaws are nearly equal in length. Anal fin with 14–16 rays, pelvics with 8. Color is yellowish to brown or gray above grading to a whitish underside. The thin skin permits the septa between the lateral muscles and on the midline of the body to be visible as thin but obvious lines. Fins are all dusky and not blotched or barred. Less than 3 inches in length.

Distribution:

The lower, base-level streams of the Mississippi drainage, Great Lakes tributaries, and the east coast from New York to Florida. In Oklahoma found throughout the Red River system as far west as Lake Altus and in the Poteau system.

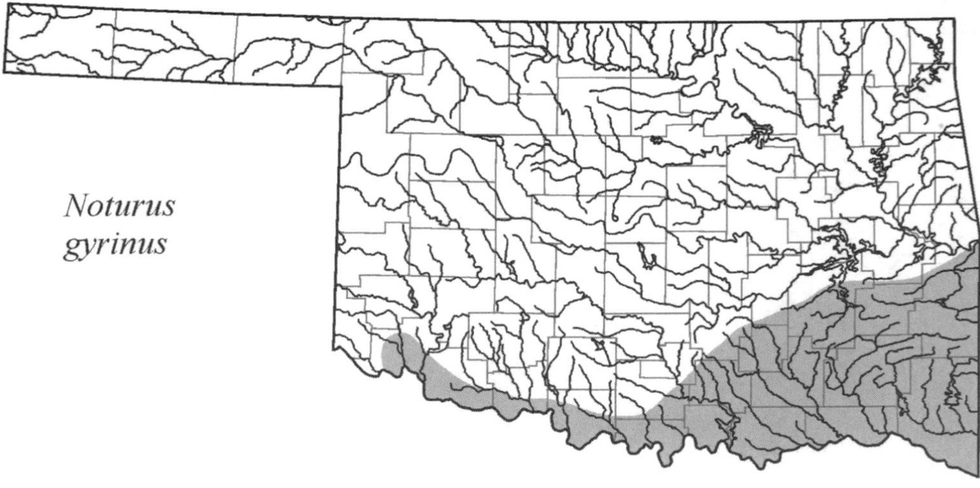

Habitat and Biology:

The tadpole madtom is nearly unique among madtoms in preferring the quiet water of small, weedy streams and springs, oxbows, and sluggish rivers. Although it is not very tolerant of turbid water, it lives in areas with soft mucky bottoms, abundant detritus, and decaying organic matter. It hides in such litter during the day and forages at night on small organisms like aquatic insect larvae, oligochaetes, snails, algae, small fish, and crustaceans. It spawns in June and July, selecting nest sites in various secluded niches. One or both parents stay with the eggs until they hatch.

BRINDLED MADTOM

Noturus miurus Jordan

Description:

A small, conspicuously banded and mottled madtom with barbed pectoral spines. The adipose fin is relatively high but only moderately notched at the caudal origin. Upper jaw is longer than the lower. Anal rays 13–15, pelvic rays 8–9. Four prominent dark saddles are located on the occiput, at the dorsal origin, behind the dorsal fin and on the center of the adipose fin. The adipose saddle extends to the distal edge of the fin. Small dark blotches are scattered along the yellowish sides, and the belly is whitish. A black spot occurs on the anterior part of the dorsal fin, and there are black bands near the margin and at the base of the caudal fin. Some black to dusky markings are also present near the edge of the anal fin. Less than 3 inches long. (See also color plate.)

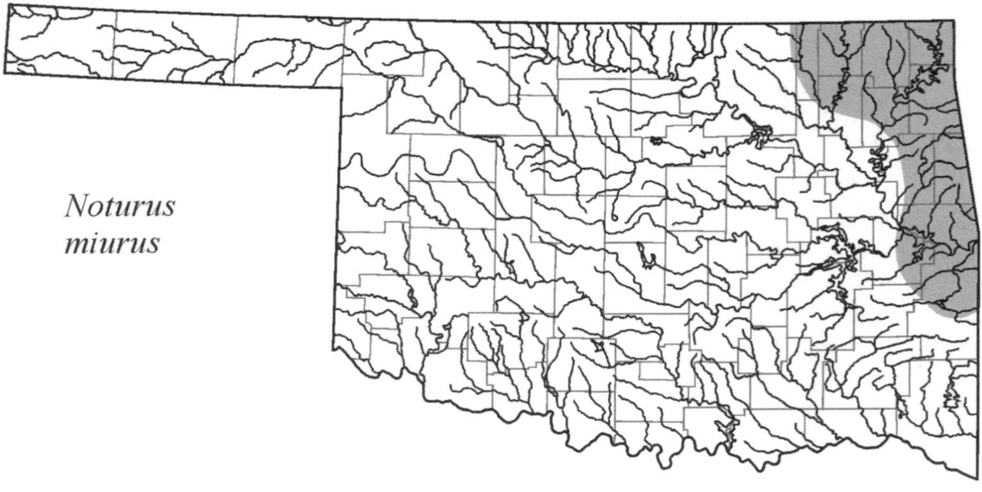

Distribution:

From New York through the Ohio River basin to the lower half of the Mississippi Valley south to eastern Oklahoma and Mississippi. Found in Oklahoma only in the Ozark uplands of the northeast.

Habitat and Biology:

The brindled madtom is very sensitive to siltation but appears to be less of a riffle inhabitant than some other *Noturus*. Generally it can be found in association with organic detritus and other materials deposited in quiet pools over relatively silt-free bottoms. Foods consist of aquatic insect larvae and adult isopods. This species spawns in June and July in Illinois. Pitlike depressions are constructed under flat rocks in quiet pools and are guarded by males. This bright little fish is not widely encountered in Oklahoma.

Freckled Madtom

Noturus nocturnus Jordan and Gilbert

Description:

A moderately stout madtom lacking large blotches or saddle markings. The adipose fin is low and barely notched, and the pectoral fin spines are toothless. There are 16–18 anal rays and 8–9 pelvic rays. Color is brownish or grayish above, lighter below, and whitish on the belly. Underparts are finely speckled. The bases of all fins but the caudal are flecked with pigment, which becomes more diffuse distally. Median fins are typically edged with white. Chin barbels are dark-pigmented near the bases. Individuals are usually less than 3 inches long. Maximum size 5.9 inches.

Distribution:

The central and lower Mississippi Valley and several rivers along the Gulf Coast from Alabama to Texas. Found in both the Red and Arkansas River drainages in about the eastern half of Oklahoma, occurring westward in the Red River system to Rainy Mountain Creek in Kiowa County.

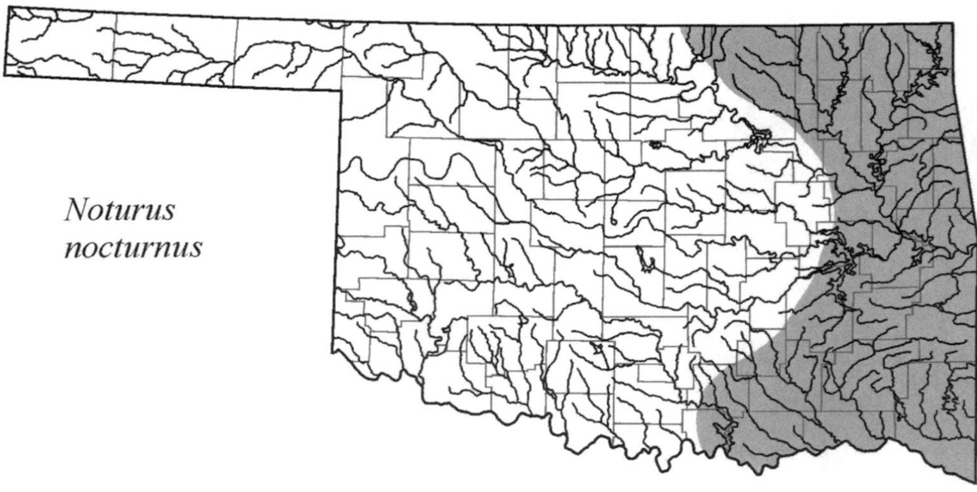

Habitat and Biology:

The freckled madtom is usually an inhabitant of small to medium-sized streams with moderate current over gravel or sand substrates but is found at times in quieter waters with soft bottoms. It tends to occur where twigs, leaves, and associated debris accumulate. Burr and Mayden (1982b) studied the life history of this species in Illinois. Spawning occurred in June and July with nests constructed in shallow areas with some current. Foods taken were primarily immature aquatic insects such as mayflies, caddisflies, midges and *Simulium*. Cross (1967) suggests that *N. nocturnus* may be a competitor of *N. gyrinus* and *N. exilis*, since it is never found with these species.

Neosho madtom

Noturus placidus Taylor

Description:

A rather heavy-bodied, mottled madtom with toothed pectoral spines. The adipose fin is moderately high with a black blotch only at its base and with a fairly good connection to the caudal fin. The adipose notch is generally nearer the end of the depressed dorsal fin than the tip of the caudal fin. Color is yellowish with four brownish saddles on the back (positions as in *N. miurus*) and scattered mottling on the sides. There is a broad dark submarginal band on the dorsal fin, and the caudal fin has two crescent-shaped brown bands, one subterminal and the other in the middle of the fin. Less than 3 inches long. (See also color plate.)

Distribution:

Neosho, Cottonwood, and Spring rivers in Kansas, Oklahoma, and Missouri.

Habitat and Biology:

The Neosho madtom is a federally threatened species that inhabits gravel riffles and runs in the main channels of the rivers where it occurs. It is listed as

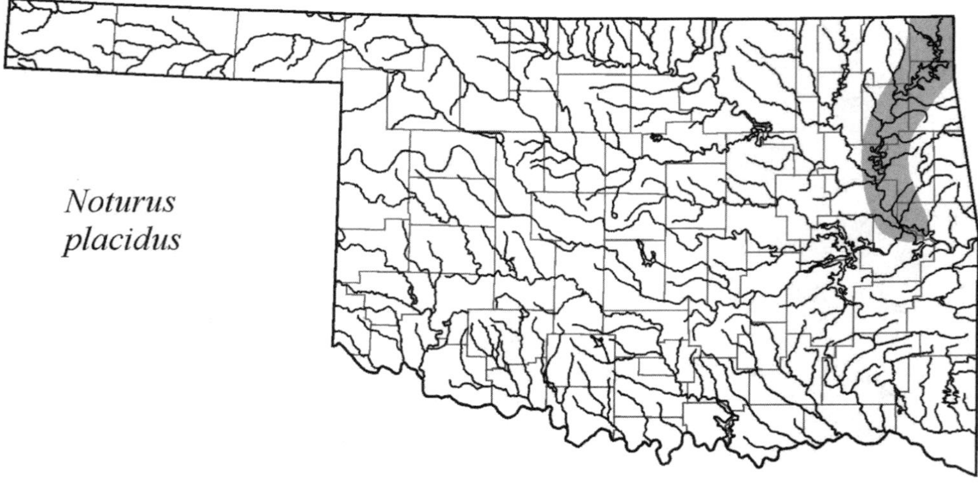

endangered in Oklahoma. Bulger (1999) studied the population structure, habitat, and breeding behavior of this species. Young of the year use shallower areas with slower flow and looser substrate than areas frequented by adults (Bulger and Edds, 2001). Breeding adults are found in more loosely compacted substrate than nonbreeding adults. Bulger and Edds (2001) suggest that most individuals may live only one year, dying after breeding. A nest cavity is constructed by the male and female, and approximately 30–60 eggs are deposited. Spawning begins in March and continues through July (Moss 1981). Spawning behavior is described as identical to that of the brown madtom. Males guard the cavity until after hatching. Individuals hide under stones and in the interstices of the gravel, from which they come out at night to feed.

FLATHEAD CATFISH

Pylodictis olivaris Rafinesque

Description:

A large, flat-headed catfish that can be distinguished easily from all other species on the basis of the broad flat head and the following characteristics: the caudal fin is slightly notched (not forked), with a white triangle on the upper rays of younger fish; the anal fin is rounded and short (14–17 rays); the lower jaw clearly protrudes beyond the upper; and the pectoral spine is serrate on both edges. Adults are yellow to dark brown on the back, mottled with the same colors on the sides, and yellowish to whitish below. The young are darker, and the white dorsal area of the caudal fin is more prominent in the young. May achieve 70 pounds or more. State record: 71 lb., 49 in., from Oologah Lake.

Distribution:

The Mississippi basin north to the Dakotas and Pennsylvania and westward to Texas and northern Mexico. Common in larger streams and lakes across Oklahoma.

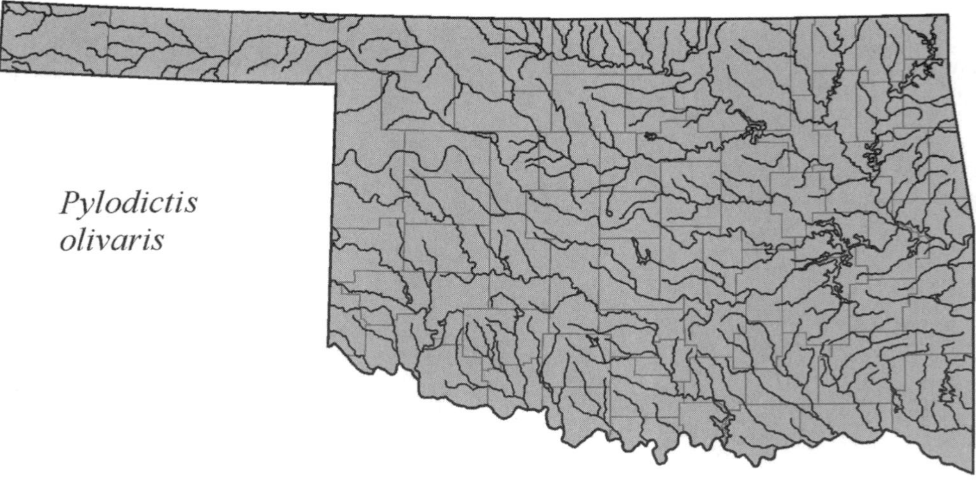

Habitat and Biology:

Flatheads are successful fish in both quiet and flowing waters and tolerate a wide range of turbidity. They seem to prefer the deep holes and channels of the rivers and lakes they inhabit and are effective piscivores. Although the adults feed almost exclusively on fish, particularly shad in reservoirs (Turner and Summerfelt 1971), younger flatheads feed on bottom invertebrates and small fish. As most anglers know, flatheads clearly prefer live fish as bait, rarely taking baits that would easily entice channel catfish. Spawning occurs in late spring and early summer in nest depressions and holes. The young form dense schools for a week or so then apparently scatter.

PIKES

FAMILY ESOCIDAE

Key

1a. Opercle with upper half scaled; lower jaw with 5 or more sensory pores .... *Esox lucius*

1b. Opercle completely scaled; lower jaw with 4 sensory pores 2

2a. Dark bar beneath eye angled slightly backward; branchiostegal rays usually 11 or 12; snout long, 2.2 to 2.4 times into head length .... *Esox americanus*

2b. Dark bar beneath eye usually vertical; branchiostegal rays usually 13 or 14; snout short, 2.4 to 3.1 times into head length .... *Esox niger*

REDFIN PICKEREL
Esox americanus Gmelin

Description:

A moderately large (to 12 inches), elongate, compressed fish with a flat, wedge-shaped snout and median fins located far back on the body. The mouth is large, with jaws well equipped with large canine teeth. Branchiostegals 11–12. Dorsal rays 12–13; anal fins with 11–12 rays. Opercles and cheeks are fully scaled, and there are 104–109 scales in the lateral line. Color is olivaceous above grading to a yellowish or whitish underside. Darker bars and vermiculations are present on the sides. A darker bar extends downward from the eye. Maximum size about 14 inches and ¾ pound. (See also color plate.)

Distribution:

The redfin pickerel is found in the Mississippi basin and lower Great Lakes from the St. Lawrence River west to Iowa and south to Texas and Alabama on the Gulf of Mexico. Limited in Oklahoma to the Poteau, Red, and Little River systems of the southeast.

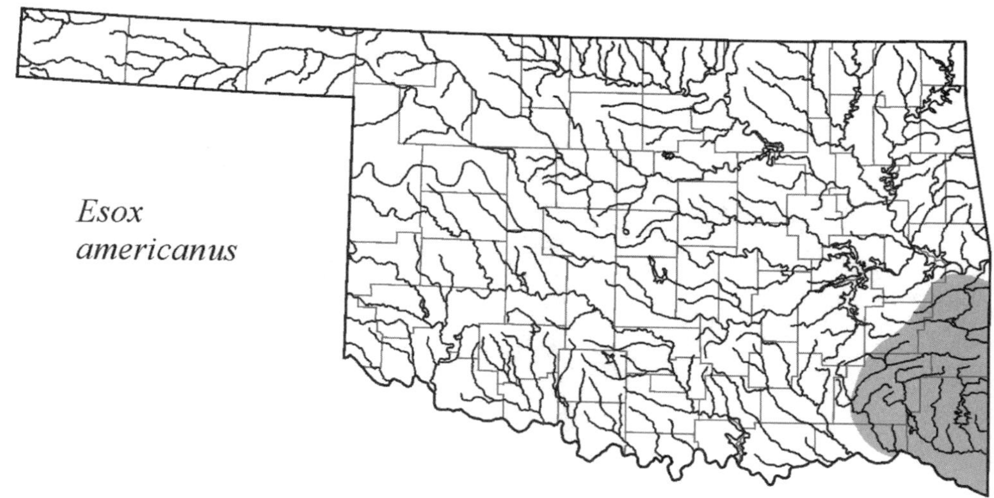

Habitat and Biology:

The redfin pickerel is most commonly found in dense beds of aquatic vegetation in small headwaters or backwaters, generally away from the current. Occasionally it can be found among large rocks or boulders or beneath tangled brush or tree roots. Younger fish feed mainly on crustaceans and insects, while adults are basically piscivorous. Redfin pickerel spawn from late February through early March in Oklahoma, but some populations have been found to spawn in late November or early December. Spawning typically occurs at water temperatures of 40–53 degrees F. Females lay several hundred adhesive eggs over submerged vegetation or objects on the bottom. Eggs hatch in 11–15 days. Growth rate for the winter-spawned fry is slower initially. In Oklahoma, few individuals live more than three years, although some have been reported to live up to eight years in Canada. The redfin pickerel is quite a handsome, beautifully adapted predator, but it does not grow large enough to be important as a food or game fish. It can be an interesting aquarium pet but must be fed live food frequently.

NORTHERN PIKE

Esox lucius Linnaeus

Description:

Similar to the pickerels in being elongate and moderately compressed, with a large, flat, wedge-shaped head. It differs in growing to much larger size (over 4 ft. and 40 pounds), in having the cheek and only the upper half of the gill cover scaled, and in lacking the dark bar below the eye. Scales in lateral series 119–128. Branchiostegal rays 14–16. The back is dark green shading to a lighter green on the sides and to white on the belly. Many white or yellowish spots are scattered along the sides. Young (to 7 inches) have vertical bars on the sides. State record: 36 lb., 8 oz., 44 in., from Lake Carl Etling.

Distribution:

A northern species occurring throughout most of Canada and the northern United States as far south as New England, the Great Lakes drainages, and Missouri. Has been introduced into Lakes Carl Etling, Carl Blackwell, and numerous others in Oklahoma. Presently reduced to a small population in Lake Carl Etling (K. Erickson, pers. comm.). The distribution map for this species is omitted.

Habitat and Biology:

This magnificent game fish is a voracious predator on fishes and any other live animals it can capture (mice, snakes, small ducks, etc.). It spends most of the year in shallow, weedy habitats like those used by the pickerels but moves into deep waters with the cold weather. Spawning occurs in early spring in shallow waters with rushes or other emergent plants. Females scatter adhesive eggs over submerged vegetation or debris on the bottom. Individuals generally live 13–24 years; specimens in zoos have survived to age 75. Pike strike readily at a variety of artificial lures and should prove a most interesting addition to Oklahoma's game fish fauna.

CHAIN PICKEREL
Esox niger (Lesueur)

Description:

Similar to all esocids in having an elongate, compressed body, dorsal fin far back, and wedge-shaped head. Like the grass pickerel, it has fully scaled cheeks and opercles and a dark suborbital bar. It differs in having a longer snout and reaching a larger size, up to 25 inches and 7 pounds. The chain pickerel also has more scales in the lateral line (about 125), more dorsal rays (14), and more anal (13) rays. Branchiostegals 13–14. Color pattern is quite distinct: a chainlike pattern of reticulations on the sides makes adults easily recognizable. State record: 2 lb., 10 oz., 22½ in., from the Mountain Fork River.

Distribution:

Found in a wide band along the East Coast from New Brunswick to Florida, west along the Gulf Coast to Texas, and north up the Mississippi Valley to Missouri and Tennessee. Specimens from Pushmataha County and

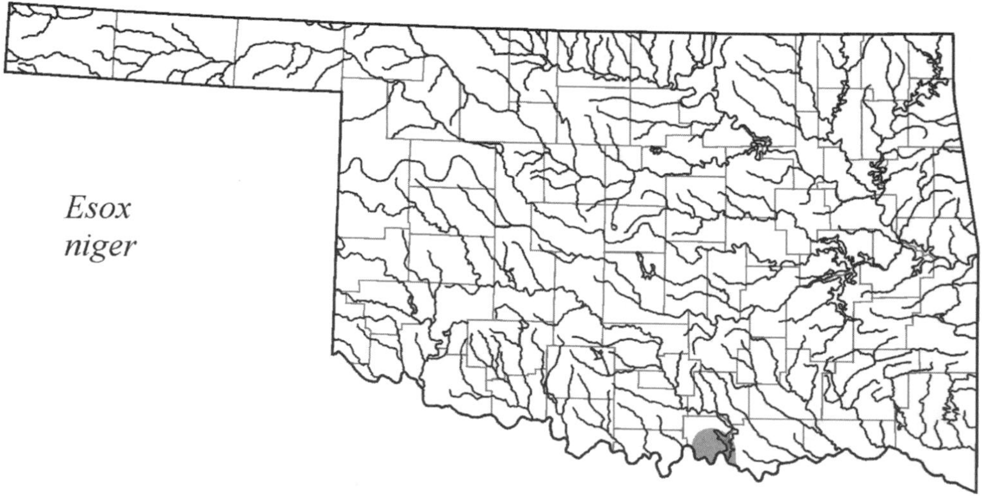

Lake Texoma are known, but the species is probably extremely rare in Oklahoma, though it may occur sporadically in the Red River system.

Habitat and Biology:

The chain pickerel is similar to the grass pickerel in preferring quiet, weedy waters but may be slightly more of a lake fish. Because of their larger size, chain pickerel probably tend to inhabit larger waters with larger prey fishes forming the staple of their diet. They are fierce predators and can grow to large size under proper conditions, though they seldom do in southern waters. They spawn in early spring, scattering their eggs over vegetation in shallow marshy habitats. Maximum life span is eight to nine years. Because of their rare occurrence, they are of little consequence to Oklahoma anglers.

TROUTS

FAMILY SALMONIDAE

Key

1a. Dark spots on caudal fin well developed; sides without reddish or orange spots in life, but having a pink or red midlateral stripe; caudal fin forked; anal rays usually 10–12 . . . . *Oncorhynchus mykiss*

1b. Dark spots on caudal fin faint or absent; sides with distinct reddish or orange spots in life but without a pink or red midlateral stripe; caudal fin not forked; anal rays usually 9 . . . . *Salmo trutta*

Rainbow trout

Oncorhynchus mykiss (Walbaum)

Description:

A beautifully streamlined fish with moderately compressed body, relatively large mouth, and a conspicuous adipose fin. The caudal fin is slightly forked. There are teeth on the jaws, roof of the mouth, and tongue. The ground color is bluish or greenish above, silvery on the sides, and white below. Small black spots occur over most of the upper part of the body, on top of the head, and on dorsal, caudal, adipose, and anal fins (sparse on the anal). A pink to reddish band runs the length of the side from behind the eye to the caudal base. State record: 10 lb., 4 oz., 27 in., from the Illinois River. (See also color plate.)

Distribution:

Originally limited to the western slope of the Rocky Mountains, the rainbow has been widely introduced throughout North America. In Oklahoma it has been introduced into the Blue, Mountain Fork, and Illinois rivers, on a

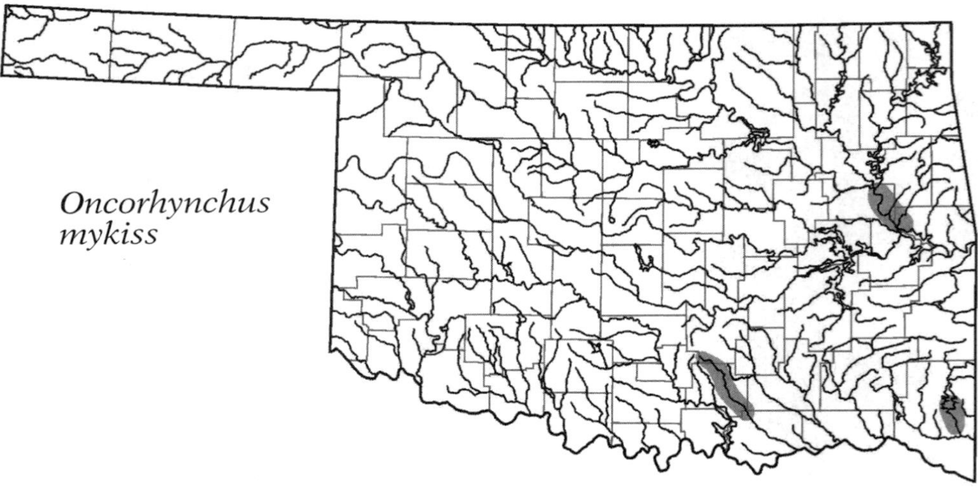

put-and-take fishing basis, and it has been stocked in Lake Carl Etling and several other lakes and ponds, often on a fee-fishing basis.

Habitat and Biology:

Rainbows are cold-water fish that rarely survive water temperatures above 70 degrees F, which limits them to a few places in Oklahoma. They provide a good winter fishery in the Illinois and Blue rivers, but few survive the summer months in the Blue River. They are active predators, feeding on a variety of aquatic and terrestrial invertebrates and small fishes. They tend to grow larger in lakes than in streams, and 4-pound fish were recorded from Lake Etling in 1963. They spawn in winter and early spring in shallow, gravelly streams, but natural reproduction is rare if it occurs at all in Oklahoma.

Brown trout

Salmo trutta Linnaeus

Description:

A streamlined fish with a moderately compressed body and a large mouth, the upper jaw barely extending behind the eye. Teeth are present on the jaws, on palatine bones in the roof of the mouth, and on the tip of the tongue. Lateral-line scales 120–140. The caudal fin is not deeply forked. Dorsal rays number 10–13 (usually 11 or 12), anal rays 9–12, and gill rakers 14–17. Axillary process present at base of pelvic fin. Breeding males develop a hook on the lower jaw. The back and upper sides are dark olive brown with scattered dark spots on the body. Sides have red or orange spots, usually with blue halos; no lateral orange or red band is present. The underside is yellowish white. Dorsal and adipose fins have black spots; the caudal fin is without spots or has only a few on the dorsal portion; and the adipose fin is orange to

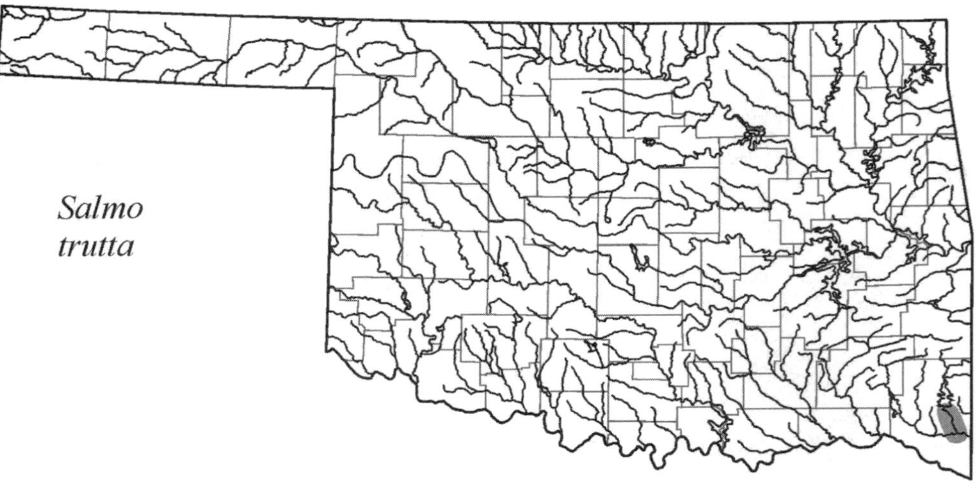

orange-red. State record: 7 lb., 12 oz., 25¼ in., from the Mountain Fork River. (See also color plate.)

Distribution:

The brown trout is presently stocked only in the lower Mountain Fork River below Mountain Fork Lake and in the lower Illinois River below Lake Tenkiller. Some brown trout may have been stocked in other Oklahoma streams by fishing clubs but they are unlikely to persist in such areas. This species, native to Europe, has been stocked throughout the United States in cold-water streams and lakes.

Habitat and Biology:

The brown trout does best in streams and rivers and seems to prefer deeper waters below riffles and areas of dense cover. It prefers cool water but can tolerate higher temperatures, though not as well as the rainbow trout. The young feed on a variety of aquatic invertebrates, while adults prefer fish and crayfish. Pflieger (1997) noted that the brown trout is more secretive than the rainbow, staying in cover during the day and feeding primarily at dusk and dawn. Spawning occurs in fall and early winter, although the success of reproduction in the Mountain Fork River has not been well documented. The female digs a shallow pit in the gravel substrate of a riffle. Eggs are deposited in it and then are fertilized by the male. Thrashing movements by the female bury the eggs in the gravel, and the nest is deserted.

PIRATE PERCHES

FAMILY APHREDODERIDAE

PIRATE PERCH

Aphredoderus sayanus (Gilliams)

Description:

A stout little fish of less than 5 inches with a nearly cylindrical body and a large dorsal fin that has 3 spines. Its most striking characteristic is the position of the anus, which is found between the pelvic fins in very young fish but well forward of the pelvics in the throat (jugular) region of adults. There are two spines in the anal fin and one pelvic spine. Scales are small and strongly ctenoid, and no lateral line is present. Color is slate gray, darker above and

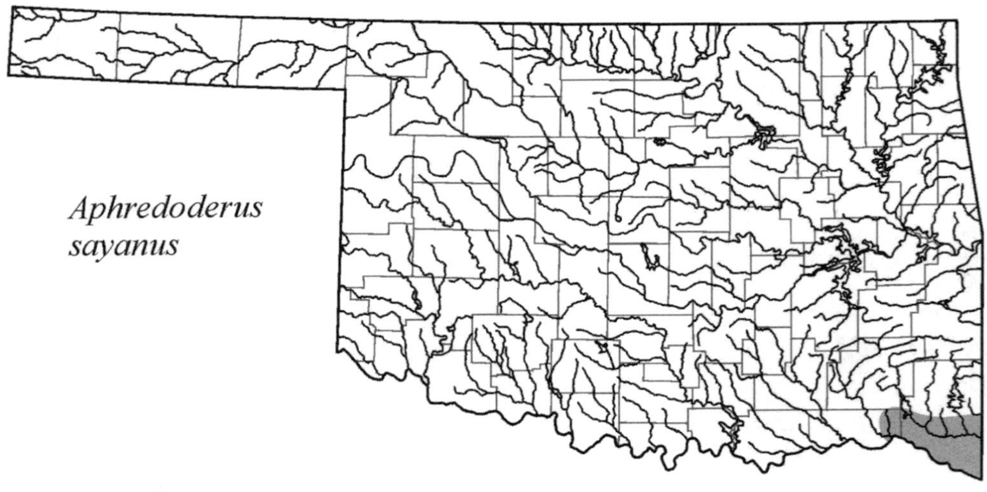

lighter below, with a characteristic purple to pink caste. A dark bar may be present on the caudal peduncle.

Distribution:

From Minnesota south through the Mississippi Valley, across the Gulf coast to Florida, and north along the Atlantic Coast to New York. Occurs in the southeastern corner of Oklahoma in the easternmost tributaries of the Red River.

Habitat and Biology:

The pirate perch is found in quiet water such as ponds, oxbows, swamps, and sluggish streams. It is a voracious predator on small fishes, crustaceans, and other invertebrates that inhabit the dense beds of detritus and thick weeds found in quiet, mud-bottomed pools. Spawning occurs in spring in a nest guarded by the parents, which protect the young until they are several centimeters long. Pirate perch are aggressive in aquaria and must be kept by themselves.

CAVE FISHES

FAMILY AMBLYOPSIDAE

OZARK CAVEFISH

Amblyopsis rosae (Eigenmann)

Description:

This form is typical of a small group of fishes in the family Amblyopsidae that are true troglobites—obligatory cave inhabitants. It resembles other cavefishes in having an elongate, whitish body, elongate and flattened head, projecting jaw, similar fin positions and shapes, and no eyes or pelvic fins. *A. rosae*, however, has no postcleithrum bone, and sensory papillae occur in two or three rows on the upper and lower half of the caudal fin. The lateral-line sense organs (neuromasts) that constitute what appear to be papillae on the head and sides are fewer in number in *Amblyopsis* and their cupulae (tips)

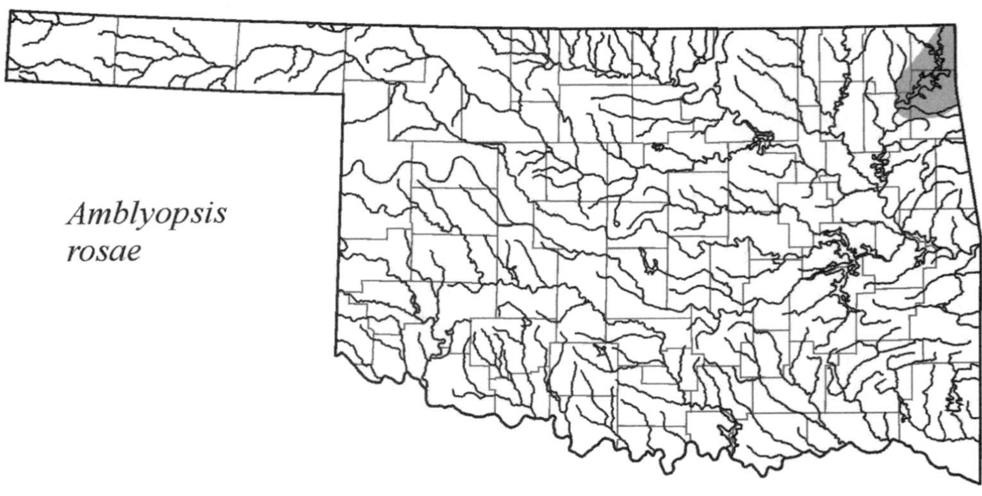

are symmetrical and tapered toward the apex rather than having a swollen apex. The number and size of melanophores are also reduced in *Amblyopsis*. Up to 2 inches long.

Distribution:

Caves of southwestern Missouri, northwestern Arkansas, and northeastern Oklahoma.

Habitat and Biology:

Of all amblyopsids, this interesting little troglobite is probably the most highly specialized for cave existence. It tends to occur in the flowing waters of small cave streams rather than quiet pools and prefers areas with chert rubble over those with silt or sand bottom. Copepods form the great bulk of its diet, though small salamanders and various small invertebrates are also eaten. *A. rosae* has been discovered in Oklahoma relatively recently from caves in Delaware, Mayes, and Ottawa counties and is a rare member of the state's fish fauna.

PUPFISHES

FAMILY CYPRINODONTIDAE

Red River Pupfish

Cyprinodon rubrofluviatilis Fowler

Description:

Like most pupfishes, this species is short and deep-bodied, stout anteriorly but more compressed posteriorly. The mouth is rather small and supplied with tricuspid teeth. Scales are large with about 24–26 in the lateral series. The breast is naked. The caudal fin is square, and the dorsal (9 rays), anal (8–9 rays), and pelvic fins are relatively small. Color is olivaceous above and whitish below. There are about 8–11 dark vertical bars or V-shaped

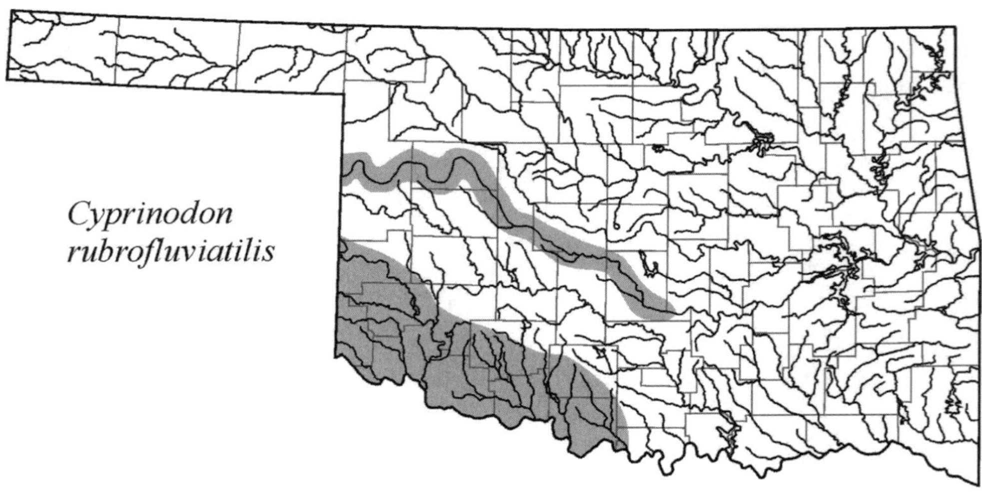

markings on the sides; a thin, dark, vertical bar on the caudal fin near its base; and a small black spot on the dorsal fin of young. Breeding colors of males are quite striking, with brassy green iridescence on top of the head, the median fins yellow to orange, the anal fin with a reddish border, pelvics bright orange, and the pectorals yellow. To about 2 inches. (See also color plate.)

Distribution:

This pupfish occurs in the Brazos and Red River drainages of Texas and southwestern Oklahoma and has been introduced to Canadian and Cimarron River drainages, where it is well established in some places.

Habitat and Biology:

The Red River pupfish is common in the sandy-bottomed rivers and streams of southwestern Oklahoma. Since temperature, salinity, and alkalinity can be high in many of these streams, the pupfish must be a hardy species. It is typically found in quieter pools and backwaters, where it feeds on midge and other insect larvae. It is a summer spawner.

TOPMINNOWS AND KILLIFISHES

FAMILY FUNDULIDAE

Key

1a. Dorsal origin over or ahead of origin of anal fin; scales in lateral series usually 40 or more; dorsal fin rays 13–16. 2

1b. Dorsal origin distinctly behind origin of anal fin; scales in lateral series usually 38 or less; dorsal fin rays 6–11 3

2a. Dorsal origin over or slightly ahead of origin of anal fin; scales in lateral series 41–49; sides with fine parallel horizontal streaks . . . . *Fundulus catenatus*

2b. Dorsal origin distinctly ahead of origin of anal fin; scales in lateral series 55–63; sides with 12–26 vertical bars. . . . . *Fundulus zebrinus*

3a. Sides with a single black lateral band 4

3b. Sides without a single black band. 5

4a. Dorsolateral spots discrete, more intense; lateral band even-edged without crossbars; predorsal stripe weak in young, lacking in adults . . . . *Fundulus olivaceus*

4b. Dorsolateral spots inconspicuous, diffuse, less distinct; lateral band tending to form crossbars; predorsal stripe present. . . . . *Fundulus notatus*

5a. Anal fin rays 8–10; dorsal fin rays 7; sides with 7–8 longitudinal rows of spots 6

5b. Anal fin rays 12–14; dorsal fin rays 10–12; sides plain, without rows of spots . . . . *Fundulus sciadicus*

6a. Subocular black blotch below eye . . . . *Fundulus blairae*

6b. No subocular black blotch below eye . . . . *Fundulus chrysotus*

WESTERN STARHEAD TOPMINNOW

Fundulus blairae Wiley and Hall

Description:

This diminutive, deep-bodied topminnow has a rounded caudal fin and a prominent solid dark bar extending downward below the eye. Males and females lack dark vertical bars on sides of body. The male has many scattered irregular dark dashes and specks on the sides, while the female has many scattered irregular horizontal dark stripes. The front of the dorsal fin base is situated above the front of the anal fin base. Lateral line is absent; 30–36 scales in lateral series. Dorsal fin rays 7 (6–8) and anal rays usually 10 (8–11). Maximum size is 2 inches. (See also color plate.)

Distribution:

This form is found only in the Little River drainage of southeastern Oklahoma.

Habitat and Biology:

An inhabitant of quiet, heavily vegetated waters of small creeks and swampy backwater overflow areas of rivers, this topminnow prefers clear water over soft mud and detritus substrates and heavy concentrations of submerged aquatic vegetation. We have collected this species from oxbows and roadside ditches of southeastern McCurtain County. It is undoubtedly a surface-feeding insectivore, but its biology has not been studied to date.

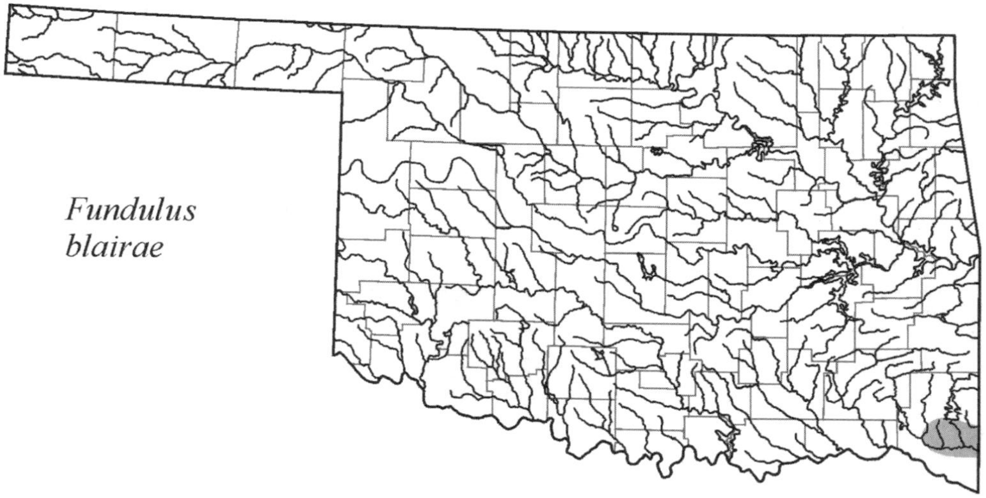

Northern studfish

Fundulus catenatus (Storer)

Description:

A small, elongate, moderately compressed fish with a flattened head and rounded caudal fin. The head and eye are large, lips are large and fleshy, and the mouth is terminal. No lateral-line pores are present, and there are 41–49 lateral scale rows. The dorsal fin has 13–16 rays, the anal 15–18, and both are rounded. Dorsal fin base is situated over or in front of anal fin base. Color is bluish to greenish above, lighter below. Breeding males are spectacular and have orange spots, while females have brown spots on the scales. The spots form 8–10 faint horizontal lines extending the length of the sides, but in many specimens these lines are broken up. The caudal fin of the male has a dark submarginal band. Maximum size about 6 inches.

Distribution:

Upland portions of the Tennessee, Cumberland and Green rivers, and the Ozark uplands, including Missouri, Arkansas, and Oklahoma. Occurs in the

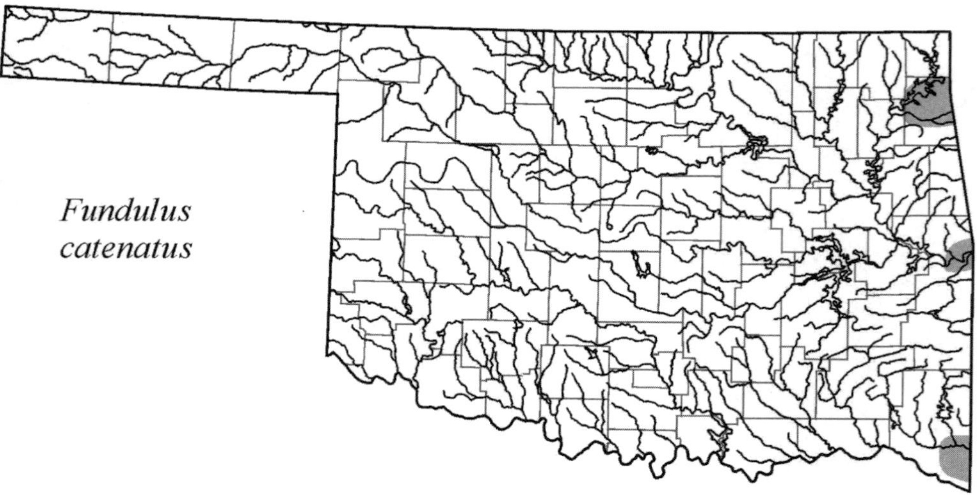

northeast corner of Oklahoma, where it is common in Spavinaw Creek (Neosho drainage) and Buffalo Creek (Elk River drainage).

Habitat and Biology:

This pugnacious topminnow is found in clear, mainly rock- and gravel-bottomed streams in Oklahoma. The studfish is generally found away from swift current in shallow pools and backwaters. Its diet features more foods from the bottom than in other topminnows, including aquatic insects and some snails. Peak feeding occurs in the morning and late afternoon. Studfish breed from April to July with males establishing small territories in shallow, quiet waters over gravel bottoms. Eggs are deposited on the gravel substrate. Life span may be five years.

GOLDEN TOPMINNOW

Fundulus chrysotus (Gunther)

Description:

A small, compressed killifish with deep caudal peduncle and no lateral band or suborbital bar. Lateral line is absent, scales in lateral series numbering 31–35. Dorsal rays 7–9, anal rays 9–11. The species shows pronounced sexual dimorphism in both body shape and color. Sides are plain in females but have 6–9 narrow vertical bars in males, most prominent in preserved specimens. Females are olivaceous above. Males are yellowish green with reddish brown spots and smaller golden flecks, their fins yellow with reddish brown spots. Dorsal and anal fins of males are larger. The back is slightly arched. Dorsal is inserted slightly behind anal origin in males, with more anterior dorsal origin in females. Maximum size about 2.5 inches.

Distribution:

Found along the coastal plain from South Carolina west to Texas and north in Mississippi drainages to Missouri and Tennessee. In Oklahoma it is found only in Little River and Red River tributaries in McCurtain County.

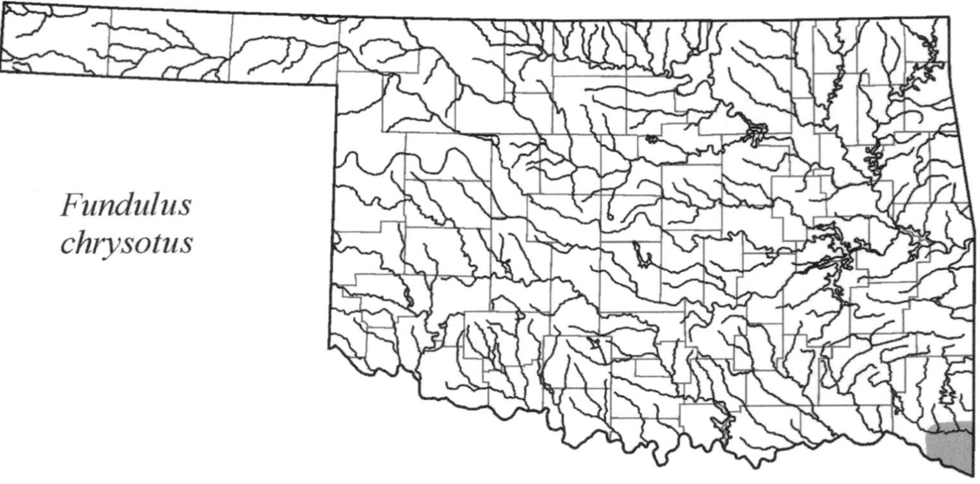

Habitat and Biology:

The golden topminnow is a species of sluggish streams, backwaters of lakes, and swampy overflows of rivers. It prefers quiet, shallow water with abundant vegetation and a soft muddy bottom covered with detritus. It feeds on insects and other aquatic invertebrates near the surface. Nothing is known of its biology in Oklahoma, as it has only recently been recognized as part of our fauna (Cashner and Matthews 1988).

BLACKSTRIPE TOPMINNOW

Fundulus notatus (Rafinesque)

Description:

An elongate, fairly terete topminnow with a rounded tail and with a broad black lateral band extending the length of the body to the caudal fin base. The scales are large, 30–35 in the lateral series, with no lateral-line pores. The dorsal fin is short (usually 9 rays) and relatively low, while the anal fin usually has 12 rays. The body is olivaceous in color above the stripe and whitish below. The lateral band is nearly straight-edged in females but usually has vertical streaks extending from it in males. Dark spots on the

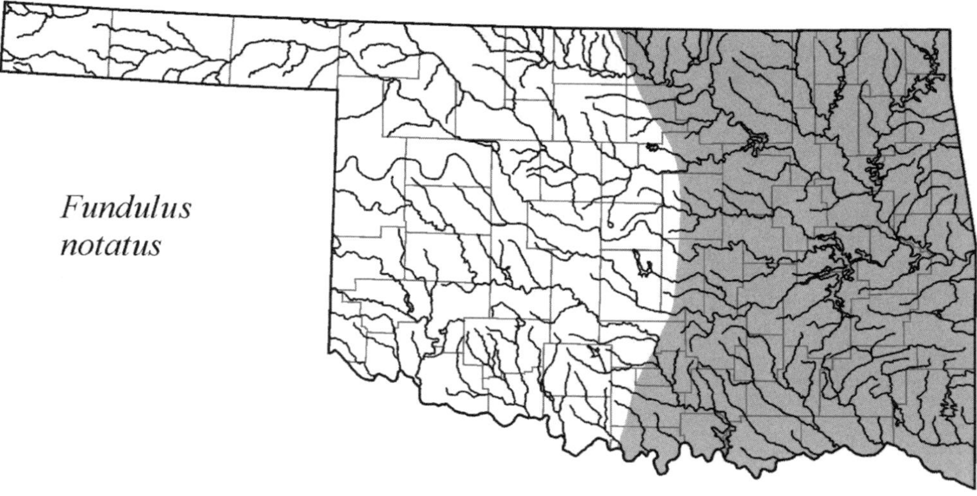

body above the lateral line are diffuse and indistinct when present. This species is similar to *F. olivaceous*, but in *F. notatus* the dorsolateral spots are inconspicuous, diffuse, and less distinct, and the lateral band tends to form crossbars. A predorsal stripe is also present in *F. notatus*. Maximum size is about 3 inches.

Distribution:

The entire lower Mississippi Valley north to Iowa. Found in about the eastern half of Oklahoma.

Habitat and Biology:

Fairly common in many small, slow-flowing eastern streams, where it prefers the quiet water along the edges of pools and backwaters. It is a surface feeder, mainly eating insects and crustaceans, although snails and algae are also consumed. Breeding occurs in spring and summer with 20–30 eggs deposited singly on vegetation, algae, tree roots, or similar substrates. In Illinois *F. notatus* differs from *F. olivaceus* in preferring quieter waters and is often found in oxbows, floodplain sloughs, and lakes. It is not restricted to such habitats in Oklahoma, however, and the overlap in habitats is appreciable. See Moore and Paden (1950) for a discussion of their occurrence together in the Illinois River.

BLACKSPOTTED TOPMINNOW

Fundulus olivaceus (Storer)

Description:

The blackspotted topminnow is similar to the blackstripe topminnow in being an elongate form with a conspicuous black lateral band. It differs in being somewhat more slender, in having the lateral band more intense and smooth-edged in both sexes, and in having the spots on the dorsum darker and more distinct. A predorsal stripe is faint in the young, absent in adults. Lateral line is absent, with 33–37 scales in lateral series. Dorsal rays 9 or 10

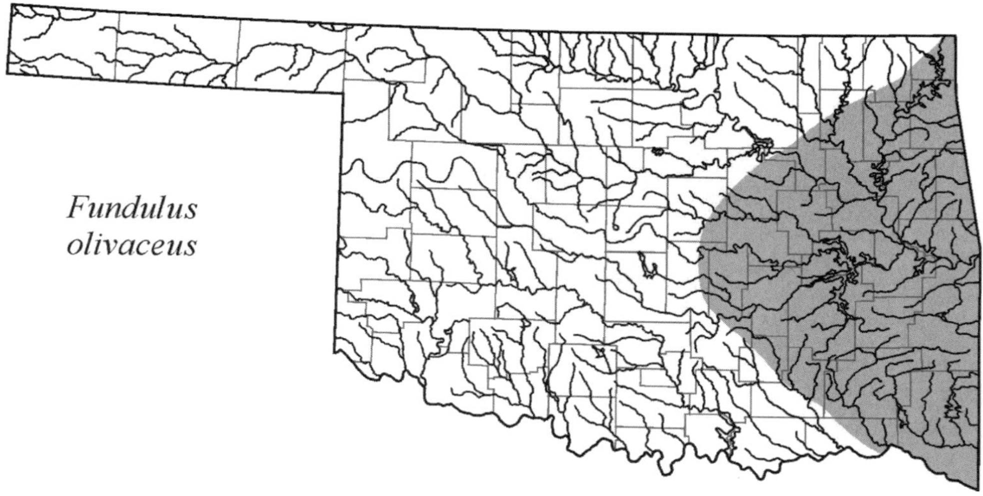

and anal rays usually 11. Adults reach maximum size of about 4 inches. (See also color plate.)

Distribution:

Florida west to Texas and up the lower and middle Mississippi Valley to Illinois. Found in about the eastern third of Oklahoma but not common in the Red River drainage.

Habitat and Biology:

Basically similar to those of several topminnows, especially the blackstripe topminnow. This form is a surface-feeding species, taking insects and small crustaceans. It tends to avoid swifter portions of the streams and rivers it inhabits. Although Braasch and Smith (1965) found *F. olivaceus* mainly in fast, clear upland streams, which is where this species generally occurs in the Ozarks, we have found *F. notatus* in the Mountain Fork River in clear, gravel-bottomed habitats almost identical to those inhabited by *F. olivaceus* in the Barren Fork River. A careful study of the ecology of these two species is required before it can be determined how it is possible for two such similar species to inhabit the same areas without forming hybrids. Coexistence in the same streams seems to be rather rare, but see Moore and Paden (1950) for data on Illinois River populations.

Plains topminnow

Fundulus sciadicus Cope

Description:

A deep-bodied, fairly compressed topminnow with a moderately rounded tail and deep caudal peduncle. It has fairly large scales (about 34–36 in a lateral row), no lateral line, and about 10–12 dorsal rays and 12–14 anal rays. Color is plain olivaceous above, grading at about the midline of the side into a lighter olive, then into a white underside. There are no spots or bars on the body, though some dusky markings are present on the dorsal and anal fins. Usually 2 inches or less in length.

Distribution:

The plains states from Wyoming and South Dakota to Oklahoma. Found in the Neosho River drainage in northeastern Oklahoma.

Habitat and Biology:

We have found this species in a small, weedy, spring-fed pool near Cloud Creek in Delaware County. It seems to be associated with slow-moving, clear water with sandy or gravel bottom and ample vegetation, but it is not very

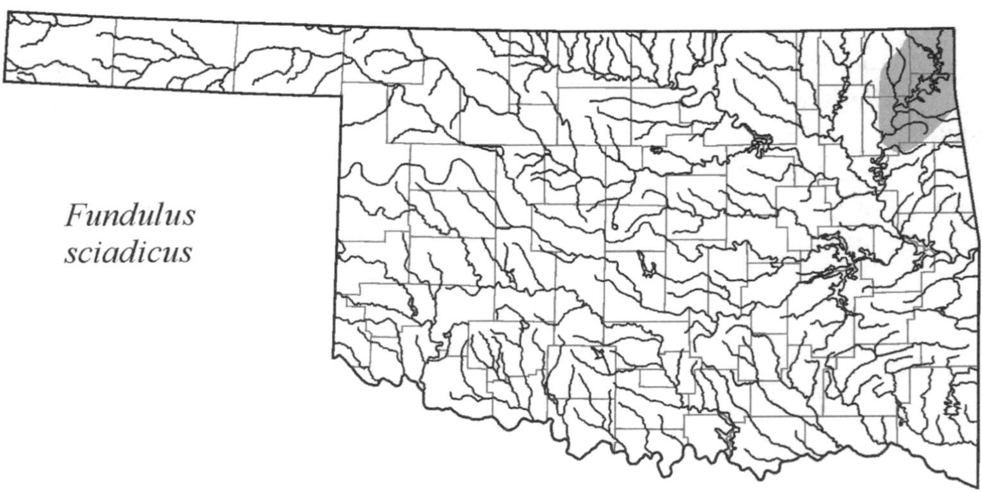

abundant anywhere in Oklahoma. Because of its somewhat unusual habitat in this part of its range, we might surmise that its biology differs from that of its big-stream relatives. Kaufmann and Lynch (1991) described courtship and breeding behavior in captivity and observed embryos in algal mats in Clear Creek, Nebraska, in May and June. They suggested that breeding occurs at temperatures of 18–22 degrees C.

PLAINS KILLIFISH

Fundulus zebrinus Jordan and Gilbert

Description:

A fairly sturdy barred topminnow with a square tail. The head is large and flat dorsally, and the mouth is terminal. Dorsal and anal fins are large; the dorsal has about 14 rays, and the anal has 13 or 14 rays. Scales are small, about 54–63 in the lateral series, with no lateral-line pores. Color is usually light brown to tan above grading to yellowish or white below. A series of thin dark vertical bars (15–26) are located along the sides and dorsum. These are

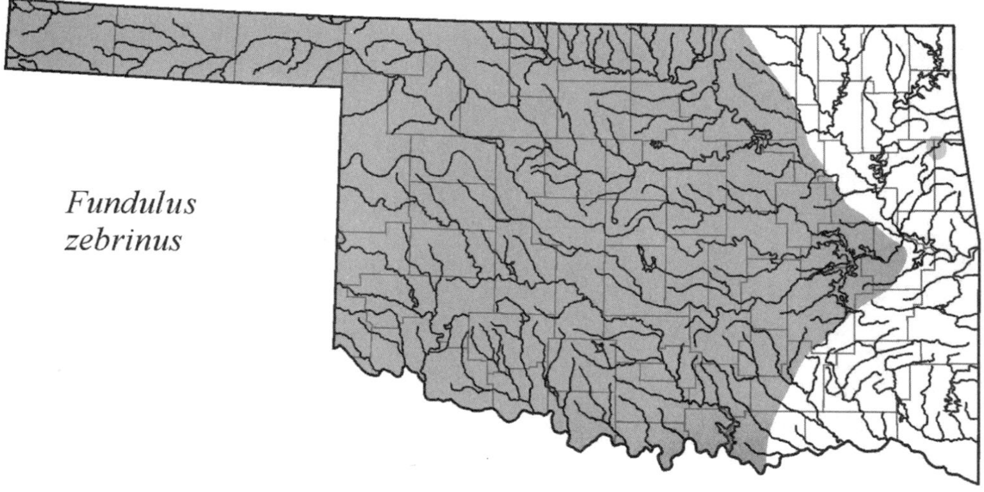

fewer and wider in males. Fins on the underside may become yellow to bright orange in breeding fish. Rarely larger than 3 inches. (See also color plate.)

Distribution:

Found throughout the Great Plains from Texas to South Dakota. Occurs in about the western two-thirds of Oklahoma, and in some salty streams and ponds in eastern Oklahoma.

Habitat and Biology:

This species is found mainly in shallow, sandy-bottomed western streams and rivers. It is very resistant to high alkalinity and salinity and is not easily harmed by turbidity, though usually it is found in fairly clear streams. Plains killifish can live in faster waters, but they tend to be most common in shallow pools, where they feed on surface insects and various invertebrates. Spawning occurs in summer in small pools, where the eggs are deposited over the sandy bottom. An isolated population of this fish is known to exist in the Salt branch of Saline Creek, a tributary of Grand Lake near Salina, and indicates the possible preference of this species for saline waters.

LIVEBEARERS

FAMILY POECILIIDAE

Western mosquitofish
Gambusia affinis (Baird and Girard)

Description:

This small, robust, round-tailed fish is the only livebearer in Oklahoma. The sexes are easily distinguishable by the presence of a highly modified anal fin in the male. Anterior rays of the anal are elongate, producing a rodlike copulatory organ. In general body form and morphology *Gambusia* resembles the topminnows, but *Gambusia* has only 7–8 dorsal rays (vs. 9 or more) and fewer than 10 anal rays (vs. 12 or more). The scales are large (29–32 in lateral series), and there are no pored scales. Color is olivaceous above grading to whitish on the underside. A dark suborbital bar and predorsal stripe are generally conspicuous. Some flecks forming faint bars on the median fins are the

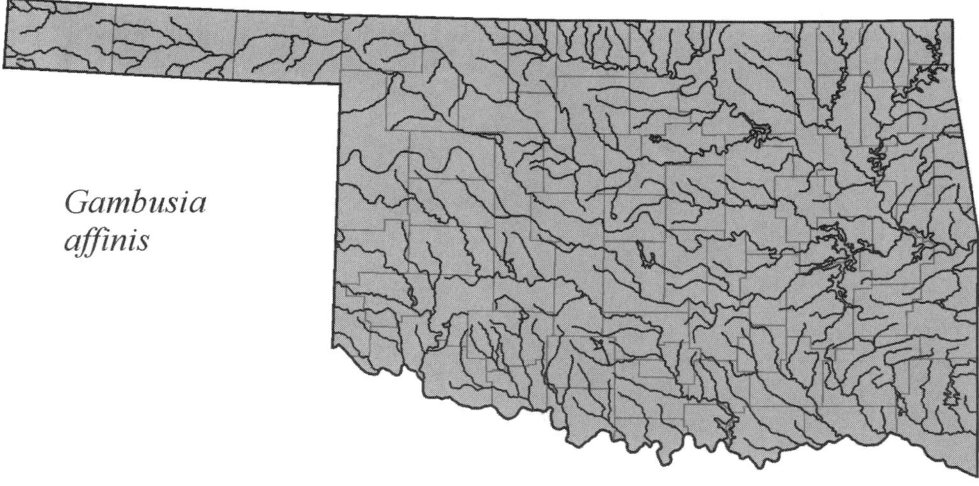

only markings on the body except for a dark blotch near the anus of females. To about 2 inches. (See also color plate.)

Distribution:

The Mississippi Valley from Illinois south to Western Alabama, across the Gulf Coast, and west to Mexico. Widely introduced elsewhere. Scattered throughout most of Oklahoma.

Habitat and Biology:

The western mosquitofish is found in all kinds of quiet, often shallow pools and backwaters of small to moderate-sized creeks and along the edges of larger rivers. It is a surface feeder, eating mainly terrestrial insects and their larvae but also various small crustaceans and other invertebrates. Females give birth to living young, producing several broods a year. Its interesting courtship and breeding habits and the ease with which it can be maintained make *Gambusia* an ideal aquarium fish for young people studying biology.

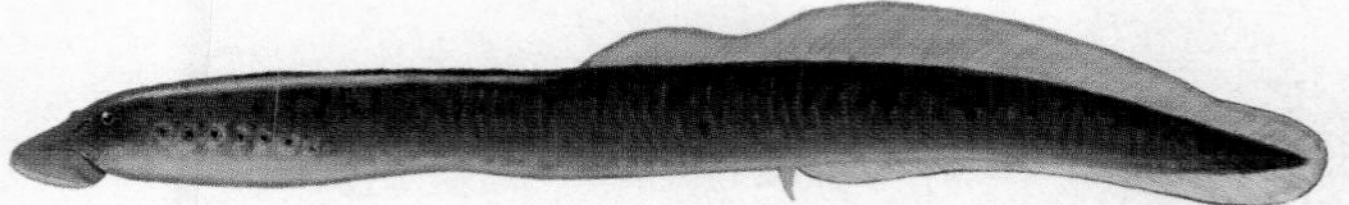

Chestnut lamprey, *Ichthyomyzon castaneus*, large adult.

Central stoneroller, *Campostoma anomalum*, breeding male.

Red shiner, *Cyprinella lutrensis*, breeding male.

Blacktail shiner, *Cyprinella venusta*, adult.

Steelcolor shiner, *Cyprinella whipplei*, adult.

Ozark minnow, *Dionda nubila*, breeding male.

Plains minnow, *Hybognathus placitus*, adult.

Ribbon shiner, *Lythrurus fumeus*, adult.

Ouachita Mountain shiner, *Lythrurus snelsoni*, adult.

Redfin shiner, *Lythrurus umbratilis*, breeding male.

Prairie chub, *Macrhybopsis australis*, adult.

Silver chub, *Macrhybopsis storeriana*, adult.

Arkansas River shiner, *Notropis girardi*, adult.

Wedgespot shiner, *Notropis greenei*, adult.

Bluehead shiner, *Notropis hubbsi*, breeding male.

Taillight shiner, *Notropis maculatus*, breeding male.

Kiamichi shiner, *Notropis ortenburgeri*, adult.

Carmine shiner, *Notropis percobromus*, breeding male.

Suckermouth minnow, *Phenacobius mirabilis*, adult.

Southern redbelly dace, *Phoxinus erythrogaster*, breeding male.

Slim minnow, *Pimephales tenellus*, adult.

Blue sucker, *Cycleptus elongatus*, adult.

Northern hog sucker, *Hypentelium nigricans*, adult.

Golden redhorse, *Moxostoma erythrurum*, adult.

Yellow bullhead, *Ameiurus natalis*, adult.

Channel catfish, *Ictalurus punctatus*, adult.

Slender madtom, *Noturus exilis*, adult.

Brindled madtom, *Noturus miurus*, adult.

Neosho madtom, *Noturus placidus*, adult.

Redfin pickerel, *Esox americanus*, adult.

Rainbow trout, *Oncorhynchus mykiss*, adult.

Brown trout, *Salmo trutta*, adult.

Red River pupfish, *Cyprinodon rubrofluviatilis*, breeding male.

Western starhead topminnow, *Fundulus blairae*, adult.

Blackspotted topminnow, *Fundulus olivaceus*, adult.

Plains killifish, *Fundulus zebrinus*, adult.

Western mosquitofish, *Gambusia affinis*, adult female.

White bass, *Morone chrysops*, adult.

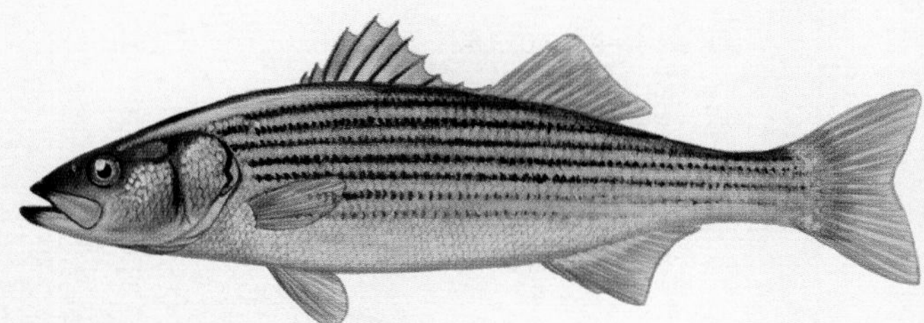

Striped bass, *Morone saxatilis*, adult.

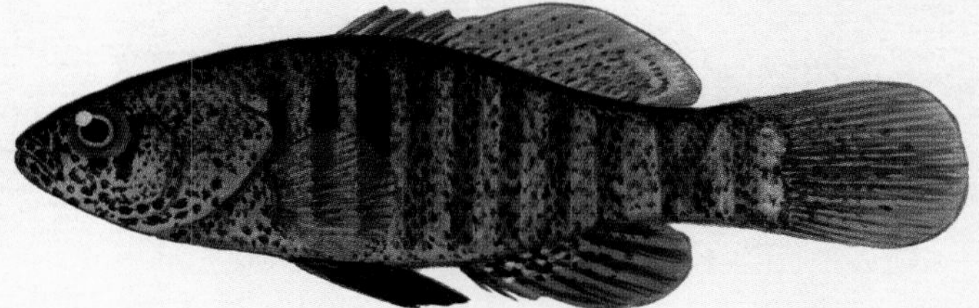

Banded pygmy sunfish, *Elassoma zonatum*, adult.

Flier, *Centrarchus macropterus*, young adult.

Redbreast sunfish, *Lepomis auritus*, adult.

Green sunfish, *Lepomis cyanellus*, breeding male.

Orangespotted sunfish, *Lepomis humilis*, breeding male.

Bluegill, *Lepomis macrochirus*, breeding male.

Dollar sunfish, *Lepomis marginatus*, adult.

Longear sunfish, *Lepomis megalotis*, breeding male.

Redspotted sunfish, *Lepomis miniatus*, adult.

Smallmouth bass, *Micropterus dolomieu*, adult.

Spotted bass, *Micropterus punctulatus*, adult.

Largemouth bass, *Micropterus salmoides*, adult.

White crappie, *Pomoxis annularis*, adult.

Black crappie, *Pomoxis nigromaculatus*, adult.

Crystal darter, *Crystallaria asprella*, adult.

Redspot darter, *Etheostoma artesiae*, breeding male.

Greenside darter, *Etheostoma blennioides*, breeding male.

Slough darter, *Etheostoma gracile*, early breeing male.

Harlequin darter, *Etheostoma histrio*, adult.

Least darter, *Etheostoma microperca*, breeding male.

Cypress darter, *Etheostoma proeliare*, breeding male.

Stippled darter, *Etheostoma punctulatum*, breeding male.

Orangebelly darter, *Etheostoma radiosum*, breeding male.

Orangethroat darter, *Etheostoma spectabile*, breeding male.

Speckled darter, *Etheostoma stigmaeum*, breeding male.

Redfin darter, *Etheostoma whipplei*, breeding male.

Banded darter, *Etheostoma zonale*, breeding male.

Logperch, *Percina caprodes*, adult.

Channel darter, *Percina copelandi*, adult.

Slenderhead darter, *Percina phoxocephala*, adult.

River darter, *Percina shumardi*, adult.

MULLETS

FAMILY MUGILIDAE

STRIPED MULLET
Mugil cephalus Linnaeus

Description:

A slightly compressed, elongate fish with two well-separated dorsal fins (the first with 4 spines), adipose eyelids, and a small subterminal mouth with thin lips. It superficially resembles the silversides but differs in having a shorter head, stouter body, adipose eyelids, blunter snout, and no silvery stripe on the side. It also grows to a much larger size (up to 2 feet). The anal fin has 2 or 3 spines and 8 or 9 rays, and the pectoral fins are located high on the body. Color is usually blue-gray above grading to a silvery white below. Lateral scales have dark spots that form horizontal lines the length of the body.

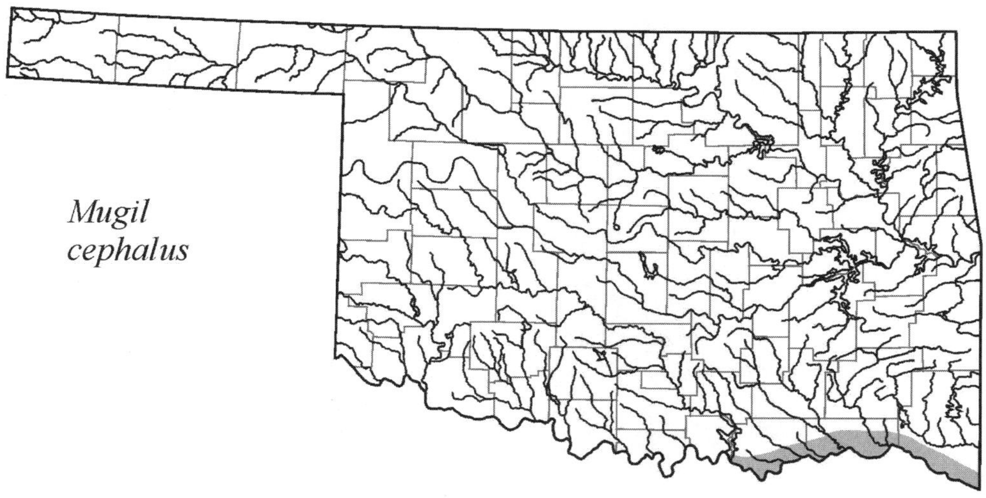

Distribution:

Widespread in marine waters, the striped mullet enters fresh waters in several of the Gulf states and California and penetrates up the Mississippi basin at least as far as the dam below Lake Texoma. Mainly a spring and summer visitor in the Red River below the dam.

Habitat and Biology:

Basically a marine species, the striped mullet travels in schools, which apparently move up the Red River fairly frequently in the spring and summer. Although mullet grow quite large, they feed on plankton and algae and are thus not susceptible to capture by angling, except perhaps by foul-hooking. They probably do not spawn in Oklahoma waters and must be considered relatively insignificant visitors.

SILVERSIDES

FAMILY ATHERINOPSIDAE

Key

1a. Premaxilla when viewed from above is triangular and produced as a beak; predorsal scales small, more than 30; anal soft rays 20–22; scales in lateral series 74–80. . . . . *Labidesthes sicculus*

1b. Premaxilla when viewed from above is neither triangular nor produced as a beak; predorsal scales large, fewer than 30, usually 19; anal soft rays 15 or 16; scales in lateral series 38–40 . . . . *Menidia beryllina*

Brook Silverside

Labidesthes sicculus (Cope)

Description:

A very elongate, terete fish with a long, pointed snout and two dorsal fins, the first containing 4–5 thin, flexible spines. The second dorsal has 10 or 11 soft rays and the anal fin has 20–22 rays. The head is relatively small, the eye is large, and the elongate jaws are protractile. The pectoral fins are inserted

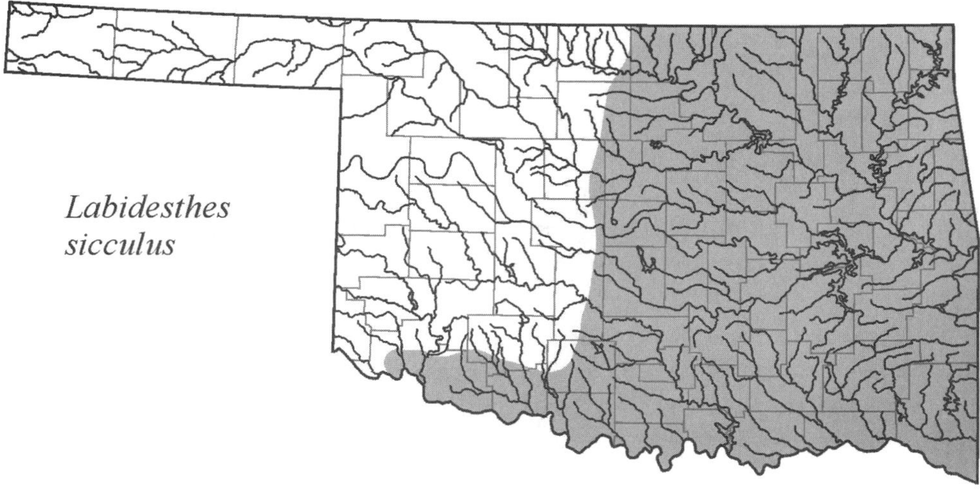

high on the body near the upper angle of the gill opening. Scales are small, with fewer than 30 predorsal scales and 74–78 scales in the lateral series. Color is greenish to straw yellow above and whitish to silvery white below, with a narrow silvery stripe on the side. Fins are transparent.

Distribution:

Throughout most of eastern United States and the Mississippi Valley to Minnesota but not found on the East Coast. Common in most of eastern Oklahoma and occasionally occurring in some western rivers and streams.

Habitat and Biology:

The brook silverside is one of the more common surface and midwater inhabitants of clear eastern streams and lakes. It tends to prefer calm pools and backwaters in streams. Food consists largely of chironomids and other insects that fly near the surface of the water but may include aquatic invertebrates as well. Spawning occurs in late spring and summer when eggs with adhesive threads are deposited on the stalks of aquatic plants or other solid objects. Silversides school as strongly as any of our native fishes, and can be seen leaping from the water at times, especially when they are chased by a predator (or a net).

INLAND SILVERSIDE

Menidia beryllina (Cope)

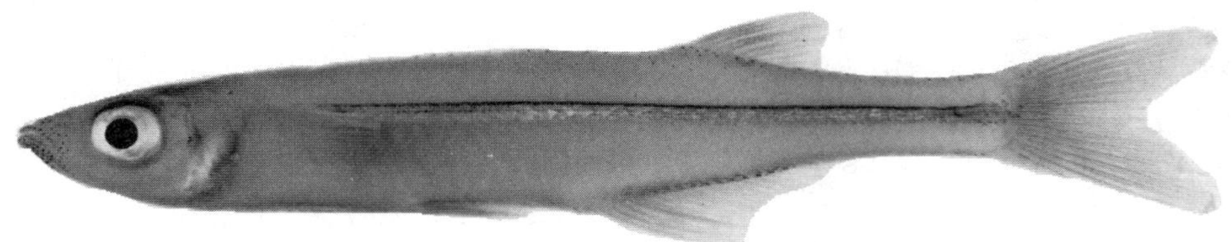

Description:

Superficially similar to the brook silverside with an elongate silvery body, long anal fin, and two dorsal fins. The large eye, high pectoral fin, and broad silvery band are common to both species, but they differ in several trenchant characteristics. The snout of *M. beryllina*, when viewed from above, is rounded rather than pointed as in *L. sicculus*; the scales are larger (about 19 before the dorsal and 38–40 in the lateral series); and *M. beryllina* usually has 9 dorsal rays and 15–16 anal rays. Coloration is similar in the two species: straw-colored to greenish above and whitish below. Usually less than 4 inches in length.

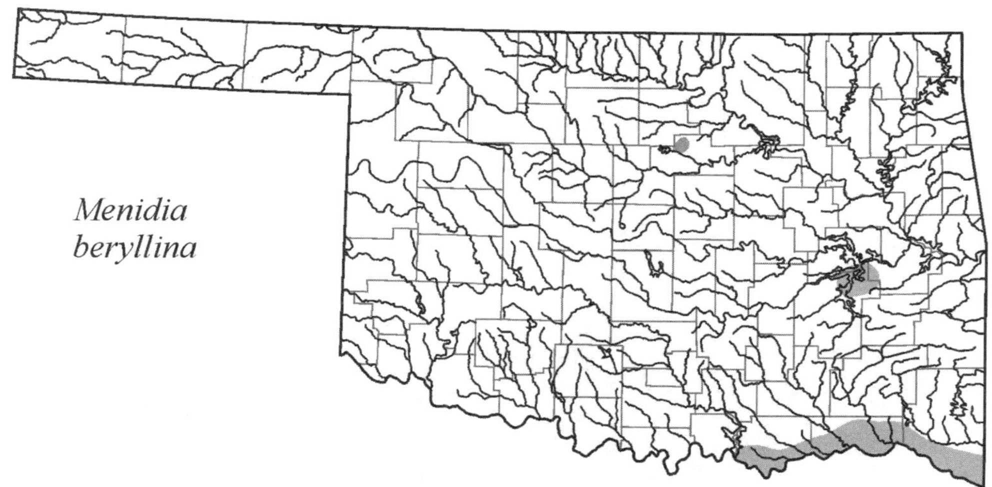

Distribution:

Brackish waters of the Gulf Coast and up the lower Mississippi basin north to Oklahoma and Tennessee. In Oklahoma it is found in the Red River basin west to Lake Texoma, where a well-established population exists. A successful introduction into Boomer Lake (Payne County) has been made, and a few other transplants may also have been successful.

Habitat and Biology:

The two species of silversides seem to have fairly similar behavior and feeding habits. They feed on insects and plankton, though *M. beryllina* may be somewhat more of a plankton feeder. Spawning occurs from late March or April through July in Oklahoma. In Lake Texoma this species has nearly replaced the brook silverside, suggesting that it may be a more successful lake resident.

SCULPINS

FAMILY COTTIDAE

BANDED SCULPIN

Cottus carolinae (Gill)

Description:

The banded sculpin is a most striking fish with its large flattened head, large eyes, and large mouth. The heavy, wedge-shaped body is naked, but there is a sharp spine on the preopercle. The first dorsal fin has 7–9 weak spines, the second dorsal fin has 16–18 soft rays, and the anal fin has 12–14 rays. All median fins are rounded, with tips of the rays extending beyond the membranes. Body color is brown or yellowish, with 4 prominent blackish or dark brown saddles extending down the sides. The fins are yellowish to orange with darker mottlings. Most specimens are less than 5 inches long.

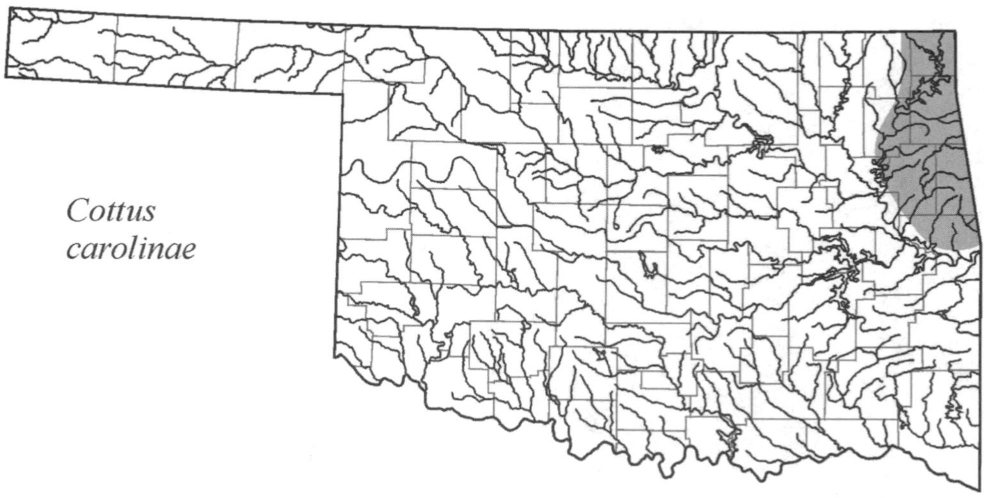

Distribution:

Occurs widely in the southeastern United States from West Virginia and Georgia in the east to Kansas and Mississippi in the west, mostly in upland streams. Common in many Oklahoma Ozark streams.

Habitat and Biology:

The banded sculpin is a characteristic inhabitant of the riffles in clear, gravel-bottomed streams in the Ozark uplands. Living in the interstices between stones and rubble, it feeds mainly on larval insects, small crustaceans, and occasionally small fish. Spawning in late winter and early spring, it has rather unusual breeding habits. The female attaches her eggs to the undersides of stones, while the male stands guard in the depression below the eggs until they hatch. Although sculpins are utilized as food by trout in western states and are good bait fish in some areas, their value as forage fish for centrarchids in eastern Oklahoma streams is unknown.

TEMPERATE BASSES

FAMILY MORONIDAE

Key

1a. Dorsal fins slightly connected, joined by a membrane; second anal spine about the same length as third anal spine; anal rays 10; lateral stripes abruptly broken and offset posteriorly; hyoid teeth absent . . . . *Morone mississippiensis*

1b. Dorsal fins distinctly separated; second anal spine much shorter than third anal spine; anal rays 11–13; lateral stripes continuous; hyoid teeth present. 2

2a. Hyoid teeth in 1 patch; body depth going into standard length less than 3 times; longest anal spine equal to or greater than half the length of longest anal ray . . . . *Morone chrysops*

2b. Hyoid teeth in 2 patches; body depth going into standard length more than 3 times; longest anal spine shorter than half the length of longest anal ray . . . . *Morone saxatilis*

WHITE BASS

Morone chrysops (Rafinesque)

Description:

A streamlined, robust fish with a moderately deep and compressed body. It has two separate dorsal fins, the first with 9 spines, the second with 1 spine and 13 rays. The anal has 3 spines, with the second clearly shorter than the third, and 11–13 rays. The head is small, the mouth is large, and the lower jaw projects beyond the upper. Generally 51–56 scales in the lateral line. Steely blue to grayish above with silvery sides and a white ventrum. Sides with 6–10 longitudinal dark stripes (those above more continuous than the

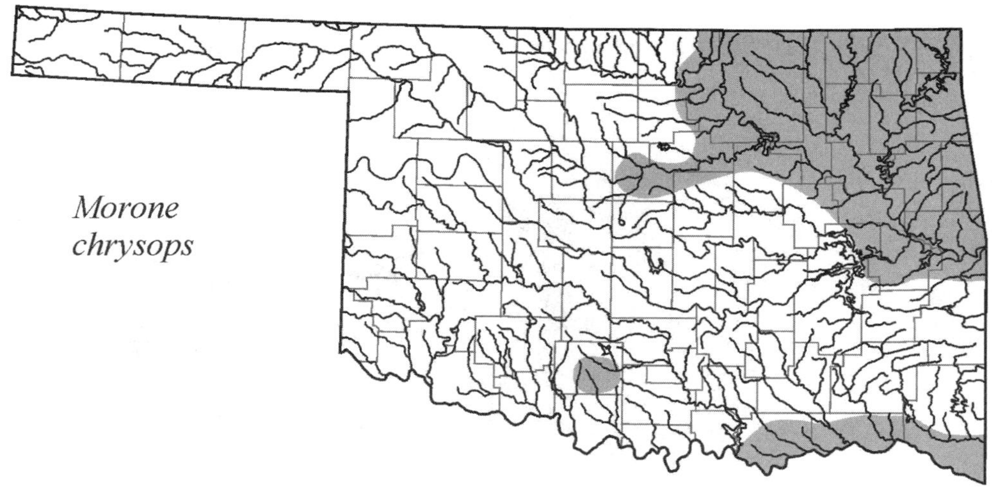

lower ones, which are broken up). Pectoral and pelvic fins whitish to transparent, other fins more dusky. State record: 5 lb., 4 oz., 21 in., from Lake Eufaula. (See also color plate.)

Distribution:

Throughout the southern Great Lakes and the Mississippi Valley, from Minnesota to Texas, and across the Gulf states to Florida. Found in many rivers and lakes in the eastern half of Oklahoma and in scattered lakes in the western part of the state.

Habitat and Biology:

White bass are often called "sand bass" in Oklahoma and are among our most popular game and food species. They do well in both rivers and lakes and are typically found in large schools, which actively move about in search of the smaller fishes (like gizzard or threadfin shad) on which they feed. It is readily taken on a variety of artificial lures. Spawning is in early spring, mainly March and April, with large schools moving into small, gravel-bottomed streams, where the males often precede the females. In lakes, spawning occurs over shallow gravel areas, with eggs and sperm being shed randomly over the bottom.

YELLOW BASS

Morone mississippiensis Jordan and Eigenmann

Description:

Similar to the white bass in being a husky, streamlined predator with a moderately compressed body. It differs from that species in being smaller (rarely exceeding 15 inches), in having the spiny dorsal fin connected to the soft dorsal by a membrane, and in having the second anal spine equal or nearly equal in size to the third anal spine. Further, there are only 10 anal rays and the lower jaw is more nearly equal in length to the upper jaw. Color pattern differs also. The yellow bass is olive greenish above, yellowish on the sides, and white below. There are 6–8 prominent dark longitudinal stripes along the side, and those below the lateral line usually are interrupted. Lateral-line scales 51–55.

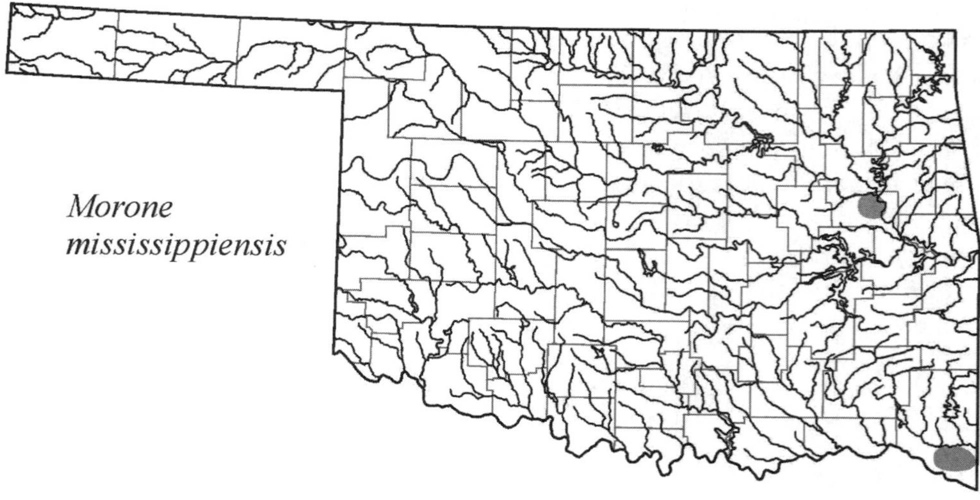

Distribution:

The Mississippi Valley north to Minnesota and Indiana and the Gulf Coast from Texas to Alabama. In Oklahoma it is known only from a few lakes in Wagoner, Muskogee, and McCurtain counties.

Habitat and Biology:

Because of their limited distribution, we know little of the biology of the yellow bass in Oklahoma. Elsewhere they are known to feed on fishes, crustaceans, and insects, both adults and larvae. They breed in spring over gravel and rocky shallows, probably in a manner similar to that of white bass. Apparently the yellow bass is somewhat more of a lake fish, and the spectacular stream spawning runs that white bass make in the spring seem not to occur in the yellow bass. It is considered superior to the white bass as a table fish.

Striped bass

Morone saxatilis (Walbaum)

Description:

The striped bass resembles the white bass more closely than the yellow bass in having the spiny dorsal clearly separated from the second dorsal fin and in being a silver color rather than yellowish or golden. It differs from the white bass, however, in being somewhat more streamlined: the body is not as deep, and the back is not as sharply elevated. There are 7–8 distinct horizontal dark lines along the side, which are more conspicuous than in white bass and not broken up into shorter lines as in that species. In addition the longest anal spine in striped bass is shorter than half the length of the longest anal ray, whereas in white bass it is equal to or greater than half the length of the longest anal ray. The dorsum is greenish or bluish above, sides are silvery, and the belly is white. Most specimens weigh less than 10 pounds, but indi-

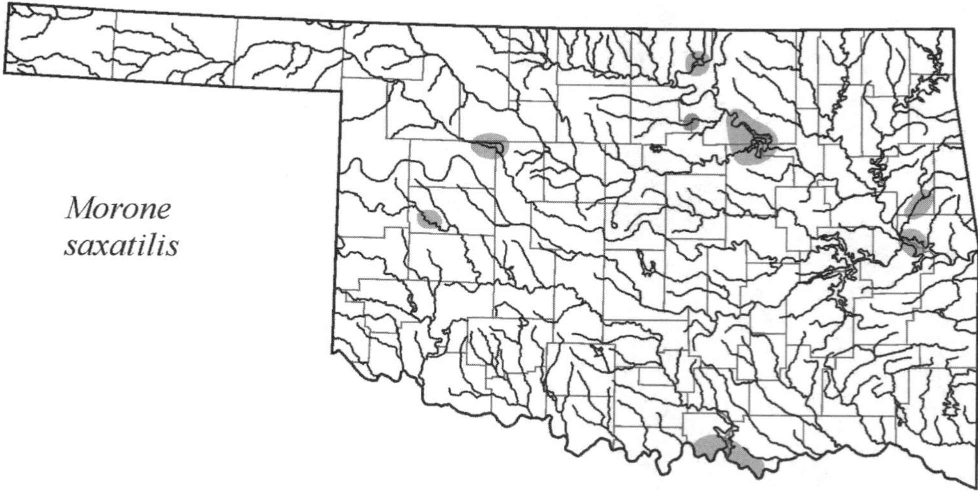

viduals can grow to 30 pounds or more in fresh water. State record: 47 lb., 8 oz., 48 in., from the lower Illinois River. (See also color plate.)

Distribution:

Essentially a marine and estuarine fish of the Atlantic coast, the striped bass runs up numerous coastal rivers to spawn. It has been widely stocked elsewhere, and good populations exist in California and in many inland lakes. At one time or another it has been planted in Lake Murray, Canton Lake, Great Salt Plains Reservoir, and elsewhere, with spectacularly successful stockings in lakes Texoma and Keystone, where successful spawning has been reported. Some records exist from the Red River drainage west to its North Fork. The Oklahoma Department of Wildlife Conservation has been stocking hybrid striper/white bass in lakes across the state.

Habitat and Biology:

A top-level carnivore, the striped bass feeds mainly on fish and crustaceans. It requires rivers with moderately strong currents in which to spawn, and has semi-buoyant eggs that may be carried considerable distances. Stripers may travel in large schools, where local populations are large enough to maintain such activity. The species is an excellent sport and food fish.

PYGMY SUNFISHES

FAMILY ELASSOMATIDAE

Banded pygmy sunfish

Elassoma zonatum Jordan

Description:

A very small, dark, perchlike fish with a moderately elongate body and rounded tail. The color is dark olive green to brown, with breeding males becoming almost black. A fine black speckling covers the body, and 10 or 11 dark vertical bands are often visible on the sides. The lateral line is degenerate. A conspicuous black spot about the size of the eye is present on each side below the origin of the dorsal fin. Less than 1 inch long. (See also color plate.)

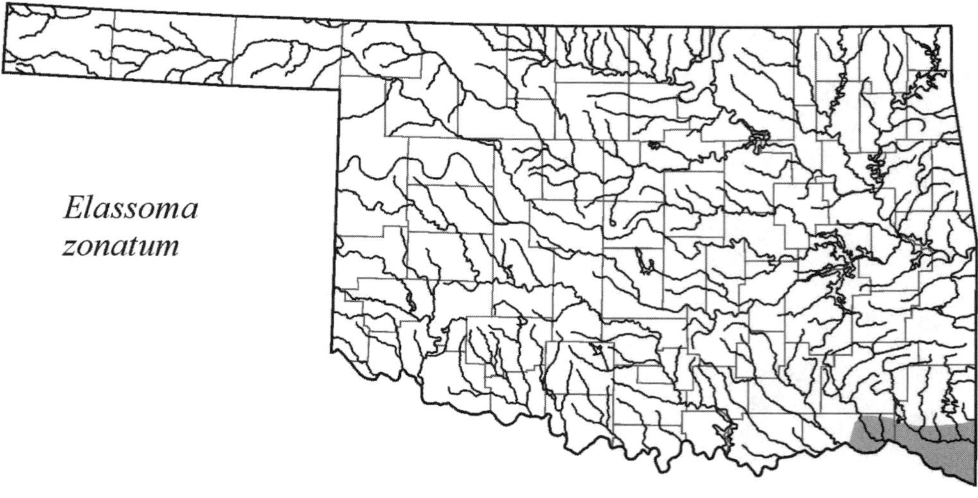

Distribution:

Through the low swampy waters of the Mississippi drainage from southern Illinois to Texas, across the Gulf Coast to Florida, and north to North Carolina. In Oklahoma the species is found only in tributaries of the Red River in McCurtain and Choctaw counties.

Habitat and Biology:

Pygmy sunfish are usually found only in swamps, quiet backwaters of lowland streams, and springs. Dense vegetation is present in the best *Elassoma* habitats, which may account for the fact that the species was not discovered in Oklahoma until 1947. It feeds mainly on small crustaceans and larval insects and does well in aquaria on a diet of daphnia. The males defend territories in the vegetation, often near the surface, and the eggs are deposited directly on strands of plants such as *Ceratophyllum*. Males guard territories for several days and spawn with all ripe females that enter. This pattern of breeding is quite distinct from that of most centrarchids. The unique breeding pattern and several morphological differences support the idea that *Elassoma* should be placed in a separate family.

SUNFISHES

FAMILY CENTRARCHIDAE

Key

1a. Anal spines 3; branchiostegals 6 2

1b. Anal spines 5–8; branchiostegals 6 or 7 14

2a. Body long and slender, not deep and compressed; opercle emarginate; lateral line with 55 or more scales 3

2b. Body deep and compressed; opercle rounded behind; lateral line with less than 55 scales 5

3a. Dorsal fin with a deep notch, the shortest posterior spine about one-half as long as the longest; cheek scales in 9–12 rows; upper jaw extending well behind rear of eye (in adults); dark longitudinal stripe on sides . . . . *Micropterus salmoides*

3b. Dorsal fin with a shallow notch, the shortest posterior spine more than one-half as long as the longest; cheek scales in more than 12 rows; upper jaw not extending well behind rear of eye; with or without dark longitudinal stripe on sides 4

4a. Dorsal soft rays 13–15; sides without lateral band but plain or with vertical bars or mottlings, which may be indistinct; lateral-line scales 67–81; no ventrolateral streaks. . . . . *Micropterus dolomieu*

4b. Dorsal soft rays 12; sides with lateral band usually broken into blotches; lateral-line scales 60–68 (55–72); a dark streak along each ventrolateral scale row . . . . *Micropterus punctulatus*

5a. Tongue with teeth; well-developed supramaxilla; several dark lines radiating backward from eye; mouth large. . . . . *Lepomis gulosus*

5b. Tongue toothless; supramaxilla inconspicuous; no distinct dark lines radiating backward from eye; mouth small (except in green sunfish) 6

6a. Opercle with red margin; pectoral fins very long and pointed, reaching almost to or to the dorsal origin . . . . *Lepomis microlophus*

6b. Opercle without red margin; pectoral fins usually not long and pointed but if long, seldom reach to dorsal origin 7

7a. Opercle stiff to its margin (not including membranes), not fimbriate along posterior edge; ear flap not greatly elongated (see fig. 22) 8

7b. Opercle produced into a thin, flexible, elongated projection, usually fimbriate or fringed along posterior edge (see fig. 22) 10

8a. Body slender and elongated; head length greater than body depth; mouth large; lateral line complete; dorsal and anal fins with dark blotch posteriorly . . . . *Lepomis cyanellus*

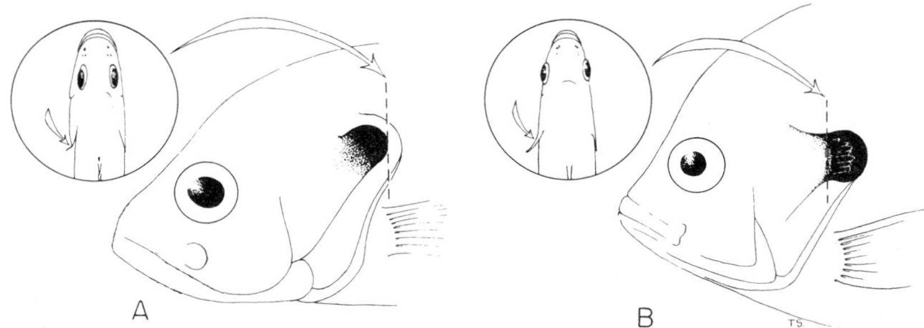

FIGURE 22. Differences in flexibility of opercles in sunfishes. (From Cross 1967)

A. Opercle inflexible posteriorly, its bony edge sharply defined where joined by the marginal gill membrane (as in the warmouth, green sunfish, and redear).

B. Opercle flexible posteriorly, attenuated as a thin, fimbriate, cartilaginous extension into the gill membrane (as in the bluegill, longear, and orangespotted sunfish).

8b. Body deep; head length less than body depth; mouth smaller; lateral line complete or incomplete 9

9a. Lateral line usually complete; soft dorsal without dark spot posteriorly . . . . *Lepomis miniatus*

9b. Lateral line incomplete, nearly one-half of scales unpored; soft dorsal with distinct dark spot posteriorly. . . . . *Lepomis symmetricus*

10a. Gill rakers short, when depressed not extending beyond first gill raker below (except in young); pectorals short, obovate. 11

10b. Gill rakers long, when depressed extending to second gill raker below (third in young); pectorals moderate to long and pointed 13

11a. Opercular membrane dark to its margin; palatine teeth present . . . . *Lepomis auritus*

11b. Opercular membrane white or greenish at the edge; palatine teeth absent 12

12a. Pectoral rays 12 (rarely 13); cheek scales in 4 (3–5) rows; body more rounded, tapering less toward caudal peduncle; anal base convex . . . . *Lepomis marginatus*

12b. Pectoral rays 14 (rarely 13 or 15); cheek scales in 6 (5–7) rows; body more sharply tapering toward caudal peduncle; anal base nearly straight . . . . *Lepomis megalotis*

13a. Palatine teeth present; anal rays 7–9; sensory cavities well developed, enlarged chambers of the interorbital canals wider than interspaces between them . . . . *Lepomis humilis*

13b. Palatine teeth absent; anal rays 10–12; sensory cavities small, the interorbital canal chambers narrower than the interspace . . . *Lepomis macrochirus*

14a. Dorsal spines 11–13 15
14b. Dorsal spines 5–8 16
15a. Preopercle with smooth edge; anal rays usually 10–11; mouth large; body elongated and mottled .... *Ambloplites rupestris*
15b. Preopercle finely serrate; anal rays usually 13–15; mouth small; body compressed with longitudinal rows of spots .... *Centrarchus macropterus*
16a. Dorsal spines usually 6; dorsal fin base shorter than distance from dorsal origin to eye.................................. *Pomoxis annularis*
16b. Dorsal spines usually 7 or 8; dorsal fin base equal to or longer than distance from dorsal origin to eye........... *Pomoxis nigromaculatus*

ROCK BASS
Ambloplites rupestris (Rafinesque)

Description:

An elongate, olivaceous sunfish that may attain a length of 12 inches and weigh over a pound. It is easily recognized by the 5 or 6 anal spines, large mouth, red eye, and color pattern. Horizontal lines are formed by single black spots at the bases of the lateral scales. Dark lateral blotches on the sides may be inconspicuous in adults but are well developed in the young. The opercle flap is short and the pectoral fin is short and rounded. Lateral line usually with fewer than 41 scales (36–44). Breast scale rows usually 20 or more (18–24). Cheek scale rows usually eight, often 9 (6–10). Dorsal spines 11–13; dorsal rays 11–13. Anal spines 5 or 6; anal rays 9–11. The back and sides are olivaceous, grading to a dusky white belly. Median fins are mottled with brown, and the anal of the male has a black marginal band.

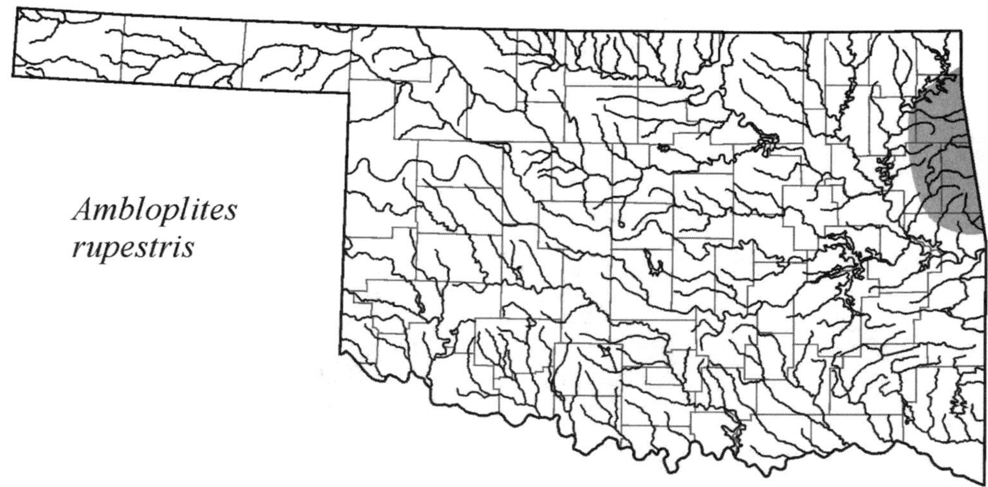

Distribution:

Throughout central North America from Manitoba and Quebec south through the Great Lakes and the Mississippi Valley to Arkansas and the northern Gulf states. Found in the Ozark uplands of northeastern Oklahoma, primarily in the Illinois River system.

Habitat and Biology:

This species is well named, for it definitely prefers the clear, rocky-bottomed streams of eastern Oklahoma. It is similar to other sunfishes in spawning habits and feeding preferences (insects, crustaceans, molluscs, and fishes) but differs in that it seeks out areas with rubble, boulders, and exposed bedrock. The cracks and step-offs in such habitats offer excellent shelter. In winter rock bass can often be found "hibernating" under leaves and debris in backwaters and among the roots of trees. They are caught easily on live baits and in larger streams can attain a size large enough to make them a preferred panfish. The young are brightly blotched and are often found in weed-choked backwaters.

Note:

In the first edition of this book, we called all rock bass in the state *Ambloplites rupestris*. Later, state populations were considered *A. ariommus* (Cashner 1980; Robison and Buchanan 1988) based on the morphological findings of Cashner and Suttkus (1977). However, recent molecular studies have not supported the morphological data that *A. ariommus* occurs in Oklahoma, and thus we return to the use of *A. rupestris* for all state populations of rock bass.

Flier

Centrarchus macropterus (Lacepede)

Description:

The flier is a relatively small, deep-bodied sunfish that rarely exceeds 6 inches in length. It can be distinguished from all other sunfishes by the 11 to 13 dorsal spines and 7 or 8 anal spines. The color is greenish above and yellowish below, with horizontal lines formed on the sides by conspicuous dark brown spots. A black spot (ocellus) with reddish to pale edges occurs on the

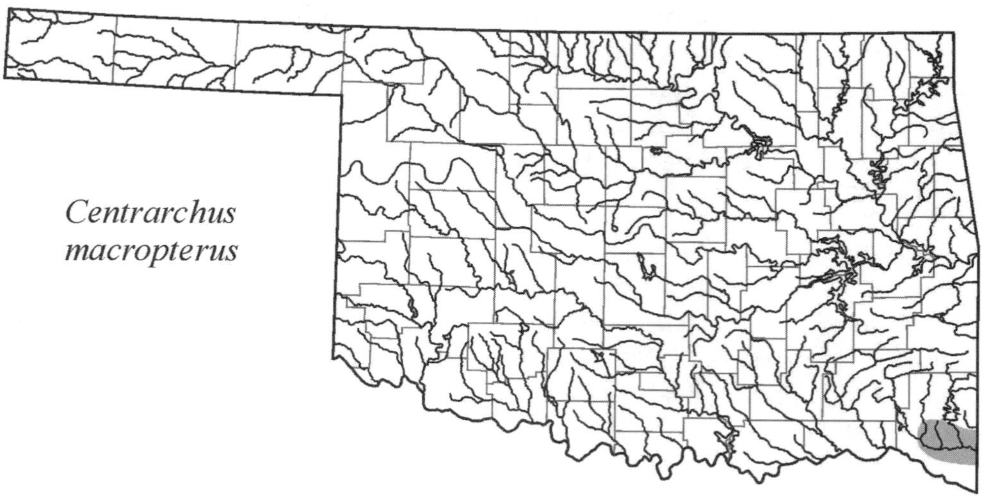

posterior rays of the dorsal fin of young fish; however, it fades with age. (See also color plate.)

Distribution:

Lowland waters from Virginia to Louisiana and northward through the Mississippi basin to southern Illinois. In Oklahoma found only in McCurtain County, typically in swampy waters and oxbow lakes.

Habitat and Biology:

Little is known about the life history of this fish in Oklahoma. Elsewhere it feeds on insects, snails, and other animal foods and is known to construct a shallow nest similar to that of other sunfish. Rarely found in fast-flowing water, the flier usually prefers living among the stumps and sunken logs of quiet, brown-water swamps and associated streams and ponds. Its small size limits its importance as a game or food fish in Oklahoma.

REDBREAST SUNFISH

Lepomis auritus (Linnaeus)

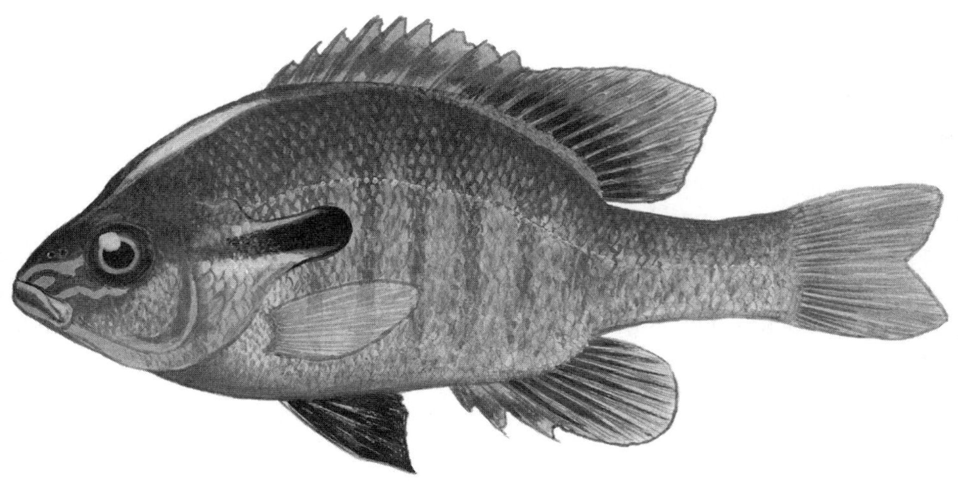

Description:

A fairly large sunfish best identified by the long, narrow opercular flap, which is uniformly black to its margin. The mouth is small; gill rakers are short. Pectoral fin is short and rounded. Lateral line scales number 43–50. The back is olivaceous, grading into the orange or reddish underside. There is no black blotch on the posterior dorsal rays. Although large specimens

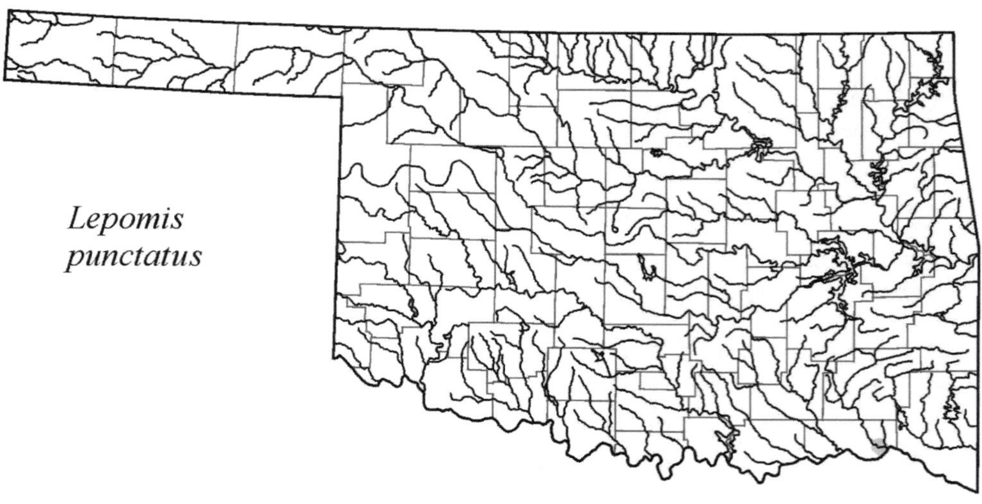

may reach 10 inches in length, relatively few exceed 6 inches. (See also color plate.)

Distribution:

Eastern coastal streams from Maine to Louisiana. Introduced and now fairly widespread in some parts of Texas. Reliable records from three counties in southeastern Oklahoma (McCurtain, Love, Muskogee) may increase as this introduced species becomes more widespread. As yet, however, the species is not encountered in natural waters regularly sampled in this area.

Habitat and Biology:

The redbreast (known as yellowbelly in some parts of its range) is primarily a stream fish, though it does well in some lakes and ponds. It feeds mainly on insects, small molluscs, and small fish. Perhaps because it is best adapted for stream habitats, it tends to be less of a colonial spawner than most other sunfishes, though nest construction and spawning are basically similar to those of congeners. If the redbreast becomes established in Oklahoma, it will probably prove to be one of the more desirable panfishes.

Green sunfish

Lepomis cyanellus Rafinesque

Description:

A rather thick-bodied, elongate *Lepomis*, the green sunfish can generally be distinguished by its unusually large mouth, olivaceous coloring, and the black spots at the bases of the posterior rays of both dorsal and anal fins. The opercle is only moderately long and is stiff to its margin. The mouth is large with iridescent bluish or greenish "worm tracks" on the cheeks. Lateral line scales 41–52. Gill rakers are long and slender. Pectoral fins are short and rounded. Adults usually 8–10 inches and about one pound. State record: 2 lb., 7 oz., 13 in., from a Pontotoc County pond. (See also color plate.)

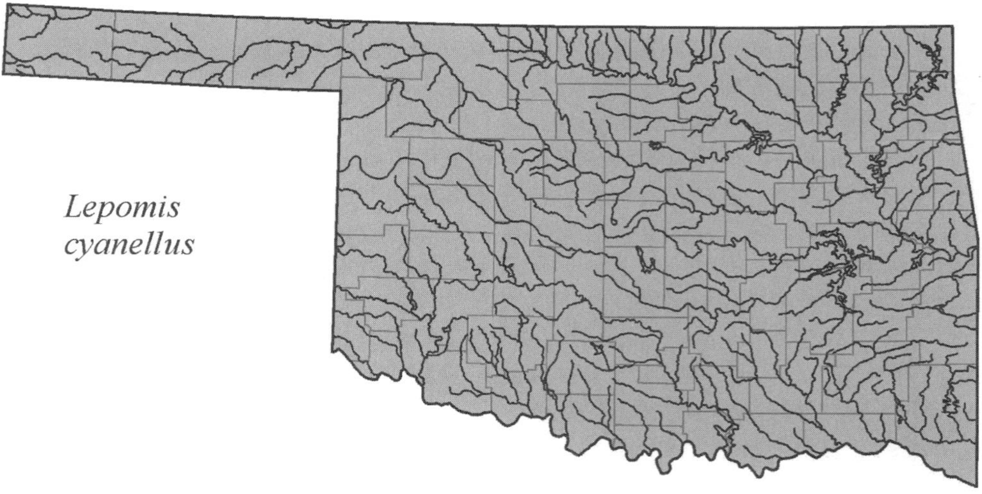

Distribution:

Ponds, lakes, and streams from Colorado through the Great Lakes to southern Ontario and New York, throughout most of the southeastern United States, and west to New Mexico. Found throughout Oklahoma.

Habitat and Biology:

Although the green sunfish can be found in a variety of waters in Oklahoma, it seems to prefer small streams and ponds and can survive in habitats too small or temporary to support most other sunfish. It feeds primarily on insects and fish, and because of its large mouth and voracious appetite, it can often be caught on lures intended for bass. Like most other sunfishes, the green sunfish spawns primarily from May through early summer in a shallow nestlike bottom depression formed by the male, which uses lateral sweeping movements of the tail to displace silt, mud, and loose detritus from the nest site. Males defend these nests vigorously during the breeding season and can often be observed fanning newly laid eggs with rhythmic movements of the pectoral fins. Because of their relatively small size (generally less than 10 inches) in most habitats, they are a marginal food and game fish, mainly of local importance.

WARMOUTH

Lepomis gulosus (Cuvier)

Description:

A brown sunfish that differs from other members of the genus *Lepomis* in having teeth on the tongue and a larger supramaxillary bone. The brown of its back and sides grades into a yellowish belly, and several mottled, dark vertical bars are usually visible on the sides. The opercle flap is short with a black spot, the eye is red, and the mouth is relatively large. Conspicuous brown and yellow streaks extend from the eye to the margin of the gill covers, providing this fish its most obvious external identification characteristic. Although indi-

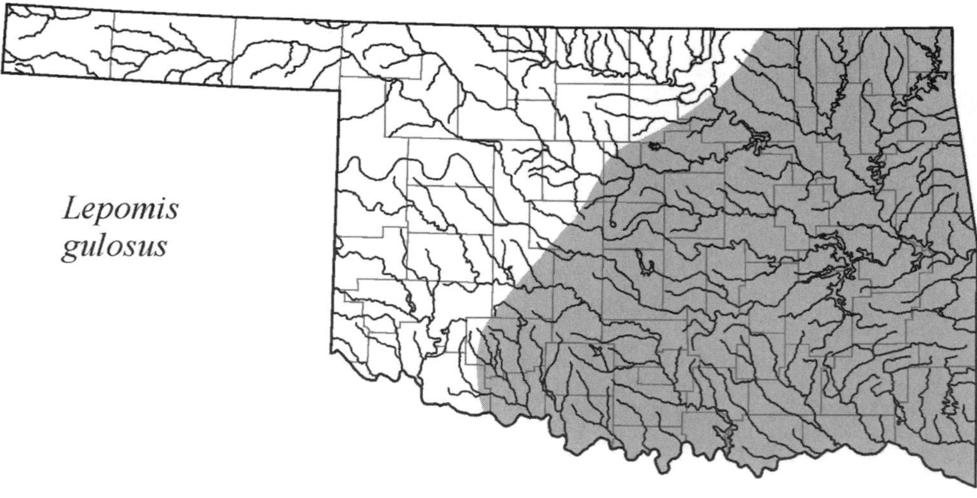

viduals may reach a pound in weight and 10 inches in length, they rarely exceed 6–8 inches in Oklahoma.

Distribution:

Most of the eastern United States from Wisconsin, Michigan, and Ohio south through the Mississippi Valley to Texas and the Gulf states. On the East Coast from Florida to New York. In Oklahoma the warmouth occurs in all of the eastern counties and extends up the three major river systems to Comanche, Cleveland, and Payne counties. Probably introduced elsewhere.

Habitat and Biology:

Basically a pond and lake fish, the warmouth can often be found in pools of sluggish streams and rivers as well. Fish, crayfish, and larval aquatic insects are preferred foods. Its large mouth permits capture of larger organisms than many other sunfish can utilize. The warmouth seems to prefer weedy or brushy habitats in quiet waters and is less colonial in its nesting habits than most *Lepomis*. Spawning occurs from May through September but is mainly concentrated in spring and early summer.

Note:

In the previous edition of this book this species was listed as *Chaenobryttus gulosus*. Bailey and colleagues (1970) included this species in the genus *Lepomis* and most authors have followed this. Studies by Merriner (1971) on intergeneric centrarchid hybrids, however, have suggested that *Chaenobryttus* is more closely related to *Micropterus* than *Lepomis*, and a final decision on the systematic status of this species must await more definitive study.

ORANGESPOTTED SUNFISH

Lepomis humilis (Girard)

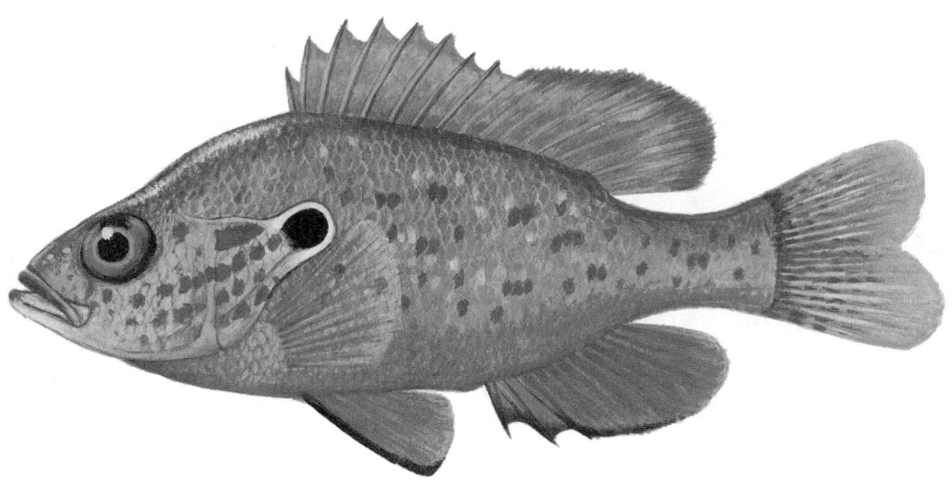

Description:

A small, brightly colored sunfish with irregularly spaced brownish or orange spots on the sides and a long, white-edged opercular flap. Breeding males have the belly and median fins flushed with bright orange, with the anal and pelvic fins edged with black pigment. The iris is red or orange and in breeding males the sides of the head are an iridescent bluish color streaked with bright orange. Mouth is moderately large. The gill rakers are long and the pectoral fin is moderately long and pointed. Lateral line scales 32–39. Adults rarely exceed 4 inches. (See also color plate.)

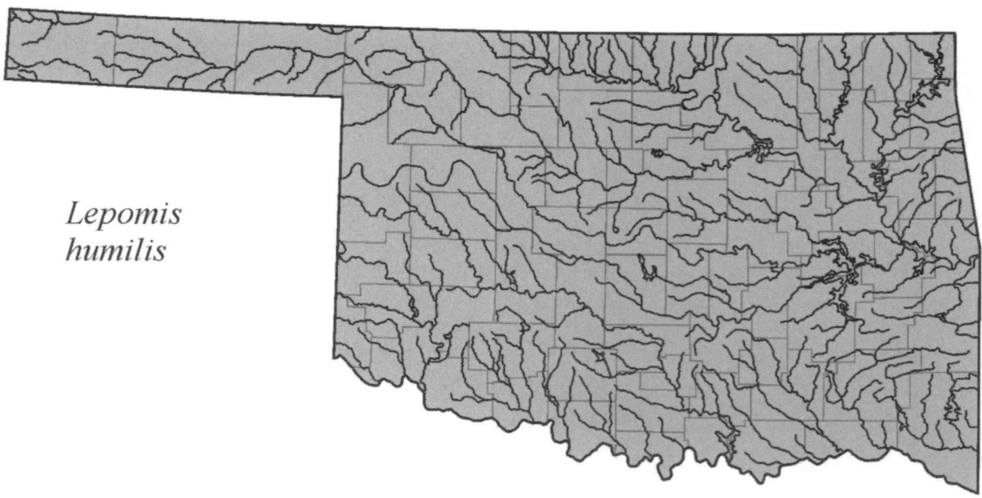

Distribution:

From North Dakota east to Ohio and southward through the Mississippi basin to Alabama and Louisiana. Throughout the Great Plains from Texas to the Dakotas, including all of Oklahoma.

Habitat and Biology:

Primarily an inhabitant of small, sandy or mud-bottomed streams, the orangespotted sunfish is better adapted than most other sunfish for life in the turbid streams and lakes of our region. Perhaps the enlarged sensory openings of the lateral-line system of the head permit a more delicate detection mechanism for pressure waves, which compensates for the lack of vision in turbid waters. A spring and early summer spawner with breeding behavior similar to that of other sunfishes, the orangespotted sunfish tends to be somewhat more gregarious than some other *Lepomis*, such as the green sunfish. Because of its small size, this sunfish is of little food or game significance.

Bluegill

Lepomis macrochirus Rafinesque

Description:

A relatively large, deep-bodied sunfish with a small mouth, slender gill rakers, a black opercular flap, and a black spot at the base of the posterior dorsal rays. Body color is olivaceous with bluish iridescence above and silvery below. Breeding males develop a bright orange to red flush on the breast, more intense coloration of the body, and darker pelvic and anal fins. The lower edge of the gill cover is usually bluish, intensely so in breeding males. Lateral-line scales 39–44. Usually less than 8 inches long but reaching 10 inches and 2 pounds. State record: 2 lb., 6 oz., 12¾ in., from a Kay County pond. (See also color plate.)

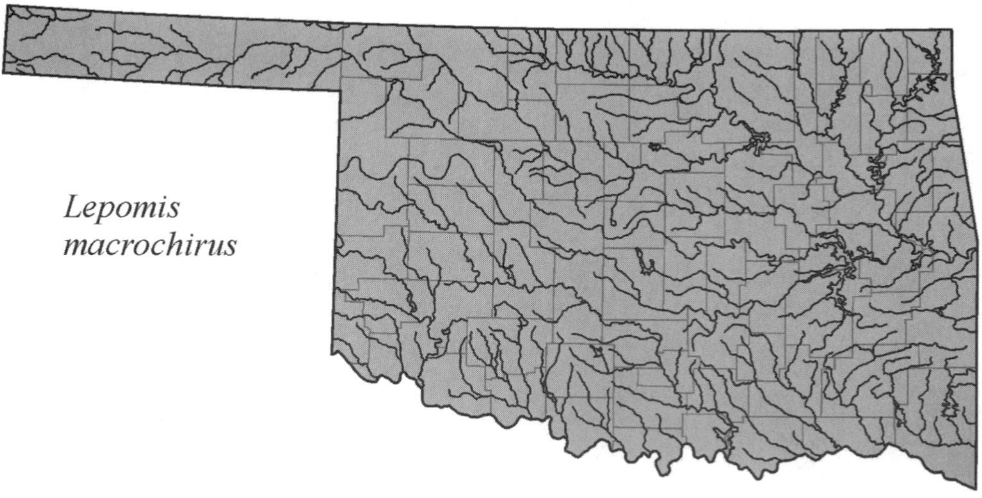

Distribution:

Throughout the eastern United States westward to the plains states and introduced widely over the entire country. Found throughout Oklahoma, the bluegill has been widely introduced in ponds and lakes and occurs in many flowing waters in the western part of the state due to escapes from stocked ponds. Probably native in eastern Oklahoma.

Habitat and Biology:

This species seems to do best in clear, quiet waters with limited vegetation. In turbid ponds it often stunts and loses condition. Bluegills feed mainly on microcrustaceans and insects, though larger individuals take small fish. More gregarious than the green sunfish, a species with which they often hybridize, bluegills typically build and defend their nests in large colonies. Spawning occurs mainly in May and June but may extend from April to August or September. In large lakes and well-balanced ponds bluegills grow to 8 inches in length or more and are good pan fish.

DOLLAR SUNFISH

Lepomis marginatus (Holbrook)

Description:

A small sunfish that superficially resembles the longear. The two can be distinguished by the dollar sunfish having 3–4 rows of cheek scales (vs. usually 6 in the longear) and 12 rays in the pectoral fin (vs. 14). Scales on the sides of adults have rather uniform dark spots, giving the fish a more dusky general appearance than many sunfishes. The opercular flap has a somewhat

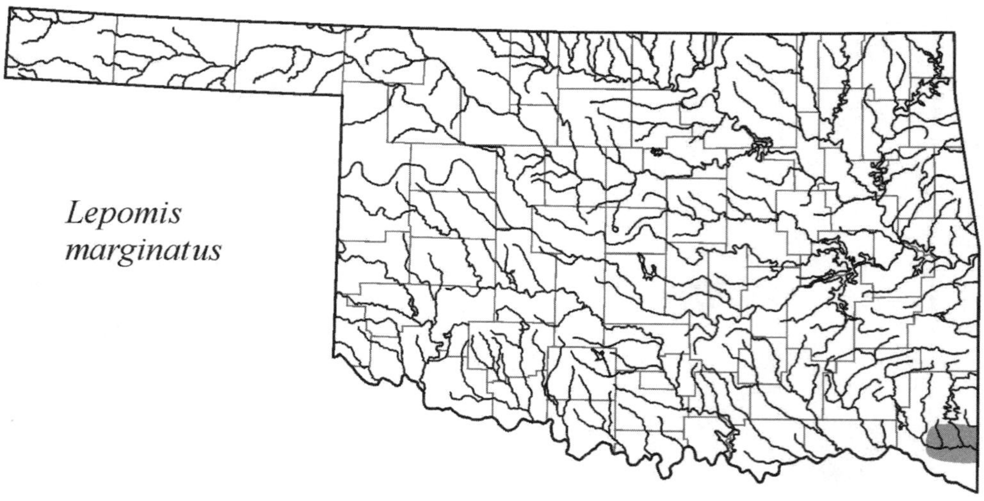

greenish margin. The mouth is small, gill rakers are short and stubby, and pectoral fin is short and rounded. Lateral-line scales 35–42. Most specimens are less than 4 inches long. (See also color plate.)

Distribution:

Southern coastal drainages from South Carolina to Texas and north through the Mississippi drainage to Tennessee and Arkansas. Found in Oklahoma only in McCurtain County.

Habitat and Biology:

Although this species was not discovered in Oklahoma until 1947, it is fairly well established in the swamps and sluggish streams of McCurtain County. It is known to feed on immature aquatic insects and small crustaceans. Spawning occurs from mid-May to early August. Nests are constructed by males on firm sand bottoms with little aquatic vegetation. Minimum breeding size is 2.4 inches.

LONGEAR SUNFISH

Lepomis megalotis (Rafinesque)

Description:

A small, deep-bodied sunfish with a long, flexible opercular flap that is generally edged with white. The pectoral fin is short and rounded with 13–15 rays. Gill rakers are short and knoblike. Mouth is relatively small. Cheek scales usually in 6 rows (5–7). Lateral-line with 36–43 scales. Color is olivaceous above, the breast usually some shade of orange in adults and pale in juveniles. Breeding males become iridescent green above and bright orange

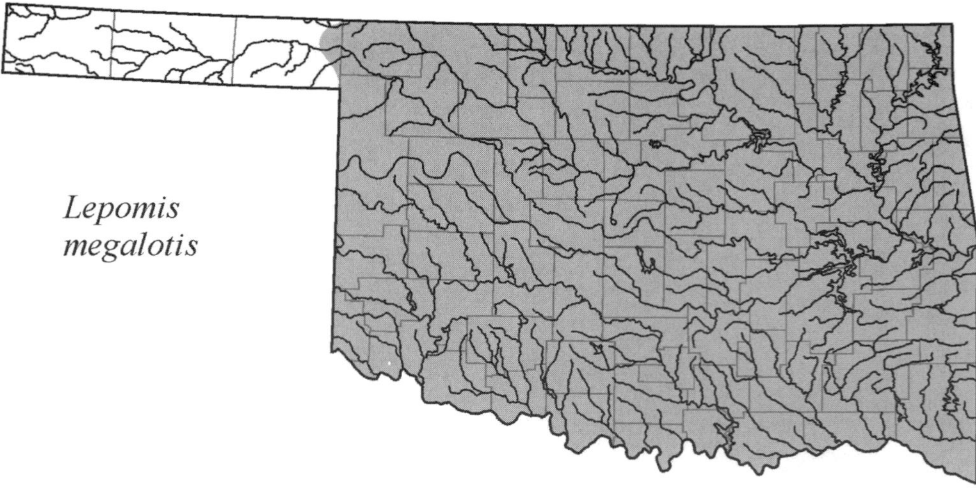

below, but there are no scattered, discrete orange spots on the sides. Adults rarely exceed 5 inches in length. Maximum length is 7 inches and 1 pound, 12 ounces. (See also color plate.)

Distribution:

Occurs in a belt from Ontario and western New York in the east throughout the Mississippi basin and extending westward through Minnesota and Nebraska and south into Texas. Found in most Oklahoma counties outside the panhandle. Distinct forms (subspecies) are found in the Red River and Arkansas River drainages.

Habitat and Biology:

The longear sunfish seems to do best in the clear waters of the eastern part of the state, apparently preferring quiet pools in clear, hard-bottomed low-gradient streams. It feeds mainly on aquatic and terrestrial insects but will take other invertebrates or even small fish. Spawning occurs from May to August. Nests are typically circular depressions in the substrate constructed by males. While this is one of the most beautiful of Oklahoma's fishes, especially in the spring, it is of limited interest to most anglers because of its small size.

Redear sunfish

Lepomis microlophus (Gunther)

Description:

A well-proportioned sunfish that can grow to 9 inches in length and half a pound in weight. The mouth is relatively small. Gill rakers are short and stout. Lateral-line scales 34–43. Color is usually pale olivaceous above and more silvery below, with young specimens having about 8 dark vertical bars on the side. The redear is readily distinguished by the short opercular flap with a bright red posterior crescent and by the long, pointed pectoral fin. The dorsal fin is uniformly colored with no black blotch on the posterior rays. State record: 2 lb., 1 oz., 12¾ in., from a Logan County pond.

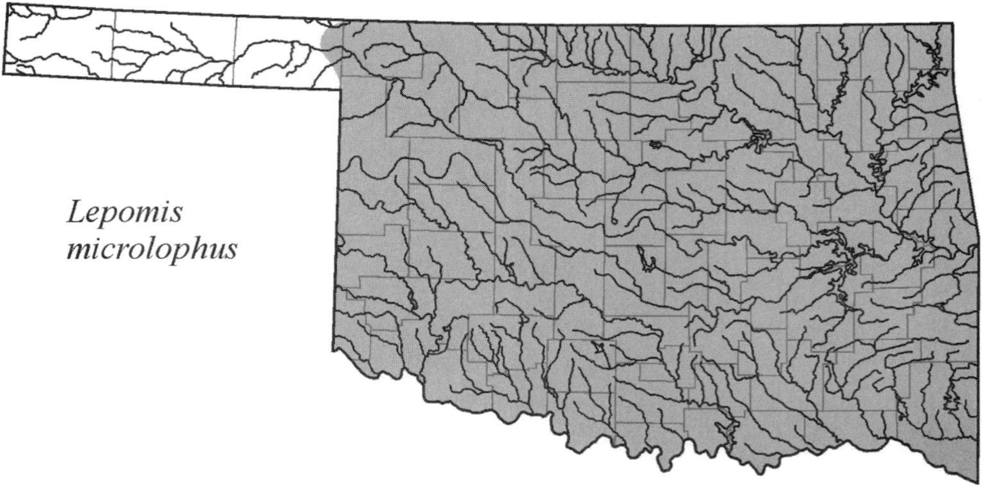

Distribution:

The Mississippi basin from Indiana and Missouri south to the Gulf states and Florida. Widely introduced elsewhere, including Oklahoma, where it now can be found irregularly distributed throughout most of the state.

Habitat and Biology:

Primarily introduced in farm ponds and impoundments, the redear has escaped to many streams and rivers of Oklahoma. Nonetheless, it does best in large lakes and ponds. In some parts of its eastern range, the tendency of this species to congregate about brush and stumps has led to adoption of the name "stumpknocker." Spawning occurs from April to August. Breeding behavior of the redear is similar to that of other sunfishes. It feeds on most kinds of small invertebrates, though its preference for eating snails has led to the use of another common name: "shellcracker." The broad, flat pharyngeal teeth are well suited for crushing mollusc shells. In well-balanced ponds and lakes the redear becomes a highly valued panfish.

Redspotted sunfish

Lepomis miniatus (Jordan)

Description:

A small, deep-bodied sunfish with a dusky brown overall appearance. Body scales each have a brown to reddish spot, which often produces an overall effect of dark horizontal lines running the length of the body. The opercular flap is short and stiff to its margin, and the large dark opercular spot is not confined to the bony flap as is true in green sunfish. The membranous edge of the flap is usually lighter. Mouth is moderate sized. Gill rakers

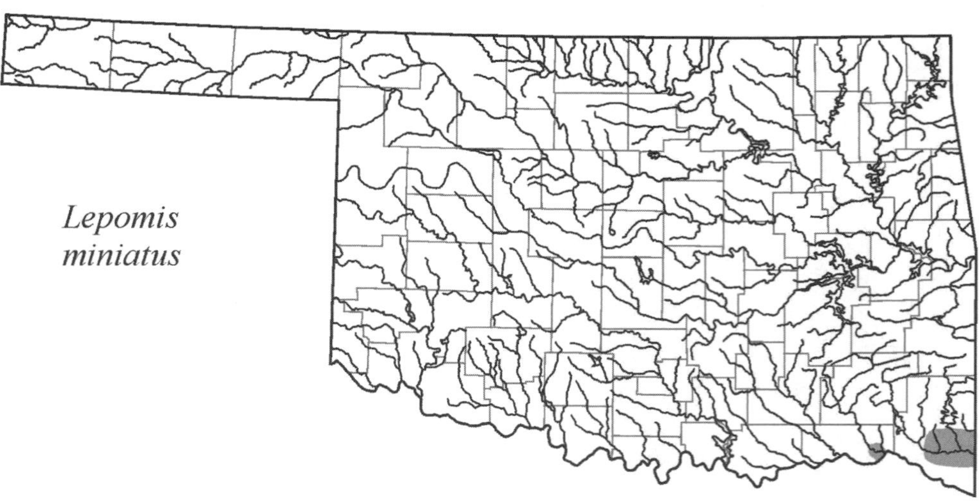

are short and rounded, as are the pectoral fins. Lateral-line scales 36–39. Rarely exceeds 5 or 6 inches in length. Maximum size 8 inches and 7 ounces. (See also color plate.)

Distribution:

From Indiana and Missouri through the Mississippi basin to the Gulf states eastward to North Carolina. In Oklahoma the species is known only from pools and swamps in the Little River system in McCurtain County.

Habitat and Biology:

The redspotted sunfish seems to prefer the sluggish, swampy lowland waters of the Little River drainage. Spawning tends to occur from April to August. Studies in Florida showed that the breeding habits of *L. punctatus* (formerly considered a subspecies, as was the Oklahoma form) were basically similar to those of other sunfish, but that in constant-temperature springs, some scattered winter breeding did occur; this is most unlikely in Oklahoma. Florida fish seemed to show relatively little movement except a nocturnal shift closer to shore. In Oklahoma the redspotted sunfish tends to be found in clear, quiet, brown water. It feeds on aquatic insects and various other invertebrates.

Bantam sunfish

Lepomis symmetricus Forbes

Description:

One of the smallest sunfishes, rarely exceeding 3 inches in length. Ground color is olivaceous, with brown spots at the base of each scale forming horizontal lines. A dark spot at the posterior base of the dorsal fin is most conspicuous in young fish. The lateral line is incomplete or interrupted with up to 18 scales lacking pores. The dark opercle flap is short with a light margin, and the gill rakers are long. Pectoral fins are short and rounded.

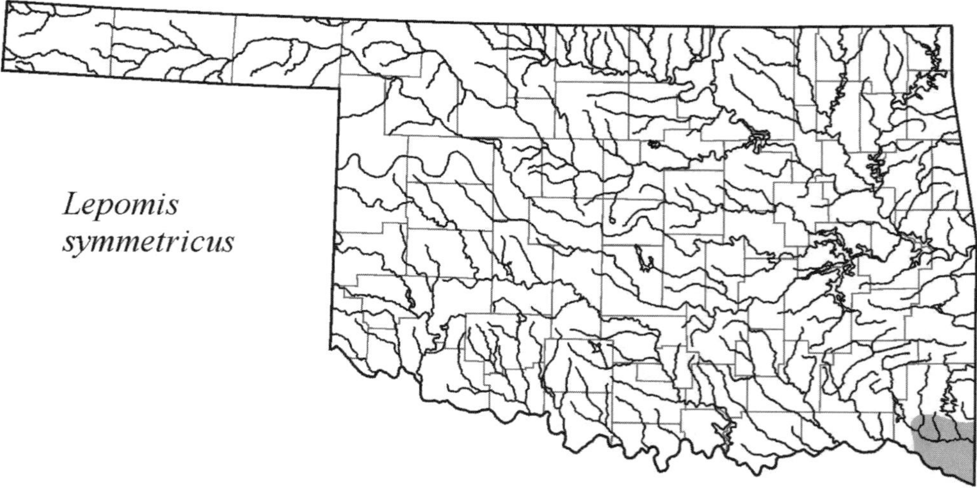

Distribution:

Throughout the Mississippi Valley from southern Illinois to Mississippi, Louisiana, and Texas. In Oklahoma found only in the swamps of McCurtain County.

Habitat and Biology:

This diminutive sunfish has a decided preference for quiet, well-vegetated, swampy waters. It feeds on small crustaceans and immature and adult insects, including terrestrial insects. Bantam sunfish can be kept in aquaria on a diet of *Daphnia* and small earthworms for at least several months. Spawning occurs in April and May; however, nestbuilding and spawning behavior have not been observed. Sexual maturity is reached at age 1.

Smallmouth bass
Micropterus dolomieu Lacepede

Description:

A large, elongate centrarchid with a low spinous dorsal joined broadly to the soft-rayed portion of the dorsal fin. The mouth is large for a centrarchid but smaller than that of the largemouth bass (see key). Lateral-line scales 68–76. Color is bronze or olivaceous, often with diffuse vertical dark bars on the sides. No dark lateral band is present on the sides. Young have an orange band at the caudal base and a black submarginal band on the caudal fin. Three dark bars on the cheek are conspicuous. State record: 7 lb., 8 oz., 23 in. long, from Lake Texoma. (See also color plate.)

Distribution:

From the Great Lakes and southeastern Canada west to South Dakota and Iowa and south to Oklahoma, Arkansas, and northern Alabama. The

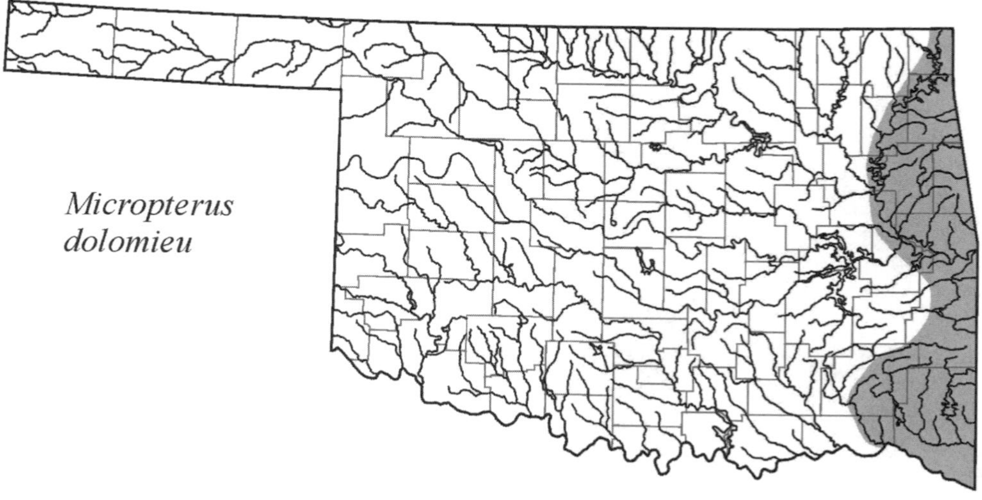

species is found in the eastern upland areas of Oklahoma, though records from Comanche County and possibly other western areas may occasionally occur as a result of transplantation.

Habitat and Biology:

This outstanding game fish (also called the "brown bass") is a species of cool, clear, rocky streams. In Ohio most populations are found in streams having gradients of 4–25 feet per mile with bottoms of clean gravel, boulders, and bedrock. Oklahoma smallmouths appear to be similar, with our best streams in the Illinois, Mountain Fork, and Glover drainages. Smallmouths feed mainly on crayfish, fish, and aquatic insects. Spawning occurs in April and May after construction of a fairly typical centrarchid nest. The male fans the nest with his pectoral fins and guards the developing eggs and hatchlings as long as they remain near the nest. The smallmouth male does not appear to move about and protect the young after they leave the nest, as do largemouth males. This is probably due to the fact that smallmouths select spawning sites in flowing waters, where the integrity of a school of hatchlings would be difficult to maintain.

Spotted bass

Micropterus punctulatus (Rafinesque)

Description:

A large, slim, elongate centrarchid with a series of dark blotches forming a longitudinal band along the side. The low spinous dorsal fin is fairly broadly joined to the rayed portion of the dorsal. The body is olivaceous to green dorsally, grading to a white underside. Scales on the underside have dark spots that form a series of dark horizontal lines. Dark cheek stripes are less conspicuous than in the smallmouth. The caudal fin of young has orange at its base and a black band submarginally. Usually 10 dorsal spines and 12 dorsal rays. Resembles the largemouth in many respects but rarely exceeds 1.5 pounds and 15 inches in length. State record: 8 lb., 2 oz., 23½ in., from a pond in Pittsburg County. (See also color plate.)

Distribution:

South-central United States from Kansas and Texas in the west to Illinois and Pennsylvania in the north and south to Georgia and the Gulf states.

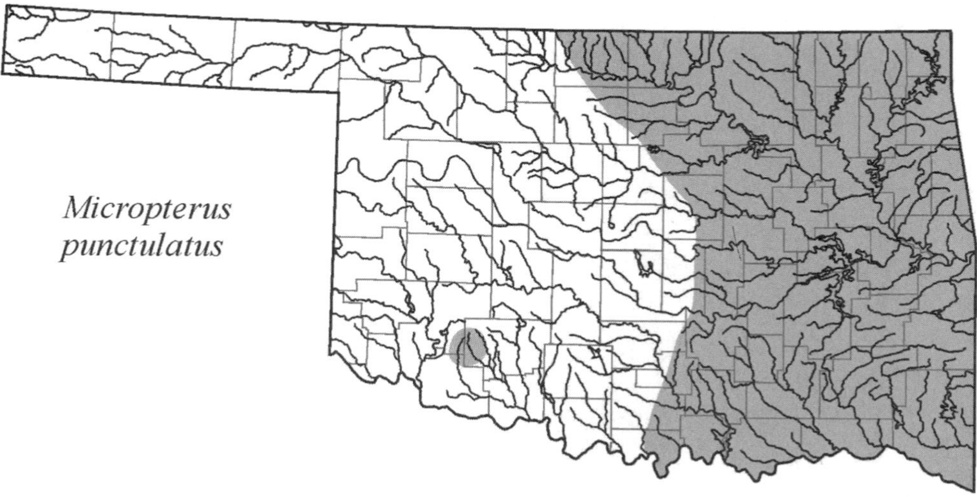

Found in about the eastern half of Oklahoma and recorded from Comanche County in the southwest.

Habitat and Biology:

Although they do fairly well in some clear lakes, spotted bass are best adapted for relatively small, clear, spring-fed streams. They tolerate turbid waters with silt bottoms better than do smallmouths, hence their wider distribution. Crayfish seem to be a major component of the diet, but insects and small fish are also eaten in most areas. Spotted bass breed in April and May, and in at least some Arkansas lakes they exhibit courtship movements not seen in largemouth or smallmouth bass.

LARGEMOUTH BASS

Micropterus salmoides (Lacepede)

Description:

A robust, elongate centrarchid that can reach 11 pounds in weight and 25 inches in length in Oklahoma. Olivaceous above and white on the underside, the body has a dark lateral band running its length. The spinous dorsal fin is barely connected to the soft-rayed dorsal fin, and the shortest dorsal spine is less than half the length of the longest dorsal spine. The mouth is large and the upper jaw extends back beyond the posterior edge of the eye. Usually 9 dorsal spines and 12 or 13 dorsal rays. State record: 14 lb., 11 oz., 28 in., from Broken Bow Reservoir. (See also color plate.)

Distribution:

Originally distributed across most of the eastern United States from southeastern Canada to Mexico and Florida. Now introduced in many places

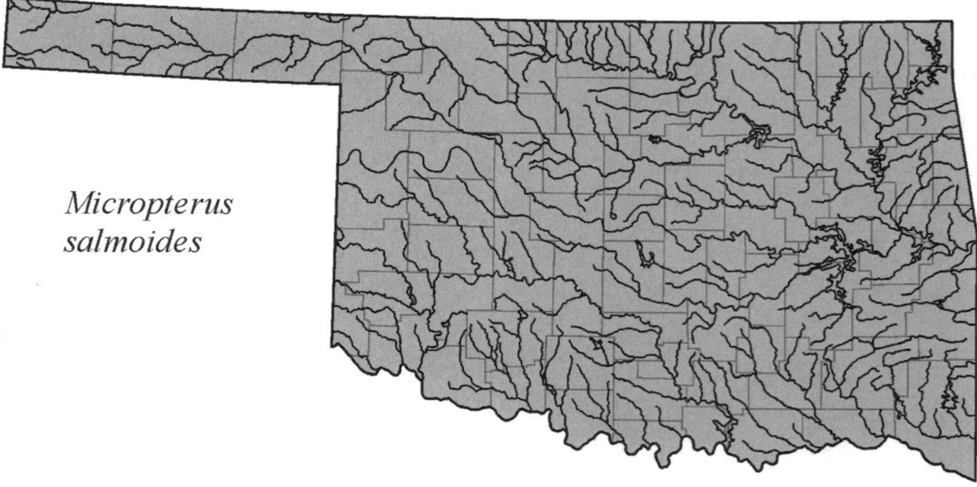

elsewhere in the country, the species can be found in ponds and lakes throughout Oklahoma.

Habitat and Biology:

The largemouth is a highly successful lake and pond fish in Oklahoma but can also do well in the deeper, quiet pools of large streams. It is the species most commonly stocked in farm ponds and probably the most sought-after game fish in the state. In larger lakes and ponds there appear to be two kinds of individuals: one type that is essentially solitary and continuously associated with cover, like a stump or clump of lily pads, and another that congregates in groups and may move regularly about the perimeter of a pond. Experienced anglers quickly learn to find the "hotspots" in a lake, where appropriate cover seems to guarantee presence of a resident fish. The largemouth feeds mainly on fish, crayfish, and insects and spawns in spring when the water temperature rises above 65 degrees F. The male guards the nest and defends the dense schools of young for some time after they leave the nest.

WHITE CRAPPIE
Pomoxis annularis Rafinesque

Description:

A deep-bodied, fairly elongate sunfish with a large mouth and overall silvery appearance. The dorsum is olivaceous but the sides are silvery with faint, dark vertical bars. Median fins are lightly mottled. The white crappie is most easily separated from the black crappie by the 6 dorsal spines (vs. 7 or 8) and the vertical bars on the silvery sides (vs. an irregular blotched pattern in black crappie). The lower jaws of both species protrude more than in most other sunfishes. May grow to 2 or 3 pounds in weight. (See also color plate.)

Distribution:

From southern Ontario west to Minnesota and Nebraska, south through the Mississippi basin to the Gulf states, and north along the East Coast to

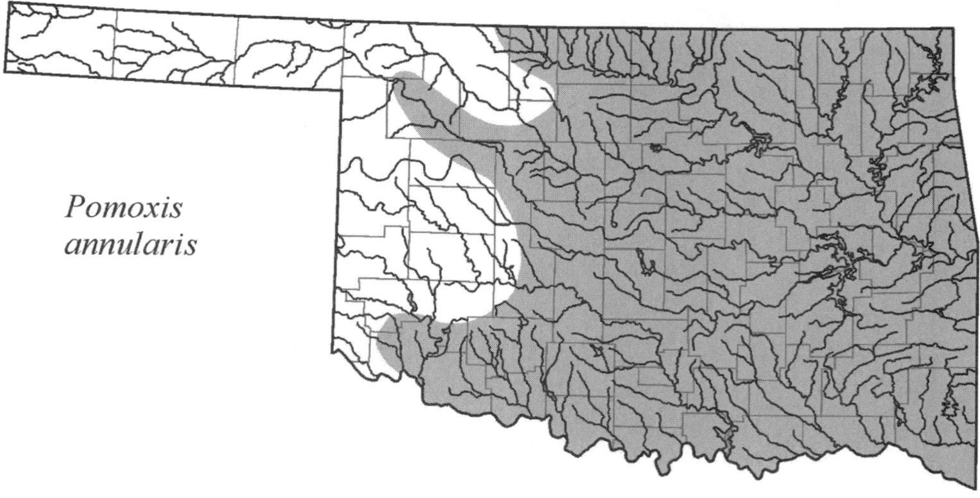

North Carolina. In Oklahoma it is widely distributed in most tributaries of the major river systems and has been introduced in many lakes and ponds throughout the state.

Habitat and Biology:

The white crappie is quite tolerant of turbidity, and as a result it has proven one of the most successful and prolific of Oklahoma centrarchids. It can be found in almost all kinds of waters and often seems to congregate about brush piles or submerged trees. Preferred food of adults is fish, and anglers have maximum success with minnows or jigs. Crappie spawn in April over nests that are less well developed than those of *Lepomis* species. Some kind of plant material or vegetation is usually found in or near the nests, and nests are typically clustered densely in rather shallow water (often less than 2 feet deep). Unfortunately, crappie are often stunted in small ponds, so they are most attractive as inhabitants of larger impoundments.

Black crappie

Pomoxis nigromaculatus (Lesueur)

Description:

A deep-bodied centrarchid that differs from the white crappie in its darker overall color, with irregular blotching on the sides, and its longer dorsal fin (7–8 dorsal spines vs. 6 in white crappie). Anal spines number 6–7 and soft rays 16–19. Lateral-line scales 35–41. The pattern of blotches on the median fins often gives the appearance of white spots on a black background. Body color is basically silvery on the sides with black blotches superimposed. The black crappie is a handsome fish that may occasionally exceed 3 pounds

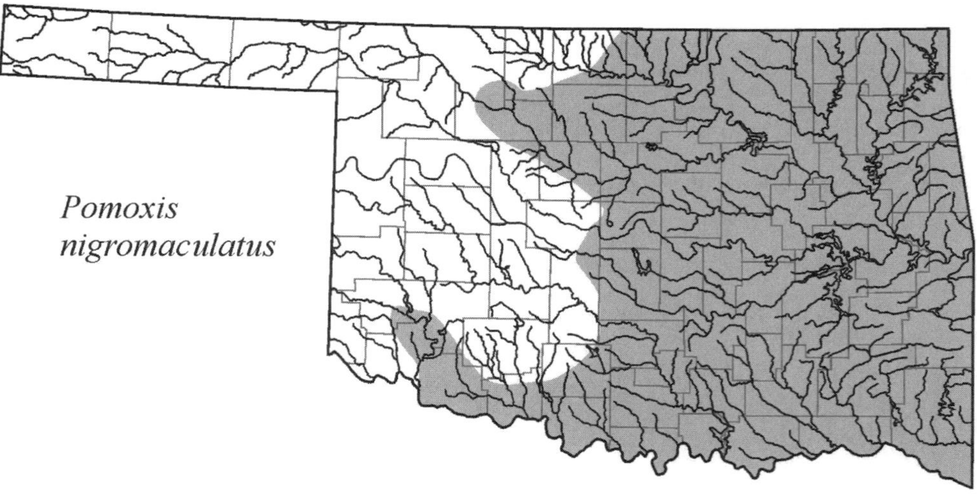

in weight. State record: 4 lb., 10 oz., 20 in., from an Ottawa County pond. (See also color plate.)

Distribution:

Widely distributed through the eastern United States, from southern Canada to Texas and Florida, and widely introduced elsewhere. It may be found in larger impoundments through much of Oklahoma but is most common in the east and in clear waters; less so in flowing and turbid waters.

Habitat and Biology:

Black crappie do best where competition with white crappie is limited and definitely prefer clear water with more vegetation than is true of white crappie. They appear to do best in large, clear lakes and are not often found in flowing waters in the western part of the state. They feed on small fish and aquatic insects and usually build their nests among vegetation, as white crappie do. Black crappie are also partial to brush piles and similar sources of cover, from which they can often be caught throughout the year.

PERCHES

FAMILY PERCIDAE

Key

1a. Preopercle strongly serrate; mouth large, upper jaw extending at least to below middle of eye; branchiostegals 7 or 8; large size, adults usually more than 10 inches 2

1b. Preopercle smooth-edged or very weakly serrate; upper jaw not extending below middle of eye; branchiostegals 5 or 6 4

2a. Body with conspicuous vertical crossbands; canine teeth absent; pelvic fins close together, the interspace less than the length of the fin base . . . . *Perca flavescens*

2b. Body without conspicuous crossbands; canine teeth present; pelvic fins separated by a space about equal to the length of the fin base (*Stizostedion*) 3

3a. Spinous dorsal with a conspicuous large black blotch on posterior end; dorsal fins with indistinct dusky mottlings or streaks parallel to spines; cheeks imperfectly scaled; soft dorsal rays 19–22. . . . *Stizostedion vitreum*

3b. Spinous dorsal without large black blotch on posterior end; dorsal fins with many round black spots; cheeks usually closely scaled; soft dorsal rays 17–20. . . . . *Stizostedion canadense*

4a. Body very long and slender, body depth contained 7 or more times in standard length; anal with a single spine; dorsal fins well separated; belly naked 5

4b. Body deep, body depth contained fewer than 7 times in standard length; anal usually with 2 spines; dorsal fins close together; belly scaled or with single row of enlarged scales 7

5a. Back crossed by 4 dark crossbars running forward and downward; lateral-line scales about 80 or more; anal soft rays 12–14; premaxillae with a narrow frenum; teeth on vomer and palatine . . . . *Crystallaria asprella*

5b. Back not crossed by crossbars but with a series of round spots; lateral-line scales fewer than 80; anal soft rays 8–10; premaxillae protractile; vomer and palatine toothless (*Ammocrypta*) 6

6a. Opercle with a sharp, pinlike spine; nape wholly naked (sometimes a few scales on midline); sides with row of spots indistinct or absent. . . . . *Ammocrypta clara*

6b. Opercle with a flat, triangular spine; nape scaled, at least a few scales near occiput; sides with distinct row of well-developed spots. . . . . *Ammocrypta vivax*

7a. Midline of belly with a single row of specialized scales (see fig. 23), which may be shed, leaving a naked strip (in *P. shumardi* belly naked anteriad and crossed by a bridge of scales posteriad); pelvic fins separated by a space at least ¾ as wide as a pelvic fin base; lateral line complete (*Percina*) 8

7b. Midline of belly usually scaled but lacking specialized scales (see fig. 23); pelvic fins separated by a space less than ¾ as wide as a pelvic fin base (except in *E. nigrum*, *E. chlorosomum*, and *E. histrio*); lateral line complete or incomplete (*Etheostoma*) 16

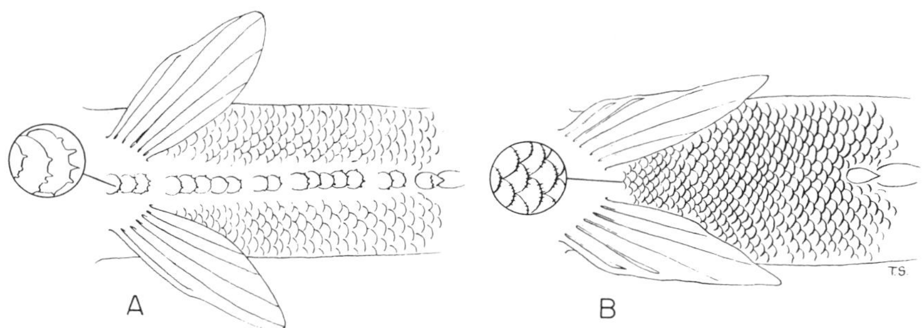

FIGURE 23. Differences in scales on the belly and in bases of the pelvic fins in darters. (From Cross 1967)

A. Belly with a median row of modified scales that are sometimes lost, leaving a naked strip; pelvic fins separated by a space about as wide as the basal length of each pelvic fin (genus *Percina*).

B. Belly with scales like those on sides (sometimes partly naked anteriorly but never with a median scaleless strip); pelvic fins separated by a space less than the basal length of each fin (genus *Etheostoma*).

8a. Snout pointed or extended conelike, usually farther forward than upper lip; sides with many vertical dark bars 9

8b. Snout not extended conelike farther forward than upper lip; sides never with conspicuous vertical dark bars 10

9a. Top of head scaleless; snout conical, bulbous, and fleshy, usually projecting well in front of upper lip; breast scaleless, except for 1 or 2 enlarged scales at pelvic fin base . . . . *Percina caprodes*

9b. Top of head fully scaled; snout pointed, not fleshy, rarely protrudes past front of upper lip; breast scales present . . . . *Percina macrolepida*

10a. Premaxillae protractile (narrow frenum sometimes present). 11

10b. Premaxillae nonprotractile, a broad frenum present 12

11a. Belly mostly naked but with scales before anus; scale row on belly midline weakly specialized; cheeks scaled; gill membranes connected, their juncture nearer pelvic fin base than snout tip . . . . *Percina shumardi*

11b. Belly scaled; cheek usually naked; gill membranes separate, their juncture nearer snout tip than pelvic fin base . . . . *Percina copelandi*

12a. Preopercular posterior edge finely serrate . . . . *Percina sciera*

12b. Preopercular posterior edge not serrate 13

13a. Snout very long and pointed, 3–3.6 into head length, width of snout less than ¾ its length . . . . *Percina nasuta*

13b. Snout shorter, 3.3 or more into head length; snout width greater than ⅔ its length 14

14a. Distance from pelvic insertion to union of gill membranes 1.1–1.5 into distance from tip of mandibles to union of gill membranes; length of eye 2.5–3.2 into distance from tip of mandibles to union of gill membranes . . . . *Percina phoxocephala*

14b. Distance from pelvic insertion to union of gill membranes 0.5–1.2 into distance from tip of mandibles to union of gill membranes; length of eye 1.5–2.2 into distance from tip of mandible to union of gill membranes 15

15a. Scales larger, 62–77 in lateral line; 7–10 scales above and 9–15 scales below the lateral line; fewer than 32 scales around caudal peduncle; background color in young olive brown . . . . *Percina maculata*

15b. Scales smaller, 81–94 in lateral line; 9–11 scales above and 16–18 scales below the lateral line; about 32 around the caudal peduncle; background color in young white. . . . . *Percina pantherina*

16a. Premaxillae protractile, the skin of the forehead separated from the upper jaw by a groove or with a narrow frenum 17

16b. Premaxillae nonprotractile, the skin of the forehead continuous with that of upper jaw; no groove crossing midline 21

17a. Single anal spine, thin and flexible; dorsal spines usually 9 18

17b. Anal spines 2, thick and rather stiff; dorsal spines 11–14 19

18a. Lateral line complete or nearly complete; cheeks usually naked; spinous dorsal only slightly separated from soft dorsal; dark bridle on snout interrupted at middle of upper lip . . . . *Etheostoma nigrum*

18b. Lateral line incomplete, not extending past about the middle of the soft dorsal; cheeks scaled; spinous dorsal separated from soft dorsal by a wider space; dark bridle on snout continuous across snout on upper lip . . . . *Etheostoma chlorosomum*

19a. Gill membranes scarcely connected across the isthmus . . . . *Etheostoma stigmaeum*

19b. Gill membranes broadly connected across the isthmus 20

20a. Maxillary adnate to the preorbital; breast naked; belly fully scaled; sides with conspicuous W-markings . . . . *Etheostoma blennioides*

20b. Maxillary not adnate to the preorbital; breast and anterior portion of belly naked; side without W-markings . . . . *Etheostoma histrio*

21a. Lateral line absent or incomplete, with no more than about 7 pores near head 22

21b. Lateral line present, with many more than 7 pores 23

22a. Opercles and cheeks scaled; a few (2–7) lateral-line pores present near head . . . . *Etheostoma proeliare*

22b. Opercles and cheeks naked; lateral line absent . . . *Etheostoma microperca*

23a. Lateral line elevated anteriorly in an arc 24

23b. Lateral line extending more directly downward and backward midlaterally 25

24a. Parietal region scaly; infraorbital canal incomplete . . . . *Etheostoma fusiforme*

24b. Parietal region scaleless; infraorbital canal complete . . . . *Etheostoma gracile*

25a. Dorsal fins low, spinous dorsal of male with fleshy knobs; gill membranes broadly connected . . . . *Etheostoma flabellare*

25b. Dorsal fins relatively high, never with knobs; gill membranes broadly connected or not 26

26a. Sides marked with conspicuous white or yellowish line along lateral line . . . . *Etheostoma parvipinne*

26b. Sides not marked with conspicuous white or yellowish line 27

27a. Gill membranes broadly connected . . . . *Etheostoma zonale*

27b. Gill membranes connected to a slight extent or not at all 28

28a. Lateral line markedly incomplete with 14 (7–20) pored scales; sides marked with a series of elongate blotches; underparts finely dotted . . . . *Etheostoma cragini*

28b. Lateral line more nearly complete; its pores not fewer than 29; variously colored but if spots are present on underparts they are coalesced into conspicuous blotches 29

29a. Underparts with conspicuous blotches; sides marked with broad bars extending downward and backward . . . . *Etheostoma punctulatum*

29b. Underparts without conspicuous blotches; sides without broad bars . . . 30

30a. An enlarged black humeral spot present over postcleithrum; no conspicuous longitudinal line on sides and dorsum 31

30b. Enlarged humeral spot absent over postcleithrum; conspicuous, longitudinal lines formed by dark spots, 1 per scale, on sides and dorsum 33

31a. Adults with red spots interspersed in a reticulum of black pigment on sides; lateral-line scales usually more than 61 (59–70) 32

31b. Adults without red spots, the body suffused with orange with a series of lateral blotches forming bars posteriad, lateral-line scales usually fewer than 62 (49–62) . . . . *Etheostoma radiosum*

32a. Lateral-line scales 59–73; caudal peduncle scales usually 27–31; breeding males with somewhat muted red spotting on sides of body; Arkansas River drainage . . . . *Etheostoma whipplei*

32b. Lateral-line scales 50–63; caudal peduncle scales usually less than 26; breeding males develop brilliant and higher degree of red spotting on sides of body; Red River drainage . . . . *Etheostoma artesiae*

33a. Cheeks naked or nearly so; infraorbital canal incomplete just below eye; anal soft rays 5–7. . . . . *Etheostoma spectabile*

33b. Cheeks scaled; infraorbital canal complete, tube continuous under eye; anal soft rays usually 7–9. 34

34a. Dorsum with 8–9 saddles, 3 or 4 of which are much darker than others; humeral spot small and dark; prepectoral area naked; spinous dorsal fin of breeding male with wide reddish orange band; posterior side with 5–7 bars indistinct above lateral line . . . . *Etheostoma collettei*

34b. Dorsum with 8 or 9 saddles of about equal intensity; humeral spot faint or absent; prepectoral area scaled; spinous dorsal fin of breeding males with narrow reddish orange band; posterior side with 6–8 bars distinct above lateral line . . . . *Etheostoma asprigene*

WESTERN SAND DARTER

Ammocrypta clara Jordan and Meek

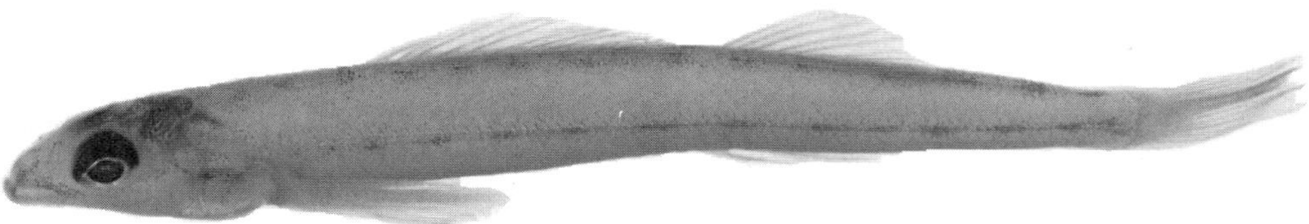

Description:

An extremely long, slender, pellucid darter with relatively long and high fins and very little pigmentation on the body. Characteristics separating it from *Crystallaria asprella* are given in the description of that species. It is most readily distinguished from *Ammocrypta vivax* by its naked nape, the presence of only 3–5 rows of scales along the side (including the lateral-line scale row) and the presence of a sharp, pinlike opercular spine. There are about 75 scales in the lateral line. A thin dark line runs the length of the body just below the lateral-line scale row, and about 12 dark blotches are present on the dorsum. In some specimens dark blotches also occur laterally; when

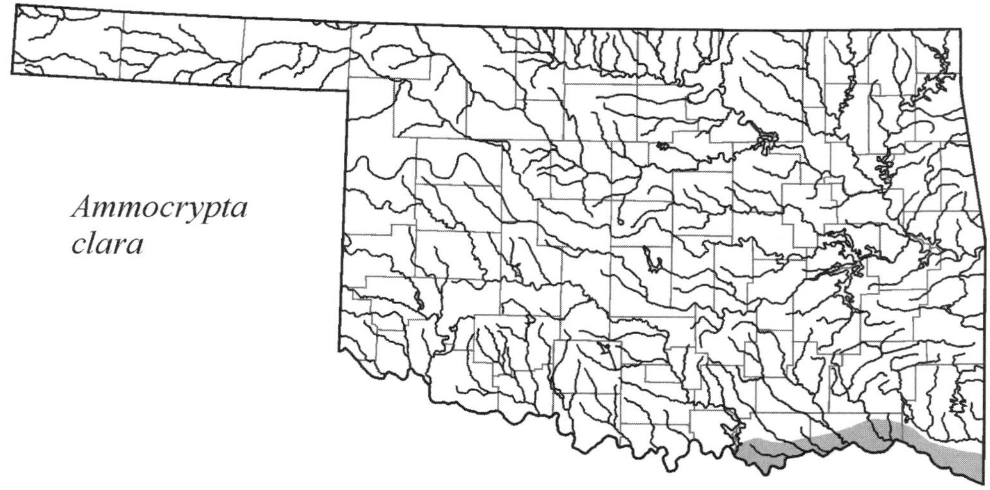

present, they tend to be longer than they are deep. May reach 3 inches in length.

Distribution:

Generally west of the Mississippi River from Minnesota to Texas. In Oklahoma known from the Red River as far west as Bryan County.

Habitat and Biology:

An inhabitant of medium to large streams and rivers, *A. clara* is generally found over sand bottoms in moderate currents. It feeds mainly on aquatic insects and may spend much of its time buried in sand when not actively feeding. Breeding season is probably July to August based on nuptial tuberculation (Williams 1975). Foods consist of small aquatic insects (midge larvae).

SCALY SAND DARTER

Ammocrypta vivax Hay

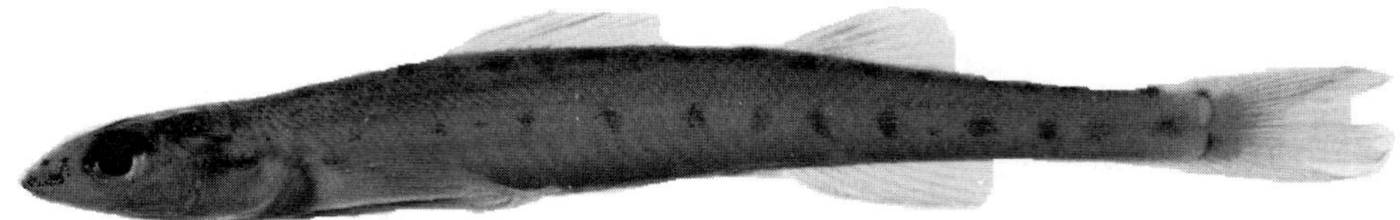

Description:

A very long, slim pellucid darter similar to *A. clara* but differing from that species in having scales on the nape (at least a few near the occiput), more than 5 rows of scales on the sides, and a flattened opercular spine. In addition to being more completely scaled, *A. vivax* tends to have more dark pigment on the body and fins. There are 10–14 dark blotches on the dorsum and 10–12 somewhat less intense dusky spots along the side. The horizontal line seen in *A. clara* is absent, and in *A. vivax* the lateral spots tend to be deeper than they are long. There is also some pigment on top of the head and snout and a dark band at the base of the soft dorsal fin. In some specimens there is conspicuous pigmentation on the basal half of the pelvic fins. Up to 2.5 inches in length.

Distribution:

From Alabama north to Missouri and west to eastern Oklahoma and Texas. In Oklahoma known from the Poteau, Kiamichi, Mountain Fork, and Little rivers and the Red River west to Bryan County.

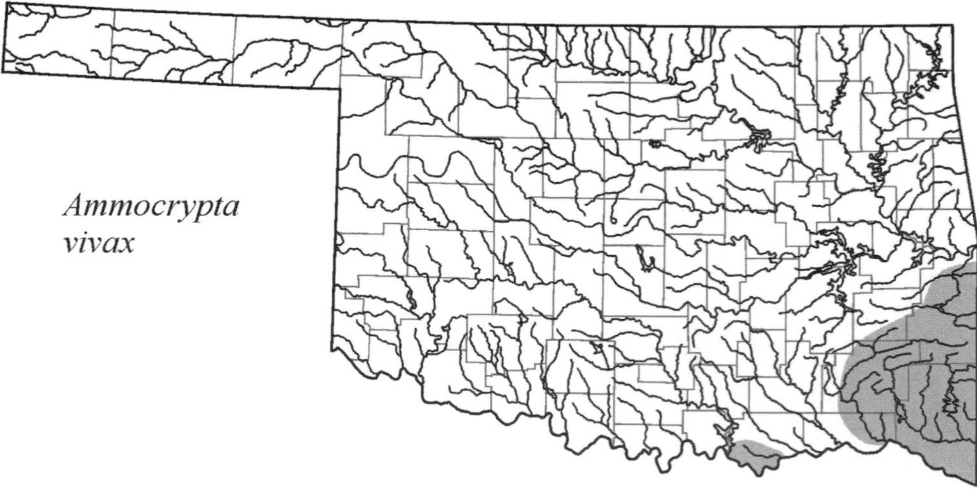

Habitat and Biology:

Like the other sand darters, *A. vivax* is found in larger rivers and streams in moderate currents over shifting sand bottoms. In captivity individuals burrow readily and spend much of their time buried in the sand, darting out to feed on drifting prey items and then returning to the sand. Such behavior is seen as providing shelter from the current and thus energy conservation in addition to camouflage (Williams 1975). Presumably this species feeds on small aquatic insects, as do other *Ammocrypta*. Miller has collected intensely colored specimens from the Amite River in Louisiana in early May with the water temperature 21 degrees C. Gravid females are known from late May in Arkansas. This suggests that *A. vivax* may be a late spring or early summer spawner in Oklahoma, but significant data on its biology are lacking.

CRYSTAL DARTER

Crystallaria asprella (Jordan)

Description:

The crystal darter may be distinguished from all *Ammocrypta* and most other percids on the basis of the following complex of characteristics. It is a large, extremely slender, pellucid darter with large eyes and well-developed premaxillary frenum (there is no frenum in *Ammocrypta*). Except for breast and belly, the entire body is covered with small, rough scales, with more than 82 scales in the lateral line (fewer than 80 in *Ammocrypta*). Median fins are extremely high with 13–15 dorsal spines (vs. 7–11), 13–15 dorsal rays (vs. 9–11), a single anal spine, and 12–14 anal rays (vs. 7–10). A series of 8–11 roundish to oblong black blotches along the lateral line may become confluent in some specimens, and 3 or 4 large, variously developed dark saddle markings straddle the back and extend obliquely forward until they contact the lateral blotches. Breeding males develop tubercles on anal and pelvic fins. Maximum length 6 inches. (See also color plate.)

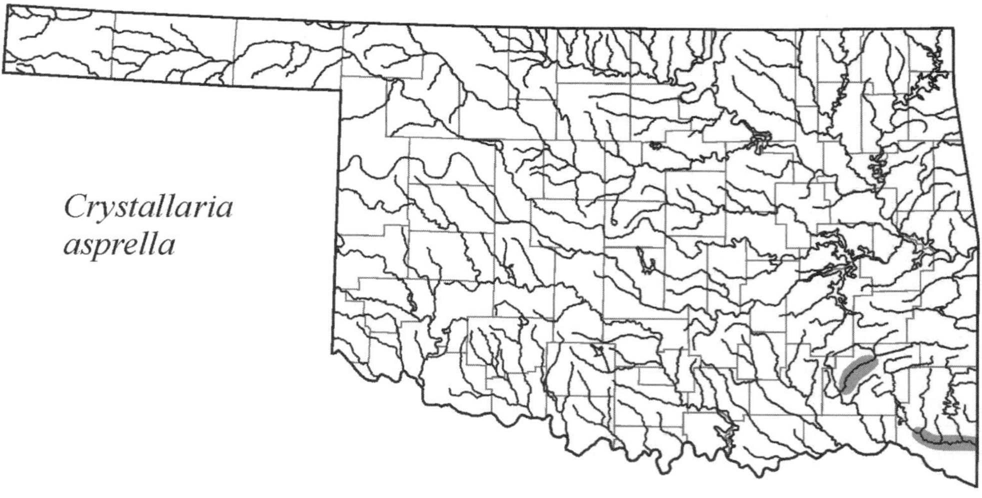

Distribution:

The larger rivers and streams of the Mississippi basin from Minnesota and Ohio south to Louisiana. Also occurs in some of the Gulf coastal rivers. Known in Oklahoma from the Little River in McCurtain County and recently collected from the Kiamichi River between Jack Fork Creek and Hugo Reservoir by Taylor and colleagues (1993).

Habitat and Biology:

The crystal darter inhabits deep riffles over silt-free sandy or fine gravel bottoms in larger rivers and streams. Like the sand darters, *Crystallaria* may burrow into the sand with only its eyes protruding and dart out when a small prey organism comes into view (observed by Miller in captive fish from the Pearl River in Louisiana). Foods consist of aquatic insects (heptageniid mayfly nymphs). In Arkansas, *C. asprella* spawns when one year old from late January to mid-April over gravel without constructing a nest (George et al. 1996). Eggs are dispersed by the current shifting the fine gravel and sand substrates. Life expectancy in the Saline River, Arkansas, is at least two years. This species has been seriously depleted throughout its former range and has been listed by the American Fisheries Society as a species of "special concern"; however, no official action has been taken by the U.S. Fish and Wildlife Service (1994) to list it as either threatened or endangered.

Note:

Although Bailey and Gosline (1955) considered the crystal darter as a member of the genus *Ammocrypta* Jordan, we follow Moore (1968) and Simons (1991) in retaining this form in a separate genus, *Crystallaria* Jordan and Gilbert. Simons (1991) hypothesized that subgenera *Crystallaria* and *Ammocrypta* are phylogenetically remote based on morphological comparisons, with *Crystallaria* sister to a lineage containing all other darters.

REDSPOT DARTER

Etheostoma artesiae (Hay)

Description:

The redspot darter is very similar to the redfin darter, from which it has been separated only recently (Piller et al. 2001). It is a moderately deep-bodied, compressed species with a fairly large head and pointed snout. The mouth is large and oblique and a premaxillary frenum is present. Scales are somewhat larger than in *E. whipplei*, with fewer lateral-line scales (less than 63) and caudal peduncle scales (less than 26). Dorsal with 10–12 spines and 13–15 rays, and anal with 2 spines and 8 or 9 rays. Color is olivaceous with irregular dark markings on the sides and dorsum; traces of 8–10 saddles on dorsum can be seen in some specimens. Three basicaudal spots are present in preserved specimens, and light spots are scattered on the sides of preserved males. Breeding males have bands of blue, white, and red (proximally) on the median fins. Nuptial males develop more numerous and brighter red spots on the sides than in *E. whipplei*. Maximum size about 3 inches. (See also color plate.)

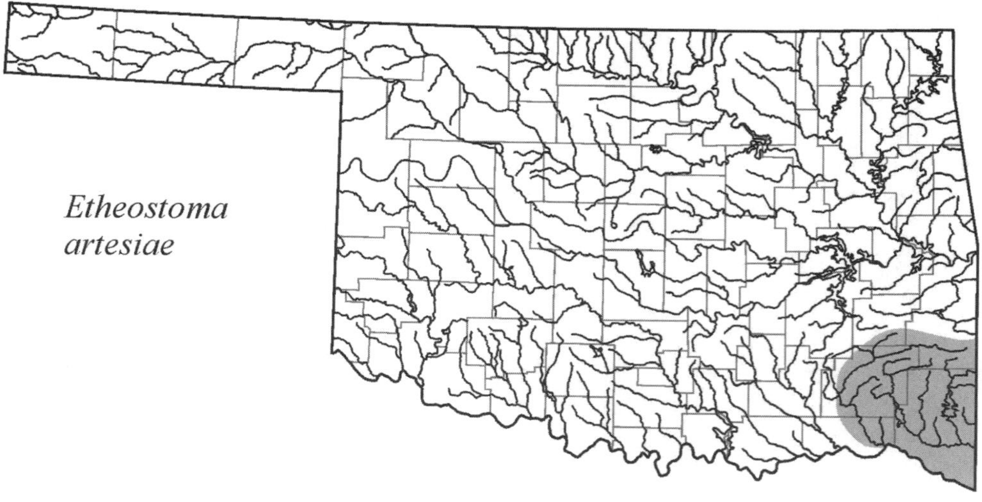

Distribution:

Gulf Coast drainages from the Chattahoochie River system in Alabama west to Oklahoma. Found in small to moderate-sized streams in the Red and Ouachita River systems of southeastern Oklahoma.

Habitat and Biology:

Moore and Rigney (1952) noted that where *E. artesiae* (then considered as *E. whipplei*) occurred in the same system with *E. radiosum,* the latter preferred smaller, high-gradient, gravel-cobble-bottomed streams, whereas the former preferred larger, low-gradient, slower-flowing, gravel-sand-bottomed streams. Like all other Oklahoma darters, this species spawns in spring, but little else is known of its biology.

MUD DARTER
Etheostoma asprigene (Forbes)

Description:

A small, relatively compressed darter usually less than 2 inches long, with 5 or 6 squarish dark saddles on the dorsum and about 9 lateral blotches (sometimes indistinct in preserved specimens). Among Oklahoma darters, it is most similar to *E. spectabile* and *E. collettei.* It differs from *E. spectabile* in having scaled cheeks, a complete infraorbital lateral-line canal, and usually 8 anal rays, though sometimes 7 (vs. 7 or fewer in *spectabile*). It differs from *E. collettei* in having all dorsal saddles of about equal coloration (vs. 4 saddles much darker than others), a faint or absent humeral spot, and posterior bars distinct above the midside; and breeding *E. asprigene* males lack tubercles on lower body sides. Color is olivaceous above, with dorsal blotches brownish or greenish, lateral bars greenish tending to become obscure anteriorly, and the spaces between them reddish or orange. The belly is orange and the head olivaceous with dark lines before and under the eye. Concentrations of dark pigment form irregular spots on the body, in front of the pectoral fin, and on the

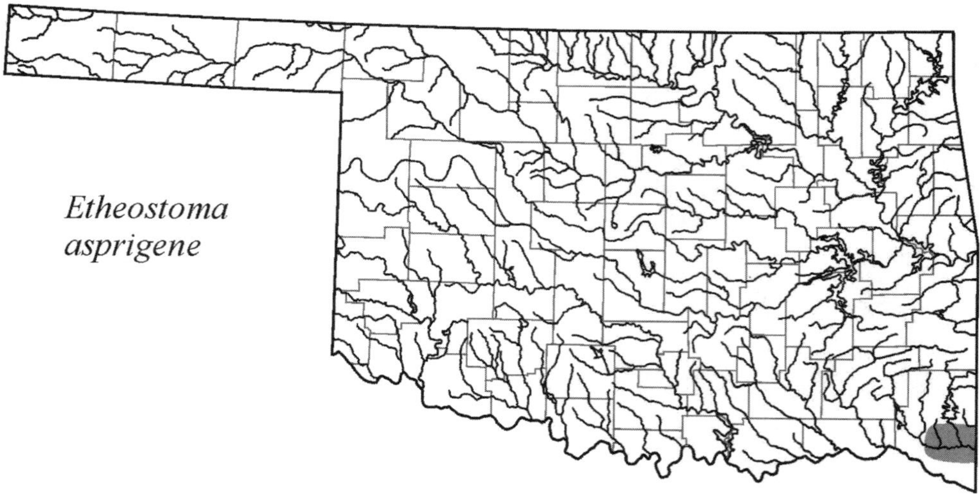

chin and gular region. The spinous dorsal fin lacks a broad blue or green band near the distal edge. Soft dorsal and caudal fins are barred.

Distribution:

Lower reaches of the Mississippi basin from Minnesota to the Gulf states. Known in Oklahoma only in McCurtain County.

Habitat and Biology:

The mud darter is an inhabitant of sloughs, lakes, swamps, and lowland rivers and streams. Although similar to the orangethroat darter, it has a much more specialized niche and is not often taken with that species in our collections. Cummings and colleagues (1984) studied the life history of the mud darter in Illinois. It feeds on chironomids, simuliids, mayfly nymphs, caddisfly larvae, isopods, and other small aquatic macroinvertebrates. Spawning occurs in Illinois from early March to early May in shallow riffles containing an abundance of detritus and even cypress tree stumps. Males did not establish territories in aquarium spawnings but courted females until spawning commenced over sticks, leaves, or vegetation, with the male mounting vertically on the back of the female. No parental care was noted.

Greenside darter
Etheostoma blennioides Rafinesque

Description:

A large, terete, sturdy darter with a moderately short head (about 4 into SL). Its characteristically blunt snout (slightly longer than the eye) overhangs the inferior mouth. The premaxillaries are protractile, but the maxilla is adnate to the preorbital bone. Gill membranes are broadly united across the isthmus. Body scales are relatively small (70–82 in the lateral line) and the breast is naked. There are 12–14 dorsal spines, 12–14 dorsal rays, and 7–9 anal rays. The most characteristic feature of this species is its color pattern. On a ground color of light olive above and whitish below is superimposed a series of 7–9 dark lateral chevrons (V- or W-shaped). There are 6–8 dark saddles on the dorsum, and scattered small dark blotches occur above the chevrons. Breeding males have bright green bars on the sides and much green on the fins. Red spots are scattered on the upper sides, and reddish spots are present on the bases of the greenish dorsal fins. Up to 5.5 inches in length. (See also color plate.)

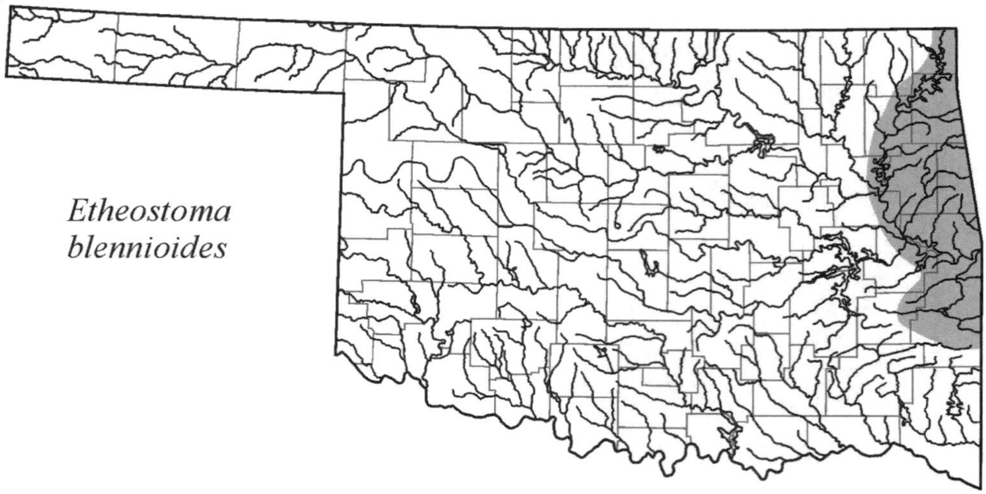

Distribution:

From the lower Great Lakes region (New York and Michigan) throughout the Ohio and Tennessee systems south and west to Oklahoma and Arkansas. Found in eastern Oklahoma in the Poteau, Illinois, and Neosho rivers and their tributaries.

Habitat and Biology:

The greenside is a large, often spectacularly colored darter that prefers rivers or streams with moderate to fast current, low turbidity, and substrates of gravel and rocky rubble. It is often found in areas where algae (*Cladophora* especially) and aquatic moss (*Fontinalis*) are abundant on rocks in riffle areas. It spawns in the algae from late February to late March (Hubbs 1985). Greenside darters feed on aquatic insect larvae and other invertebrates and seem not to occur in dense populations anywhere in Oklahoma.

Bluntnose darter
Etheostoma chlorosomum (Hay)

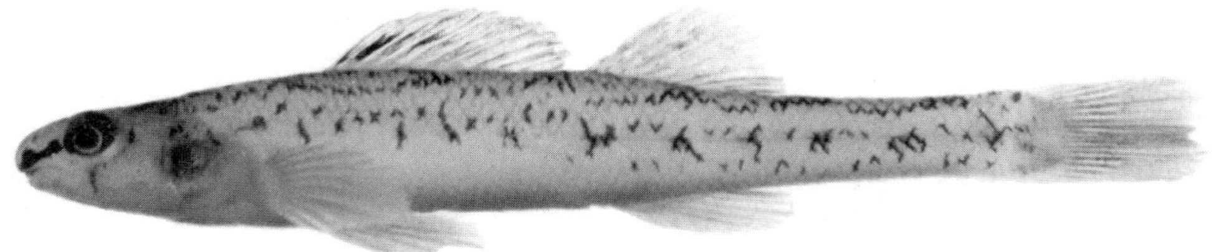

Description:

A slender little darter less than 2 inches long with a short rounded snout, no premaxillary frenum, and a small head (3.9–4.2 into SL). The bluntnose darter is fairly similar to the speckled darter but has only a single anal spine (vs. 2), a scaled cheek, and no prominent square blotches on the side. It is most similar to the johnny darter but differs in having fully scaled cheeks, operculum, and breast and an incomplete lateral line with about 53–57 scales (28–36 pored). Additionally, in *E. chlorosomum* the preorbital bar extends continuously around the snout just above the upper lip (preorbital bars are not continuous in *E. nigrum*). Color is pale brown to straw, with 6 fairly small, faint dorsal saddles, 8–10 small W- or XX-shaped blotches along the sides, and irregular vermiculate markings dorsolaterally. Dorsal and caudal fins are barred. Breeding males become somewhat darker but develop no bright chromatic patterns.

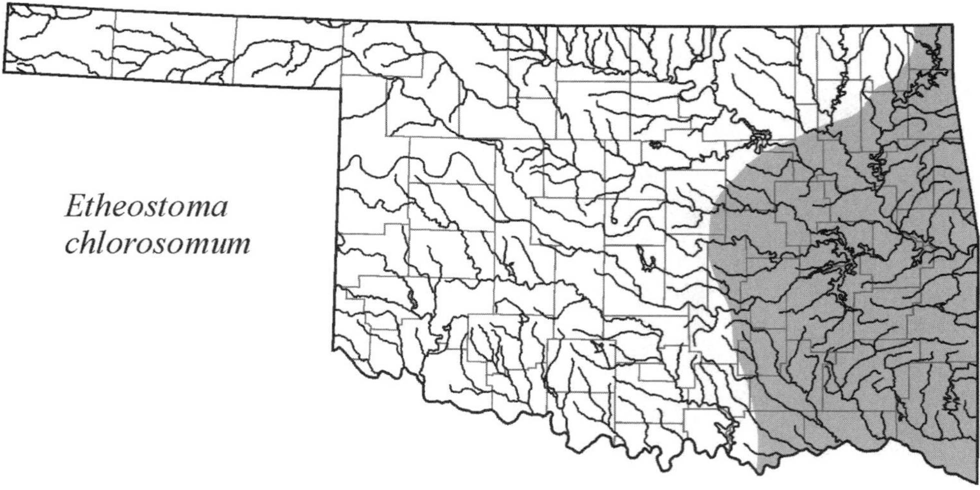

Distribution:

The central Mississippi Valley from Minnesota to Texas and along the coast to Alabama. Found in both the Arkansas and Red River systems in about the eastern third of Oklahoma.

Habitat and Biology:

The bluntnose darter lives in quiet water in sluggish streams with soft, muddy bottoms and in some oxbows and lakes. It is obviously adapted for a different ecological niche than most Oklahoma darters. Diet consists primarily of aquatic insects. It probably spawns in late April or May, as nuptial specimens have been taken in Illinois on April 30 (Page et al. 1982); placed in an aquarium, the males courted females the next day. One to three eggs were subsequently laid on algae, twigs, and leaves during each spawning act.

CREOLE DARTER

Etheostoma collettei Birdsong and Knapp

Description:

A small (2.5 inches long), relatively compressed darter with 8 or 9 brown saddles on the dorsum, 4 of which are much darker than others, and 5–7 vertical bars developed posteriorly on the sides with bars indistinct above the midside. Distinct rows of small dark spots occur on the upper sides. Gill membranes are separate or slightly joined across the throat. Premaxillary frenum is present. Opercle scaled, and lower half of cheek usually scaled. Lateral line is incomplete, usually with 47–52 scales in the lateral series, 32–42 of which are pored. This species is most similar to *E. spectabile* and *E. asprigene*, but differs from *spectabile* in having an uninterrupted infraorbital canal and 4 dorsal saddles of about equal intensity. From *asprigene* it can be distinguished in having 4 dorsal saddles much darker than others, humeral spot large and black (vs. faint or absent), and breeding males with tubercles on lower body sides (vs. no tubercles). Males in breeding color have dark blue or turquoise bars posteriorly with bright orange areas between bars. The belly is orange and the head is dark blue-green, as are anal and pelvic fins.

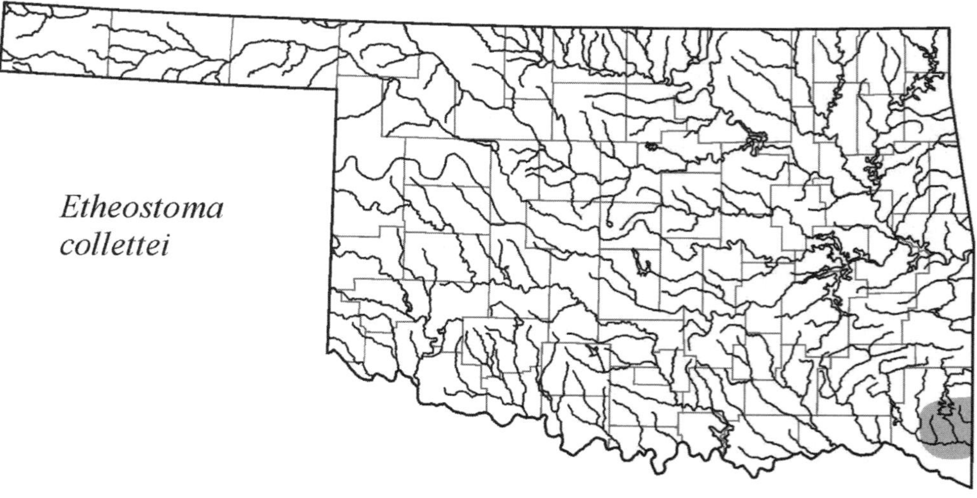

The first dorsal fin has a narrow blue marginal band, wide red submarginal band, and blue basal band. Second dorsal fin is red and blue.

Distribution:

Found in Arkansas, Oklahoma, and Louisiana in the Ouachita River, Little River, and Red River drainages. In Oklahoma it is known only in McCurtain County.

Habitat and Biology:

The creole darter inhabits headwater creeks and small rivers in swift current over gravel bottoms or in rocky chutes with heavy submergent vegetation. It feeds primarily on aquatic insects, especially mayfly nymphs. Spawning occurs in March and April in shallow gravel riffles in Arkansas. Males guard spawning territories and females spawn with several males.

ARKANSAS DARTER

Etheostoma cragini Gilbert

Description:

A small, moderately terete darter usually less than 2.5 inches long, with a short blunt snout and large head (3–3.2 into SL). *E. cragini* is most similar to *E. punctulatum* but differs in the following characteristics: the lateral line is markedly incomplete with fewer than 20 of the 44–57 lateral-line scales pored; there are usually 9 spines in the first dorsal fin and 12 rays (11–13) in the second (vs. 10 or 11 spines and 13–15 rays); the back has 6–9 small dusky saddles, while 12–14 dusky bars occur along the midside; and the underside is covered with very tiny dark spots. The broad saddles and large lateral blotches of *E. punctulatum* are never present. Breeding males develop bright orange on the branchiostegal membranes and underside of the body, and median fin rays also exhibit some orange. Well-developed breeding tubercles form on the anal rays.

Distribution:

Tributaries of the Arkansas River in Colorado, Kansas, Oklahoma, and Missouri. Found in Oklahoma mainly in the Grand River system in the north-

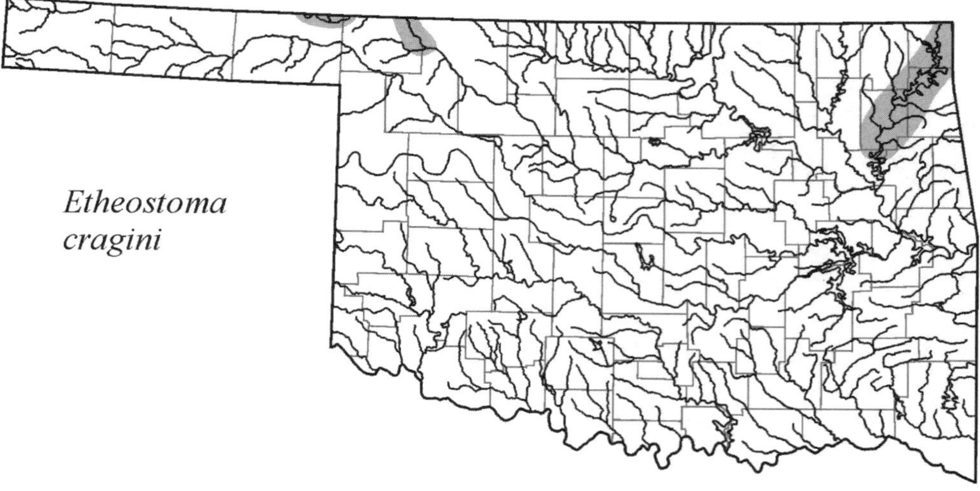

east and in the Cimarron River and tributaries in Harper, Woods, and Beaver counties in the northwest (Pigg and Gibbs 1994).

Habitat and Biology:

This highly specialized darter is known primarily from springs and spring streams having an abundance of watercress and other aquatic plants, although Matthews and McDaniel (1981) and Cross (pers. comm.) reported it in turbid streams with sand and mud bottoms away from nearby springs. Snails comprise a large part of its diet in Kansas (Distler 1972); however, in Missouri it feeds on isopods, mayflies, and midges (Taber et al. 1986). It has been captured in breeding color from mid-February to April and spawns from March to April in Arkansas and into July in Missouri. Females may spawn more than once. Distler (1972) detailed spawning behavior of this species in aquaria.

FANTAIL DARTER

Etheostoma flabellare Rafinesque

Description:

A deep-bodied, highly compressed darter with an unusually short, deep caudal peduncle. The head is moderate in length (about 3.5 into SL) and comparatively conical, tapering to a symmetrical pointed snout and terminal oblique mouth. A well-developed frenum is present, and the gill membranes are broadly united across the isthmus. The head, nape, and breast lack scales and the lateral line is incomplete. One of the most characteristic features is the unusually low spinous dorsal (7–10 spines). The soft dorsal is also quite low and long (13–15 rays). Color is brownish to olivaceous with black horizontal streaks (made up of spots on each scale) running the length of the body. Dark dorsal saddles and/or lateral bars are faint to clearly visible in some specimens. The caudal fin is heavily banded. In breeding males the head becomes very dark, the bases of both dorsal fins become inky black, and the tips of the spines of the first dorsal fin develop yellowish fleshy knobs. About 2 inches long.

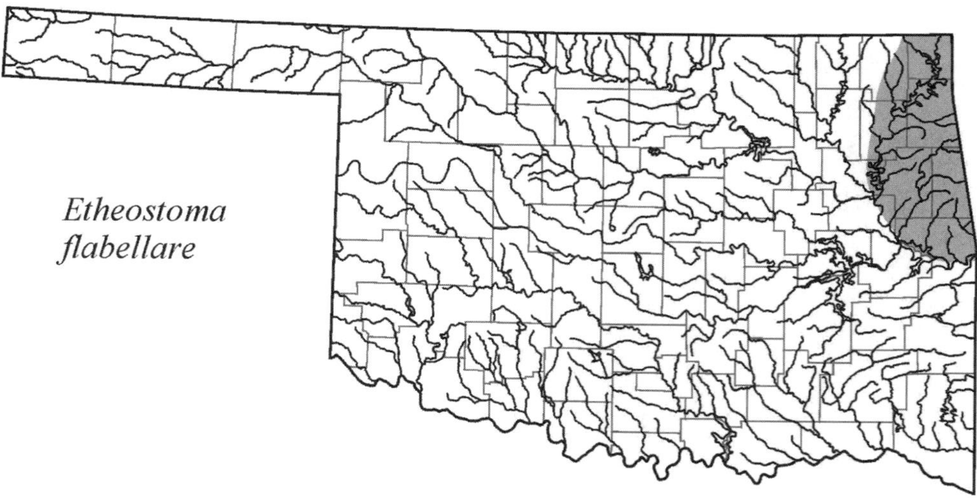

Distribution:

From the St. Lawrence drainage west through the Great Lakes to Minnesota and south to Oklahoma, Louisiana, Alabama, and North Carolina. Occurs in the northeastern corner of Oklahoma.

Habitat and Biology:

The fantail darter is found in small, clear gravelly upland streams and spring brooks. It can usually be found in gentle currents over gravel or gravel and rubble bottoms in water less than 15 inches deep. Its food consists mainly of mayfly and midge larvae and other larval insects or microcrustaceans. Breeding occurs from late March or April to May, when the male constructs a nest and defends a territory beneath rocks. The eggs are deposited on the underside of the stone, and the male remains with them until they hatch. The knobs on the dorsal fin of the male are used to keep the eggs free of silt.

SWAMP DARTER

Etheostoma fusiforme (Girard)

Description:

Although some earlier authors (e.g., Moore 1968) considered this form to be distinct from the northeastern swamp darter (*E. f. fusiforme*) and refer it to the species *E. barratti* (Holbrook), the scalyhead darter, we follow Collette (1962) in considering the two forms as subspecies. The swamp darter is most similar to the slough darter in Oklahoma but can be distinguished by its incomplete infraorbital lateral-line canal; the presence of scales on nape, breast, and top of the head; and the presence of four dark spots at the caudal fin base. There are 52–58 scales in the lateral line, of which 13–20 are pored. Color is dark olivaceous to brown above with dark reticulations or spots over most of the body. From 9 to 12 more or less distinct lateral blotches occur on the sides, and about 9 dorsal saddles are usually visible. Median fins are all spotted or barred. Maximum size is about 2 inches.

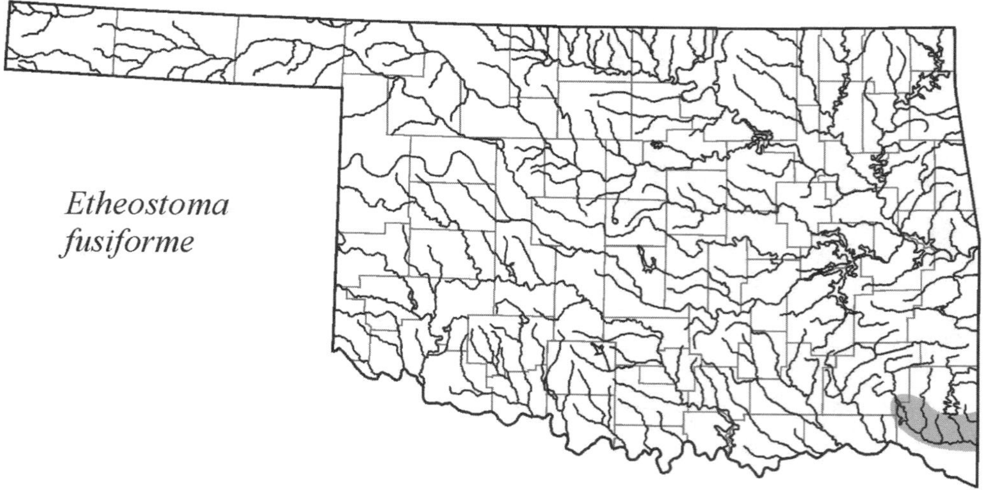

Distribution:

Coastal streams from North Carolina to Louisiana and north in the Mississippi basin to Oklahoma and Tennessee. Found in Oklahoma only in the Little River system in McCurtain County.

Habitat and Biology:

E. fusiforme is found in swamps, lakes, oxbows, and in the backwaters of lowland streams, generally occurring in association with dense vegetation. The swamp darter seems to be one of Oklahoma's rarest fishes. Foods consist mainly of aquatic insect larvae and small crustaceans (Schmidt and Whitworth 1979). Collette (1962) described spawning behavior but indicated that no territoriality was observed. Eggs are laid singly on plant leaves and fertilized. This darter is probably an early spring spawner, but little is known of its timing.

Slough darter

Etheostoma gracile (Girard)

Description:

The slough darter and swamp darter are members of the subgenus *Hololepis*, the swamp darters, and differ from other darters in having the lateral line conspicuously arched anteriorly. The slough darter is a small, slender species of up to 2 inches, with a short, rounded snout and moderately short head (3.5–4.0 into SL). It can be distinguished from the swamp darter by the complete infraorbital lateral-line canal and the naked breast and nape. The cheeks and opercles are scaled, and the lateral line is incomplete with 47–51 scales, of which 17–23 are pored. There are 8–10 spines in the first dorsal fin, 9–13 rays in the second, and 2 spines and 6 or 7 rays in the anal fin. Color is olivaceous above with brownish reticulations covering most of the body. About 9 indistinct lateral blotches are sometimes present. In breeding males green bars appear on the sides, the bases of the membranes of the spinous dorsal become black, and a red-orange band develops submarginally on the

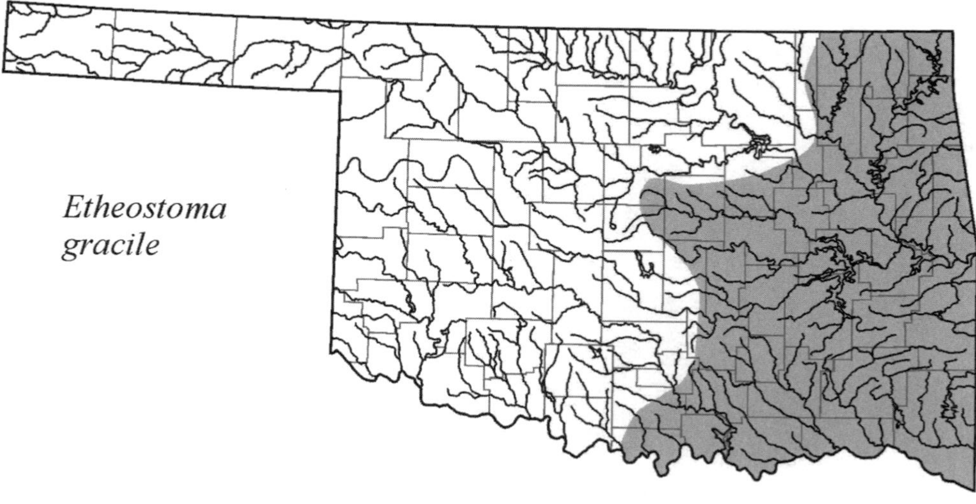

spinous dorsal. Soft dorsal and caudal fins are barred, and three dark spots occur at the base of the caudal fin. (See also color plate.)

Distribution:

From southern Illinois through the lower Mississippi basin to Oklahoma and Louisiana and coastal streams in eastern Texas. Found in about the eastern third of Oklahoma, it extends west to Carter County in the Red River system.

Habitat and Biology:

The slough darter is found in quiet or slow-moving waters, often swampy creeks or oxbows, where the bottom is generally soft and covered with organic debris, and vegetation is fairly dense. It feeds mainly on midge larvae, mayfly larvae, and copepods. Breeding occurs in April when the female deposits one egg at a time on small twigs or other objects after the male has stimulated her by rubbing the top of her head and nape with his tuberculate chin (Braasch and Smith 1967). No postspawning parental behavor has been observed in this species.

HARLEQUIN DARTER
Etheostoma histrio Jordan and Gilbert

Description:

A small, slim, terete darter usually less than 1.5 inches long, with a short blunt snout and short head (4.2 into SL). The mouth is ventral and only slightly oblique. Besides being one of our least common darters, it is one of the most distinctive in color pattern. The olivaceous body is covered with 6 or 7 large dark brownish blotches on the dorsum (the second and fourth smaller than the others) and about 8 on the sides. There are also many small irregular spots and blotches on the underside of the head, breast, and caudal peduncle. All fins, including the pectoral and pelvic fins, are conspicuously spotted. There are 46–58 lateral-line scales, 9–11 dorsal spines, 11–14 dorsal rays, and 6–8 anal rays. The two large basicaudal blotches alone are adequate to distinguish this species from all other *Etheostoma* in the state. Maximum size is 3 inches. (See also color plate.)

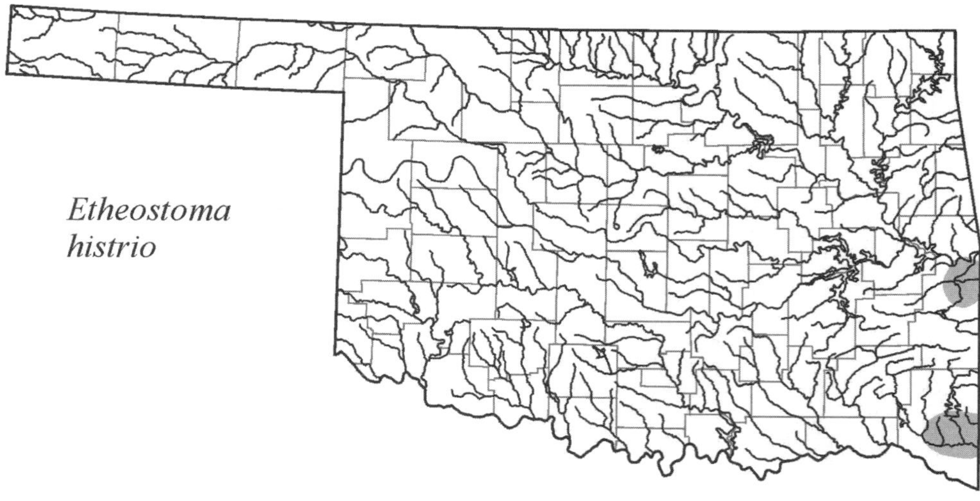

Distribution:

Found from southern Indiana to Alabama and western Florida in the east, to Oklahoma and Texas in the west, and Louisiana and Mississippi in the south. Found in the Poteau, Little, and Mountain Fork rivers in Oklahoma.

Habitat and Biology:

This species seems to be spottily abundant throughout its range (Tsai 1968). Generally collected in riffles of streams having gravel or rock bottoms, the harlequin darter nonetheless seems to be a lowland species. We have collected it near the mouth of the Mountain Fork River in very swift riffles about 18 inches deep. *E. histrio* tends to inhabit sand-detritus habitats such as those found in association with embedded logs, submerged snags, leaf packs, and brush. Thus while a stream section may consist predominantly of gravel, the harlequin darter may be found only where the sand-detritus microhabitat exists. Foods eaten are primarily aquatic insect larvae and nymphs. Spawning occurs from February to March.

LEAST DARTER

Etheostoma microperca Jordan and Gilbert

Description:

A relatively short, moderately compressed darter with high, short dorsal fins and a fairly large head (3.2–3.4 into SL). The snout is short and rounded, and the mouth is small and oblique. Scales are large, but the nape, cheeks, opercle, and breast are naked. The most distinctive characteristic of this species is the total absence of a lateral line (*E. proeliare* has at least 2–7 pored scales). There are 32–35 scales in the lateral series. The first dorsal fin has 6 or 7 spines, the second 9 or 10 rays, and the anal fin has 2 spines and 5 or 6 rays. Color is somewhat dusky olive above, more yellowish below. No dorsal saddles are present, but about 6–9 small dusky blotches occur along the mid-side, and the whole body is speckled with small brown spots. Soft dorsal and caudal fins are prominently barred. The spinous dorsal of breeding males is black near its base and its tip, with orange-brown or reddish spots on the basal half of the fin. Some orange may also be present on the anal and pelvic fins. Usually less than 1.5 inches long. (See also color plate.)

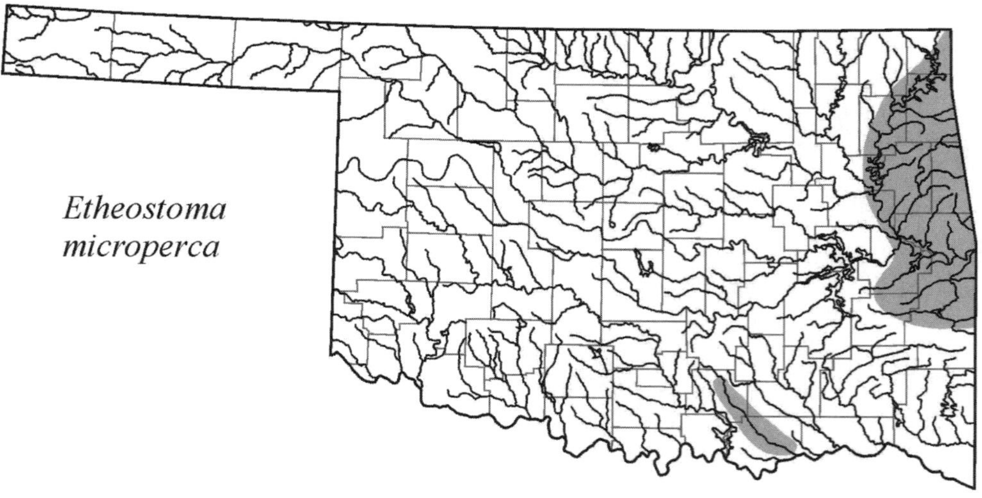

Distribution:

The lower Great Lakes and upper Mississippi drainages from Minnesota and Ohio south and west to Oklahoma. In Oklahoma known mainly from Spavinaw, Saline, and Spring creeks in the Arkansas basin and the Blue River in the Red River system.

Habitat and Biology:

Found only in clear, cold streams, where it prefers the dense vegetation (water cress and filamentous algae) of backwaters and edges of quiet pools. It feeds mainly on microcrustaceans (copepods) and other tiny invertebrates, with peak feeding at midday. Spawning occurs in April or May. According to Winn (1958a) and Burr and Page (1979), *E. microperca* spawns in an almost vertical (upright) position, the female depositing her eggs on the stems and leaves of aquatic plants. The male does not tend the eggs but does defend a weak territory including the spawning site.

Johnny Darter

Etheostoma nigrum Rafinesque

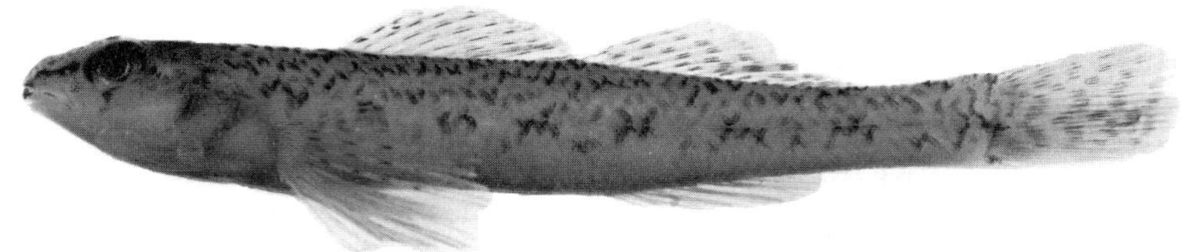

Description:

A relatively small, slender fish usually less than 2 inches long, with a short blunt snout and small head (3.7–4 into SL). It differs from *E. stigmaeum* in having a single anal spine, complete lateral line, and scaleless cheeks, breast, and nape, and in not having the preorbital dark bars continuous around the snout—a small clear gap is present on the tip of the snout. The dorsal fins have 8–10 spines and 11–13 rays, and the anal fin has 1 spine and 7–9 rays. Color is straw to light brown with about 6 faint small dorsal saddles and 8 or 9 W-shaped lateral blotches. Irregular vermiculations or V-shaped markings occur dorsolaterally. Breeding males become very dark and develop traces of yellow on the soft dorsal and caudal fins.

Distribution:

Most of the northeastern and north-central United States from the Great Lakes to Louisiana and from Georgia to Oklahoma. Known from both the Arkansas (Poteau River) and Red (Kiamichi, Little River) River basins in extreme eastern Oklahoma.

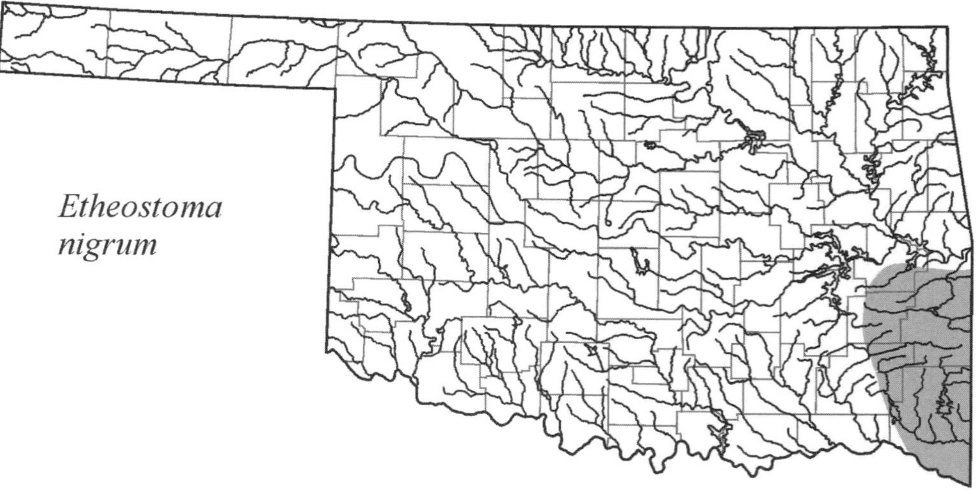

Habitat and Biology:

Johnny darters prefer relatively small, clear streams with sandy gravel or gravel bottoms and moderate to high gradient but can often be found near the edge of the current in pools. They feed on insect larvae and other small invertebrates. Breeding takes place in April or May, when spawning migrations occur and males establish breeding territories under stones prior to the arrival of the females. Bart and Page (1991) suggested that egg mimicking by males using the swollen tips of the dorsal fin may be important in courtship. Females enter the area periodically, the spawning pair inverts, and the eggs are deposited on the underside of the stones. The male stays to guard the eggs until they hatch.

GOLDSTRIPE DARTER
Etheostoma parvipinne Gilbert and Swain

Description:

A rare darter less than 2 inches long, with a fairly terete body and relatively small head (3.4–3.6 into SL). It differs from our other darters in having a generally dark upper body, which is traversed from the opercle to the caudal peduncle by a longitudinal pale stripe formed by the absence of pigment on the lateral-line scales. There are 3 or 4 basicaudal spots, but the one nearest the median is most distinct. In most specimens a single dark spot is present on the body scales except on the belly. Superimposed on this pattern is a series of 10–12 fairly faint dorsolateral bars, which are essentially bisected by the gold stripe. A well-developed suborbital bar is present, and the median fins are all finely speckled or barred. There are 49–55 scales in the lateral line, of which 44–52 are pored. There are 9–10 spines in the first dorsal, usually 10 rays in the second dorsal, and usually 2 spines and 8 rays in the anal fin.

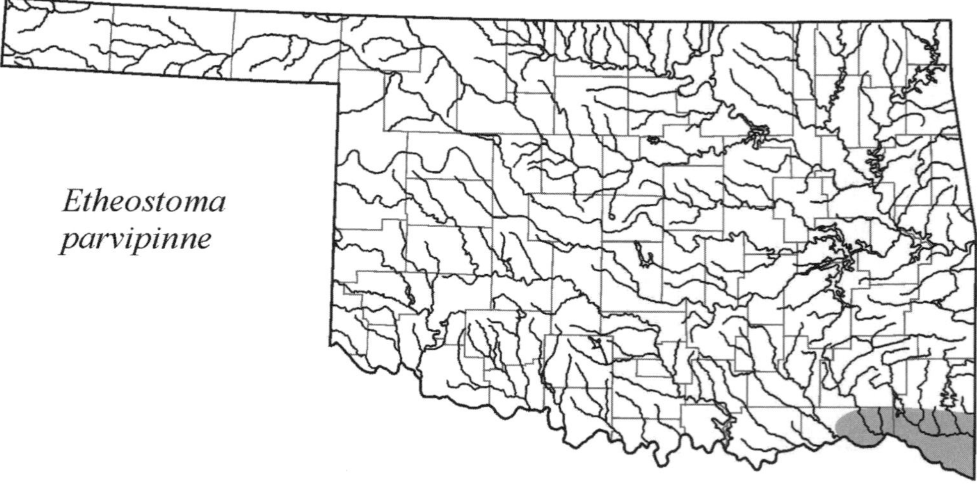

Distribution:

From Oklahoma and Texas east along the Gulf Coast to Georgia. Known in Oklahoma from Gates Creek in Choctaw County and the Mountain Fork River in McCurtain County.

Habitat and Biology:

Little is known about the life history of this rare little darter. In Arkansas (Robison 1977b) it occurs in spring-fed, shallow feeder streams or spring branches of low to moderate gradient. In Oklahoma. Moore and Cross (1950) found this species in Gates Creek, which they described as a clear, spring-fed creek with sand, gravel, and rubble-bottomed areas with nearby beds of filamentous algae. Johnston (1994) described spawning in captivity of fishes taken from a spring in the Little Tallahatchie River system in Mississippi. Males were aggressive but nonterritorial and mounted the females in typical darter fashion. Spawning took place mainly on the stems, leaves, and roots of submerged plants, with adhesive eggs being released singly as the pair vibrated.

CYPRESS DARTER

Etheostoma proeliare (Hay)

Description:

The cypress darter and least darter are members of the subgenus *Microperca* and are similar in being short (less than 1.5 inches), moderately stout, and dusky-colored. The cypress darter can be distinguished from its relative in usually having 4–6 (extremes 2–7) pored lateral-line scales, scales on the cheeks and opercles, 8 spines in the first dorsal, and 11 rays in the second dorsal fin. There are 2 spines and 6 rays in the anal fin and 35 or 36 scales in the lateral series. Color is olive above and lighter below, with fairly large brown spots distributed uniformly, one per scale, over most of the body. There are 9–11 brownish spots of varying intensity along the side. Dorsal saddles are absent or very faint. Dark mottlings on the dorsal and caudal fins tend to form bars, while the other fins are finely speckled. (See also color plate.)

Distribution:

From Illinois and Missouri south to Texas and western Florida. In Oklahoma known from Sallisaw Creek and the Poteau River southward to McCurtain

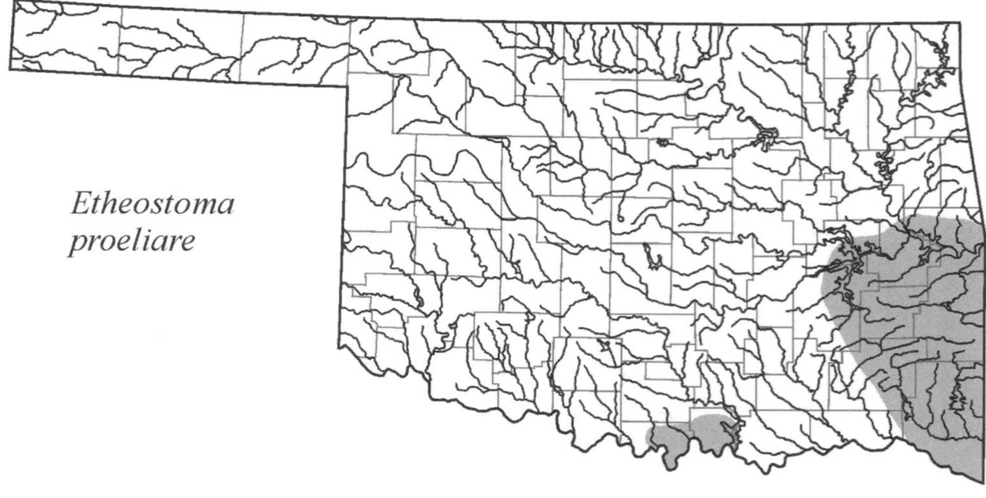

County. Found as far west in the Red River drainage as Limestone Creek in Marshall County.

Habitat and Biology:

The cypress darter is mainly a lowland stream inhabitant, though we have collected it in the upper reaches of the Kiamichi River. It seems to prefer weedy habitats along the edges of clear streams with rocky or gravel bottoms. It feeds on small crustaceans and midge larvae. Breeding takes place from mid-March to early June in Illinois (Burr and Page 1978) and as early as January in Louisiana (Kuehne and Barbour 1983). Eggs are not guarded by either sex.

STIPPLED DARTER

Etheostoma punctulatum (Agassiz)

Description:

A fairly large, stout darter reaching 3 inches, with a relatively long, conical snout and large head (3–3.2 into SL). The mouth is relatively large, and a premaxillary frenum is present. Cheeks and breast are scaleless, and the lateral line is incomplete with about 60–67 scales (40–50 pored). The most distinctive features of this darter are associated with pigmentation. Color above is olivaceous to brown with four conspicuous dark saddles on the back, one before the spinous dorsal, one at the end of the spinous dorsal, one near the end of the soft dorsal, and one (faint) at the end of the caudal peduncle. The underside is lighter but thoroughly sprinkled with conspicuous spots formed by aggregations of tiny punctules. The cheeks, opercles, and underside of the head are similarly spotted. All fins are spotted or barred. A dark, large lateral blotch is present behind the head, and 2–4 large blotches are present on the sides of the caudal peduncle. Breeding males become darker, and their undersides become bright salmon. Some orange also appears in their fins. (See also color plate.)

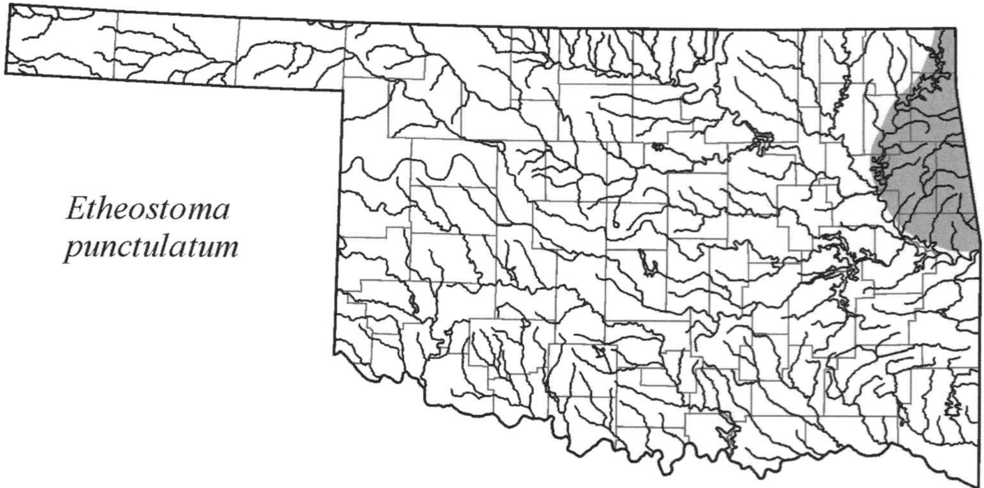

Distribution:

Southeastern Kansas, southwestern Missouri, and northeastern Oklahoma, where it is found in Ozark tributaries of the Arkansas River.

Habitat and Biology:

In Oklahoma this fish is generally found in clear cool creeks or spring brooks with vegetation present in quiet water. It is usually found in vegetation or in detritus away from the main current. Its diet consists of isopods, mayfly nymphs, and caddisfly larvae, although amphipods, crayfish, and earthworms are taken. In Oklahoma,we have collected fish in breeding condition in early May. Spawning occurs from early February to late May in Missouri and Arkansas and from mid-February through mid-May (Hubbs 1985) in springs or spring environments. Breeding habits are unknown. Maximum life span is more than four years (Hotalling and Taber 1987).

Note:

According to Mayden (1985), the species we have been calling *Etheostoma punctulatum* is actually an undescribed new species; however, until it is formally described, we continue to recognize Oklahoma populations as *E. punctulatum* to avoid confusion.

ORANGEBELLY DARTER

Etheostoma radiosum (Hubbs and Black)

Description:

A slender to moderately deep-bodied, compressed darter with a large head (3.2 into SL) and orange belly. Originally described as a subspecies of *E. whipplei*, it is similar to that form and the recently elevated *E. artesiae* but can be distinguished from them by several characteristics. The scales are larger in *E. radiosum* than in *E. whipplei*, usually varying from 49 to 62 in the lateral series versus 59–70 in *whipplei*. Although coloration of the fins is similar, and the tesselated or mottled body markings of some *E. radiosum* specimens are similar to those of both *whipplei* and *artesiae*, most *radiosum* exhibit a much clearer pattern of 9–10 fairly conspicuous dorsal saddles and 8–12 lateral blotches that are often most pronounced below the lateral line. Sometimes the blotches may be attenuated to form bars on the caudal peduncle. In life *E. radiosum* can always can be distinguished from the other two by the absence of red spots on the sides. *E. radiosum* and *E. whipplei* are also geographically separated in Oklahoma (see maps). Where *radiosum* and *artesiae*

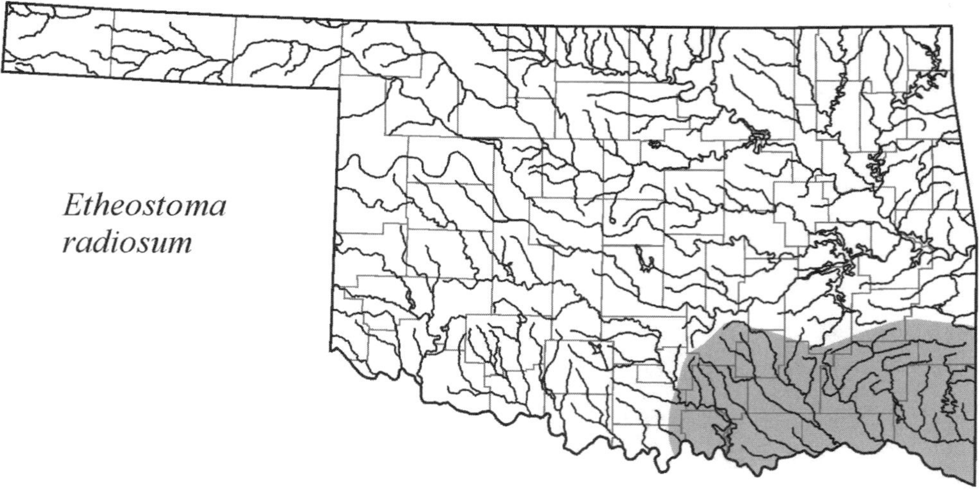

occur in the same stream system, *radiosum* generally inhabits smaller, high-gradient, swift-flowing, gravel- and cobble-bottomed streams, whereas *artesiae* occurs in larger streams of lower gradient, more moderate flow, and gravel and sand bottoms (Moore and Rigney 1952). Up to 2.5 inches in length. (See also color plate.)

Distribution:

From the Ouachita River of southwestern Arkansas to the tributaries of the Red River in southeastern Oklahoma and westward to the Washita River in Oklahoma.

Habitat and Biology:

This species seems to have a broad ecological niche, since it occurs in a variety of habitats from small, gravelly, high-gradient streams to larger, more sluggish lowland rivers. It seems to be most common, however, in gravel-bottomed streams with moderate to high gradient. Spawning occurs in early spring, perhaps commencing as early as February in some places. This is a very attractive fish that does fairly well in aquaria if a supply of live food (*Tubifex*, white worms, or *Daphnia*) is available.

Note:

Matthews and Gelwick (1988) reviewed variation and systematics of the orangebelly darter. They recognized three subspecies: *E. radiosum radiosum* (Ouachita and Little rivers, Arkansas and Oklahoma), *E. r. paludosum* (Kiamichi, Boggy, and Washita rivers in Oklahoma), and *E. r. cyanorum* (Blue River), which were originally named by Moore and Rigney (1952).

ORANGETHROAT DARTER

Etheostoma spectabile (Agassiz)

Description:

A relatively robust darter with a moderate to deep compressed body and large head. The lateral line is incomplete with about 46–53 scales, about 29–33 pored. Most similar in Oklahoma to *E. asprigene* and *E. collettei*, it differs from *asprigene* in having a naked cheek (or with only 1 or 2 scales) and an interrupted infraorbital lateral-line canal. It also tends to have fewer anal rays (5–7, vs. 8 in *asprigene*), usually fewer than 35 pored lateral-line scales (vs. more than 35), and differs in its color pattern. *E. spectabile* can be distinguished from *E. collettei* by its interrupted infraorbital canal and dorsal saddles of about equal intensity (4 saddles much darker in *collettei*). Color of males is olivaceous above with 7 or 8 darker brown saddles and usually 8 or 9 dark blue-green bars on the side. In males in or near breeding condition, the bars are brilliant, with more or less bright orange between them. Branchiostegals are usually orange, and the belly varies from whitish or gray to orange. Females are generally drab, show little color, and exhibit dark longitudinal streaks formed

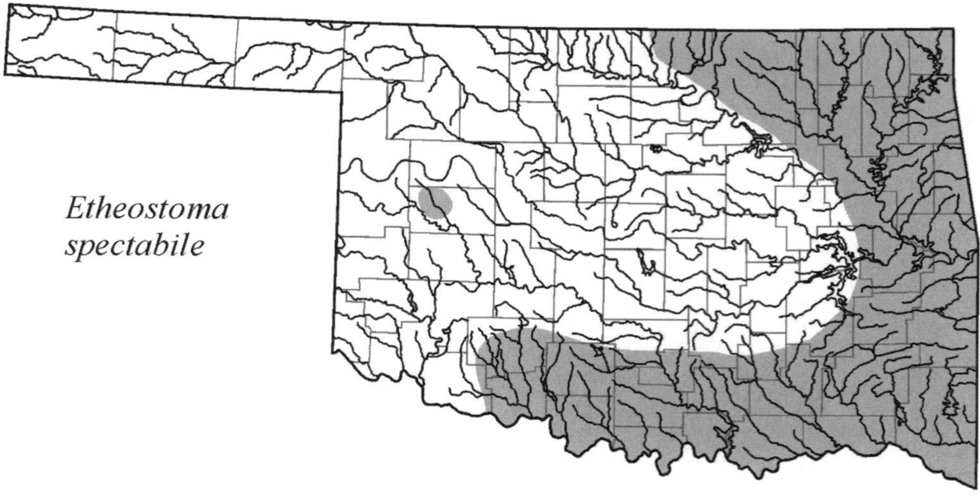

by spots of pigment on several successive scales. Preserved males tend to show these short streaks (dashes) more clearly than do live ones. Maximum size about 2.5 inches. (See also color plate.)

Distribution:

From Michigan west to Colorado and south to Texas and Tennessee. Found in hilly regions of Oklahoma in both the Red River and Arkansas drainages.

Habitat and Biology:

This is one of the most common and attractive of our native darters (see color plate). Two fairly distinctive subspecies occur in the state: *E. s. squamosum* in the Ozark tributaries of the Arkansas River (moderately scaled anteriorly) and *E. s. pulchellum* elsewhere (nearly naked anteriorly; Distler 1968). Both seem to prefer small, gravel-bottomed streams, where they are usually found in riffle areas. Ocurrence in several areas in western Oklahoma indicates a tolerance of intermittent siltation and low flow. We have not collected them, however, in streams with mud or silt bottoms. They feed on caddisfly and other insect larvae and fish eggs. Life history aspects have been summarized by Page (1983). Spawning occurs in shallow gravel riffles from late February or March to May, depending on location in the state.

Speckled Darter
Etheostoma stigmaeum (Jordan)

Description:

A small, slender darter less than 2 inches long with a short blunt snout and short head (3.7–4.2 into SL). The mouth is horizontal, and there is no premaxillary frenum. There are 10–12 spines in the first dorsal fin, 10–12 rays in the second, and 2 spines and 8 or 9 rays in the anal fin. The lateral line is incomplete with 45–55 scales, of which 27–34 are pored. This species is most similar to two other members of the subgenus *Boleosoma*, *E. nigrum* and *E. chlorosomum*. It can be separated from them on the basis of its 2 anal spines and much more colorful and distinctive body and fin pigmentation. Six dark dorsal saddles tend to be more conspicuous than those found in the other two species, and the 8 or 9 square blotches on the side are unique. Fine dark reticulations are present above and below the lateral blotches. The preorbital bars do not connect at the tip of the snout as they do in *E. chlorosomum*. In breeding males the lateral blotches become iridescent light blue to blue-green, the head develops some bluish coloration, and the spinous dorsal develops a black band centrally, an orange band more distally, and a narrow dark band on the margin. (See also color plate.)

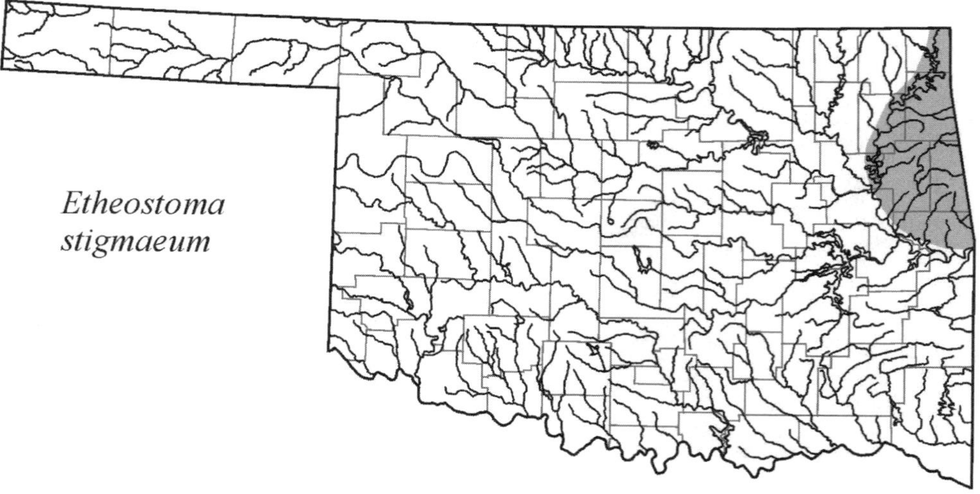

Distribution:

From Kansas and Oklahoma east to Kentucky and western Florida and south to Louisiana. Found in the Ozark tributaries of the Arkansas River in Oklahoma.

Habitat and Biology:

Blair (1959) indicates that this species is usually found in slow or moderate currents over silty bottoms in relatively clear streams. Most of the year speckled darters inhabit pools, moving into riffles to spawn in the spring. We have also collected them in moderately deep raceways with fine gravel bottom where the current was moderate. They spawn from March through April using the typical darter spawning actions (Winn 1958a, 1958b).

Note:

In an unpublished dissertation on the subgenus *Doration*, Layman (1994) recognized the Oklahoma populations of *Etheostoma stigmaeum* as part of a new species he called the "highland darter"; however, until it is formally described, we continue to recognize Oklahoma populations as *E. stigmaeum*.

Redfin darter
Etheostoma whipplei (Girard)

Description:

The redfin darter is a moderately deep-bodied, compressed darter with a pointed snout and fairly large head (3–3.5 into SL). The mouth is fairly large and moderately oblique, and a premaxillary frenum is present. Scales are small, 59–70 in the incomplete lateral line, and are absent from the cheeks and breast. The spinous dorsal fin has 10–12 spines, the soft dorsal has 13–15 rays, and the anal fin has 2 spines and 8 or 9 rays. Color is olivaceous to brownish with irregular dark markings along the sides and dorsum. Faint traces of 8–10 saddles are barely visible in some preserved specimens. Three basicaudal spots are also evident in preserved specimens. Scattered light yellowish spots, bright red in living males, occur on the sides. Breeding males have bands of blue, white, and red (proximally) on the median fins. Reaches 2.5 inches in length. Separable from *E. artesiae* by the higher lateral-line count (59 or higher) and higher number of caudal peduncle circumference scales (26 or higher). (See also color plate.)

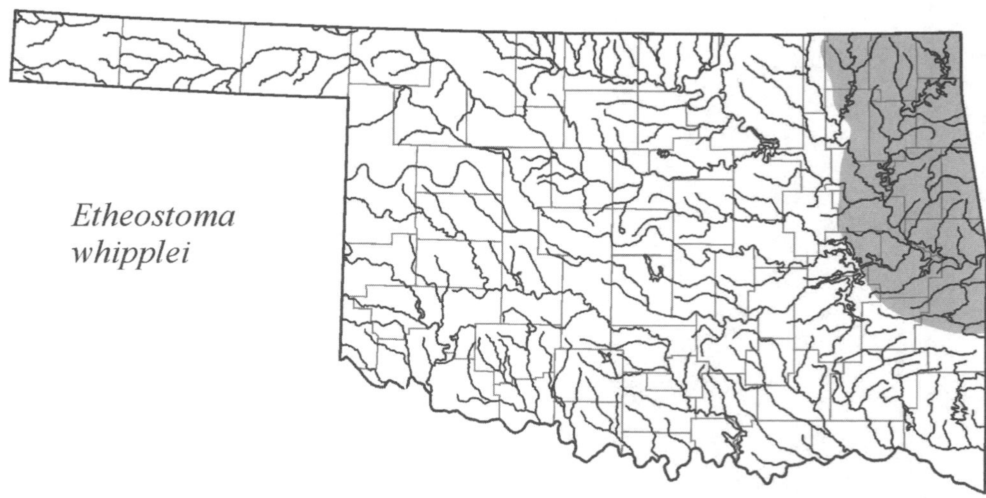

Distribution:

The Arkansas River system in eastern Oklahoma and Kansas and western Missouri and Arkansas. A similar form from the lowland streams of the Red and Ouachita River systems in Arkansas and Oklahoma is now recognized as a distinct species, *E. artesiae* (Piller et al. 2001).

Habitat and Biology:

Redfin darters are generally found in medium-sized clear streams with low to moderate gradients and sand or sand and gravel bottom. They occur primarily in shallow riffle areas. Like most darters, they spawn in early spring and feed on microinvertebrates, though the details of their life history have not yet been studied.

BANDED DARTER
Etheostoma zonale (Cope)

Description:

A slim to moderately deep-bodied, compressed darter with a short blunt snout and relatively small head (about 4 into SL). The mouth is small, subterminal, and slightly oblique. A premaxillary frenum is present and the gill membranes are broadly united across the isthmus. The nape, cheeks, opercles, and breast are scaled, and the lateral line is complete with 52–57 scales. The dorsal fin has 10–12 spines and 10 or 11 rays; the anal has 2 spines and 7 or 8 rays. Light olivaceous to straw colored above and whitish below, the body is marked with 6 or 7 brownish dorsal saddles and 9–13 greenish or brownish blotches on the side. In breeding males these lateral blotches become brilliant green vertical bars extending the full depth of the body. The spinous dorsal fin develops brick-red basal spots on the membranes and a greenish black submarginal band. Reddish spots also occur at the base of the soft dorsal. The anal fin becomes bright green. In preserved specimens there

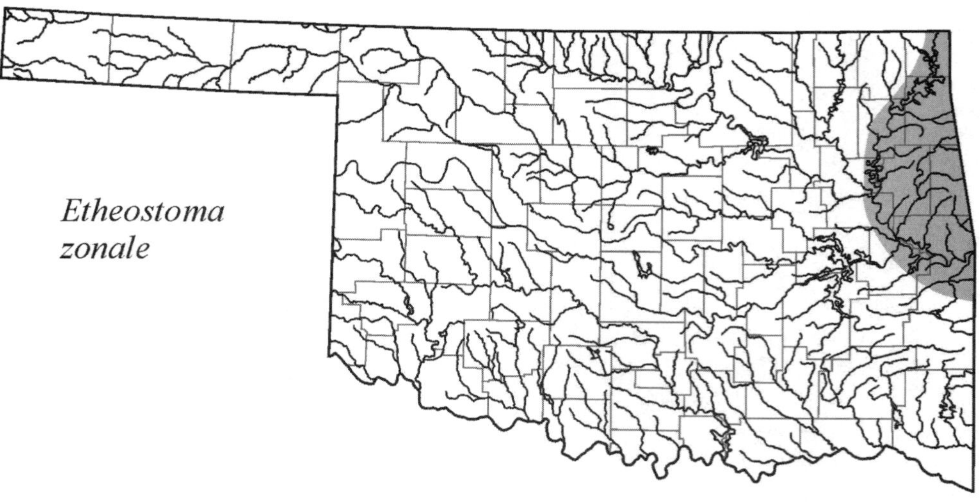

are 3 or 4 conspicuous basicaudal spots. Up to 2.8 inches in length. (See also color plate.)

Distribution:

From Pennsylvania west to Minnesota and south to Georgia and Louisiana. Found in the easternmost tributaries of the Arkansas River.

Habitat and Biology:

Banded darters occur most abundantly in Ozark streams of moderate size, with moderate to high gradients, and with an abundance of algae on larger stones in fairly deep, swift riffle areas. They spawn in these algae clumps during April and May, but little is known of their behavior. Food consists primarily of immature aquatic insects (Chironomidae and *Simulium*) taken from the stream bottom.

Yellow perch

Perca flavescens (Mitchill)

Specimens of this species have not been caught for many years. We now consider it to be extirpated from the state.

Logperch

Percina caprodes (Rafinesque)

Description:

Morris and Page (1981) studied variation in western logperches and reported two subspecies in Oklahoma. The nominate form, *P. caprodes caprodes*, occupies only the extreme southwest corner of the state in the Little River drainage, while *P. c. fulvitaenia*, the Ozark logperch, inhabits the rest of Oklahoma in the Arkansas River system and the Blue River and Mill Creek in the Red River drainage of Oklahoma. The logperch is the largest Oklahoma darter and is easily recognized by its conical head, which terminates in a long, pointed snout. The head is fairly short, the mouth is inferior, the body is streamlined and terete, and the fins are relatively high. The breast is naked and the midline of the belly is either naked or has a row of large scales. The complete lateral line contains 83–89 scales. Ground color is olivaceous to yellow with 15–20 dark bars along the side. Alternate bars are longer and more prominent, and a conspicuous black spot is present at the base of the caudal fin. Breeding males have an orange band near the distal edge of the

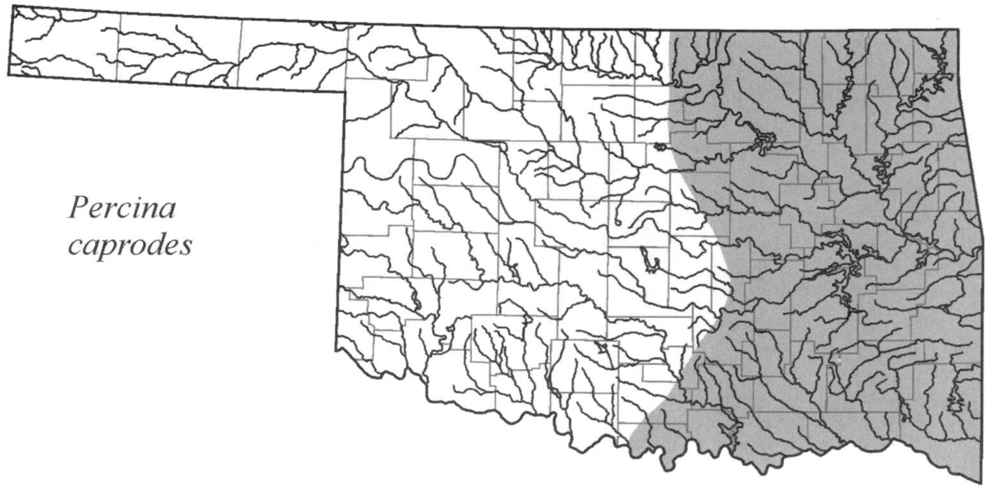

spinous dorsal fin. Maximum size 7 inches. *Percina caprodes* is very similar to *P. macrolepida*, but can be distinguished by its conical, bulbous, and fleshy snout, usually projecting well in front of the upper lip (*P. macrolepida* has a pointed, nonfleshy snout that rarely protrudes prominently past the upper lip). The absence of scales in the prepectoral area, on the edge of the preopercle, and on top of the head in *caprodes* contrasts with *macrolepida* having scales in all those areas. (See also color plate.)

Distribution:

From southern Canada through the Great Lakes to the Mississippi basin and south to Louisiana and Texas. Most common in the eastern half of Oklahoma but present in scattered localities throughout most of the state.

Habitat and Biology:

The logperch is most common in lakes or in clear streams with gravel, rocky, or clear sand bottoms. It tends to be found mainly over gravel in fairly deep riffle areas. It feeds mainly on larval insects and other small invertebrates. Spawning occurs in swift riffle areas or raceways during late March or April. There is little or no territory defense by the male, and spawning involves the male perching on the female's back with his anal region curving down next to the female's side. Eggs and sperm are extruded into the sand or gravel bottom, where they develop with no parental care.

Channel darter
Percina copelandi (Jordan)

Description:

A rather small, drab darter with a slim body and short blunt snout. The head is short, and the large eye is about equal in diameter to snout length. The mouth is rather small and nearly horizontal, and there is usually a distinct groove between the premaxillary (upper jaw) and the snout. Scales are absent on the anterior nape and breast, and the lateral line is complete with 53–60 scales. Dorsal fins have 11–12 spines and 11–12 rays; anal fin has 2 spines and 8–9 rays. Color is olivaceous above with 8 faint darker dorsal saddles, scattered faint X- or V-shaped markings dorsolaterally, and 9–12 dark, horizontally elongate blotches forming an interrupted lateral band on the side. The belly is yellowish to whitish. A preorbital band is prominent, and a suborbital bar is variously developed. The base of the spinous dorsal is black, and a less intense band is present near the distal edge of that fin. About 2 inches in length. (See also color plate.)

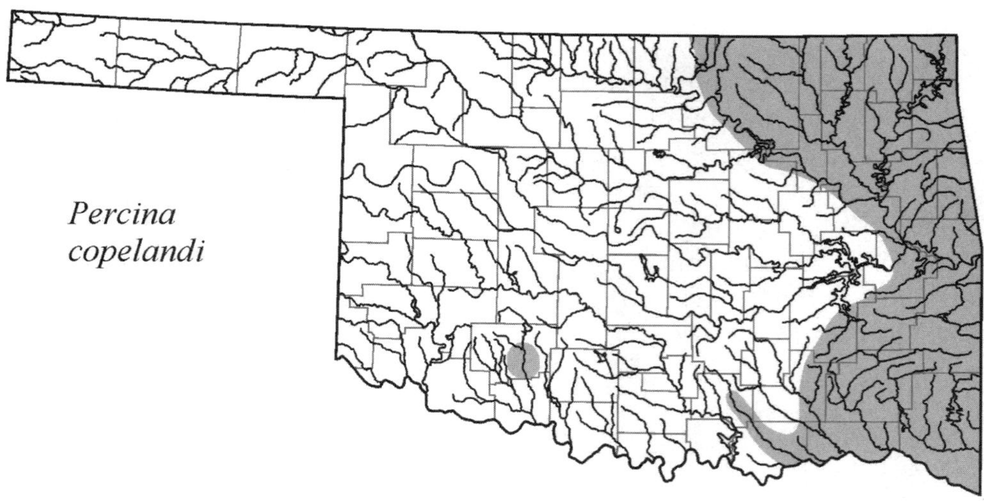

Distribution:

From the upper St. Lawrence basin through Ohio and southern Michigan south through the Ohio basin to the Alabama River system and Red River system of Oklahoma. Found in both the Arkansas and Red River systems in about the eastern half of Oklahoma. Recently found in East Cache and Medicine creeks at Fort Sill (Brown et al. 1997).

Habitat and Biology:

The channel darter tends to prefer quieter water than many darters. Throughout its range it is often found over clear sand or gravel along the shores of lakes or in gravelly sections of streams with relatively slower currents. Cross (1967) found this darter mainly at the interface between riffles and pools. It feeds primarily on chironomids and other tiny larval insects or microcrustaceans. In Oklahoma spawning occurs in June (Hubbs and Bryan 1975), with males showing more intense dark coloration and defending bottom territories less than a meter in diameter in areas of swift current over gravel and sand. Spawning is in the typical darter manner, the male perched on the female's back, caudal peduncle curved down beside the female. The slightly adhesive eggs are buried in the substrate and deserted, although the male maintains a surrounding territory for a short while. Hatching occurs in 6–10 days at 15–20 degrees C.

Bigscale logperch

Percina macrolepida Stevenson

Description:

A light-colored logperch with a protruding snout, a small head, 15–20 vertical dark lateral bars extending over the dorsum to join those on the opposite side. There are scales on the nape, on top of the head, on the breast, and in front of the pectoral fin. Body is terete and streamlined with relatively high fins. Lateral-line scales 77–90. Ground color is olivaceous and a conspicuous black spot is present at the base of the caudal fin. Breeding males lack the submarginal yellow-orange band near the distal edge of the spinous dorsal fin. Maximum size 4.5 inches. *Percina macrolepida* is very similar to *P. caprodes*, but can be distinguished by its pointed, nonfleshy snout, which rarely protrudes prominently past the front of the upper lip. (Snout of *caprodes* is conical, bulbous, fleshy, and protruding in front of the upper lip.) Scales are present in the prepectoral area, on the edge of the preopercle, and on top of the head in *macrolepida* but absent in those areas in *caprodes*).

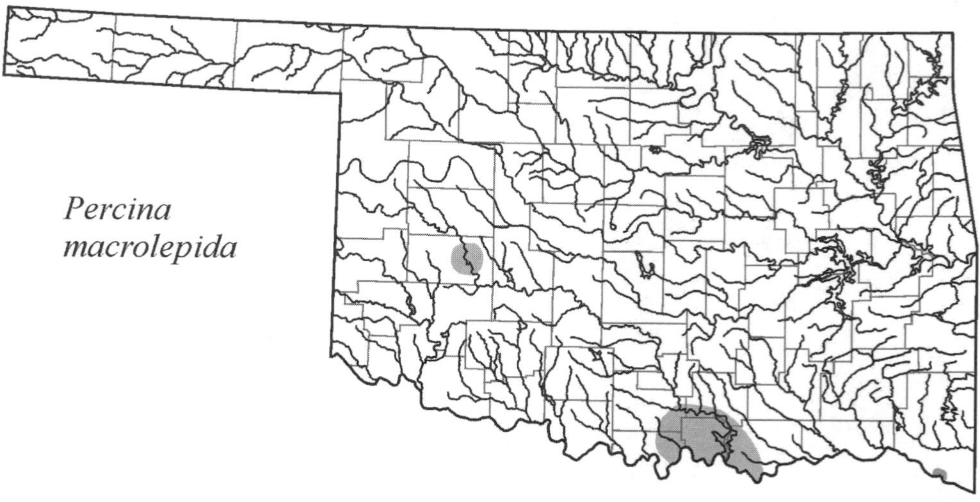

Distribution:

From the Sabine River in eastern Texas and western Louisiana northwest to the Red and Washita rivers in Oklahoma and west to the Rio Grande drainage in Texas, New Mexico, and Mexico. Also introduced in California. Occurs in the Arkansas River throughout Arkansas. In Oklahoma, this species occurs in both the Red River system and western reaches of the North Canadian River system (Buchanan and Stevenson 2003).

Habitat and Biology:

The bigscale logperch occurs in small to medium-sized rivers and tends to inhabit gravel and sand runs and pools but avoids typical riffles. An opportunistic feeder, it eats aquatic insect larvae, amphipods, planktonic crustaceans (copepods, cladocerans), and fish eggs. Moyle (1976) reported spawning in aquaria in February in California. Males were not strongly territorial, and females spawned in a vertical position, depositing eggs on the stems of aquatic plants. This behavior—so different from that of other *Percina* species, which generally spawn in gravelly riffles—may explain why this species has become so adundant in sloughs (Moyle 1976).

Blackside darter

Percina maculata (Girard)

Description:

A medium-sized (to 3.5 inches), slender darter with streamlined body and conical head. The snout is more pointed than in *P. copelandi*, and a well-developed frenum is present connecting the premaxillary and the snout. The preopercle is not serrate (unlike in *P. sciera*). Gill membranes are separate, and the breast and belly are naked except for a single line of enlarged scales down the midline (sometimes absent). The lateral line is complete with 62–77 scales. Color is light olivaceous above, slightly lighter below, with a conspicuous series of 7–8 horizontal dark blotches along the side, a small black spot at the base of the caudal fin, dark vermiculations along the dorsolateral part of the body, and a less conspicuous series of 8–9 dark saddles along the back. Fins are dusky, with second dorsal and caudal lightly barred.

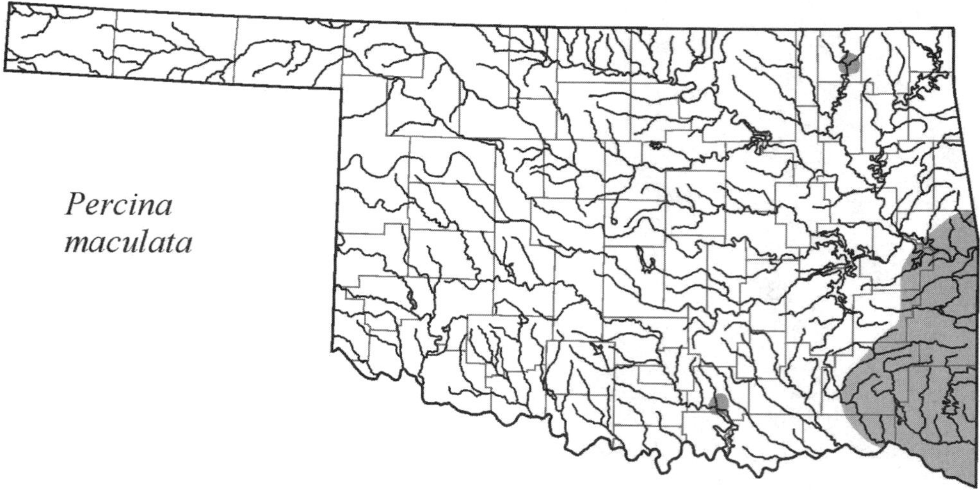

Distribution:

From southern Manitoba through the southern Great Lakes to the Ohio and Mississippi drainages between the eastern plains states and the Alleghenies, south to Louisiana. Mainly limited to the southeastern third of Oklahoma, especially the Poteau and Little River drainages but known from other streams connecting to the Red River. There is one record from the Verdigris drainage.

Habitat and Biology:

An inhabitant of clear, gravel-bottomed streams, this darter is not commonly found in swift currents or riffle areas. Instead, it occupies pools and riffles of slow to moderate current over gravel and rock bottoms. Trautman (1957) reported it swimming at midwater and even feeding at the surface. It feeds primarily on insect larvae and other small invertebrates but does so at a wider variety of depths than most darters. Spawning occurs in spring over sand or gravel when the water temperature rises above 60 degrees F. No nest is constructed, and there is little courtship. The typical darter spawning posture is used, and the eggs are buried in the substrate and deserted.

Longnose darter

Percina nasuta (Bailey)

Description:

The longnose darter is most closely related to *P. phoxocephala* and shares with that form its slender body, slim head, orange submarginal band on the spinous dorsal, and generally similar body markings. However, it can be distinguished by its 7 branchiostegal rays, rather than the 6 usual in darters, and by its longer head and snout (head 3–3.2 into SL; snout 3–3.6 into head). The fins are lower and shorter than in *P. phoxocephala*, and the scales are smaller (73–83 in the lateral line). Coloration is dull yellowish above and lighter below, with 10–14 vertical blotches along the side and numerous crossbands and smaller blotches on the dorsum. There is no subocular bar. The caudal fin has 3 dark bars. To about 2.5 inches long.

Distribution:

The Ozark region of southern Missouri, northern and western Arkansas, and eastern Oklahoma (Poteau River and Lee Creek).

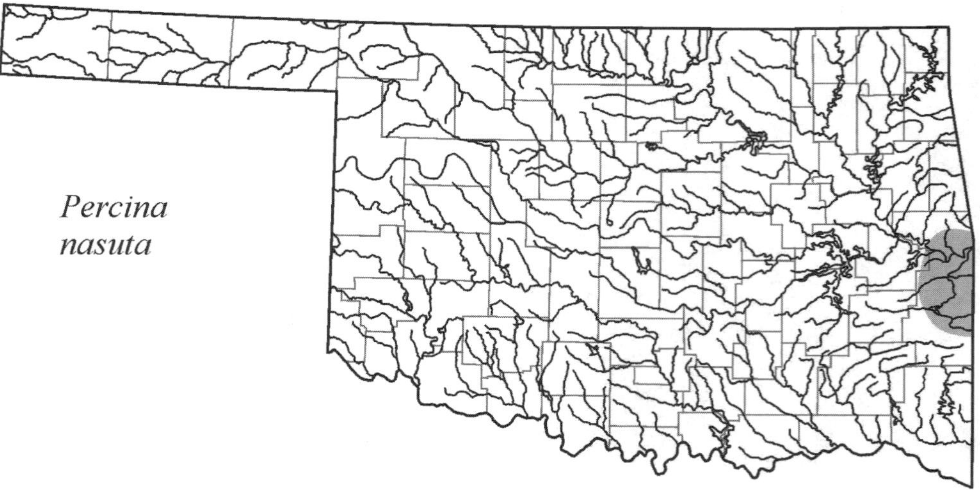

Habitat and Biology:

The longnose darter is one of Oklahoma's rarest species. It occurs in a few clear, silt-free upland streams of the Ozark region and prefers pool areas of cobble and gravel bottom substrates. In the spring individuals move into the riffles and raceway areas of pools having moderate to strong current at depths of 1–3 feet. Later in the summer, they move into deeper pool regions. Although spawning occurs in mid-May in Arkansas, Thompson (1977) believes peak spawning occurs in April.

Leopard Darter

Percina pantherina (Moore and Reeves)

Description:

This species is closely related to the blackside darter (*P. maculata*) but readily distinguishable from the latter on the basis of two main characteristics: scales are smaller (81–94 in lateral line vs. 62–77) and the 11–14 dark blotches along the lateral band are square or round and tend to be deeper than they are long (vs. longer than they are deep). The eye is dark, and there are well-developed preorbital, suborbital, and postorbital bars. Dark spots or blotches connect the major lateral spots, and numerous irregular dark blotches and saddles cover the dorsum. Color is light olive above and whitish below. Some specimens have faint traces of three bars on the caudal fin but relatively little pigment on the other fins (see color plate). To about 3 inches in length.

Distribution:

The Little River system in southern Oklahoma and southwestern Arkansas. Found widely distributed in the upper Little River and Mountain Fork River drainages in Oklahoma as well as throughout the Glover River drainage.

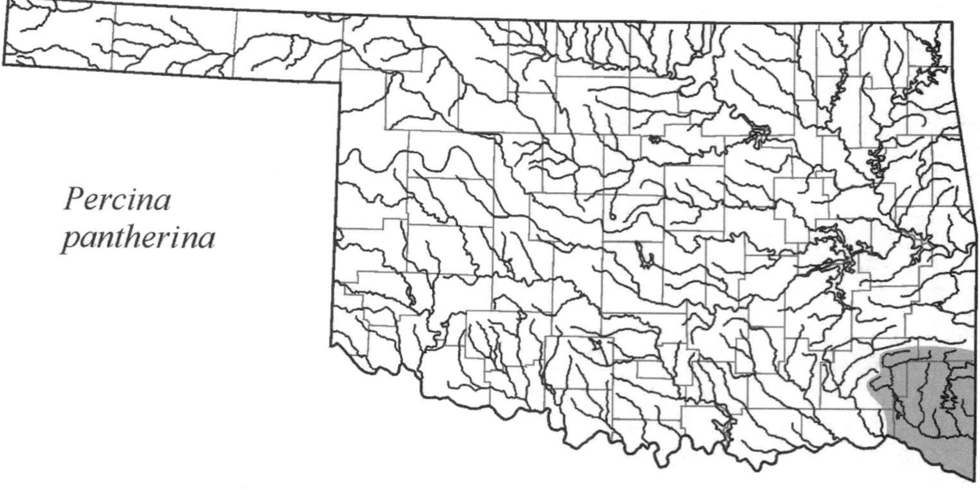

Habitat and Biology:

Rarely captured, the leopard darter is federally listed as a threatened species. It inhabits the swift, clear upper reaches of the Little and Mountain Fork rivers and their tributaries as well as the Glover River system. This darter shows a decided preference for pools of large and intermediate-sized streams and rivers during summer, autumn, and winter (Jones et al. 1984) Individuals move to riffles to spawn from mid-March to mid-May when water temperatures reach 12–20 degrees C (James et al. 1991). Females usually spawn with a single male, although occasionally up to three males may spawn simultaneously with one female. We have captured this species among coarse gravel and rubble with associated emergent plants along the borders of the stream channel. Diet of the leopard darter includes mayfly nymphs, blackfly larvae, midge larvae, coleopterans, chaoborids, and Chlorophyta.

SLENDERHEAD DARTER
Percina phoxocephala (Nelson)

Description:

A slender, handsome darter with a slim head and long, pointed snout. The snout is longer than the eye but not as long as in *P. nasuta* (usually more than 3.5 into head length vs. 3.0 in *nasuta*). Gill membranes are united, and the breast and belly are nearly naked (some enlarged median scales may be present). Scales are larger than in *P. nasuta*, with about 70–73 in the lateral line. Color varies considerably, with ground color brown to tan above, sides yellowish, and belly light yellow to whitish. There are 11–15 dark blotches along the side, often deeper than they are long, and with anterior blotches typically longer and slimmer. Darker blotches and saddles on the dorsum are highly variable in size and intensity. Cross (1967) points out that much of the variation in color pattern is due to size, with juveniles having numerous contrasting dorsal crossbars and lateral blotches, while adults become generally plainer and darker than young. The spinous dorsal has an orange submarginal

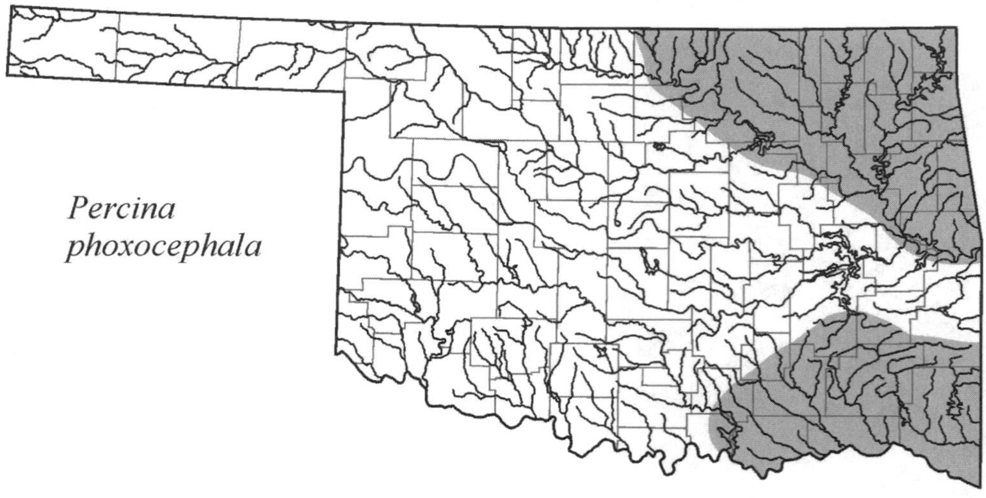

band, and the soft dorsal and caudal fins are lightly barred. Usually to 3 inches in length. Maximum size is about 4 inches. (See also color plate.)

Distribution:

The central Ohio and Mississippi basins from Minnesota to Pennsylvania south to Oklahoma and Tennessee. Occurs in both the Arkansas and Red River drainages, mainly in the eastern half of the state.

Habitat and Biology:

An inhabitant of the larger streams and rivers of Oklahoma, the slenderhead darter is somewhat more tolerant of turbid conditions than are many darters. Nonetheless, it is usually taken in swift water over clear gravel and sand bottoms and cannot survive in muddy water habitats. It feeds on chironomids and other insect larvae (mayflies and caddisflies) and breeds from March to June over large gravel beds in swift current in moderately deep riffles (15–20 inches). Males move to the spawning habitat prior to the arrival of females, indicating territoriality. Following spawning, adults return to deeper water (Page and Smith 1971). Breeding behavior has not been described.

DUSKY DARTER

Percina sciera (Swain)

Description:

A sturdy, moderately deep-bodied *Percina* that can be distinguished from others in the genus in Oklahoma by having both a well-developed frenum (fleshy bridge connecting the premaxillary bone with the snout) and serrations on the preoperculum. The body is somewhat compressed in deeper specimens, and the head is relatively short and deep. The scales are small, nearly absent on the breast, and number 66–72 in the lateral line. Basic ground color is light olivaceous with about 8–10 large, well-developed dark blotches along the side. The blotches tend to be deeper than they are long, but variation is great. Smaller, often less intense blotches sometimes occur between the large blotches, giving the impression of an irregular, nearly complete lateral band. Crossing the dorsum are 7 or 8 small dark saddles, and irregular dark vermiculations fill the space between saddles and lateral blotches. In some intensely colored specimens, faint dark blotches occur on the underside as well. Reaches more than 3 inches in length.

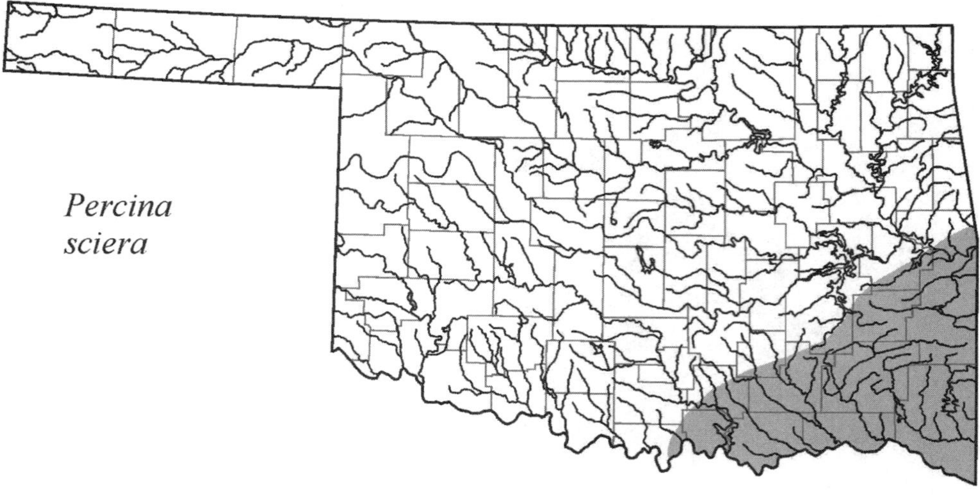

Distribution:

Throughout the lower Ohio and Mississippi drainages from Ohio through Tennessee and Missouri south to Texas and Alabama. Found in about the southeastern third of Oklahoma. Fairly widespread in the Red River system west to Rainy Mountain Creek in Kiowa County and also known from the Poteau drainage.

Habitat and Biology:

Usually found in moderate-sized to larger streams over sandy areas and gravel beds in riffles and raceways, this species is often associated with some kind of cover, such as large boulders, emergent plants, downed trees, or other debris. Foods consist entirely of aquatic insects (Page and Smith 1970). The dusky darter is a spring spawner, but its spawning behavior has not yet been described.

River darter
Percina shumardi (Girard)

Description:

A relatively stout, terete *Percina* with a moderately large head, large eyes, and short blunt snout. The premaxillary is separate from the snout or has only a narrow, sometimes obscure frenum. The species is readily identified by the following complex of characteristics: unusually long anal fin rays, which extend past the end of the dorsal rays, especially in adult males; naked breast and belly, except for a few scales before the anus; and more or less conspicuous black blotches on the membranes between the first and second and the last three dorsal spines. The pattern of 8–13 lateral blotches is also fairly distinctive, with anterior blotches deeper and slimmer than they are long, whereas posterior blotches are longer and wider than they are deep. About 7–12 dark saddles on the dorsum. Scales are moderate, 52–57 in the lateral line. May reach 3 inches in length. (See also color plate.)

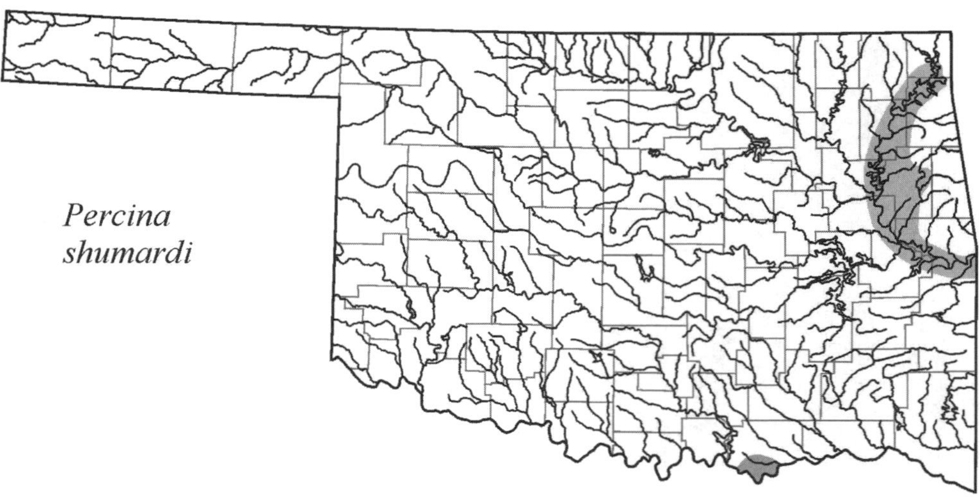

Distribution:

From southern Manitoba through parts of the Great Lakes and Ohio drainages south through the Mississippi basin to Alabama and Texas. Known primarily from the Grand River and Illinois River systems in northeastern Oklahoma and the Blue River in the south. Probably more widely distributed in the main streams of our clearer eastern rivers.

Habitat and Biology:

Definitely an inhabitant of large streams, the river darter is generally found over gravel and rubble in deeper riffles and raceways; it is rarely captured in less than 3 feet of water. Because of this predilection for deep, fast water, relatively few have been collected in the state. Thomas (1970) studied river darter biology in Illinois, where spawning occurs during April and May. In Tennessee this darter may spawn as early as February (Etnier and Starnes 1993). Foods consist primarily of midge and hydropsychid caddisfly larvae as well as microcrustaceans.

Sauger

Stizostedion canadense (Smith)

Description:

One of the two largest members of the family Percidae, the sauger is a streamlined predator with relatively high fins, moderately large eyes, and a large mouth containing impressive canine teeth as well as small villiform teeth. The most prominent recognition characteristics are the well-developed black spots occurring in rows on the dorsal fins and the absence of a black blotch at the posterior end of the first dorsal. There are 17–20 soft dorsal rays (vs. 19–22 in *S. vitreum*). Color is olivaceous above with a white belly. Three or four dark, saddlelike bands may cross the back and extend down the side, but these may be indistinct. To about 15 inches in length. State record: 5.5 lb., 23 in., from Kerr Reservoir.

Distribution:

From the Hudson Bay region of Canada west to Montana, east to New Brunswick, and south through the Great Lakes and Mississippi basin to

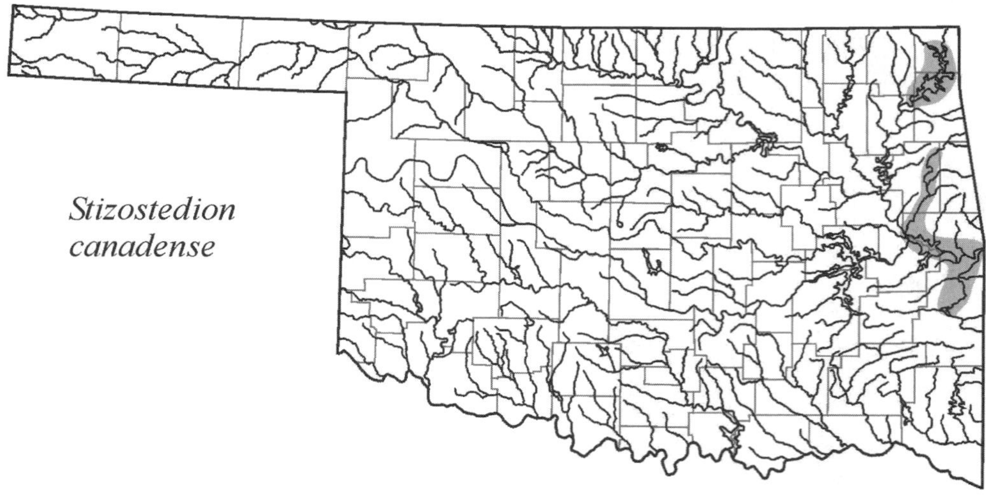

Louisiana. Found in the Poteau, Illinois, Red, and Neosho rivers in Oklahoma and in several lakes and reservoirs around the state.

Habitat and Biology:

In Oklahoma the sauger is primarily a river and stream fish, preferring the clear eastern rivers. It is not abundant anywhere and seems to be rare in the tailwaters below Lake Texoma. The eyes of this species give off an eerie glow due to the tapetum lucidum, a reflective layer on the retina. This adaptation is for feeding at night in low light levels. Adults feed largely on fish, the young mainly taking invertebrates and small fish. The sauger is a spring spawner, but little is known about its biology in Oklahoma. Spawning occurs at night and is completed within two weeks. Eggs are scattered over a firm substrate by females, with multiple males attending each female. No nest is constructed and no parental care is provided. Adults tend to congregate near spawning runs in late winter, and that is a prime time for anglers to take them. Known as to fishermen as "jack salmon," the sauger may once have been significant as a game fish in the Illinois River.

Note:

We continue to use the generic name *Stizostedion* despite the fact that some workers are using *Sander* for the pikeperches. In our view, the latter was a buried name and probably intended as a common name by its author, Oken 1817. The international rules of zoological nomenclature do not favor use of such a name, so we believe *Stizostedion* is the valid name for the pikeperches.

WALLEYE
Stizostedion vitreum (Mitchill)

Description:

Like the sauger, the walleye is a large, streamlined perch with high fins and a large mouth containing both villiform and large canine jaw teeth. It is distinguishable from the sauger on the basis of the following complex of characteristics: the spinous dorsal fin has a well-developed black blotch on the posterior membranes, but other spots are faint or absent; 19–22 soft dorsal rays; and a white tip on the lower lobe of the caudal fin. Coloration is quite different from that of the sauger. Instead of having large blotches, the walleye has 6–8 dark saddles on the dorsum over an olivaceous ground color, which grades to a white underside. Up to 27 inches long. State record: 12 lb., 10 oz., 29½ in., from Altus-Lugert Lake.

Distribution:

Essentially a northeastern species found from Great Slave Lake to Labrador and south through the Dakotas to Arkansas, Louisiana, and Missis-

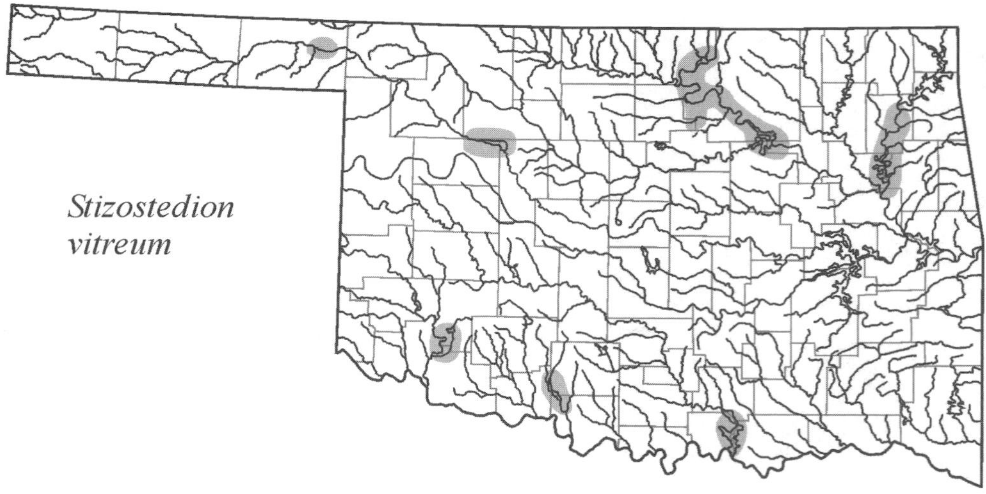

sippi. Present in Oklahoma in numerous reservoirs and streams, mainly as a result of recent hatchery planting. It may have been present in the eastern part of the state (in the Arkansas River system) in earlier times. The Oklahoma Department of Wildlife Conservation has produced walleye-sauger hybrids (saugeye) in quantity and has stocked them around the state.

Habitat and Biology:

An inhabitant of deep, fairly clear water, the walleye has done reasonably well in Canton Lake and a few other places in the state. Although it is relatively intolerant of heavy silt loads, at the same time it avoids strong light, hence its occurrence in deep water or weedy areas. Its eyes, like those of the sauger, have the reflective layer called the tapetum lucidum, an adaptation for vision in dim light, giving the fish a "wall-eyed" appearance. Adult walleyes feed mainly on fishes, although a variety of vertebrates and invertebrates are eaten by the young. Breeding occurs in early spring (February–March), mainly in the rocky areas of lakes and over gravel beds in streams. Spawning activity is apparently triggered by a sudden rise in water level following a heavy rain (Robison and Buchanan 1988).

DRUMS

FAMILY SCIAENIDAE

FRESHWATER DRUM

Aplodinotus grunniens (Rafinesque)

Description:

Aplodinotus is a freshwater representative of a large group of marine fishes (Sciaenidae) characterized by a highly developed lateral-line system and the ability to make loud booming sounds by contracting muscles along the walls of the gas bladder. It has a deep, compressed body with a high, arching back, blunt snout, subterminal mouth, and cavernous lateral-line canals on the head. The lateral line (48–53 scales) runs the length of the body and extends out onto the rounded or triangular caudal fin. The dorsal fin is

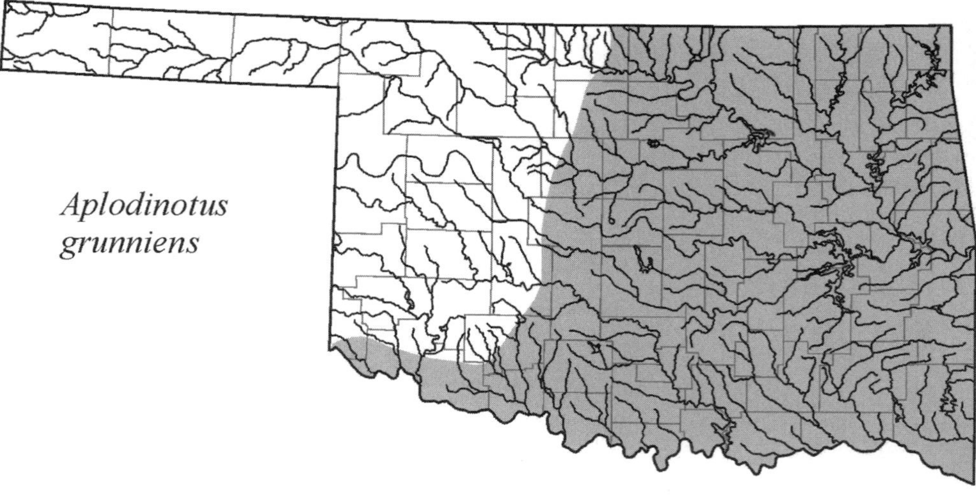

continuous and deeply notched, with 10 spines and about 31 soft rays. Color is silvery over most of the body with the dorsum grayish and the belly white. Oklahoma drum reach a weight of 25 pounds and length of 34 inches at 14 years of age. State record: 38 lb., 41¾ in., from Tenkiller Lake.

Distribution:

The entire Mississippi basin and southern Great Lakes south into Central America. Found throughout most of Oklahoma but probably uncommon or absent in the northwest.

Habitat and Biology:

Freshwater drum are most common in the deeper pools of rivers and in many lakes. While they can tolerate turbid waters, they seem to do best in clear waters, especially lakes, and grow fastest in smaller impoundments. Chironomids (midge larvae), small crustaceans, and other bottom fauna constitute their major food, though they feed on molluscs and small fish where these are available. Spawning occurs in late spring (April–May), when schools of this pelagic spawner gather. Eggs are released and float at the surface until hatching, which may occur in 24–48 hours. Although the drum is a fine table fish, those usually caught by anglers tend to be small and are often discarded.

BIBLIOGRAPHY

Able, K. W. 1984. Cyprinodontiformes: Development. Pp. 362–68 in H. G. Moser et al., eds., *Ontogeny and Systematics of Fishes*. Amer. Soc. Ichthy. & Herp. Spec. Pub. no. 1.

Adams, C. C., and T. L. Hankinson. 1928. The ecology and economics of Oneida Lake fish. *Roosevelt Wild Life Annals* 1(3–4):235–548.

Adamson, S. W., and T. E. Wissing. 1977. Food habits and feeding periodicity of the rainbow, fantail, and banded darters in Four Mile Creek. *Ohio J. Sci.* 77(4):164–69.

Ali, M. A., R. A. Ryder, and M. Anctil. 1977. Photoreceptors and visual pigments as related to behavioral responses and preferred habitats of perches (*Perca* spp.) and pikeperches (*Stizostedion* spp.). *J. Fish. Res. Bd. Canada* 34:1475–80.

Al-Rawi, A. H., and F. B. Cross. 1964. Variation in the plains minnow, *Hybognathus placitus* Girard. *Trans. Kansas Acad. Sci.* 67: 154–68.

Amemiya, C. T., and J. R. Gold. 1990. Chromosomal NOR phenotypes of seven species of North American Cyprinidae, with comments on cytosystematic relationships of the *Notropis volucellus* species-group, *Opsopoeodus emiliae,* and the genus *Pteronotropis*. *Copeia* 1990:68–78.

Applegate, R. L., and J. W. Mullan. 1967a. Food of the black bullhead (*Ictalurus melas*) in a new reservoir. *Proc. 20th Ann. Conf. Southeastern Assoc. Game and Fish Comm.* 288–92.

———. 1967b. Food of young largemouth bass, *Micropterus salmoides* in a new and old reservoir. *Trans. Amer. Fish Soc.* 96(1):74–77.

Ashbaugh, N. A., R. K. Reichert, S. E. Franklin, M. N. Mercer, H. A. Lanman, and B. S. Mantooth. 1996. A comparative study of the ichthyofauna in selected streams on the Salt Plains National Wildlife Refuge in Oklahoma. *Proc. Okla. Acad. Sci.* 76:17–21.

Atema, J., J. H. Todd, and J. E. Bardach. 1969. Olfaction and behavioral sophistication in fish. Pp. 241–51 in C. Pfaffman, ed., *Olfaction and Taste: Proceedings of the Third International Symposium*. New York: Rockefeller University Press.

Atmar, G.L., and K.W. Stewart. 1972. Food, feeding selectivity and ecological efficiencies of *Fundulus notatus*. *Amer. Midl. Nat.* 88:76–89.

Avise, J. C., G. S. Helfmann, N. C. Saunders, and L. S. Hales. 1986. Mitochondrial DNA differentiation in North Atlantic eels: Population genetic consequences of an unusual life history pattern. *Proc. Nat. Acad. Sci. USA* 83:4350–54.

Avise, J. C., and M. H. Smith. 1974a. Biochemical genetics of sunfish. I. Geographic variation and subspecific intergradation in the bluegill, *Lepomis macrochirus*. *Evolution* 28:42–56.

———. 1974b. Biochemical genetics of sunfish. II. Genic similarity between hybridizing species. *Amer. Nat.* 108:458–72.

———. 1977. Gene frequency comparisons between sunfish (Centrarchidae) populations at various stages of evolutionary divergence. *Syst. Zool.* 26:319–35.

Avise, J. C., D. O. Straney, and M. H. Smith. 1977. Biochemical genetics of sunfish. IV. Relationships of centrarchid genera. *Copeia* 1977:250–58.

Baglin, R. E., Jr., and L. G. Hill. 1977. Fecundity of white bass, *Morone chrysops* (Rafinesque), in Lake Texoma. *Amer. Midl. Nat.* 98:233–38.

Bailey, R. M. 1941a. *Hadropterus nasutus*, a new darter from Arkansas. Occas. Papers Mus. Zool. Univ. Mich. no. 440. 8 pp.

———. 1941b. Records of lampreys (*Ichthyomyzon gagei*) in Oklahoma. *Copeia* 1941(2): 146.

———. 1956. A revised list of the fishes of Iowa, with keys for identification. Pp. 326–77 in *Iowa Fish and Fishing*. Des Moines: Iowa Conserv. Comm.

Bailey, R. M., and M. O. Allum. 1962. *Fishes of South Dakota*. Misc Pub. Mus. Zool. no. 119. Ann Arbor: University of Michigan. 131 pp.

Bailey, R. M., and F. B. Cross. 1954. River sturgeons of the American genus *Scaphirhynchus*: Characters, distribution, and synonymy. *Papers Mich. Acad. Sci. Arts, Let.* 39:169–208.

Bailey, R. M., and D. A. Etnier. 1988. Comments on the subgenera of darters (Percidae) with descriptions of two new species of *Etheostoma (Ulocentra)* from southeastern United States. Misc. Pub. Mus. Zool. no. 175. Ann Arbor: University of Michigan. 48 pp.

Bailey, R. M., J. E. Fitch, E. S. Herald, E. A. Lachner, C. C. Lindsey, C. R. Robins, and W. B. Scott. 1970. *A List of Common and Scientific Names of Fishes from the United States and Canada*. 3rd ed. Amer. Fish. Soc. Spec. Pub. no. 6. 150 pp.

Bailey, R. M., and W. A. Gosline. 1955. Variation and systematic significance of vertebral counts in the American fishes of the family Percidae. Misc. Publ. Mus. Zool. Univ. Mich. no. 93. 5–44.

Bailey, R. M., and C. L. Hubbs. 1949. The black basses (*Micropterus*) of Florida, with description of a new species. Occas. Papers Mus. Zool. Univ. Mich. no. 516. 40 pp.

Bailey, R. M. and H. W. Robison. 1978. *Notropis hubbsi*, a new cyprinid fish from the Mississippi River basin. Occas. Papers Mus. Zool. Univ. Mich. no. 683. 21 pp.

Bailey, R. M., H. E. Winn, and C. L. Smith. 1954. Fishes of the Escambia River, Alabama and Florida, with ecologic and taxonomic notes. *Proc. Acad. Nat. Sci. Philadelphia* 106:109–64.

Bailey, W. M., and R. L. Boyd. 1970. A preliminary report on spawning and rearing of grass carp (*Ctenopharyngodon idella*) in Arkansas. *Proc. 24th Ann. Conf. Southeastern Assoc. Game and Fish Comm.* 560–69.

Baker, C. D., and E. H. Schimtz. 1971. Food habits of adult gizzard shad and threadfin shad in two Ozark reservoirs. Pp. 3–11 in G. E. Hall, ed., *Reservoir Fisheries and Limnology.* Amer. Fish. Soc. Spec. Pub. no. 8..

Balon, E. K. 1975. Reproductive guilds of fishes: A proposal and definition. *J. Fish. Res. Bd. Canada* 32(6):821–64.

Balon, E. K., W. T. Momat, and H. A. Regier. 1977. Reproductive guilds of percids: Results of paleogeographical history and ecological succession. *J. Fish. Res. Bd. Canada* 34: 1910–21.

Barila, T. Y. 1980a. *Stizostedion canadense*, Sauger. P. 745 in Lee et al., *Atlas* (see Lee et al., 1980).

———. 1980b. *Stizostedion vitreum*, walleye. Pp. 747–48 in Lee et al., *Atlas* (see Lee et al., 1980).

Barney, R. L., and B. J. Anson. 1920. Life history and ecology of the pygmy sunfish, *Elassoma zonatum*. *Ecology* 1(4):241–56.

———. 1922. Life history and ecology of the orange-spotted sunfish, *Lepomis humilis*. Append. 15, Rpt. U.S. Comm. Fish. 1922, Bur. Fish. Doc. 938. 16 pp.

Barnikol, P. G. 1941. Food habits of *Gambusia affinis* from Reelfoot Lake, Tennessee, with special reference to malarial control. Rpt. Reelfoot Biol. Sta. (*J. Tenn. Acad. Sci.*) 5:5–13.

Bart, H. L., Jr., and L. M. Page. 1991. Morphology and adaptive significance of the fin knobs in egg clustering darters. *Copeia* 1991: 80–86.

Bass, J. C., and C. D. Riggs. 1959. Age and growth of the river carpsucker, *Carpiodes carpio* Rafinesque of Lake Texoma. *Proc. Okla. Acad. Sci.* 39:50–69.

Bauer, B. H. 1980. *Lepomis megalotis* (Rafinesque), longear sunfish. P. 600 in Lee et al., *Atlas* (see Lee et al., 1980).

Beach, M. L. 1974. Food habits and reproduction of the taillight shiner, *Notropis maculatus* (Hay), in central Florida. *Florida Scientist* 37(1):5–6.

Beamish, F. W. H., and E. J. Thomas. 1984a. Potential and actual fecundity of the "paired" lampreys, *Ichthyomyzon gagei* and *I. castaneus*. *Copeia* 1983(2):367–74.

———. 1984b. Metamorphosis of the southern brook lamprey, *Ichthyomyzon gagei*. *Copeia* 1984:502–15.

Beamish, R. J. 1973. Determination of age and growth of populations of the white sucker (*Catostomus commersoni*) exhibiting a wide range in size at maturity. *J. Fish. Res. Bd. Canada* 30:607–16.

Becker, G. C. 1983. *Fishes of Wisconsin*. Madison: University of Wisconsin Press. 1,052 pp.

Beckham, E. C. 1986. Systematics and redescription of the blackside darter, *Percina maculata* (Girard), (Pisces: Percidae). Occas. Papers Mus. Zool. La. St. Univ. no. 62. 11 pp.

Behmer, D. J. 1965. Spawning periodicity of the river carpsucker, *Carpiodes carpio*. *Iowa Acad. Sci.* 72:253–62.

Behnke, R. J. 1966. Relationships of the far eastern trout, *Salmo mykiss* Walbaum. *Copeia* 1966:346–48.

———. 1990. Still a rainbow—by any other name. *Trout* (Winter 1990): 41–45.

Bemis, W. E., E. K. Findeis, and L. Grande. 1997. An overview of the Acipenseriformes. *Environ. Biol. Fishes* 48:25–71.

Berg, L. S. 1940. *Classification of Fishes Both Recent and Fossil*. Travaux Inst. Zool. de Acad. Sci. USSR. English transl., 1947, Ann Arbor, Mich.: Edwards Press. 517 pp.

———. 1964. *Freshwater Fishes of the USSR and Adjacent Countries*. 4th ed. Vol. 2. Jerusalem: Israel Program for Scientific Translations.

Berner, L. M. 1948. The intestinal convolutions: New generic characteristics for the separation of *Carpiodes* and *Ictiobus*. *Copeia* 2:140–41.

Berra, T. M. 1981. *An Atlas of Distribution of the Freshwater Fish Families of the World*. Lincoln: University of Nebraska Press. 197 pp.

Berra, T. M., and G. E. Gunning. 1972. Seasonal movement and home range of the longear sunfish, *Lepomis megalotis* (Rafinesque) in Louisiana. *Amer. Midl. Nat.* 88:368–75.

Binderim, G. E. 1977. Fishes of Mill Creek, a tributary of the Washita River, Johnston and Murray counties, Oklahoma. *Proc. Okla. Acad. Sci*. 57:1–11.

Birdsong, R. S., and L. W. Knapp. 1969. *Etheostoma collettei*, a new darter of the subgenus *Oligocephalus* from Louisiana and Arkansas. *Tulane Studies in Zoology and Botany* 15(3): 106–12.

Birkhead, W. S. 1972. Toxicity of stings of ariid and ictalurid catfishes. *Copeia* 1972 (4):790–807.

Birstein, V. J. 1993. Sturgeons and paddlefishes: Threatened fishes in need of conservation. *Conserv. Biol.* 7:773–87

Black, D. A., and W. M. Howell. 1979. The North American mosquitofish, *Gambusia affinis*: A unique case in sex chromosome evolution. *Copeia* 1979:509–13.

Black, J. D. 1945. Natural history of the northern mimic shiner, *Notropis volucellus volucellus* Cope. *Invest. Indiana Lakes and Streams* 2(18):449–69.

Blair, A. P. 1959. Distribution of the darters (Percidae; Etheostomatinae) of northeastern Oklahoma. *Southwestern Nat.* 4(1):1–13.

Blair, A. P., and J. Windle. 1961. Darter associates of *Etheostoma cragini* (Percidae). *Southwestern Nat.* 6(3–4): 201–202.

Blair, W. F., and T. H. Hubbell. 1938. The biotic districts of Oklahoma. *Amer. Midl. Nat.* 20(2):425–54.

Blumer, L. S. 1985. Reproductive natural history of the brown bullhead *Ictalurus nebulosus* in Michigan. *Amer. Midl. Nat.* 114(2):318–30.

Bockstael, J. 1983. Spawning the logperch, a native Canadian darter. *American Currents* (July–August): 5–7.

Boltz, J. M., and J. R. Stauffer, Jr. 1986. Branchial brooding in the pirate perch, *Aphredoderus sayanus* (Gilliams). *Copeia* 1986(4):1030–31.

———. 1993. Systematics of *Aphredoderus sayanus* (Teleostei: Aphredoderidae). *Copeia* 1993:81–98.

Bottrell, C. E., R. H. Ingersol, and R. W. Jones. 1964. Notes on the embryology, early development, and behavior of *Hybopsis aestivalis tetranemus* (Gilbert). *Trans. Am. Micros. Soc.* 83:391–99.

Bowman, M. L. 1970. Life history of the black redhorse, *Moxostoma duquesnei* (Lesueur), in Missouri. *Trans. Amer. Fish. Soc.* 99(3):546–59.

Braasch, M. E., and P. W. Smith. 1965. Relationships of the topminnow *Fundulus notatus* and *Fundulus olivaceus* in the upper Mississippi River Valley. *Copeia* 1965 (1):46–53.

———. 1967. The life history of the slough darter, *Etheostoma gracile* (Pisces: Percidae). Ill. Nat. Hist. Surv. Biol. Notes no. 58. 12 pp.

Branson, B. A. 1962. Comparative cephalic and appendicular osteology of the fish family Catostomidae, Part 1: *Cycleptus elongatus* (Lesueur). *Southwestern Nat.* 7(2):81–153.

———. 1967. Fishes of the Neosho River system in Oklahoma. *Amer. Midl. Nat.* 78(1): 126–54.

Branson, B. A., and G. A. Moore. 1962. The lateralis components of the acoustico-lateralis system in the sunfish family Centrarchidae. *Copeia* 1962:1–108.

Breder, C. M., Jr., and D. E. Rosen. 1966. *Modes of Reproduction in Fishes*. New York: Natural History Press. 941 pp.

Brezner, J. 1958. Food habits of the northern river carpsucker in Missouri. *Prog. Fish-Culturist* 20(4):170–74.

Brown, B. E., and J. S. Dendy. 1961. Observations of the food habits of the flathead and blue catfish in Alabama. *Proc. 15th Ann. Conf. Southeastern Assoc. Game and Fish Comm.* 219–22.

Brown, M. D., A. H. Claborn, L. M. Lofer, T. G. Heger, and J. D. Tyler. 1997. The occurrence of the channel darter (Perciformes: Percidae) in the east Cache Creek system of southwest Oklahoma. *Proc. Okla. Acad. Sci.* 77:127–29.

Bower, C. A., Jr. 1980. The life history of the brindled madtom *Noturus miurus* (Jordan) in Salt Creek, Hocking and Vinton counties, Ohio. M.S. thesis, Ohio State University, Columbus.

Buchanan, T. M., and M. M. Stevenson. 2003. Distribution of bigscale logperch, *Percina macrolepida* (Percidae), in the Arkansas River basin. *Southwestern Nat*. 48(3):454–60.

Bulger, A. G. 1999. Population structure, habitat use, and breeding behavior of the Neosho madtom, *Noturus placidus*. M.S. thesis, Emporia State University, Emporia, Kans. 83 pp.

Bulger, A. G., and D. R. Edds. 2001. Population structure and habitat use in Neosho madtom (*Noturus placidus*). *Southwestern Nat*. 46(1):8–15.

Burgess, G. H. 1980. *Morone saxatilis* (Walbaum), striped bass. P. 576 in Lee et al., *Atlas* (see Lee et al., 1980).

Burkhead, N. M., and J. D. Williams. 1989. Current status of the exotic minnow, *Scardinius erythrophthalmus*, in the United States. *Assoc. SE Biol. Bull.* 36:93 (abstract).

———. 1991. An intergeneric hybrid of a native minnow, the golden shiner, and an exotic minnow, the rudd. *Trans. Amer. Fish. Soc*. 120:781–95.

Burr, B. M. 1977. The bantam sunfish, *Lepomis symmetricus*: Systematics and distribution, and life history in Wolf Lake, Illinois. *Ill. Nat. Hist. Surv. Bull.* 31(10):437–65.

———. 1978. Systematics of the percid fishes of the subgenus *Microperca*, genus *Etheostoma*. *Bull. Alabama Mus. Nat. Hist*. 4:1–53.

Burr, B. M., and R. C. Cashner, and W. L. Pflieger. 1979. *Campostoma oligolepis* and *Notropis ozarcanus* (Pisces: Cyprinidae), two additions to the known fish fauna of the Illinois River, Arkansas and Oklahoma. *Southwestern Nat.* 24(2):381–403.

Burr, B. M., and W. W. Dimmick. 1983. Redescription of the bigeye shiner, *Notropis boops* (Pisces: Cyprinidae). *Proc. Biol. Society of Washington* 96(1): 50–58.

Burr, B. M., and R. C. Heidinger. 1983. Reproductive behavior of the bigmouth buffalo *Ictiobus cyprinellus* in Crab Orchard Lake, Illinois. *Amer. Midl. Nat.* 110(1):220–21.

Burr, B. M., and R. L. Mayden. 1982a. Status of the cypress minnow, *Hybognathus hayi* Jordan, in Illinois. Natural History Miscellanea, Chicago Acad. of Sci. no. 215. 10 pp.

———. 1982b. Life history of the freckled madtom, *Noturus nocturnus*, in Mill Creek, Illinois (Pisces: Cyprinidae). Occas. Papers Mus. Nat. Hist. Univ. Kansas no. 98. 15 pp.

———. 1982c. Life history of the brindled madtom, *Noturus miurus* in Mill Creek, Illinois (Pisces: Ictaluridae). *Amer. Midl. Nat.* 107(1):25–41.

———. 1984. Reproductive biology of the checkered madtom (*Noturus flavater*) with observations on nesting in the Ozark (*N. albater*) and slender (*N. exilis*) madtoms (Siluriformes: Ictaluridae). *Amer. Midl. Nat.* 112:408–14.

Burr, B. M., and M. A. Morris. 1977. Spawning behavior of the shorthead redhorse, *Moxostoma macrolepidotum*, in Big Rock Creek, Illinois. *Trans. Amer. Fish. Soc.* 106(1):80–92.

Burr, B. M., and L. M. Page. 1975. Distribution and life history notes on the taillight shiner, *Notropis maculatus* in Kentucky. *Trans. Kentucky Acad. Sci.* 36:71–74.

———. 1978. The life history of the cypress darter, *Etheostoma proeliare*, in Max Creek, Illinois. Ill. Nat. Hist. Surv. Biol. Notes no. 106. 15 pp.

———. 1979. The life history of the least darter, *Etheostoma microperca*, in the Iroquois River, Illinois. Ill. Nat. Hist. Surv., Biol. Notes no. 106. 15 pp.

———. 1991. Morphology and adaptative significance of fin knobs in egg-clustering darters. *Copeia* 1991(1):80–86.

Burr, B. M., and P. W. Smith. 1976. Status of the largescale stoneroller, *Campostoma oligolepis*. *Copeia* 1976(3):521–31.

Burr, B. M., and J. N. Stoeckel. 1999. The natural history of madtoms (Genus *Noturus*) North America's diminuitive catfishes. *Amer. Fish. Soc. Symp.* 24: 51–101.

Buth, D. G. 1979. Biochemical systematics of the cyprinid genus *Notropis*. I: The subgenus *Luxilus*. *Biochem. Syst. Ecol.* 7:69–79.

———. 1980. Evolutionary genetics and systematic relationships in the catostomid genus *Hypentelium*. *Copeia* 1980:280–90.

Buth, D. G., and R. L. Mayden. 1981. Taxonomic status and relationships among populations of *Notropis pilsbryi* and *N. zonatus* (Cypriniformes: Cyprinidae) as shown by the glucosephosphate isomerase, lactate dehydrogenase and phosphoglucomutase enzyme systems. *Copeia* 1981(3):585–90.

Butler, R. L. 1962. The life history and ecology of the sheepshead, *Aplodinotus grunniens* Rafinesque, in the commercial fishery of the upper Mississippi River. Ph.D. diss., University of Minnesota, Minneapolis. 178 pp.

Campbell, R. D., and B. A. Branson. 1978. Ecology and population dynamics of the black bullhead, *Ictalurus melas* (Rafinesque), in central Kentucky. *Tulane Studies in Zoology and Botany* 29(3–4):99–136.

Campos, H. H. and C. Hubbs. 1973. Taxonomic implications of the karyotype of *Opsopoeodus emiliae*. *Copeia* 1973(1):161–63.

Carlander, K. D. 1977. *Handbook of Freshwater Fishery Biology*. Vol. 2. Ames: Iowa State University Press. 431 pp.

Carlson, D. M., W. L. Pflieger, L. Trial, and P. S. Harerland. 1985. Distribution, biology and hybridization of *Scaphirhynchus albus* and *S. platorynchus* in the Missouri and Mississippi rivers. *Environ. Biol. Fishes* 14:51–59.

Carnes, W. C., Jr. 1958. Contributions to the biology of the eastern creek chubsucker, *Erimyzon oblongus oblongus* (Mitchill). M.S. thesis, North Carolina State College, Raleigh. 69 pp.

Carpenter, C. C. 1975. Functional aspects of the notochordal appendage of young-of-the-year gar (*Lepisosteus*). *Proc. Okla. Acad. Sci.* 55:57–64.

Carr, M. H. 1946. The breeding habits of the eastern stumpknocker, *Lepomis punctatus punctatus* (Cuvier). *Quart. Jour. Fla. Acad. Sci.* 9:101–106.

Carranza, J., and H. E. Winn. 1954. Reproductive behavior of the black stripe topminnow, *Fundulus notatus*. *Copeia* 1954(4):273–78.

Case, B. 1970. Spawning behavior of the chestnut lamprey (*Ichthyomyzon castaneus*). *J. Fish. Res. Bd. Canada* 27:1872–74.

Cashner, R. C. 1980a. *Ambloplites ariommus* Viosca, shadow bass. P. 578 in Lee et al., *Atlas* (see Lee et al., 1980).

———. 1980b. *Ambloplites rupestris*, rockbass. P. 581 in Lee et al., *Atlas* (see Lee et al., 1980).

Cashner, R. C., and W. J. Matthews. 1988. Changes in the known Oklahoma fish fauna from 1973 to 1988. *Proc. Okla. Acad. Sci.* 68:1–7.

Cashner, R. C., and R. D. Suttkus. 1978. The status of the rock bass population in Blue Spring, New Mexico, with comments on the introduction of rock bass in the western United States. *Southwestern Nat.* 23(3):463–72.

Cavender, T. M. 1986. Review of the fossil history of North American freshwater fishes. Pp. 699–724 in C. H. Hocutt and E. O. Wiley, eds., *The Zoogeography of North American Freshwater Fishes*. New York: John Wiley and Sons. 866 pp.

Cavender, T. M., and M. M. Coburn. 1985. Interrelationships of North American cyprinidae, part 2. *65th Ann. Meet. Amer. Soc. Ichthy. & Herp.*, p. 49 (abstract).

———. 1987. The *Phoxinus* group and its relationship with North American cyprinids. *67th Ann. Meet. Amer. Soc. Ichthy. & Herp.*, p. 38 (abstract).

———. 1988. Relationships of the cyprinid genus *Hybognathus*. *68th Ann. Meet. Amer. Soc. Ichthy. & Herp.*, p. 74 (abstract).

———. 1989. Relationships of American cyprinidae. *69th Ann. Meet. Amer. Soc. Ichthy. & Herp.*, p. 74 (abstract).

Ceas, P. A., and L. M. Page. 1997. Systematic studies of the *Etheostoma spectabile* complex, with descriptions of four new species. *Copeia* 1997:496–522.

Chernoff, B., J. V. Conner, and C. F. Bryan. 1981. Systematics of the *Menidia beryllina* complex (Pisces: Atherinidae) from the Gulf of Mexico and its tributaries. *Copeia* 1981:319–36.

Clemens, H. P., and K. E. Sneed. 1957. The spawning behavior of the channel catfish *Ictalurus punctatus*. U.S. Fish and Wildl. Serv. Spec. Sci. Rept. Fish. no. 219. 11 pp.

Clemmer, G. H. 1971. The systematics and biology of the *Hybopsis amblops* complex. Ph.D. diss., Tulane University, New Orleans. 155 pp.

———. 1980a. *Hybopsis amblops*, bigeye chub. P. 181 in Lee et al., *Atlas* (see Lee et al., 1980).

———. 1980b. *Notropis amnis* (Hubbs and Greene), pallid shiner. P. 224 in Lee et al., *Atlas* (see Lee et al., 1980).

Coburn, M. M., and T. M. Cavender. 1992. Interrelationships of North American cyprinid fishes. Pp. 328–73 in R. L. Mayden, ed., *Systematics, Historical Ecology, and North American Freshwater Fishes*. Stanford, Calif.: Stanford University Press.

Cochran, P. A. 1996. Cavity enhancement by madtoms (genus *Noturus*). *J. Freshwater Ecology* 11:521–22.

———. 2000. The spotfin shiner (*Cyprinella spiloptera*): A fish that spawns in trees. *American Currents* 26(4):7–8.

Cofer, L. M. 1995. Invalidation of the Wichita spotted bass, *Micropterus punctulatus wichitae*, subspecies theory. *Copeia* 1995:487–90.

Cole, K. S., and R. J. F. Smith. 1992. Attraction of female fathead minnows, *Pimephales promelas*, to chemical stimuli from breeding males. *J. Chem. Ecol.* 18:1269–84

Collette, B. B. 1962. The swamp darters of the subgenus *Hololepis*. (Pisces: Percidae). *Tulane Studies in Zoology and Botany* 9(4):115–211.

Collette, B. B., M. A. Ali, K. E. F. Hokanson, M. Nagiec, S. A. Smirnov, J. E. Thorpe, A. H. Weatherley, and J. Willemson. 1977. Biology of the percoids. *J. Fish. Res. Bd. Canada* 34(10):1891–97.

Collette, B. B., and L. W. Knapp. 1966. Catalog of type specimens of the darters (Pisces: Percidae, Etheostomatini). *Proc. U.S. Natl. Mus.* 119(3550):1–88.

Conley, J. M. 1966. Ecology of the flier, *Centrarchus macropterus* (Lacepede) in southeast Missouri. M.A. thesis, University of Missouri, Columbia. 119 pp.

Conner, J. V., R. P. Gallagher, and M. F. Chatry. 1980. Larval evidence for natural reproduction of the grass carp (*Ctenopharyngodon idella*) in the lower Mississippi River. Proc. 4th Ann. Larval Fish. Conf. Biol. Serv. Prog. National Power Plant Team, Ann Arbor, Michigan. FWS/OBS-80/43:1–19.

Cook, K. D. 1979. Fish population study of West Cache Creek with emphasis on search for the Witchita spotted bass, *Micropterus punctulatus wichitae*. *Proc. Okla. Acad. Sci.* 59:1–3.

Cooper, E. L., ed. 1987. *Carp in North America*. Bethesda, Md.: American Fisheries Society. 84 pp.

Courtenay, W. R., Jr. and J. R. Stauffer, Jr. 1984. *Distribution, Biology, and Management of Exotic Fishes*. Baltimore: Johns Hopkins University Press. 430 pp.

Cowell, B. C., and B. S. Barnett. 1974. Life history of the taillight shiner, *Notropis maculatus*, in central Florida. *Amer. Midl. Nat.* 91(2):282–93.

Craddock, J. R. 1965. Some aspects of the life history of the banded sculpin, *Cottus carolinae carolinae* in Doe Run, Meade County, Kentucky. Ph. D. diss., University of Louisville. 157 pp.

Cross, F. B. 1950. Effects of sewage and of a headwater impoundment on the fishes of Stillwater Creek in Payne County, Oklahoma. *Amer. Midl. Nat.* 43(1):128–45.

——. 1967. *Handbook of Fishes of Kansas*. Misc. Pub. Mus. Nat. Hist. Univ. Kansas no. 45. 357 pp.

———. 1970. Occurrence of the Arkansas River shiner, *Notropis girardi* Hubbs and Ortenburger, in the Red River system. *Southwestern Nat.* 14(3):370.

Cross, F. B., R. L. Mayden, and J. D. Stewart. 1986. Fishes in the western Mississippi Basin (Missouri, Arkansas and Red Rivers). Pp. 362–412 in C. H. Hocutt and E. O. Wiley, eds., *The Zoogeography of North American Freshwater Fishes*. New York: John Wiley and Sons. 866 pp.

Cross, F. B., and G. A. Moore 1952. The fishes of the Poteau River, Oklahoma and Arkansas. *Amer. Midl. Nat.* 47(2):396–412.

Cross, F. B., and R. E. Moss. 1987. Historic changes in fish communities and aquatic habitats in plains streams of Kansas. Pp. 155–65 in W. J. Matthews and D. C. Heins, eds., *Community and Evolutionary Ecology of North American Stream Fishes*. Norman: University of Oklahoma Press. 310 pp.

Crossman, E. J. 1966. A taxonomic study of *Esox americanus* and its sub-species in eastern North America. *Copeia* 1966:1–20.

———. 1978. Taxonomy and distribution of North American esocids. Pp. 13–26 in Amer. Fish. Soc. Spec. Pub. no. 11.

Cummings, K. S., J. M. Grady, and B. M. Burr. 1984. The life history of the mud darter, *Etheostoma asprigene*, in Lake Creek, Illinois, Ill. Nat. Hist. Surv. Biol. Notes no. 122. 16 pp.

Curd, M. R. 1960. On the food and feeding habits of the catfish *Schilbeodes exilis* (Nelson) in Oklahoma. *Proc. Okla. Acad. Sci.* 1959:26–29.

Curry, K. D., and A. Spacie. 1984. Differential use of stream habitat by spawning catostomids. *Amer. Midl. Nat.* 11:267–79.

Daiber, F. C. 1952. The food and feeding relationships of the freshwater drum, *Aplodinotus grunniens* Rafinesque in western Lake Erie. *Ohio J. Sci.* 52(1):35–46.

Darnell, R. M., and R. R. Meierotto. 1965. Diurnal periodicity in the black bullhead, *Ictalurus melas* (Rafinesque). *Trans. Amer. Fish. Soc.* 94(1):1–8.

Davis, B. J., and R. J. Miller. 1967. Brain patterns in minnows of the genus *Hybopsis* in relation to feeding habits and habitat. *Copeia* 1967(1):1–39.

De Leon, F. J. G., L. Gonzalez-Garcia, J. M. Herrera-Castillo, K. O. Winemiller, and A. Banda-Valdes. 2001. Ecology of the alligator gar, *Atractosteus spathula*, in the Vincente Guerrero Reservoir, Tamaulipas, Mexico. *Southwestern Nat.* 46(2):151–57.

Deacon, J. E., and 24 others. 1979. Fishes of North America: Endangered, threatened, or of special concern. *Fisheries* 4:29–44.

Dendy, J. S., and D. C. Scott. 1953. Distribution, life history, and morphological variations of the southern brook lamprey, *Ichthyomyzon gagei*. *Copeia* 1953(3):152–62.

Dillard, J. G., L. K. Graham, and T. R. Russell, eds. 1986. The paddlefish: Status, management and propagation. Northcentral Div. Amer. Fish. Soc., Spec. Pub. no. 7. 59 pp.

Dimmick, W. W. 1987. Phylogenetic relationships of *Notropis hubbsi, N. welaka* and *N. emiliae* (Cypriniformes: Cyprinidae). *Copeia* 1987:316–25.

———. 1988. Ultrastructure of North American cyprinid maxillary barbels. *Copeia* 1988(1):72–79.

———. 1993. A molecular perspective on the phylogenetic relationships of the barbeled minnows, historically assigned to the genus *Hybopsis* (Cyprinidae: Cypriniformes). *Mol. Phylogenet. Evol.* 2:173–84.

Dimmick, W. W., and B. M. Burr. 1999. Phylogenetic relationships of the suckermouth minnows, genus *Phenacobius*, infuence from parsimony analysis of nucleotide sequence, allozymic and morphological data (Cyprinidae: Cypriniformes). *Biochemical Systematics and Ecology* 27:469–85.

Dimmick, W. W., and L. M. Page. 1992. Systematic significance of lactate dehydrogenase variation at the generic level in percids. *Copeia* 1992:535–37.

Dingerkus, G. and W. M. Howell. 1976. Karyotypic analysis and evidence of tetraploidy in the North American paddlefish, *Polyodon spathula*. *Science* 194:842–44.

Dion, R. 1994. Spawning patterns and interspecific mating of sympatric white (*Catostomus commersoni*) and longnose (*C. catostomus*) suckers from the Gouin reservoir system, Quebec. *Can. J. Zool.* 72:195–200.

Distler, D. A. 1968. Distribution and variation of *Etheostoma spectabile* (Agassiz) (Percidae. Teleostei). *Univ. Kansas Sci. Bull.* 48(5):143–208.

———. 1972. Observations on the reproductive habits of captive *Etheostoma cragini* Gilbert. *Southwestern Nat.* 16:439–41.

Douglas, N. H. 1974. *Freshwater Fishes of Louisiana*. Baton Rouge: Claitors Publ. Div. 443 pp.

Dowling, T. E., and W. M. Brown. 1989. Allozymes, mitochondrial DNA, and levels of phylogenetic resolution among four minnow species (*Notropis*: Cyprinidae). *Syst. Zool.* 38:126–43.

Dowling, T. E., W. R. Hoeh, G. R. Smith, and W. M. Brown. 1992. Evolutionary relationships of shiners in the genus *Luxilus* as determined by analysis of mitochondrial DNA. *Copeia* 1992:306–22.

Dowling, T. E., and W. S. Moore. 1984. Level of reproductive isoloation between two cyprinid fishes, *Notropis cornutus* and *N. chrysocephalus*. *Copeia* 1984:617–28.

———. 1985. Genetic variation and divergence of the sibling pair of cyprinid fishes, *Notropis cornutus* and *N. chrysocephalus*. *Biochem. Syst. Ecol.* 13:471–76.

———. 1986. Absence of population subdivision in the common shiner, *Notropis cornutus* (family Cyprinidae). *Environ. Biol. Fishes* 15:151–55.

Dowling, T. E., and G. J. P. Naylor. 1997. Evolutionary relationships of minnows in the genus *Luxilus* as determined from cytochrome b sequences. *Copeia* 1997:758–65.

Dowling, T. E., G. R. Smith, and W. M. Brown. 1989. Reproductive isolation and introgression between *Notropis cornutus* and *Notropis chrysocephalus* (family Cyprinidae): Comparison of morphology, allozymes, and mitochondrial DNA. *Evolution* 43:620–34.

Echelle, A. A. 1968. Food habits of young-of-year longnose gar in Lake Texoma, Oklahoma. *Southwestern Nat.* 13(1):45–50.

Echelle, A. A., A. F. Echelle, and L. G. Hill. 1972. Interspecific interactions and limiting factors of abundance and distribution in the Red River pupfish, *Cyprinodon rubrofluvitalis*. *Amer. Midl. Nat.* 88:109–30.

Echelle, A. A., A. F. Echelle, M. H. Smith, and L. G. Hill. 1975. Analysis of genic continuity in a headwater fish, *Etheostoma radiosum*. *Copeia* 1975:197–204.

Echelle, A. A., and J. B. Mense. 1968. Forage value of Mississippi silversides in Lake Texoma. *Proc. Okla. Acad. Sci.* 47:392–96.

Echelle, A. A., and C. D. Riggs. 1972. Aspects of the early life history of gars (*Lepisosteus*) in Lake Texoma. *Trans. Amer. Fish. Soc.* 101(1):106–12.

Echelle, A. A., J. R. Schenck, and L. G. Hill. 1974. *Etheostoma spectabile-E. radiosum* hybridization in Blue River, Oklahoma. *Amer. Midl. Nat.* 91(1):182–94.

Edds, D. R., W. J. Matthews, and F. P. Gelwick. 2002. Resource use by large catfishes in a reservoir: Is there evidence for interactive segregation and innate differences? *Journal of Fish Biology* 60:739–50.

Eder, S., and C. A. Carlson. 1977. Food habits of carp and white suckers in the South Platte and St. Vrain Rivers and Goosequill Pond, Weld Country, Colorado. *Trans. Amer. Fish. Soc.* 106(4):339–46.

Eisenhour, D. J. 1997. Systematics, variation and speciation of the *Macrhybopsis aestivalis* complex (Cypriniformes: Cyprinidae) west of the Mississippi River. Ph.D. diss., Southern Illinois University, Carbondale.

———. 1999. Systematics of *Macrhybopsis tetranema* (Cypriniformes: Cyprinidae). *Copeia* 1999:969–80.

Eley, R. L., J. C. Randolph, and J. Carroll. 1981. A comparison of pre- and post-impoundment fish populations in the Mountain Fork River in souhteastern Oklahoma. *Proc. Okla. Acad. Sci.* 61:7–14.

Eley, R. L., J. C. Randolph, and R. J. Miller. 1975. Current status of the leopard darter, *Percina pantherina*. *Southwestern Nat.* 20(3):343–54.

Etnier, D. A., and W. C. Starnes. 1993. *The Fishes of Tennessee*. Knoxville: University of Tennessee Press. 681 pp.

Evenhuis, B. L. 1970. Seasonal and daily food habits of goldeye, *Hiodon alosoides* (Rafinesque), in the Little Missouri Arm of Lake Sakakawea, North Dakota. M.S. thesis, University of North Dakota. 41 pp.

Evermann, B. W. 1892. A report upon investigations made in Texas in 1891. *U. S. Fish. Comm.* 9(1891): 61–90.

Facey, D. E., and G. W. Labar. 1981. Biology of American eels in Lake Champlain, Vermont. *Trans. Amer. Fish. Soc.* 110:396–402.

Fahy, W. E. 1954. The life history of the northern greenside darter, *Etheostoma blenniodes blennioides* Rafinesque. *J. Elisha Mitchell Soc.* 70(2):139–205.

Farringer, R. T., A. A. Echelle, and S. F. Lehtinen. 1979. Reproductive cycle of the red shiner, *Notropis lutrensis*, in central Texas and south-central Oklahoma. *Trans. Amer. Fish. Soc.* 108:271–76.

Felley, J. D. 1980. Analysis of morphology and asymmetry in bluegill sunfish (*Lepomis macrochirus*) in the southeastern United States. *Copeia* 1980(1):18–29.

———. 1984. Piscivorous habits of the chub shiner, *Notropis potteri* (Cyprinidae). *Southwestern Nat.* 29(4):495–96.

Felley, J. D., and E. G. Cochran. 1981. *Notropis bairdi* (Cyprinidae) in the Cimarron River, Oklahoma. *Southwestern Nat.* 25:564.

Fingerman, S. W. and R. D. Suttkus. 1961. Comparison of *Hybognathus hayi* Jordan and *Hybognathus nuchalis* Agassiz. *Copeia* 1961(4):462–67.

Finnell, J. C. 1955. Growth of fishes in cutoff lakes and streams of the Little River system, McCurtain County, Oklahoma. *Proc. Okla. Acad. Sci.* 35:61–66.

Finnell, J. C., and R. M. Jenkins. 1954. Growth of channel catfish. Okla. Fish. Res. Lab Report 41. 37 pp.

Flack, S., and R. Chipley, eds. 1996. *Troubled Waters: Protecting our Aquatic Heritage*. Arlington, Va.: Nature Conservancy. 17 pp.

Flemer, D. A., and W. S. Woolcott. 1966. Food habits and distribution of the fishes of Tuckahoe Creek, Virginia, with special emphasis on the bluegill, *Lepomis m. machrochirus* Rafinesque. *Chesapeake Sci.* 7(2):75–89.

Fletcher, D. E., and B. M. Burr. 1992. Reproductive biology, larval description, and diet of the North American bluehead shiner, *Pteronotropis hubbsi*, with comments on conservation status. *Ichthyological Explorations in Freshwater* 3:193–218.

Flittner, G. A. 1964. Morphometry and life history of the emerald shiner *Notropis atherinoides* Rafinesque. Ph.D. diss., University of Michigan, Ann Arbor. 213 pp.

Fogle, N. E. 1959. Some aspects of the life history of the brook silverside, *Labidesthes sicculus*, in Lake Fort Smith, Arkansas. M.S. thesis, University of Arkansas, Fayetteville. 22 pp.

Folkerts, G. W. 1997. State and fate of the world's aquatic fauna. Pp. 1–16 in G. W. Benz and D. E. Collins, eds., *Aquatic Fauna in Peril: The Southeastern Perspective*. Decatur, Ga.: Lenz Design and Communications. 554 pp.

Fontaine, P. A. 1944. Notes on the shovelhead catfish, *Pylodictis olivaris* (Rafinesque). *Copeia* 1944: 50–51.

Forbes, S. A., and R. E. Richardson. 1920. *The Fishes of Illinois*. 2nd ed. Urbana: Illinois Natural History Survey. 357 pp.

Force, E. R. 1928. Fish of the ponds and streams of Okmulgee county. *Proc. Okla. Acad. Sci.* (1927):137.

Forney, J. L. 1955. Life history of the black bullhead *Ameiurus melas* (Rafinesque), of Clear Lake, Iowa. *Iowa State College Jour. Sci.* 30(1):145–62.

Fowler, H. W. 1904. Notes on fishes from Arkansas, Indian Territory, and Texas. *Proc. Acad. Nat. Sci. Philadelphia* (1904): 242–49.

Fowler, J. F., P. W. James, and C. A. Taber. 1984. Spawning activity and eggs of the Ozark Minnow, *Notropis nubilus*. *Copeia* 1984(4):992–96.

Fowler, J. F., and C. A. Taber. 1985. Food habits and feeding periodicity in two sympatric stonerollers (Cyprinidae). *Amer. Midl. Nat.* 113(2):217–24.

Franklin, D. R., and L. L. Smith. 1963. Early life history of the northern pike (*Esox lucius* L.) with special reference to the factors influencing strength of year classes. *Trans. Amer. Fish. Soc.* 92(2):91–110.

Frazer, K. S., H. T. Boschung, and R. L. Mayden. 1989. Diet of juvenile bowfin, *Amia calva* Linnaeus, in the Sipsey River, Alabama. *Proc. SE Fishes Council* 20: 13–15.

Fuchs, E. H. 1967. Life history of the emerald shiner, *Notropis atherinoides* in Lewis and Clark Lake, South Dakota. *Trans. Amer. Fish. Soc.* 96(3):247–56.

Fuselier, L., and D. Edds. 1994. Seasonal variation in habitat use by the Neosho madtom (Teleostei: Ictaluridae: *Noturus placidus*). *Southwestern Nat.* 39:217–223.

Gale, W. F., and G. L. Buynak. 1982. Fecundity and spawning frequency of the fathead minnow, a fractional spawner. *Trans. Amer. Fish. Soc.* 111:35–40.

Gale, W. F., and C. A. Gale. 1976. Selection of artificial spawning sites by the spotfin shiner (*Notropis spilopterus*). *J. Fish. Res. Bd. Canada* 33:1906–13.

———. 1977. Spawning habits of spotfin shiner (*Notropis spilopterus*), a fractional, creavice spawner. *Trans. Amer. Fish. Soc.* 100(2):170–77.

Garcia de Leon, L. Gonzalez-Garcia, J. M. Herrera-Castillo, K. D. Winemiller, and A. Banda-Valdes. 2001. Ecology of the alligator gar, *Atractosteus spathula*, in the Vicente Guerrero Reservoir, Tamaulipas, Mexico. S. W. nat. 46(2): 151–57.

George, S. G., W. T. Slack, and N. H. Douglas. 1996. Demography, habitat, reproduction, and sexual dimorphism of the crystal darter, *Crystallaria asprella*, from south-central Arkansas. *Copeia* 1996:68–78.

Gibbs, R. H., Jr. 1957a. Cyprinid fishes of the subgenus *Cyprinella* of *Notropis*. 1: Systematic status of the subgenus *Cyprinella* with a key to the species exclusive of the *lutrensis-ornatus* complex. *Copeia* (3):185–95.

———. 1957b. Cyprinid fishes of the subgenus *Cyprinella* of *Notropis*. 2: Distribution and variation of *Notropis spilopterus*, with description of a new subspecies. *Lloydia* 20(3):186–211.

———. 1957c. Cyprinid fishes of the subgenus *Cyprinella* of *Notropis*. 3: Variation and subspecies of *Notropis venustus* (Girard). *Tulane Studies in Zoology and Botany* 5(8):175–203.

———. 1961. Cyprinid fishes of the subgenus *Cyprinella* of *Notropis*. 4: The *Notropis galacturus–camurus* complex. *Amer. Midl. Nat.* 66(2):337–54.

———. 1963. Cyprinid fishes of the subgenus *Cyprinella* of *Notropis*. The *Notropis whipplei-analostanus-chloristius* complex. *Copeia* 1963:511–28.

Gilbert, C. R. 1961. Hybridization versus intergradation: An inquiry into the relationship of two cyprinid fishes. *Copeia* 1961:181–92.

———. 1964. The American cyprinid fishes of the subgenus *Luxilus* (Genus *Notropis*). *Bull. Florida State Mus., Biol. Sci.*, 8(2):95–194.

———. 1978. Type catalog of the North American cyprinid fish genus *Notropis*. *Bull. Florida State Mus., Biol. Sci.* 23(1):1–104.

———. 1980b. *Notropis chrysocephalus*, striped shiner. P. 256 in Lee et al., *Atlas* (see Lee et al., 1980).

———. 1980g. *Percina shumardi* (Girard), river darter. P. 741 in Lee et al., *Atlas* (see Lee et al., 1980).

———. 1998. *Type Catalogue of Recent and Fossil North American Freshwater Fishes: Families Cyprinidae, Catostomidae, Ictaluridae, Centrarchidae, and Elassomatidae.* Florida Mus. Nat. Hist., Special Pub. 1. 284 pp.

Gilbert, C. R., and R. M. Bailey. 1962. Synonymy, characters and distribution of the American cyprinid fish, *Notropis shumardi*. *Copeia* 1962(4):807–19.

———. 1972. Systematics and zoogeography of the American cyprinid fish *Notropis* (*Opsopoeodus*) *emiliae*. Occas. Papers Mus. Zool. Univ. Mich. no. 664. 35 pp.

Gilbert, C. R., and J. D. Williams. 2002. *National Audubon Society Field Guide to Fishes*. Rev. ed. New York: Alfred A. Knopf. 607 pp.

Girard, C. 1856. Researches upon the cyprinoid fishes inhabiting the freshwaters of the United States of America, west of the Mississippi Valley, from specimens in the museum of the Smithsonian Institution. *Proc. Acad. Nat. Sci. Philadelphia* 8: 165–213.

———. 1858. Fishes (in general report on the zoology). *U.S. Pacific Railroad Surveys* 10(4): 1–400.

Glazier, J. R., and C. A. Taber. 1980. Reproductive biology and age and growth of the Ozark minnow, *Dionda nubila*. *Copeia* 1980(3):547–50.

Gleason, C. A., and T. M. Berra. 1993. Demonstration of reproductive isolation and observation of mismatings in *Luxilus cornutus* and *L. chrysocephalus* in sympatry. *Copeia* 1993:614–28.

Glodek, G. S. 1980. *Ictalurus nebulosus*, brown bullhead. P. 443 in Lee et al., *Atlas* (see Lee et al., 1980).

Grady, J. M., R. C. Cashner, and J. S. Rogers. 1988. Distribution, variation and biochemical systematics of the *Fundulus notti* species group. *68th Ann. Meet. Amer. Soc. Ichthy. & Herp.*, p. 99 (abstract).

Grady. J. M., and W. H. LeGrande. 1992. Phylogenetic relationships, modes of speciation, and historical biogeography of the madtom catfishes, genus *Noturus*. Pp. 747–77 in R. L. Mayden, ed., *Systematics, Historical Ecology, and North American Freshwater Fishes*. Stanford, Calif.: Stanford University Press.

Greenberg, L. A., and D. A. Holtzman. 1987. Microhabitat ultilization, feeding periodicity, home range and population size of the banded sculpin, *Cottus carolinae*. *Copeia* 1987(1):19–25.

Greenwood, P. H., D. E. Rosen, S. H. Weitzman, and G. S. Myers. 1966. Phyletic studies of teleostean fishes, with a provisional classification of living forms. *Bull. Amer. Mus. Nat. Hist*. 131(4):339–456.

Hackney, P. A., G. R. Hooper, and J. F. Webb. 1970. Spawning behavior, age and growth, and sport fishery for the silver redhorse, *Moxostoma anisurum* (Rafinesque) in the Flint River, Alabama. *Proc. 24th Ann. Conf. Southeastern Assoc. Game and Fish Comm*. 569–76.

Hadley, W. F., and W. A. Carter. 1962. Fishes known from Salt Creek, Osage County, Oklahoma. *Proc. Okla. Acad. Sci*. 42:128–32.

Hale, J. G. 1970. White sucker spawning and culture of the young in the laboratory. *Prog. Fish-Culturist* 32:169.

Hale, M. C. 1963. A comparative study of the food of the shiners *Notropis lutrensis* and *Notropis venustus*. *Proc. Okla. Acad. Sci*. 43:125–29.

Hall, G. E. 1949. Fish population of the Stilling Basin below Wister Dam. *Proc. Okla. Acad. Sci*. 30(1949): 59–62.

———. 1951a. A preliminary list of the fishes of eleven Oklahoma lakes. *Proc. Okla. Acad. Sci*. 31(1950):36–40.

———. 1951b. Further collections of Oklahoma lake and pond fishes. *Proc. Okla. Acad. Sci*. 31(1950):11–20.

———. 1951c. Preimpoundment fish populations of the Wister Reservoir area in the Poteau River basin, Oklahoma. *Trans. 16th N.A. Wildl. Conf*. (1951):266–283.

———. 1952. Observations on the fishes of the Fort Gibson and Tenkiller Reservoir areas, 1952. *Proc. Okla. Acad. Sci*. (1952):55–64.

———. 1953a. A preliminary survey of Fort Gibson Reservoir, Oklahoma (Summer, 1952). Okla. Fish. Res. Lab (mimeo) 29. 53 pp.

———. 1953b. Preliminary observations on the presence of stream-inhabiting fishes in Tenkiller Reservoir, a new Oklahoma impoundment. *Proc. Okla. Acad. Sci*. 34: 34–40.

———. 1956. Additions to the fish fauna of Oklahoma with a summary of introduced species. *Southwestern Nat*. 1(1):16–26.

Hall, G. E., and R. E. Jenkins. 1952. The rate of growth of channel catfish, *Ictalurus punctatus*, in Oklahoma waters. *Proc. Okla. Acad. Sci*. 33:121–29.

Hall, G. E., and W. C. Latta. 1952. Pre- and post-impoundment fish populations in the Stilling Basin below Wister Dam. *Proc. Okla. Acad. Sci*. 32:14–19.

Hall, G. E., and G. A. Moore. 1954. Oklahoma lampreys: Their characterization and distribution. *Copeia* 1954(2):127–35.

Hambrick, P. S., and R. C. Hibbs, Jr. 1977. Feeding chronology and food habits of the blacktail shiner, *Notropis venustus* (Cyprinidae), in Bayou Sara, Louisiana. *Southwestern Nat*. 22(4):511–16.

Harlan, J. R., and E. B. Speaker. 1956. *Iowa Fish and Fishing*. 3rd ed. Des Moines: Iowa Conservation Commission. 377 pp.

Harrel, R. C., B. J. Davis, and T. C. Dorris. 1967. Stream order and species diversity of fishes in an intermittent Oklahoma stream. *Amer. Midl. Nat*. 78(2): 428–36.

Harris, J. L. 1986. Systematics, distribution, and biology of fishes currently allocated to *Erimystax* Jordan, a subgenus of *Hybopsis* (Cyprinidae). Ph.D. diss., University of Tennessee. 335 pp.

Heard, W. R. 1959. Live bait imports: *Chrosomus eos* and *Eucalia inconstans* as potential additions to Oklahoma's fish fauna. *Proc. Okla. Acad. Sci.* 37: 47–48.

———. 1960. An isolated population of the plains killifish *Fundulus kansae*, within the Ozark uplift, Mayes County, Oklahoma. *Proc. Okla. Acad. Sci.* 38:62–64.

Heidinger, R. C. 1975. Life history of the largemouth bass. Pp. 11–20 in R. H. Stroud and H. Clepper, eds., *Black Bass Biology And Management*. Washington, D.C.: Sport Fisheries Institute.

Heins, D. C., and D. R. Dorsett. 1986. Reproductive traits of the blacktail shiner, *Notropis venustus* (Girard), in southeastern Mississippi. *Southwestern Nat.* 31(2):185–89.

Heins, D. C., and M. D. Machado. 1993. Spawning season, clutch characteristics, sexual dimorphism and sex ratio in the redfin darter *Etheostoma whipplei*. *Amer. Midl. Nat.* 129:161–71.

Heins, D. C., and F. G. Rabito, Jr. 1986. Spawning performance in North American minnows: Direct evidence of the occurrence of multiple clutches in the genus *Notropis*. *J. Fish. Biol.* 28:343–57.

Helfman, G. S., D. E. Facey, L. S. Hales, and E. L. Bozeman. 1987. Reproductive ecology of the American eel. *Amer. Fish. Soc. Symp.* 1:42–56.

Henry, C. J., and R. Ruelle. 1992. A study of pallid sturgeon and shovelnose sturgeon reproduction. Pierre, S. D.: U.S. Fish and Wildlife Service, Fish and Wildlife Enhancement. 19 pp.

Hill, L. G., and M. R. Curd. 1969. Additional observations of the striped mullet, *Mugil cephalus* (Mugilidae) in Oklahoma. *Proc. Okla. Acad. Sci.* 48:36–37.

Hill, L. G., and T. A. Jenssen. 1968. A meristic study of the redbelly dace, *Chrosomus erythrogaster* (Cyprinidae), from a stream in southern Oklahoma. *Southwestern Nat.* 13(1): 55–60.

Hill, L. G., W. J. Matthews, T. Schene, and K. Asbury. 1981. Notes on fishes of Grand River, Chouteau Creek, and Pryor Creek, Mayes County, Oklahoma. *Proc. Okla. Acad. Sci.* 61:76–77.

Hlohowskj, C. P., M. M. Coburn, and T. M. Cavender. 1989. Comparison of a pharyngeal filtering apparatus in seven species of the herbivorous cyprinid genus, *Hybognathus* (Pisces, Cyprinidae). *Copeia* 1989(1):172–83.

Hocutt, C. H., and E. O. Wiley, eds. 1986. *The Zoogeography of North American Freshwater Fishes*. New York: John Wiley and Sons. 866 pp.

Hooe, M. L., and D. H. Buck. 1991. Crappie biology and management. *N. Amer. J. Fish. Mgmt*. 11:483–84.

Hotalling, D. R., and C. A. Taber. 1987. Aspects of the life history of the stippled darter *Etheostoma punctulatum*. *Amer. Midl. Nat.* 117(2):428–34.

Houser, A. 1960. Growth of the freshwater drum in Oklahoma. Okla. Fish. Res. Lab Report 78. 15 pp.

———. 1962. A trout fishery in Oklahoma. *Proc. Okla. Acad. Sci.* 42:272–74.

Houser, A., and M. G. Bross. 1959. Observations on growth and reproduction of the paddlefish. *Trans. Amer. Fish. Soc.* 88: 50–52.

Houser, A., and H. E. Bryant. 1970. Age, growth, sex composition, and maturity of white bass in Bull Shoals Reservoir. Tech. Paper Bur. Sport Fish. and Wild. no. 49. 11 pp.

Hubbs, C. 1954. A new Texas subspecies, *apristis*, of the darter *Hadropterus scierus* with a discussion of variation within the species. *Amer. Midl. Nat.* 52(1):211–20.

———. 1976. The diel reproductive pattern and fecundity of *Menidia audens*. *Copeia* 1976:386–88.

———. 1982. Life history dynamics of *Menidia beryllina* from Lake Texoma. *Amer. Midl. Nat.* 107(1)1–12.

———. 1985. Darter reproductive seasons. *Copeia* 1985(1):56–68.

Hubbs, C., and J. Pigg. 1972. Habitat preferences of the harlequin darter, *Etheostoma histrio*, in Texas and Oklahoma. *Copeia* 1972(1):193–94.

———. 1976. The effects of impoundments on threatened fishes of Oklahoma. *Ann. Okla. Acad. Sci.* 5:113–17.

Hubbs, C. L. 1930. Materials for a revision of the catostomid fishes of eastern North America. Univ. Michigan Mus. Zoology Misc. Publ. 20. 47 pp.

———. 1949. Corrected distributional records for Minnesota fishes. *Copeia* 1949:13–22.

———. 1951. *Notropis amnis*, a new cyprinid fish of the Mississippi fauna, with two subspecies. Occas. Papers Mus. Zool. Univ. Mich. no. 530. 30 pp.

Hubbs, C. L., and R. M. Bailey. 1940. A revision of the black basses (*Micropterus* and *Huro*) with descriptions of four new forms. Misc. Pub. Mus. Zool. Univ. Mich. no. 48. 51 pp.

Hubbs, C. L., and J. D. Black. 1940a. *Notropis perpallidus*, a new minnow from Arkansas. *Copeia* 1940(1):46–49.

———. 1940b. Status of the catostomid fish, *Carpiodes carpio elongatus* Meek. *Copeia* 1940(4):226–30.

———. 1940c. Percid fishes related to *Poecilichthys variatus*, with descriptions of new forms. Occas. Papers Mus. Zool. Univ. Mich. no. 416. 30 pp.

———. 1941. The subspecies of the American percid fish, *Poecilichthys whipplii*. Occas Papers Mus. Zool. Univ. Mich. no. 42. 21 pp.

———. 1947. Revision of *Ceratichthys*, a genus of American cyprinid fishes. Misc. Pub. Mus. Zool. Univ. Mich. no. 66. 56 pp.

———. 1954. Status and synonymy of the American percid fish *Hadropterus scierus*. *Amer. Midl. Nat.* 52(1):201–10.

Hubbs, C. L., and W. R. Crowe. 1956. Preliminary analysis of the American cyprinid fishes, seven new, referred to the genus *Hybopsis*, subgenus *Erimystax*. Occas. Papers Mus. Zool. Univ. Mich. no. 578. 8 pp.

Hubbs, C. L., and C. W. Greene. 1935. Two new subspecies of fishes from Wisconsin. *Trans. Wis. Acad. Sci., Arts, Let.* 29:89–101.

Hubbs, C. L., and G. A. Moore. 1940. The subspecies of *Notropis zonatus*, a cyprinid fish of the Ozark upland. *Copeia* 1940(2):91–99.

Hubbs, C. L., and A. I. Ortenburger. 1929a. Further notes on the fishes of Oklahoma with descriptions of new species of Cyprinidae. *Pub. Univ. Okla. Biol. Surv.* 1(2):17–43.

———. 1929b. Fishes collected in Oklahoma and Arkansas in 1927. Univ. of Okla. Bull., (N.S.) 434. *Pub. Univ. Okla. Biol. Surv*. 1:45–112.

Hubbs, C. L., and E. C. Raney. 1944. Systematic notes on North American siluroid fishes of the genus *Schilbeodes*. Occas. Papers Mus. Zool. Univ. Mich. no. 487. 36 pp.

Hudson, L., and T. M. Buchanan. 2001. Life history of the river shiner, *Notropis blennius* (Cyprinidae), in the Arkansas River of western Arkansas. *J. Akansas Acad. Sci.* 55: 57–65.

Hutchens, L., and G. E. Hall. 1951. Occurrence of the Ohio smelt, *Alosa ohiensis* Evermann, in eastern Oklahoma. *Copeia* 1951(1):83–84.

Huish, M. T. 1954. Life history of the black crappie of Lake George, Florida. *Trans. Amer. Fish. Soc.* 83:176–93.

Humphries, J. M., and R. C. Cashner. 1994. *Notropis suttkusi*, a new cyprinid from the Ouachita uplands of Oklahoma and Arkansas, with comments on the status of Ozarkian populations of *N. rubellus*. *Copeia* 1994:82–90.

Hunt, B. P. 1953. Food relationships between Florida spotted gar and other organisms in the Tamiami Canal, Dade County, Florida. *Trans. Amer. Fish. Soc.* 82(1952):13–33.

Hunter, J. R., and A. D. Hasler. 1965. Spawning association of the redfin shiner, *Notropis umbratilis* and the green sunfish, *Lepomis cyanellus*. *Copeia* 1965(3):265–81.

Jackson, S. W. 1954. Rotenone survey of Black Hollow on lower Spavinaw Lake, November, 1953. *Proc. Okla. Acad. Sci.* 34:10–14.

James, P. W., O. E. Maughan, and A. V. Zale. 1991. Life history of the threatened leopard darter, *Percina pantherina*, in Glover River, Oklahoma. *Amer. Midl. Nat.* 25:173–79.

Jenkins, R. E. 1970. Systematic studies of the catostomid fish tribe Moxostomatini. Ph.D. diss., Cornell University, Ithaca, N.Y. 799 pp.

Jenkins, R. E., and N. M. Burkhead. 1994. *Freshwater Fishes of Virginia*. Bethesda, Md.: American Fisheries Society. 1,079 pp.

Jenkins, R. M. 1952. Growth of the flathead catfish, *Pylodictis olivaris* in Grand Lake (Lake O' the Cherokees), Oklahoma. *Proc. Okla. Acad. Sci.* 33:11–20.

———. 1953. An eleven-year growth history of white crappie in Grand lake, Oklahoma. *Proc. Okla. Acad. Sci.* 34:40–47.

———. 1955. The effect of gizzard shad on the fish population of a small Oklahoma lake. *Trans. Amer. Fish. Soc.* 85: 58–74.

———. 1956. Growth of the blue catfish *Ictalurus furcatus* in Lake Texoma. *Southwestern Nat.* 1(4): 166–73.

Jenkins, R. M., and R. E. Elkin. 1957. Growth of the white bass in Oklahoma. Okla. Fish. Res. Lab Report 60. 21 pp.

Jenkins, R. M., E. M. Leonard, and G. E. Hall. 1952. An investigation of the fisheries resources of the Illinois River and pre-impoundment study of Tenkiller Reservoir, Oklahoma. Okla. Fish. Res. Lab Report 26. 136 pp.

Jennings, C. A., and S. J. Zigler. 2000. Ecology and biology of paddlefish in North America: Historical prospectus, management approaches, and research priorities. *Rev. Fish. Biology and Fisheries* 10:167–81.

Jennings, D. P. 1988. Bighead carp (*Hypophthalmichthys nobilis*): biological synopsis. U.S. Fish and Wildl. Serv. Biol. Report 88(29). 47 pp.

Jester, D. B., A. A. Echelle, W. J. Matthews, J. Pigg, C. M. Scott, and K. D. Collins. 1992. The fishes of Oklahoma, their gross habitats, and their tolerance of degradation in water quality and habitat. *Proc. Okla. Acad. Sci.* 72:7–19.

Johnson, D. H. 1963. The food habits of the goldeye of the Missouri River and Lewis and Clark Reservoir, South Dakota. M.S. thesis, University of South Dakota.

Johnson, R. P. 1963. Studies on the life history and ecology of the bigmouth buffalo, *Ictiobus cyprinellus* (Valenciennes). *J. Fish. Res. Bd. Canada* 20(6):1397–29.

Johnston, C. E. 1989. Spawning in the eastern sand darter, *Ammocrypta pellucida*, with comments on the phylogeny of *Ammocrypta* and related taxa. *Trans. Ill. Acad. Sci.* 82 (3–4):163–68.

———. 1994. Spawning behavior of the goldstripe darter (*Etheostoma parvipinne* Gilbert and Swain). *Copeia* 1994:823–25.

Johnston, C. E., and D. C. Johnson. 2000. Sound production in *Pimephales notatus* (Rafinesque)(Cyprinidae). *Copeia* 2000(2):527–71.

Johnston, C. E., and C. L. Knight. 1999. Life-history traits of the bluenose shiner, *Pteronotropis welaka* (Cypriniformes: Cyprinidae). *Copeia* (1):200–205.

Johnston, C. E., and L. M. Page. 1988. The spawning behavior of *Opsopoeodus emiliae*. *68th Ann. Meet. Amer. Soc. Ichthy. & Herp.*, p. 118 (abstract).

———. 1992. The evolution of complex reproductive strategies in North American minnows (Cyprinidae). In R. L. Mayden, ed., *Systematics, Historical Ecology, and North American Freshwater Fishes*. Stanford, Calif.: Stanford University Press. 969 pp.

Jones, R. N. 1987. Food of two species of darters in Glover River, Oklahoma. *Proc. Okla. Acad. Sci*. 67:73–74.

Jones, R. N., and O. E. Maughan. 1989. Food habits of the juvenile and adult orangebelly darter, *Etheostoma radiosum*, in the Glover Creek, Oklahoma. *Proc. Okla. Acad. Sci*. 69:39–43.

Jones, R. N., O. E. Maughan, R. J. Miller, and H. W. Robison. 1983. *Status of the Leopard Darter in Oklahoma and Arkansas*. Endangered Species Report no. 12. Albuquerque, N.M.: U.S. Fish and Wildlife Service. 68 pp.

Jones, R. N., D. I. Orth, and O. E. Maughan. 1984. Abundance and preferred habitat of the leopard darter, *Percina pantherina*, in Glover River, Oklahoma. *Copeia* 1984 (2): 378–84.

Jordan, D. S. 1877. *Contributions to North American Ichthyology Based Primarily on the Collections of the United States National Museum*. 2, Part A: *Notes on the Cottidae, Etheostomatidae, Percidae, Centrarchidae, Aphredoderidae, Dorysomatidae, and Cyprinidae, with Revisions of the Genera and Descriptions of New or Little Known Species*. Bull. U.S. Natl. Mus. 10. 68 pp.

Jordan, D. S., and B. W. Evermann. 1896. *The Fishes of North and Middle America*. Part 1. Bull. U.S. Natl. Mus. 47. 1240 pp.

Jordan, D. S., and C. H. Gilbert. 1886. *List of Fishes Collected in Arkansas, Indian Territory, and Texas, in September, 1884, with Notes and Descriptions*. Proc. U.S. Nat. Mus. 9(549). 25 pp.

Katula, R. 1988. Spawning of an Ozark endemic, the stippled darter. *Freshw. Mar. Aq*. 11 (September): 104–107.

———. 1990. Notes on spawning of the johnny darter. *American Currents* (September-November): 21–22.

———. 1991. Observations of spawning methods of the creole darter and the finescale saddled darter (*Etheostoma collettei* and *Etheostoma osburni*). *American Currents* (summer): 15–16.

———. 1992. The spawning mode of the pirate perch. *Tropical Fish Hobbyist* (August): 156–59.

———. 1993. Spawning the green banded darter, *Etheostoma zonale*. *Freshw. Mar. Aq*. 16 (month undetermined): 27–29.

———. 2000a. The captive maintenance of darters. *Tropical Fish Hobbyist* (August): 68–77.

———. 2000b. Crystal clear: Observation on the crystal darter, *Crystallaria asprella*. *Freshw. Mar. Aq*. 154.

Kaufmann, S. A., and J. D. Lynch. 1991. Courtship, eggs and development of the plains topminnow in Nebraska (Actinopterygii: Fundulidae) *Prairie Nat*. 23(1):41–45.

Keenlyne, K. D. 1997. Life history and status of the shovelnose sturgeon, *Scophirhynchus platorynchus*. *Environ. Biol. Fishes* 48:291–98.

Kendall, R. L. ed. 1978. *Selected Coolwater Fishes of North America*. Amer. Fish. Soc. Pub. 11. 437 pp.

Kilambi, R. V., and R. E. Baglin. 1969a. Fecundity of the gizzard shad, *Dorosoma cepedianum* (Lesueur), in Beaver and Bull Shoals reservoirs. *Amer. Midl. Nat.* 82(2): 444–49.

Kilambi, R. V., and R. E. Baglin, Jr. 1969b. Fecundity of the threadfin shad, *Dorosoma petenense*, in Beaver and Bull Shoals reservoirs. *Trans. Amer. Fish. Soc.* 98(2):320–22.

Kinney, E. C., Jr. 1954. A life history study of the silver chub, *Hybopsis storeriana* (Kirtland), in western Lake Erie with notes on associated species. Ph. D. diss., Ohio State University, Columbus. 99 pp.

Knapp, R. A., and R. C. Sargent. 1989. Egg-mimicry as a mating strategy in the fantail darter, *Etheostoma flabellare*: Females prefer males with eggs. *Behav. Ecol. Sociobiol.* 25:321–26.

Kreiser, B. R. 2001. Mitochondrial cytochrome b sequence support recognition of two cryptic species of plains killifish, *Fundulus zebrinus* and *Fundulus kansae*. *Amer. Midl. Nat*. 146:199–209.

Kreiser, B. R., J. B. Mitton, and J. D. Woodling. 2001. Phylogeography of the plains killifish, *Fundulus zebrinus*. *Evolution* 55(2):339–50.

Kristmundsdottir, A. Y., and J. R. Gold. 1996. Systematics of the blacktail shiner (*Cyprinella venusta*) inferred from analysis of mitochondrial DNA. *Copeia* 1996:773–83.

Krotzer, M. J. 1990. Variation and systematics of *Etheostoma nigrum* Rafinesque, the johnny darter (Pisces: Percidae). Ph.D. diss., University of Tennessee. 192 pp.

Kuehne, R. A., and R. W. Barbour. 1983. *The American Darters*. Lexington: University Press of Kentucky. 177 pp.

Kuhajda, B. R., and M. L. Warren, Jr. 1989. Life history aspects of the harlequin darter, *Etheostoma histrio*, in western Kentucky. *Assoc. SE Biol. Bull*. 36:66–67 (abstract).

Kwak, T. J., and T. M. Skelly. 1988. Spawning habitat and behavior and isolating mechanisms of the golden redhorse (*Moxostoma erythrurum*) and the black redhorse (*M. duquesnei*), two syntopic fishes. *68th Ann. Meet. Amer. Soc. Ichthy. & Herp.*, p. 125 (abstract).

Lachner, E. A. 1950. The comparative food habits of the cyprinid fishes *Nocomis biguttatus* and *Nocomis micropogon* in western New York. *J. Washington Acad. Sci*. 40(7):229–36.

Lachner, E. A., and R. E. Jenkins. 1967. Systematics, distribution, and evolution of the chub genus *Nocomis* (Cyprinidae) in the southwestern Ohio River system, with a description of a new species. *Copeia* 1967(3):557–80.

———. 1971. *Systematics, Distribution and Evolution of the* Nocomis biguttatus *Species Group (family Cyprinidae: Pisces) with a Description of a New Species from the Ozark Upland*. Smithsonian Contributions to Zoology 91. 35 pp.

Lachner, E. A., E. F. Westlake, and P. S. Handwerk. 1950. Studies on the biology of some percid fishes from western Pennsylvania. *Amer. Midl. Nat*. 43(1):92–111.

Lagler, K. F., C. B. Obrecht, and G. V. Harry. 1942. The food habits of gars (*Lepisosteus* spp.) considered in relation to fish management. *Invest. Indiana Lakes and Streams* 2:117–35.

Lambinon, J. 1994. Keeping and breeding the red shiner. *Aquarist and Pondkeeper* (July): 69–71.

Larimore, R. W. 1957. Ecological life history of the warmouth (Centrarchidae). Bull. Ill. Nat. Hist. Surv. 27(1):83 pp.

Larson, R. D. 1998. Present status and distribution of the Arkansas River shiner, *Notropis girardi* (Pisces: Cyprinidae), and possible causes for its decline. M. S. thesis, Oklahoma State University, Stillwater.

Laurence, G. C., and R. W. Yerger. 1966. Life history studies of the Alabama shad, *Alosa alabama*, in the Appalachicola River, Florida. *Proc. 20th Ann Conf. Southeastern Assoc. Game and Fish. Comm.* 260–73.

Layher, W. G., and O. E. Maughan. 1987. Relations between two darter species and their respective abiotic environments. *Proc. Okla. Acad. Sci.* 67:11–22.

Layman, S. R. 1994. Phylogenetic systematics and biogeography of darters of the subgenus *Doration* (Percidae: Etheostoma). Ph.D. diss., University of Alabama, Tuscaloosa.

Lee, D. S. 1980a. *Scaphhynchus platorynchus*. P. 44 in Lee et al., *Atlas* (see Lee et al. 1980).

———. 1980b. *Labidesthes sicculus*. P. 557 in Lee et al., *Atlas* (see Lee et al. 1980).

Lee, D. S., and B. M. Burr. 1985. Observations on life history of the dollar sunfish, *Lepomis marginatus* (Holbrook). *Assoc. SE Biol. Bull.* 32(2):58 (abstract).

Lee, D. S., and C. R. Gilbert. 1980. *Centrarchus macropterus* (Lacepede), flier. P. 583 in Lee et al., *Atlas* (see Lee et al., 1980).

Lee, D. S., C. R. Gilbert, C. H., Hocutt, R. E. Jenkins, D. E. McAllister, and J. R. Stauffer, Jr. 1980. *Atlas of North American Freshwater Fishes*. Raleigh: North Carolina State Museum of Natural History. 854 pp.

Lee, D. S., and J. R. Shute. 1980. *Pimephales promelas* Rafinesque, fathead minnow. P. 341 in Lee et al., *Atlas* (see Lee et al., 1980).

Lee, D. S., and S. P. Platania. 1980. *Carpiodes velifer*. P. 369 in Lee et al., *Atlas* (see Lee et al., 1980).

Leonard, E. M., and R. M. Jenkins. 1952. Growth of the basses of the Illinois river, Oklahoma. *Proc. Okla. Acad. Sci.* (33):21–30.

Le Grande, W. H. 1981. Chromosomal evolution in North American catfishes (Siluriformes: Ictaluridae) with particular emphasis on the madtoms, *Noturus*. *Copeia* 1981: 33–52.

Lehtinen, S., and A. A. Echelle. 1979. Reproductive cycle of *Notropis boops* (Pisces: Cyprinidae) in Brier Creek, Marshall County, Oklahoma. *Amer. Midl. Nat.* 102(2): 237–43.

Lemmons, R. P., and J. Pigg. 1999. Historical and new records of the goldstripe darter, *Etheostoma parvipinne*, in Oklahoma. *Proc. Okla. Acad. Sci.* 79:87–89.

Lemmons, R. P., M. J. Hood, and L. G. Hill. 1997. New Oklahoma localities for shortnose gar (*Lepisosteus platostomus*), largescale stoneroller (*Campostoma oligolepis*) and bluehead shiner (*Pteronotropis hubbsi*). *Proc. Okla. Acad. Sci.* 77:125–26.

Lewis, W. M., Jr. 1970. Morphological adaptations of cyprinodontoids for inhabiting oxygen deficient waters. *Copeia* 1970(2):319–26.

Linder, A. D. 1955. The fishes of the Blue River in Oklahoma with descriptions of two new percid hybrid combinations. *Amer. Midl. Nat.* 54(1): 173–91.

———. 1959. The American percid fishes *Ammocrypta clara* Jordan and *Ammocrypta pellucida* (Baird). *Southwestern Nat.* 4:176–84.

Lindsey, H. L., J. C. Randolph, and J. Carroll. 1983. Updated survey of the fishes of the Poteau River, Oklahoma and Arkansas. *Proc. Okla. Acad. Sci.* 63:42–48.

Luttrell, G. R., A. A. Echelle, W. L. Fisher, and D. J. Eisenhour. 1999. Declining status of two species of the *Macrhybopsis aestivalis* complex (Teleostei: Cyprinidae) in the Arkansas River Basin and related effects of reservoirs as barriers to dispersal. *Copeia* 1999(4): 981–89.

Luttrell, G. R., D. M. Underwood, W. L. Fisher, and J. Pigg. 1995. Distribution of the Red River shiner, *Notropis bairdi*, in the Arkansas River drainage. *Proc. Okla. Acad. Sci.* 75:61–62.

Luttrell, G. R., R. D. Larson, W. J. Stark, N. A. Ashbaugh, A. A. Echelle, and A. V. Zale. 1992. Status and distribution of the Neosho madtom (*Noturus placidus*) in Oklahoma. *Proc. Okla. Acad. Sci.* 72:5–6.

MacCrimmon, H. R., and W. H. Robbins. 1975. Distribution of the black basses in North America. P. 56–66 in R. H. Stroud and H. Clepper, eds., *Black Bass Biology and Management*. Washington, D.C.: Sport Fishing Institute. 534 pp.

Markus, H. C. 1934. Life history of the blackhead minnow (*Pimephales promelas*).*Copeia* 1934(3):116–22.

Marshall, C. L. 1978. The distribution of *Notropis bairdi* along the Cimarron River in Logan County, Oklahoma. *Proc. Okla. Acad. Sci.* 58:109.

Marshall, N. 1947. Studies on the life history and ecology of *Notropis chalybaeus* (Cope). *Florida Acad. Sci.* 9(1946):163–88.

Marsh-Matthews, E., and W. J. Matthews. 2000. Geographic, terrestrial, and aquatic factors: Which most influence the structure of stream fish assemblages in the midwestern United States? *Ecology of Freshwater Fish* 9:9–21.

Marsh-Matthews, E., W. J. Matthews, K. B. Gido, and R. L. Marsh. 2003. Reproduction by young-of-the-year red shiner (*Cyprinella lutrensis*) and its implications for invasion success. *Southwestern Nat.* 41(4):605–10.

Master, L. L. 1990. The imperiled status of north American aquatic animals. *Biodiversity Network News* 3:1–2, 7–8.

Mathur, D. 1972. Seasonal food habits of adult white crappie, *Pomoxis annularis* Rafinesque, in Conowingo Reservoir. *Amer. Midl. Nat.* 87:236–41.

Matthews, M. M., and D. C. Heins. 1984. Life history of the redfin shiner, *Notropis umbratilis* (Pisces: Cyprinidae) in Mississippi. *Copeia* 1984(2):385–90.

Matthews, W. J. 1985. Distribution of midwestern fishes on multivariate environmental gradients, with emphasis on *Notropis lutrensis*. *Amer. Midl. Nat.* 113:225–37.

———. 1987a. Geographic variation in *Cyprinella lutrensis* (Pisces: Cyprinidae) in the United States, with notes on *Cyprinella lepida*. *Copeia* 1987(3):616–37.

———. 1987b. Physicochemical tolerance and selectivity of stream fishes as related to their geographic ranges and local distributions. Pp. 11–120 in W. J. Matthews and D. C. Heins, eds., *Community and Evolutionary Ecology of North American Stream Fishes*. Norman: University of Oklahoma Press. 310 pp.

———. 1988. North American prairie streams as systems for ecological study. *J. of North American Benthological Soc.* 7:37–409.

———. 1995. Geographic variation in nuptial colors of red shiners (*Cyprinella lutrensis*: Cyprinidae) within the United States. *Southwestern Nat.* 40:5–10.

———. 1998. *Patterns in Freshwater Fish Ecology*. New York: Chapman and Hall. 756 pp.

Matthews, W. J., and F. Gelwick. 1988. Variation and systematics of *Etheostoma radiosum*, the orangebelly darter (Pisces, Percidae). *Copeia* 1988:543–44.

Matthews, W. J., and L. G. Hill. 1977. Tolerance of the red shiner, *Notropis lutrensis* (Cyprinidae) to environmental parameters. *Southwestern Nat.* 22(1):89–98.

———. 1979. Influence of physicochemical factors on habitat selection by red shiners, *Notropis lutrensis* (Pisces: Cyprinidae). *Copeia* 1979(1):70–81.

———. 1980. Habitat partitioning in the fish community of a southwestern river. *Southwestern Nat.* 25:51–56.

Matthews, W. J., and R. McDaniel. 1981. New locality records for some Kansas fishes, with notes on the habitat of the Arkansas darter *Etheostoma cragini*. *Trans. Kansas Acad. Sci.* 84(4):219–22.

Matthews, W. J., and H. W. Robison. 1982. Addition of *Etheostoma collettei* (Percidae) to the fish fauna of Oklahoma and of the Red River drainage in Arkansas. *Southwestern Nat.* 27(2):215–16.

Matthews, W. J., M. E. Power, and A. J. Stewart. 1986. Depth distribution of *Campostoma* grazing scars in an Ozark stream. *Environ. Biol. Fishes* 17(4):291–97.

May, E. B., and A. A. Echelle. 1968. Young-of-year alligator gar in Lake Texoma, Oklahoma. *Copeia* 1968(3):629–30.

Mayden, R. L. 1985. Biogeography of Ouachita Highland fishes. *Southwestern Nat.* 30(2):195–211.

———. 1987. Systematics of fishes in the *Etheostoma punctulatum* and *Notropis zonatus* species groups. *67th Ann. Meet. Amer. Soc. Ichthy. & Herp.* (abstract).

———. 1988a. Systematics of the *Notropis zonatus* species group, with description of a new species from the interior highlands of North America. *Copeia* 1988:153–73.

———. 1988b. Vicariance biogeography, parsimony, and evolution in North American freshwater fishes. *Syst. Zool.* 37:329–55.

———. 1989. Phylogenetic studies of North American minnows, with emphasis on the genus *Cyprinella*. Misc. Pub. Mus. Nat. Hist. Univ. Kansas no. 80.189 pp.

———. 1992. *Systematics, Historical Ecology, and North American Freshwater Fishes.* Stanford, Calif.: Stanford University Press. 969 pp.

Mayden, R. L., and B. M. Burr. 1981. Life history of the slender madtom, *Noturus exilis*, in southern Illinois (Pisces: Ictaluridae). Occas. Papers Mus. Nat. Hist. Univ. Kansas no. 93. 64 pp.

Mayden, R. L., B. M. Burr, L. M. Page, and R. R. Miller. 1992. The native freshwater fishes of North America. Pp. 827–63 in R. L. Mayden, ed., Systematics, Historical Ecology, and North American Freshwater Fishes. Stanford, Calif.: Stanford Univ. Press.

Mayden, R. L., and F. B. Cross. 1983. A re-evaluation of Oklahoma records of the southern cavefish, *Typhlichthys subterraneus* (Amblyopsidae).*Southwestern Nat.* 28: 471–73.

Mayden, R. L., and C. R. Gilbert. 1989. *Notropis ludibundus* (Girard) and *Notropis tristis* (Girard), replacement names for *N. stramineus* (Cope) and *N. topeka* (Gilbert) (Teleostei: Cypriniformes). *Copeia* 1989:1084–89.

Mayden, R. L., and R. H. Matson. 1988. Evolutionary relationships of eastern North American cyprinids: An allozyme perspective. *68th Ann. Meet. Amer. Soc. Ichthy. & Herp.*, p. 138 (abstract).

Mayden, R. L., and R. M. Wood. 1995. Systematics, species concepts, and the evolutionary significant unit in biodiversity and conservation biology. Pp. 58–113 in J. L. Nielson, ed., *Evolution and the Aquatic Environment: Defining Unique Units in Population Conservation.* Amer. Fish. Soc. Symp. 17, Bethesda, Md.

McBride, S. I., and D. Tarter. 1983. Foods and feeding behavior of sauger, *Stizostedion canadense* (Smith) (Pisces: Percidae) from Gallipolis Locks and Dam, Ohio River. *Brimleyana* 9:123–34.

McCarraher, D. B., and R. Thomas. 1968. Some ecological observations on the fathead minnow, *Pimephales promelas*, in the alkaline waters of Nebraska. *Trans. Amer. Fish. Soc.* 97(1):52–55.

McCann, J. A. 1984. Involvement of the American Fisheries Society with exotic species. Pp. 413–14 in W. N. Courtenay, Jr., and J. R. Stauffer, Jr., eds., *Distribution, Biology, and Management of Exotic Fishes*. Baltimore: Johns Hopkins University Press. 430 pp.

McCaskill, M. L., J. E. Thomerson, and P. R. Mills. 1972. Food of the northern studfish, *Fundulus catenatus*, in the Missouri Ozarks. *Trans. Amer. Fish. Soc.* 101(2):375–77.

McCleave, J. D., R. C. Kleckner, and M. Castonguay. 1987. Reproductive sympatry of American and European eels and implication for migration and taxonomy. *Amer. Fish. Soc. Symp*. 1:286–97.

McComish, T. S. 1967. Food habits of bigmouth and smallmouth buffalo in Lewis and Clark Lake and the Missouri River. *Trans. Amer. Fish. Soc.* 96(1):70–74.

McCoy, H. A. 1953. The rate of growth of flathead catfish in twenty-one Oklahoma lakes. *Proc. Okla. Acad. Sci.* 34(1953): 47–52.

McGeehan, L. T. 1985. Multivariate and univariate analyses of the geographical variation within *Etheostoma flabellare* of eastern North America. Ph.D. diss., Ohio State University, Columbus. 156 pp.

McIlwain, T. D. 1970. Stomach contents and length-weight relationships of chain pickerel (*Esox niger*) in south Mississippi waters. *Trans. Amer. Fish. Soc.* 99(2):439–40.

McMillan, V. E., and R. J. F. Smith. 1974. Agonistic and reproductive behavior of the fathead minnow (*Pimephales promelas* Rafinesque). *Z. Tierpsychol.* 34:25–58.

McPhail, J. D., and C. C. Lindsay. 1970. *Freshwater Fishes of Northwestern Canada and Alaska*. Bull. Fish. Res. Bd. Canada 173. 381 pp.

McSwain, L. E., and R. M. Gennings. 1972. Spawning behavior of the spotted sucker, *Minytrema melanops* (Rafinesque). *Trans Amer. Fish. Soc*. 101:738–40.

Meffe, G. K., and F. F. Snelson, Jr., eds. 1989. Ecology and evolution of livebearing fishes. Englewood Cliffs, N.J.: Prentice Hall. 453 pp.

Meek, S. E. 1896. A list of the fishes and mollusks collected in Arkansas and Indian Territory in 1894. *Bull. U.S. Fish. Comm.*, 15(1895):341–49.

Megrey, B. A. 1980. *Dorosoma cepedianum* (Lesueur), gizzard shad. P. 69 in Lee et al., *Atlas* (see Lee et al., 1980).

Menhinick, E. F. 1991. *The Freshwater Fishes of North Carolina*. Raleigh: North Carolina Wildlife Resources Commission. 227 pp.

Mense, J. B. 1967. Ecology of the Mississippi silversides, *Menidia audens* Hay, in Lake Texoma. Okla. Fish. Res. Lab Bull. 6. 31 pp.

Menzel, B. W., and F. B. Cross. 1977. Systematics of the bleeding shiner species group (Cyprinidae: genus *Notropis* subgenus *Luxilus*). 1977 A.S.I.H. meeting, Gainesville, Florida (abstract).

Merriner, J. V. 1971. Development of intergeneric centrarchid hybrid embryos. *Trans. Amer. Fish. Soc.* (4):611–18.

Metcalf, A. C. 1966. Fishes of the Kansas River system in relation to zoogeography of the Great Plains. *Pub. Mus. Nat. Hist. Univ. Kansas* 17:23–189.

Mettee, M. F., P. E. O'Neil, and J. M. Pierson. 1996. *Fishes of Alabama and the Mobile Basin.* Birmingham, Ala.: Oxmoor House. 820 pp.

Meyer, W. H. 1962. Life history of three species of redhorses (*Moxostoma*) in Des Moines River, Iowa. *Trans. Amer. Fish. Soc.* 91(4):412–19.

Middaugh, D. P., and M. J. Hemmer. 1992. Reproductive ecology of the inland silverside, *Menidia beryllina* (Pisces: Atherinidae) from Blackwater Bay, Florida. *Copeia* 1992:53–61.

Miller, D. R. 1953. Two additions to Oklahoma's fish fauna from Red River in Bryan County. *Proc. Okla. Acad. Sci.* 34: 33–34.

Miller, D. L. 1984. Distribution, abundance, and habitat of the Arkansas darter, *Etheostoma cragini* (Percidae) in Colorado. *Southwestern Nat*. 29(4):496–99.

Miller, G. L., and W. R. Nelson. 1974. Goldeye, *Hiodon alosoides*, in Lake Oahe: Abundance, age, growth, maturity, food, and the fishery, 1963–69. Tech. Papers U.S. Fish and Wildl. Serv. no. 79. 13 pp.

Miller, R. J. 1962. Reproductive behavior of the stoneroller minnow, *Campostoma anomalum pullum*. *Copeia* 1962 (2):407–17.

——. 1964. Behavior and ecology of some North American cyprinid fishes. *Amer. Midl. Nat.* 72(2):313–57.

———. 1967. Nestbuilding and breeding activities of some Oklahoma fishes. *Southwestern Nat.* 12(4):463–68.

———. 1968. Speciation in the common shiner: an alternate view. *Copeia* 1968(3):642–47.

———. 1979. New records of fishes from two southern Oklahoma rivers. *Proc. Okla. Acad. Sci.* 59:121–122.

———. 1984. The occurrence of *Notropis hubbsi* in Oklahoma. *Proc. Okla. Acad. Sci.* 64:45.

Miller, R. J., and H. E. Evans. 1965. External morphology of the brain and lips in catastomid fishes. *Copeia* (4):467–87.

Miller, R. J., and H. W. Robison. 1973. *The Fishes of Oklahoma*. Oklahoma State University Museum of Natural and Cultural History. Series no. 1. 246 pp.

Miller, R. R. 1960. Systematics and biology of the gizzard shad (*Dorosoma cepedianum*) and related fishes. *U.S. Fish and Wildl. Serv. Fish. Bull.* 60(173):371–92.

———. 1972. Threatened freshwater fishes of the United States. *Trans. Amer. Fish. Soc.* 101(2):239–52.

Miller, R. R., J. D. Williams, and J. E. Williams. 1989. Extinctions of North American fishes during the past century. *Fisheries* 14: 22–38.

Miller, R. V. 1967. Food of the threadfin shad, *Dorosoma petenense* in Lake Chicot, Arkansas. *Trans. Amer. Fish. Soc.* 96(3):243–46.

———. 1968. A systematic study of the greenside darter, *Etheostoma blennioides* Rafinesque (Pisces: Percidae). *Copeia* 1968(1):1–40.

Mills, J. G. 1972. Biology of the Alabama shad in northwest Florida. State of Florida Dept. of Natural Resources, Tech. Series no. 68. 24 pp.

Minckley, W. L. ,and J. E. Deacon. 1959. Biology of the flathead catfish in Kansas. *Trans. Amer. Fish. Soc.* 88:344–55.

Minckley, W. L., J. E. Johnson, J. N. Rinne, and S. E. Willoughby. 1970. Foods of buffalo fishes, genus *Ictiobus*, in central Arizona reservoirs. *Trans. Amer. Fish. Soc.* 99(2): 333–42.

Ming, A. D. 1968. Life history of the grass pickerel, *Esox americans vermiculatus* in Oklahoma. Okla. Fish. Res. Lab Bull. 8. 66 pp.

Modde, T., and J. C. Schmulbach. 1977. Food and feeding behavior of the shovelnose sturgeon, *Scaphirhynchus platorynchus*, in the unchannelized Missouri River, South Dakota. *Trans. Amer. Fish. Soc.* 106(6):602–608.

Moore, G. A. 1944. Notes on the early life history of *Notropis girardi*. *Copeia* 1944(4): 209–14.

———. 1948. *Notropis perpallidus* Hubbs and Black in Oklahoma. *Copeia* (1):63.

———. 1950. The cutaneous sense organs of barbeled minnows adapted to life in the muddy waters of the Great Plains region. *Trans. Amer. Micros. Soc.* 67(1):69–95.

———. 1968. Fishes. Pp. 22–165 in W. F. Blair et al., *Vertebrates of the United States*, 2nd ed. New York: McGraw Hill.

———. 1973. Discovery of fishes in Oklahoma (1852–1972). *Proc. Okla. Acad. Sci.* 53:1–26.

Moore, G. A., and D. H. Buck. 1953. The fishes of the Chikaskia River in Oklahoma and Kansas. *Proc. Okla. Acad. Sci.* 34:19–27.

Moore, G. A., and F. B. Cross. 1950. Additional Oklahoma fishes with validation of *Poecilichthys parvipinnis* (Gilbert and Swain). *Copeia* 1950(2):139–48.

Moore, G. A., and M. Kernodle. 1965. A new size record for the chestnut lamprey, *Ichthyomyzon castaneus* Girard in Oklahoma. *Proc. Okla. Acad. Sci.* 45:68–69.

Moore, G. A., and J. D. Mizell. 1939. A fall survey of the fishes of the Stillwater Creek drainage system (Payne and Noble counties, Oklahoma). *Proc. Okla. Acad. Sci.* 19: 43–44.

Moore, G. A., and J. M. Paden. 1950. The fishes of the Illinois River in Oklahoma and Arkansas. *Amer. Midl. Nat.* 44:76–95.

Moore, G. A., and D. D. Poole. 1948. The pygmy sunfish, *Elassoma zonatum* Jordan in Oklahoma. *Proc. Okla. Acad. Sci.* 28:37.

Moore, G. A., and J. D. Reeves. 1955. *Hadropterus pantherinus*, a new percid fish from Oklahoma and Arkansas. *Copeia* 1955(2):89–92.

Moore, G. A., and C. C. Rigney. 1952. Taxonomic status of the percid fish *Poecilichthys radiosus* in Oklahoma and Arkansas with the description of two new subspecies. *Copeia* 1952:7–15.

Moore, J. W., and F. W. H. Beamish. 1973. Food of larval sea lamprey (*Petromyzon marinus*) and American brook lamprey (*Lampetra lamottei*). *J. Fish. Res. Bd. Canada* 30:7–15.

Moos, R. E. 1978. Movement and reproduction of shovelnose sturgeon *Schphirhynchus platorynchus* (Rafinesque) in the Missouri River, South Dakota. Ph.D. diss., University of South Dakota, Vermillion. 213 pp.

Morris, M. A., and L. M. Page. 1981. Variation in western logperches (Pisces: Percidae), with description of a new subspecies from the Ozarks. *Copeia* 1981(1):95–108.

Moser, H. G., W. J. Richards, D. M. Cohen, M. P. Fehay, A. W. Kendall, and S. L. Richardson, eds. 1984. *Ontogeny and Systematics of Fishes*. Amer. Soc. Ichthy. & Herp. Spec. Pub. no. 1. 760 pp.

Moshin, A. K. M., and B. J. Gallaway. 1977. Seasonal abundance, distribution, food habitats and condition of the southern brook lamprey, *Ichthyomyzon gagei* Hubbs and Trautman, in an east Texas watershed. *Southwestern Nat.* 22(1):107–14.

Moss, R. E. 1981. Life history information for the Neosho madtom, *Noturus placidus*. Report to Kansas Department of Wildlife and Parks, Platt. 38 pp.

Moss, R. E., J. W. Scanlan, and C. S. Anderson. 1983. Observations on the natural history of the blue sucker *Cycleptus elongatus* Lesueur in the Neosho River. *Amer. Midl. Nat.* 109(1):15–22.

Moyle, P. B. 1976. *Inland Fishes of California*. Berkeley: University of California Press. 405 pp.

Moyle, P. B., and J. J. Cech, Jr. 1988. *Fishes: An Introduction to Ichthyology*. 2nd ed. Englewood Cliffs, N.J.: Prentice-Hall. 559 pp.

Moyle, P. B., and R. A. Leidy. 1992. Loss of biodiversity in aquatic ecosystems: Evidence from fish farms. Pp. 127–69 in P. L. Fielder and S. K. Join, eds., *Conservation Biolology: The theory and Protocol of Nature Conservation, Preservation, and Management*. New York: Chapman and Hall.

Mullan, J. W., R. L. Applegate, and W. C. Rainwater. 1968. Food of logperch (*Percina caprodes*) and brook silverside (*Labidesthes sicculus*), in a new and old Ozark reservoir. *Trans. Amer. Fish. Soc.* 97(3):300–305.

Muller, B. 2000. The mystery of the feeder fish, or who is rosy red? *American Currents* 26(4):19–20.

Myers, N. 1988. Threatened biota: "hot spots" in tropical forests. Environmentalist 8: 187–208.

Nelson, J. S. 1968. Life history of the brook silverside, *Labidesthes sicculus*, in Crooked Lake, Indiana. *Trans. Amer. Fish. Soc.* 97(3):293–96.

———. 1976. *Fishes of the World*. John Wiley and Sons, New York. 416 pp.

Nelson, J. S. (Chairman), E. J. Crossman, H. Espinosa-Perez, L. T. Findley, C. R. Gilbert, R. N. Lea, and J. D. Williams. 2003. Common and scientific names of fishes from the United States, Canada, and Mexico. 6th ed., , Amer. Fish. Soc. Spec. Pub. no. 20. Bethesda, Md. (in press).

Nelson, W. R. 1968. Reproduction and early life history of sauger, *Stizostedion canadense* in Lewis and Clark Lake. *Trans. Amer. Fish. Soc.* 97(2):159–66.

Netsch, N. F. 1964. Food and feeding habits of the longnose gar in central Missouri. *Proc. 18th Ann. Conf. Southeastern Assoc. Game and Fish. Comm.* 506–11.

Netsch, N. F., and A. Witt, Jr. 1962. Contributions to the life history of the longnose gar (*Lepisosteus osseus*) in Missouri. *Trans. Amer. Fish. Soc.* 91(3):251–62.

Niazi, A. D. and G. A. Moore. 1962. The weberian apparatus of *Hybognathus placitus* and *H. nuchalis*. *Southwestern Nat.* 7(1):41–50.

Ogden, J. C. 1970. Relative abundance, food habits, and age of the American eel, *Anguilla rostrata* (Lesueur) in certain New Jersey streams. *Trans. Amer. Fish. Soc.* 99(1):54–59.

Olmsted, L. L. and R. V. Kilambi. 1978. Age and growth of spotted bass (*Micropterus punctulatus*) in Lake Fort Smith, Arkansas. *Trans. Amer. Fish. Soc.* 107(1):21–25.

Olund, L. J., and F. B. Cross. 1961. Geographic variation in the North American cyprinid fish, *Hybopsis gracilis*. *Pub. Mus. Nat. Hist. Univ. Kansas* 13(7):323–48.

Ono, R. D., J. D. Williams, and A. Wagner. 1983. *Vanishing Fishes of North America*. Stone Wall Press, Inc., Washington, D. C. 257 pp.

Ortenburger, A. I., and C. L. Hubbs. 1926. A report on the fishes of Oklahoma, with descriptions of new genera and species. *Proc. Okla. Acad. Sci.* 6(1926):126–41.

Orth, D. J. 1980. Changes in the fish community of Lake Carl Blackwell, Oklahoma (1967–77) and a test of the reproductive guild concept. *Proc. Okla. Acad. Sci.* 60:10–17.

Orth, D. J., and R. N. Jones. 1980. Range extensions of the orangethroat darter (*Etheostoma spectabile*) and the freckled madtom (*Noturus nocturnus*) into western Oklahoma. *Proc. Okla. Acad. Sci.* 60:98–99.

Osborn, R. S., and J. T. Shelf. 1966. Observations on the spawning ecology of buffalos (*Ictiobus bubalus* and *I. cyprinellus*) in relation to parasitism. *Proc. Okla. Acad. Sci.* 46:54–57.

Paden, J. M. 1947. Notes on four species of fishes from Oklahoma. *Proc. Okla. Acad. Sci.* (1947):38–39.

Page, L. M. 1976. The modified midventral scales of *Percina* (Osteichthyes; Percidae*) J. of Morphology* 148(2):255–64.

———. 1983. *Handbook of Darters*. Neptune City, N.J.: TFH Publications. 271 pp.

———. 1985. Evolution of reproductive behaviors in percid fishes. *Ill. Nat. Hist. Surv. Bull.* 33:275–95.

Page, L. M., and B. M. Burr. 1991. *A Field Guide to Freshwater Fishes, North America North of Mexico*. Peterson Field Guide Series. Boston: Houghton Mifflin Company. 432 pp.

Page, L. M., and P. A. Ceas. 1989. Egg attachment in *Pimephales* (Pisces: Cyprinidae). *Copeia* 1989:1074–77.

Page, L. M., and C. E. Johnston. 1990a. The breeding behavior of *Opsopoeodus emiliae* and its phylogenetic implications. *Copeia* 1990:1176–80.

———. 1990b. Spawning in the creek chubsucker, *Erimyzon oblongus*, with a review of spawning behavior in suckers (Catostomidae). *Environ. Biol. Fishes* 27:265–72.

Page, L. M., M. A. Retzer, and R. A. Stiles. 1982. Spawning behavior in seven species of darters (Pisces: Percidae). *Brimleyana* 8:135–43.

Page, L. M., and P. W. Smith. 1970. The life history of the dusky darter, *Percina sciera*, in the Embarras River, Illinois. Ill. Nat. Hist. Surv. Biol. Notes no. 69. 15 pp.

———. 1971. The life history of the slenderhead darter, *Percina phoxocephala*, in the Embarras River, Illinois. Ill. Nat. Hist. Surv. Biol. Notes no. 74. 14 pp.

Parenti, L. R. 1981. A phylogenetic and biogeographic analysis of cypriodontiform fishes (Teleostei, Atherinomorpha). *Bull. Am. Mus. Nat. Hist.* 168(4):335–557.

Parker, A., and I. Kornfield. 1995. Molecular perspective on evolution and zoogeography of cyprinodontid killifishes. *Copeia* 1995:8–21.

Parker, H. L. 1964. Natural history of *Pimephales vigilax* (Cyprinidae). *Southwestern Nat.* 8(4):228–35.

Parker, N. C., and B. A. Simco. 1975. Activity patterns, feeding and behavior of the pirate perch, *Aphredoderus sayanus*. *Copeia* 1975(3):572–74.

Paukert, C. P., and W. L. Fisher. 2000. Abiotic factors affecting summer distribution and movement of male(?) paddlefish, *Polyodon spathula*, in a prairie reservoir. *Southwestern Nat.* 45(2):133–40.

Paukert, C. P., and J. M. Long. 1999. New maximum age for bigmouth buffalo, *Ictiobus cyprinellus*. *Proc. Okla. Acad. Sci.* 79:85–86.

Pflieger, W. L. 1965. Reproductive behavior of the minnows, *Notropis spilopterus* and *Notropis whipplei*. *Copeia* 1965:1–7.

———. 1966a. Reproduction of the smallmouth bass in a small Ozark stream. *Amer. Midl. Nat.* 76(2):410–18.

———. 1966b. Young of the orangethroat darter (*Etheostoma spectabile*) in nests of the smallmouth bass (*Micropterus dolomieu*) *Copeia* 1966(1):139–40.

———. 1971. A distributional study of Missouri fishes. *Pub. Mus. Nat. Hist. Univ. Kansas* 20(3):225–570.

———. 1997. *The Fishes of Missouri*. Jefferson City: Missouri Department of Conservation. 372 pp.

Pfingsten, D. G., and D. R. Estes. 1994. Reproductive traits of the Neosho madtom, *Noturus placidus* (Pisces: Ictaluridae). *Trans. Kansas Acad. Sci.* 97:82–87.

Phillips, G. L. 1969. Diet of minnow *Chrosomus erythrogaster* (Cyprinidae) in a Minnesota stream. *Amer. Midl. Nat.* 82(1):99–109.

Pigg, J. 1977. A survey of the fishes of the Muddy Boggy River in south central Oklahoma. *Proc. Okla. Acad. Sci.* 57:68–82.

———. 1978. The tilapia *Sarotherodon aurea* (Steindachner) in the North Canadian River in central Oklahoma. *Proc. Okla. Acad. Sci.* 58:111–12.

———. 1982. Noteworthy distribution and habitat records for four Oklahoma fishes. *Proc. Okla. Acad. Sci.* 62:93–94.

———. 1983. Three additional records for fishes rare in Oklahoma. *Proc. Okla. Acad. Sci.* 63:105.

———. 1985. Records of the Arkansas darter, *Etheostoma cragini* Gilbert, in Harper and Beaver counties in Oklahoma. *Proc. Okla. Acad. Sci.* 65:61–63.

———. 1987. Survey of fishes in the Oklahoma panhandle and Harper County, northwestern Oklahoma. *Proc. Okla. Acad. Sci.* 67:45–59.

———. 1991. Decreasing distribution and current status of the Arkansas River shiner, *Notropis girardi*, in the rivers of Oklahoma and Kansas. *Proc. Okla. Acad. Sci.* 71:5–15.

Pigg, J., and R. Gibbs. 1994. Update of the distribution records for the Arkansas River darter, *Etheostoma cragini* Gilbert, in northwestern Oklahoma. *Proc. Okla. Acad. Sci.* 74:37–38.

———. 1997. Records for northwest Oklahoma of spotted gar, *Lepisosteus oculatus* (Winchell), longnose gar, *L. osseus* (Linnaeus), and shortnose gar, *L. platostomus* Rafinesque. *Proc. Okla. Acad. Sci*. 77:119–21.

Pigg, J., R. Gibbs, and C. C. Cuningham. 1999. Decreasing abundance of the Arkansas River shiner in the South Canadian River, Oklahoma. *Proc. Okla. Acad. Sci*. 79:7–12.

Pigg, J., W. Harrison, and R. Gibbs. 1984. Red River pupfish, *Cyprinodon rubrofluviatilis* (Fowler), in the Arkansas River drainage in western Oklahoma. *Proc. Okla. Acad. Sci*. 64:48.

———. 1985. Records of the Arkansas darter, *Etheostoma cragini* Gilbert, in Harper and Beaver counties in Oklahoma. *Proc. Okla. Acad. Sci*. 65:61–63.

Pigg, J., and L. G. Hill. 1974. Fishes of the Kiamichi River, Oklahoma. *Proc. Okla. Acad. Sci*. 54:121–30.

Pigg, J., and G. Peterson. 2000. Additional records of the yellow bass, *Morone mississippiensis*, in Oklahoma. *Proc. Okla. Acad. Sci.* 80:139–140.

Pigg, J., and T. Pham. 1990. The rudd, *Scardinus erythropthalamus*, a new fish in Oklahoma waters. *Proc. Okla. Acad. Sci*. 70:37.

Pigg, J., and J. D. Tyler. 1990. Distribution of the goldeye and striped bass in the North Fork of the Red River in Oklahoma. *Proc. Okla. Acad. Sci.* 70:19–21.

Piller, K. R., H. L. Bart, Jr., and C. A. Walser. 2001. Morphological variation of the redfin darter, *Etheostoma whipplei*, with comments on the status of the subspecific populations. *Copeia* 2000(3):802–807.

Platania, S. P., and H. W. Robison. 1980. *Etheostoma collettei* Birdsong and Kapp, creole darter. P. 636 in Lee et al., *Atlas* (see Lee et al., 1980).

Polivka, K. M. 1999. The microhabitat distribution of the Arkansas River shiner, *Notropis girardi*: A habitat mosaic approach. *Environ. Biol. Fishes* 55:265–78.

Poss, S. G., and R. R. Miller. 1983. Taxonomic status of the plains killifish, *Fundulus zebrinus*. *Copeia* 1983:55–66.

Potter, G. E. 1927. Ecological studies of the short-nosed gar pike (*Lepisosteus platostomus*). *Univ. Iowa Stud. in Nat. Hist*. 11(9):17–27.

Poulson, T. L. 1963. Cave adaptation in amblyopsid fishes. *Amer. Midl. Nat.* 70:257–90.

Power, M. E., and E. J. Matthews. 1983. Algae-grazing minnows (*Campostoma anomalum*), piscivorous bass (*Micropterus* spp.), and the distribution of attached algae in a small prarie-margin stream. *Oecologia* 60:328–32.

Power, M. E., W. J. Matthews, and A. J. Stewart. 1985. Grazing minnows, piscivorous bass and stream algae: Dynamics of a strong interaction. *Ecology* 55:1448–56.

Powers, P. K., and J. R. Gold. 1992. Cytogenetic studies in North American minnows (Cyprinidae). 20: Chromosomal NOR variation in the genus *Luxilus*. *Copeia* 1992: 332–42.

Pratt, K. E. 2000. Life history of the rocky shiner, *Notropis suttkusi*. M.S. thesis, University of Oklahoma, Norman. 50 pp.

Priegel, G. R. 1967. Food of the freshwater drum, *Aplodinotus grunniens*, in Lake Winnebago, Wisconsin. *Trans. Amer. Fish. Soc.* 96(2):218–20.

———. 1970. Food of the white bass, *Roccus chrysops*, in Lake Winnebago, Wisconsin. *Trans. Amer. Fish. Soc.* 99(2):440–43.

Purkett, C. A., Jr. 1961. Reproduction and early development of the paddlefish, *Trans. Amer. Fish. Soc.* 90(2):125–29.

Pyron, M., and C. M. Taylor. 1993. Fish community of Oklahoma Gulf coastal plains. *Hydrobiologia* 257:29–35.

Rainboth, W. J., Jr., and G. S. Whitt. 1974. Analysis of evolutionary relationships among shiners of the subgenus *Luxilus* (Teleostei, Cypriniformes, *Notropis*) with the lactate dehydrogenase and malate dehydrogenase isozyme systems. *Comparative Biochemistry and Physiology* 49B:241–52.

Ramsey, J. S. 1975. Taxonomic history and systematic relationships among species of *Micropterus*. Pp. 67–75 in R. H. Stroud and H. Clepper, eds., *Black Bass Biology and Management*. Washington, D.C.: Sport Fishing Institute. 534 pp.

Randolph, J. C., and H. L. Lindsay. 1975. A new locality record for the blue sucker, *Cycleptus elongatus* (LeSueur) in Oklahoma. *Proc. Okla. Acad. Sci.* 55:55–56.

Raney, E. C. 1939. The breeding habits of the silvery minnow, *Hybognathus regius* Girard. *Amer. Midl. Nat.* 21:674–80.

Raney, E. C., and E. A. Lachner. 1946. Age, growth, and habits of the hog sucker, *Hypentelium nigricans* (Lesueur) in New York. *Amer. Midl. Nat.* 36(1):76–86.

Raney, E. C., and D. A. Webster. 1940. The food and growth of the young of the common bullhead *Ameiurus nebulosus nebulosus* (Lesueur) in Cayuga Lake, N.Y. *Trans. Amer. Fish. Soc.* 69(1939):205–209.

Rare and Endangered Species of Oklahoma Committee. 1975. *Rare and Endangered Vertebrates and Plants of Oklahoma*. Stillwater, Okla.: USDA Soil Conservation Service.

Reash, R. J., and J. Pigg. 1990. Physicochemical factors affecting the abundance of and species richness of fishes in the Cimarron River. *Proc. Okla. Acad. Sci.* 70:23–28.

Redmond, L. C. 1964. Ecology of the spotted gar (*Lepisosteus oculatus* Winchell) in southeastern Missouri. M.A. thesis, University of Missouri, Columbia. 144 pp.

Reed, B. C., W. E. Kelso, and D. A. Rutherford. 1992. Growth, fecundity, and mortality of paddlefish in Louisiana. *Trans. Amer. Fish. Soc.* 121:378–84.

Reed, J. R., and W. D. Davies. 1991. Population dynamics of black crappies in Weiss Reservoir, Alabama: implications for the implementation of harvest restrictions. *N. Amer. J. Fish. Mgmt.* 11:598–603.

Reeves, J. D. 1953. The fishes of the Little River system in Oklahoma. Ph.D. thesis, Oklahoma State University, Stillwater. 95 pp.

Reeves, J. D., and G. A. Moore. 1950. *Lepomis marginatus* (Holbrook) in Oklahoma. *Proc. Okla. Acad. Sci.* 30:41–42.

Reighard, J. 1940. The natural history of *Amia calva* Linnaeus. *Mark Anniversary Volume* 4:57–108.

Reno, H. W. 1966. The infraorbital canal, its lateral line ossicles and neuromasts in the minnows *Notropis volucellus* and *N. buchanani*. *Copeia* 1966(3):403–13.

———. 1969. Cephalic lateral-line systems of the cyprinid genus *Hybopsis*. *Copeia* 1969(4): 436–773.

Retzer, M. E., L. M. Page, and D. L. Swofford. 1986. Variation and systematics of *Etheostoma whipplei*, the redfin darter (Pisces: Percidae). *Copeia* 1986:631–41.

Ricciardi, A., and J. B. Rasmussen. 1999. Extinction rates of North American Freshwater fauna. *Cons. Biol.* 13(5):1220–22.

Richardson, L. R., and J. R. Gold. 1995. Evolution of the *Cyprinella lutrensis* species-complex. 2: Systematics and biogeography of the Edwards Plateau shiner, *Cyprinella lepida*. *Copeia* 1995:28–37.

Richter, B. D., D. P. Braun, M. A. Mendelson, and L. L. Master. 1997. Threats to imperiled freshwater fauna. *Cons. Biol.* 11(5):1081–93.

Riggs, C. D. 1954. The occurrence of *Astyanax fasciatus mexicanus* in Lake Texoma, Oklahoma. *Proc. Okla. Acad. Sci.* 33:141.

———. 1957. *Mugil cephalus* in Oklahoma and northeastern Texas. *Copeia* (2):158–59.

———. 1958. The occurrence of *Signalosa petenensii* in Lake Texoma. *Proc. Okla. Acad. Sci.* 38:64–67.

Riggs, C. D., and E. W. Bonn. 1959. An annotated list of the fishes of Lake Texoma, Oklahoma and Texas. *Southwestern Nat.* 4(4):157–68.

Riggs, C. D., and V. E. Dowell. 1956. Some recent changes in the fish fauna of Lake Texoma. *Proc. Okla. Acad. Sci.* 35:37–39.

Riggs, C. D., and G. A. Moore. 1950. Some new records of paddlefish and sturgeon for Oklahoma. *Proc. Okla. Acad. Sci.* 30:16–18.

———. 1963. A new record of *Moxostoma macrolepidotum pisolabrum*, and a range extension for *Percina shumardi*, in the Red River, Oklahoma and Texas. *Copeia* 1963(2):451–52.

Riggs, C. D., and R. Smithpeter. 1952. The fish population of a small, periodically innundated island pond in Lake Texoma, Oklahoma. *Proc. Okla. Acad. Sci.* 33:49–55.

Riggs, C. D., and W. F. Wade. 1964. *Percina shumardi* in the Illinois River of Oklahoma. *Proc. Okla. Acad. Sci.* 44:65–66.

Robertson, M. S., and K. O. Winemiller. 2001. Diet and growth of smallmouth bass in the Devil's River, Texas. *Southwestern Nat.* 46(2):216–21.

Robins, C. R. 1989. The phylogenetic relationships of the anguilliform fishes. Pp. 9–23 in *Fishes of the Western North Atlantic*. Memoirs Sears Found. Mar. Res., Yale Univ., vol. 1, no. 1, pt. 9.

Robison, H. W. 1977a. Distribution and habitat notes on the ironcolor shiner *Notropis chalybaeus* (Cope) in Arkansas. *Proc. Ark. Acad. Sci.* 31:92–94.

———. 1977b. Distribution, habitat, variation and status of the goldstripe darter, *Etheostoma parvipinne* Gilbert and Swain, in Arkansas. *Southwestern Nat.* 22(4): 435–42.

———. 1978a. Distribution and habitat of the taillight shiner, *Notropis maculatus* (Hay), in Arkansas. *Proc. Arkansas Acad. Sci.* 32:68–70.

———. 1978b. *The Leopard Darter: A Status Report*. Endangered Species Report no. 3. Albuquerque, N.M.: U.S. Fish and Wildlife Service. 28 pp.

———. 1980a. *Notropis ortenburgeri* Hubbs, Kiamichi shiner. P. 290 in Lee et al., *Atlas* (see Lee et al., 1980).

———. 1980b. *Percina pantherina* (Moore and Reeves), leopard darter. P. 735 in Lee et al., *Atlas* (see Lee et al., 1980).

———. 1985. *Notropis snelsoni*, a new cyprinid from the Ouachita Mountains of Arkansas and Oklahoma. *Copeia* 1985(1):126–34.

———. 1986. Zoogeographic implications of the Mississippi River Basin. Pp. 267–83 in C. H. Hocutt and E. O. Wiley, eds., *The Zoogeography of North American Freshwater Fishes*. New York: John Wiley and Sons. 866 pp.

Robison, H. W., and T. M. Buchanan. 1988. *Fishes of Arkansas*. Fayetteville: University of Arkansas Press. 536 pp.

Robison, H. W., and R. J. Miller. 1972. A new intergeneric cyprinid hybrid (*Notropis pilsbryi* × *Chrosomus erythrogaster*) from Oklahoma. *Southwestern Nat.* 16(3–4):442–44.

Robison, H. W., G. A. Moore, and R. J. Miller. 1974. Threatened fishes of Oklahoma. *Proc. Okla. Acad. Sci.* 54:139–46.

Rohde, F. C. 1981. *Phenacobius mirabilis* (Girard), suckermouth minnow. P. 332 in Lee et al., *Atlas* (see Lee et al., 1980).

Rohde, F. C., R. G. Arndt, and J. C. S. Wang. 1976. Life history of the freshwater lampreys, *Okkelbergia aepyptera* and *Lampetra lamottenii* (Pisces: Petromyzontidae), on the Delmarva Peninsula (East Coast, United States). *Bull. So. Calif. Acad. Sci.* 75(2): 99–111.

Rosen, R. A., and D. C. Hales. 1981. Feeding of paddlefish, *Polyodon spathula*. *Copeia* 1981(2):441–55.

Ross, S. T. 2001. *The Inland Fishes of Mississippi*. Jackson: University Press of Mississippi. 624 pp.

Rupprecht, R. J., and L. A. Jahn. 1980. Biological notes on blue suckers in the Mississippi River. *Trans. Amer. Fish. Soc.* 109:323–26.

Rutherford, D. A., and A. A. Echelle. 1985. An addition to the fish fauna of Oklahoma: *Erimyzon sucetta* (Catostomidae). *Southwestern Nat.* 30(2):305–306.

Rutherford, D. A., A. A. Echelle, and O. E. Maughan. 1992. Drainage-wide effects of timber harvesting on the structure of stream fish assemblages in southeastern Oklahoma. *Trans. Amer. Fish. Soc.* 121(6):716–28.

Ryman, N., F. Utter, and L. Lankre. 1994. Protection of aquatic biodiversity. Pp. 87–109 in C. W. Voightlander, ed., *State of the World's Fisheries Resources*. Proceedings of the World Fisheries Congress Plenary Session. New Delhi: Oxford and IBH.

Sandoz, O. 1959. Changes in the fish populations of lake Murray following the reduction of gizzard shad numbers. *Proc. Okla. Acad. Sci.* 37:174–81.

Sanford, C. P. J. 1990. The phylogenetic relationships of salmonoid fishes. *Bull. Brit. Mus. Nat. Hist. (Zool.)* 56:145–53.

Saunders, R. P. 1959. A study of the food of the Mississippi silverside, *Meidia audens* Hay, in Lake Texoma. M.S. thesis, University of Oklahoma, Norman.

Scalet, C. G. 1972. Food habits of the orangebelly darter, *Etheostoma radiosum cyanorum* (Osteichthys: Percidae). *Amer. Midl. Nat.* 87(2):515–22.

———. 1973a. Reproduction of the orangebelly darter, *Etheostoma radiosum cyanorum* (Osteichthyes: Percidae). *Amer. Midl. Nat.* 89:156–65.

———. 1973b. Stream movements and population density of the orangebelly darter, *Etheostoma radiosum cyanorum* (Osteichthyes: Percidae). *Southwestern Nat.* 17:381–87.

Schaefer, S. A., and T. M. Cavender. 1986. Geographic variation and subspecific status of *Notropis spilopterus* (Pisces: Cyprinidae). *Copeia* 1986(1):122–30.

Schmidt, J. 1922. The breeding places of the eel. *Phil. Trans. Royal Soc. London,* Ser. B. 211:179–208.

Schmidt, R. E., and W. R. Whitworth. 1979. Distribution and habitat of the swamp darter (*Etheostoma fusiforme*) in southern New England. *Amer. Midl. Nat.* 102: 408–13.

Schmidt, T. R. 1994. Phylogenetic relationships of the genus *Hybognathus*. *Copeia* 1994: 622–30.

Schmidt, T. R., J. P. Bielawski, and J. R. Gold. 1998. Molecular phylogenetics and evolution of the cytochrome b gene in the cyprinid genus *Lythrurus*. *Copeia* 1998:14–22.

Scott, W. B., and E. J. Crossman. 1973. *Freshwater Fishes of Canada*. Bull. Fish. Res. Bd. Canada 184. 966 pp.

Seagle, H. H., Jr., and J. W. Nagel. 1982. Life cycle and fecundity of the American brook lamprey, *Lampetra appendix*, in Tennessee. *Copeia* 1982(2):362–66.

Secor, S. M. 1987. The golden topminnow, *Fundulus chrysotus* (Cyprinodontidae), an addition to the fish fauna of Oklahoma. *Southwestern Nat.* 32(4):522–25.

Settles, W. H., and R. D. Hoyt. 1976. Age structure, growth patterns, and food habits of the southern redbelly dace *Chrosomus erythrogaster* in Kentucky. *Trans. Kentucky Acad. Sci.* 37(1–2):1–10.

———. 1978. The reproductive biology of the southern redbelly dace, *Chrosomus erythrogaster* Rafinesque, in a spring-fed stream in Kentucky. *Amer. Midl. Nat.* 99(2):290–98.

Shelton, W. L. 1972. Comparative reproductive biology of the gizzard shad, *Dorosoma cepedianum* (Lesueur) and *D. petenense* in Lake Texoma, Oklahoma. *Proc. 26th Ann. Conf. Southeastern Assoc. Game and Fish Comm.* 506–10.

Shepherd, M. E., and M. T. Huish. 1978. Age, growth, and diet of the pirate perch in a coastal plain stream in North Carolina. *Trans. Amer. Fish. Soc.* 107(3):457–59.

Simons, A. M. 1991. Phylogenetic relationships of the crystal darter, *Crystallaria asprella*. *Copeia* 1991:927–36.

Simons, A. M., and R. L. Mayden. 1999. Phylogenetic relationships of North American cyprinids and assessment of homology of the open posterior myodome. *Copeia* 1999: 13–21.

Sisk, M. E., and R. R. Stephens. 1964. *Menidia audens* (Pisces: Atherinidae) in Boomer Lake, Oklahoma, and its possible spread in the Arkansas River system. *Proc. Okla. Acad. Sci.* 44:71–73.

Sisk, M. E., and D. H. Webb. 1976. Distribution and habitat preference of *Etheostoma histrio* in Kentucky. *Trans. Kentucky Acad. Sci.* 37:33–34.

Smith, B. G. 1908. The spawning habits of *Chrosomus erythrogaster* Rafinesque. *Biological Bulletin* 14(6):9–18.

Smith, C. L. 1954. Pleistocene fishes of the Baerends Fauna of Beaver County, Oklahoma. *Copeia* 1954(4):282–89.

Smith, C. L., and C. R. Powell. 1971. The summer fish communities of Brier Creek, Marshall County, Oklahoma. Amer. Mus. Novitates no. 2458. 30 pp.

Smith, G. R. 1963. A late Illinoisan fish fauna from southwestern Kansas and its climatic significance. *Copeia* 1963(2):278–85.

———. 1992. Phylogeny and biogeography of the Catostomidae, freshwater fishes of North America and Asia. Pp. 778–826 in R. L. Mayden, ed., *Systematics, Historical Ecology, and North American Freshwater Fishes.* Stanford, Calif.: Stanford University Press.

Smith, G. R., and R. F. Stearley, 1989. The classification and scientific names of rainbow and cutthroat trouts. *Fisheries* 14:4–10.

Smith, P. W. 1979. *The Fishes of Illinois*. Urbana: University of Illinois Press. 314 pp.

Smith, P. W., and L. M. Page. 1969. The food of spotted bass in streams of the Wabash River drainage. *Trans. Amer. Fish. Soc.* 98(4):647–51.

Smith, R. J. F., and B. D. Murphy. 1974. Functional morphology of the dorsal pad in fathead minnows (*Pimephales promelas* Rafinesque). *Trans. Amer. Fish. Soc.* 103(1):65–72.

Smith-Vaniz, W. F. 1968. *Freshwater Fishes of Alabama*. Auburn Univ. Agri. Exper. Sta., Auburn, Ala. 211 pp.

Snedden, G. A., W. E. Kelso, and D. A. Rutherford. 1999. Diet and seasonal patterns of spotted gar movement and habitat use in the lower Atchafalaya River basin, Louisiana. *Trans. Amer. Fish. Soc.* 128:144–54.

Snelson, F. F., Jr. 1973. Systematics and distribution of the ribbon shiner, *Notropis fumeus* (Cyprinidae), from the central United States. *Amer. Midl. Nat.* 89:166–91.

Snelson, F. F., Jr., and R. E. Jenkins. 1973. *Notropis perpallidus*, a cyprinid fish from south-central United States: Description, distribution, and life history aspects. *Southwestern Nat.* 18(3):291–304.

Snelson F. F., Jr., and W. L. Pflieger. 1975. Redescription of the redfin shiner, *Notropis umbratilis*, and its subspecies in the central Mississippi River basin. *Copeia* 1975(2): 231–49.

Starnes, L. B., and W. C. Starnes. 1985. Ecology and life history of the mountain madtom, *Noturus eleutherus* (Pisces: Ictaluridae). *Amer. Midl. Nat.* 114(2):331–41.

Starrett, W. 1950. Food relationships of the minnows and darters of the Des Moines River, Iowa. *Ecology* 31(2):216–33.

———. 1951. Some factors affecting the abundance of minnows in the Des Moines River, Iowa. *Ecology* 32(1):13–27.

Stein, B. A., and R. M. Chipley, (eds.). 1996. Priorities for Conservation: 1996 Annual Report Card for U.S. Plants and Animal Species. Arlington, Va.: Nature Conservancy.

Sternburg, J. 1986. Aquarium spawning and rearing of the southern redbelly dace. *American Currents* (October): 7–9.

Strange, R. M. 1993. Season feeding ecology of the fantail darter, *Etheostoma flabellare*, from Stinking Fork, Indiana. *J. Freshwater Ecology* 8:13–18.

Stevenson, M. M. 1971. *Percina macrolepida* (Percidae, Ethesotomatinae), a new percid fish of the subgenus *Percina* from Texas. *Southwestern Nat.* 16(1): 65–83

Stevenson, M. M., and B. A. Thompson. 1978. Further distribution records for the bigscale logperch, *Percina macrolepida* (Osteichthyes: Percidae), from Oklahoma, Texas, and Louisiana with notes on its occurrence in California. *Southwestern Nat.* 23: 309–13.

Stewart, J. G. 1999. An annotated checklist of the fishes of the Tallgrass Prairie Preserve, Osage County, Oklahoma. *Proc. Okla. Acad. Sci.* 57:68–82.

Sublette, J. E., M. D. Hatch, and M. Sublette. 1990. *The Fishes of New Mexico*. Albuquerque: Univ. of New Mexico Press.

Sule, M. J., and T. M. Skelly. 1985. The life history of the shorthead redhorse, *Moxostoma macrolepidotum*, in the Kankakee River drainage, Illinois. Ill. Nat. Hist. Surv. Biol. Notes no. 123. 15 pp.

Summerfelt, R. C., and C. O. Minckley. 1969. Aspects of the life history of the sand shiner, *Notropis stramineus* (Cope), in the Smoky Hill River, Kansas. *Trans. Amer. Fish. Soc.* 98(3):444–53.

Summers, P. B. 1954. Some observations on limnology and fish distribution in the Illinois River below Tenkiller Reservoir. *Proc. Okla. Acad. Sci.* 35:15–20.

Suttkus, R. D. 1980. *Notropis candidus*, a new cyprinid fish from the Mobile Bay Basin, and a review of the nomenclatural history of *Notropis shumardi* (Girard). *Bull. Alabama Mus. Nat. Hist.* 5:1–15.

Suttkus, R. D., and M. F. Mettee. 2001. Analysis of four species of *Notropis* included in the subgenus *Pteronotropis* Fowler, with comments, relationships, origin, and dispersion. Geol. Surv. Alabama Bull. 170. 50 pp.

Swedberg, D. V. 1968. Food and growth of the freshwater drum in Lewis and Clark Lake, South Dakota. *Trans. Amer. Fish. Soc.* 97(4):442–47.

Swift, C. C. 1970. A review of the eastern North American cyprinid fishes of the *Notropis texanus* species group (Subgenus *Alburnops*), with a definition of the subgenus *Hydrophlox*, and materials for a revision of the subgenus *Alburnops*. Ph.D. diss., Florida State University, Tallahassee. 515 pp.

Taber, C. A., B. A. Taber, and M. S. Topping. 1986. Population structure, growth and reproduction of the Arkansas darter, *Etheostoma cragini* (Percidae). *Southwestern Nat.* 31(2):207–14.

Tanyolac, J. 1973. Morphometric variation and life history of the cyprinid fish *Notropis stramineus* (Cope). Occas. Papers Mus. Nat. Hist. Univ. Kansas no. 12. 28 pp.

Taylor, C. M. 2000. A large-scale comparative analysis of riffle and pool fish communities in an upland stream system. *Environ. Biol. Fishes* 58(1):89–95.

Taylor, C. M., and P. W. Lienesch. 1995. Environmental correlates of distribution and abundance for *Lythrurus snelsoni*: A range-wide analysis of an endemic fish species. *Southwestern Nat.* 40(4): 373–78.

———. 1996. Regional parapatry of the congeneric cyprinids *Lythrurus snelsoni* and *L. umbratilis*: species replacement along a complex environmental gradient. *Copeia* (2):493–97.

Taylor, C. M., and R. J. Miller. 1990. Reproductive ecology and population structure of the plains minnow, *Hybognathus placitus* (Pisce: Cyprinidae), in Oklahoma. *Amer. Midl. Nat.* 123:32–39.

Taylor, C. M., and S. M. Norris. 1992. Notes on the reproductive cycle of *Notropis hubbsi* (bluehead shiner) in southeastern Oklahoma. *Southwestern Nat.* 37:89–92.

Taylor, C. M., M. R. Winston, and W. J. Matthews. 1993. Fish species-environment and abundance relationships in a Great Plains river system. *Ecography* 16:16–23.

———. 1996. Temporal variaion in tributary and mainstem fish assemblages in a Great Plains stream system. *Copeia* 1996(2):280–89.

Taylor, C. M., M. Pyron, and M. R. Winston. 1993. Zoogeographic implications for the first record of *Crystallaria asprella* (Percidae) from the Kiamichi River drainage, and for the occurrence of *Notropis boops* (Cyprinidae) and *Luxilus chrysocephalus* (Cyprinidae) in the Wichita Mountains, Oklahoma. *Southwestern Nat.* 38(3): 302–303.

Taylor, W. R. 1969. Revision of the catfish genus *Noturus* Rafinesque, with an analysis of higher groups in the Ictaluridae. Bull. U.S. Nat. Mus. 282. 315 pp.

Thomas, D. L. 1970. An ecological study of four darters of the genus *Percina* (Percidae) in the Kaskaskia River, Illinois. Ill. Nat. Hist. Surv. Biol. Notes no. 70. 18 pp.

Thomerson, J. E. 1966. A comparative biosystematic study of *Fundulus notatus* and *Fundulus olivaceus* (Pisces: Cyprinodontidae). *Tulane Studies in Zoology and Botany* 13(1):29–48.

———. 1969. Variation and relationship of the studfishes, *Fundulus catenatus* and *Fundulus stellifer* (Cyprinodontidae, Pisces). *Tulane Studies in Zoology and Botany* 16(1):1–21.

Thompson, B. A. 1977. An analysis of three subgenera (*Hypohomus, Odontopholis*, and *Swainia*) of the genus *Percina* (tribe Etheostomatini, family Percidae). Ph.D. diss. Tulane University, New Orleans.

———. 1980. *Percina phoxocephaia*, slenderhead darter. P. 737 in Lee et al., *Atlas* (see Lee et al., 1980).

Thompson, B. A., and R. C. Cashner. 1980. *Percina ouachitae* (Jordan and Gilbert), yellow darter. P. 732 in Lee et al., *Atlas* (see Lee et al., 1980).

Thompson, W. H., H. C. Ward, and J. F. Arthur. 1951. The age and growth of white crappie, *Pomoxis annularis* (Rafinesque) from four small Oklahoma lakes. *Proc. Okla. Acad. Sci.* 30:93–101.

Todd, J. H., J. Atema, and J. E. Bardach. 1976. Chemical communication in social behavior of a fish, the yellow bullhead. *Science* 158(3801):672–73.

Tomelleri, J. R., and M. E. Eberle. 1990. *Fishes of the Central United States*. Lawrence: University Press of Kansas. 226 pp.

Trautman, M. B. 1981. *The Fishes of Ohio*. Columbus: Ohio State University Press. 638 pp.

Trautman, M. B., and R. G. Martin. 1957. *Moxostoma aureolum pisolabrum*, a new subspecies of sucker from the Ozarkian streams of the Mississippi River system. Occas. Papers Mus. Zool. Univ. Mich. no. 534. 10pp.

Tsai, C. 1968. Distribution of the harlequin darter, *Etheostoma histrio*. Copeia 1968(1): 178–81.

Tsai, C., and E. C. Raney. 1974. Systematics of the banded darter, *Etheostoma zonale* (Pisces: Percidae). *Copeia* 1974(1):1–24.

Tumlison, R., and G. R. Cline. 2002. Food habits of the banded sculpin (*Cottus carolinae*) in Oklahoma with reference to predation on the Oklahoma salamander (*Eurycea tynerensis*). *Proc. Okla. Acad. Sci.* 82:111–13.

Turner, P. R., and R. C. Summerfelt. 1971. Food habits of adult flathead catfish, *Pylodictis olivaris* (Rafinesque), in Oklahoma reservoirs. *Proc. 24th Ann. Conf. Southeastern Assoc. Game and Fish. Comm.* 387–401.

Tyler, J. D. 1987. Spotted gar with deformed mandible. *Proc. Okla. Acad. Sci.* 67:81.

———. 1990. A xanthochroistic gar in Oklahoma. *Southwestern Nat.* 35(2):225.

———. 1994. Albinistic spotted gar, *Lepisosteus oculatus*, in Oklahoma. *Proc. Okla. Acad. Sci.* 74:39.

Tyler, J. D., and M. N. Granger. 1984. Notes on food habits, size, and spawning behavior of spotted gar in Lake Lawtonka, Oklahoma. *Proc. Okla. Acad. Sci.* 64:8–10.

Tyler, J. D., and D. R. Mills. 1978. Range extensions of *Hiodon alosoides* (Rafinesque) in Oklahoma. *Proc. Okla. Acad. Sci.* 58:113.

Tyler, J. D., J. K. Webb, T. R. Wright, J. D. Hargett, K. J. Mask, and D. R. Schucker. 1994. Food habits, sex ratios, and size of longnose gar in southwestern Oklahoma. *Proc. Okla. Acad. Sci.* 74:41–42.

Van Cleve, H. J., and H. C. Markus. 1929. Studies on the life history of the blunt-nosed minnow. *American Naturalist* 63(689):530–39.

Van Oosten, J. 1961. Records, ages and growth of the mooneye, *Hiodon tergisus*, of the Great Lakes. *Trans. Amer. Fish. Soc.* 90(2):170–74.

Vives, S. P. 1987. Aspects of the life history of the slender madtom, *Noturus exilis*, in northeastern Oklahoma (Pisces: Ictaluridae). *Amer. Midl. Nat.* 117(1):167–76.

Vogele, L. E. 1975. Reproduction of spotted bass, *Micropterus punctulatus*, in Bull Shoals Reservoir, Arkansas. Tech. Papers. U.S. Fish and Wildl. Serv. no. 84. 21 pp.

Wade, W. F., and R. E. Craven. 1965. Changes in the fish fauna of Stillwater Creek, Payne and Noble counties, Oklahoma from 1938 to 1965. *Proc. Okla. Acad. Sci.* (1965): 60–66.

Wagner, B. A., A. A. Echelle, and O. E. Maughan. 1985. Status and distribution of the longnose darter, *Percina nasuta*, and the Neosho madtom, *Noturus placidus*, in Oklahoma. *Proc. Okla. Acad. Sci.* 65:59–60.

———. 1987. Abundance and habitat use of an uncommon fish, *Notropis perpallidus* (Cyprinidae): Comparison with sympatric congeners. *Southwestern Nat.* 32(2):251–60.

Wagner, B. A., D. R. Edds, and J. Pigg. 1983. Grass carp in Oklahoma streams. *Proc. Okla. Acad. Sci.* 63:106.

Wagner, C. C., and E. L. Cooper. 1963. Population density, growth and fecundity of the creek chubsucker, *Erimyzon oblongus*. *Copeia* 1963(2):350–51.

Walberg, C. H., and W. R. Nelson. 1966. Carp, river carpsucker, smallmouth buffalo, and bigmouth buffalo in Lewis and Clark Lake, Missouri. U.S. Fish and Wildl. Serv. Res. Report no. 69. 30 pp.

Wallace, C. R. 1967. Observations of the reproductive behavior of the black bullhead (*Ictalurus melas*). *Copeia* 1967(4):852–53.

Wallen, G. H. 1956. Fishes of the Verdigris River. M. S. thesis, Oklahoma State University, Stillwater. 57 pp.

Walsh, S. J., and B. M. Burr. 1984. Life history of the banded pygmy sunfish, *Elassoma zonatum* Jordan (Pisces: Centrarchidae), in western Kentucky. *Bull. Alabama Mus. Nat. Hist.* 8:31–52.

Warren, M. L., Jr. 1992. Variation of the spotted sunfish, *Lepomis punctatus* complex: Meristics, morphometrics, pigmentation and species limits. *Bull. Alabama Mus. Nat. Hist.* 12:1–47.

Warren, M. L., Jr., and B. M. Burr. 1994. Status of the freshwater fishes of the United States: Overview of an imperiled fauna. *Fisheries* 19: 6–18.

Warren, M. L., Jr., B. M. Burr, S. J. Walsh, H. L. Bart, Jr., R. C. Cashner, D. A. Etnier, B. J. Freeman, B. R. Kuhajda, R. L. Mayden, H. W. Robison, S. T. Ross, and W. C. Starnes. 2000. Diversity, distribution, and conservation status of native freshwater fishes of the southern United States. *Fisheries* 25(10):7–29.

Webb, R. G. 1970. *Reptiles of Oklahoma*. Norman: University of Oklahoma Press. 370 pp.

Weese, A. O. 1949. Age and growth of *Lepibema chrysops* in Lake Texoma. *Proc. Okla. Acad. Sci.* 30:45–58.

Westman, J. R. 1938. Studies in the reproduction and growth of the bluntnose minnow, *Hyborhychus notatus* (Rafinesque). *Copeia* 1938(2):57–61.

White, D. S., and K. H. Haag. 1977. Foods and feeding habits of the spotted sucker *Minytrema melanops* (Rafinesque). *Amer. Midl. Nat.* 98(1):137–46.

Whiteside, B. G. 1962. Biology of the white crappie, *Pomoxis annularis*, in Lake Texoma, Oklahoma. M.S. thesis, Oklahoma State University, Stillwater.

Whiteside, L. A., and B. M. Burr. 1986. Aspects of the life history of the tadpole madtom, *Noturus gyrinus* (Silurifromes: Ictaluridae), in southern Illinois. *Ohio J. Sci*. 86(4): 153–60.

Wiley, E. O. 1976. The phylogeny and biogeography of fossil and recent gars (Actinopterygii: Lepisosteidae). Misc. Pub. Mus. Nat. Hist. Univ. Kansas no. 64. 111 pp.

———. 1977. The phylogeny and sytematics of the *Fundulus nottii* species group (Teleostei: Cyprinodontidae). Occas. Papers Mus. Nat. Hist. Univ. Kansas no. 66. 31 pp.

———. 1986. A study of the evolutionary relationships of *Fundulus* topminnows (Teleostei: Fundulidae). *Amer. Zool.* 26:121–30.

Wiley, E. O., and D. D. Hall. 1975. *Fundulus blairae*, a new species of the *Fundulus nottii* complex (Teleostei, Cyprinodontidae). Amer. Mus. Novitates no. 2577. 13 pp.

Wilkinson, C., D. Edds, J. Dorlac, M. L. Wildhaber, C. J. Schmidt, and A. Allert. 1996. Neosho madtom distribution and abundance in the Spring River. *Southwestern Nat*. 41:78–81.

Williams, J. D. 1975. Systematics of the percid fishes of the subgenus *Ammocrypta*, genus *Ammocrypta*, with descriptions of two new species. *Bull. Alabama Mus. Nat. Hist.* 1:1–56.

Williams, J. D., and H. W. Robison. 1980. *Ozarka*, a new subgenus of *Etheostoma* (Pisces: Percidae). *Brimleyana* 4:149–56.

Williams, J. E., J. E. Johnson, D. A. Hendrickson, S. Contreras-Balderas, J. D. Williams, M. Navarro-Mendoza, D. E. McAllister, and J. E. Deacon. 1989. Fishes of North America endangered, threatened, or of special concern: 1989. *Fisheries* 14:2–20.

Williams, J. E., and R. J. Neves. 1992. Introducing the elements of biological diversity in the aquatic environment. *Trans. 57th North Amer. Wildlife and Natural Resources Conf.* Washington, D.C.: 345–54.

Williams, L. R., and E. E. Echelle. 1998. Collection in Oklahoma of a rare fish species, *Notropis chalybeaus* (Cyprinidae). *Proc. Okla. Acad. Sci.* 78:115–16.

Williams, R. R. G. 1987. The phylogenetic relationships of the salmoniform fishes. *67th Ann. Meet. Amer. Soc. Ichthy. & Herp.*, p. 88 (abstract).

Willis, L. D., and A. V. Brown. 1985. Distribution and habitat requirements of the Ozark cavefish, *Amblyopsis rosae*. *Amer. Midl. Nat.* 144(2):311–17.

Winn, H. E. 1953. Breeding habits of the percid fish *Hadropterus copelandi* in Michigan. *Copeia* 1953(1):26–30.

———. 1958a. Comparative reproductive behavior and ecology of fourteen species of darters (Pisces: Percidae). *Ecol. Monogr*. 28:155–91.

———. 1958b. Observations on the reproductive habits of darters (Pisces: Percidae). *Amer. Midl. Nat.* 59 (1):190–212.

Winston, M. R., C. M. Taylor, and J. Pigg. 1991. Upstream extirpation of four minnow species due to damming of a prairie stream. *Trans. Amer. Fish. Soc.* 120:98–105.

Wiseman, E. D., A. A. Echelle, and A. F. Echelle. 1978. Electrophoretic evidence for subspecific differentiation and intergradation in *Etheostoma spectabile* (Teleostei: Percidae). *Copeia* 1978(2):320–27.

Wolfe, J. C. 1969. Biological studies of the skipjack herring, *Alosa chrysochloris*, in the Apalachicola River, Florida. M.S. thesis, Florida State University, Tallahassee. 68 pp.

Wood, R. M., R. L. Mayden, R. H. Matson, B. R. Kuhajda, and S. R. Layman. 2002. Systematics and biogeography of *Notropis rubellus* species group (Teleostei: Cyprinidae). *Bull. Ala. Mus. Nat. Hist*. 22:37–80.

Woods, L. P., and R. F. Inger. 1957. The cave, spring, and swamp fishes of the family Amblyopsidae of central and eastern United States. *Amer. Midl. Nat.* 58(1):232–56.

Woodward, R. L., and T. E. Wissing. 1976. Age, growth, and fecundity of the quillback (*Carpiodes cyprinus*) and highfin (*C. velifer*) carpsuckers in an Ohio Stream. *Trans. Amer. Fish. Soc.* 105(3):411–15.

Yeager, L. E. 1936. An observation on spawning buffalofish in Mississippi. *Copeia* 1936(4):716–28.

INDEX